Nirvana Upside Down

Also by Dhiravamsa

Insight Meditation (UK: 1966, 1967)

Beneficial Factors for Meditation (UK: 1967)

The Real Way to Awakening (UK: 1968)

A New Approach to Buddhism (UK: 1971)

"Theravāda Meditation" in *Secrets of the Lotus*, edited by Donald K. Swearer (USA: 1972)

The Middle Path of Life (UK: 1974, 1980; USA: 1988)

The Way of Non-Attachment (UK: 1975, 1984)

Angenommen Sie fühlen sich elend (Austria: 1979)

Das meditative Leben. Ein neuer Weg zum Buddhismus (Germany: 1980)

La via del non attaccamento (Italy: 1980)

The Dynamic Way of Meditation (UK: 1982, 1989)

La voie du non-attachement (France: 1982, 2010)

La meditación dinámica (Argentina: 1983)

L'attention: Source de plénitude (France: 1983, 2010)

La via dinamica della meditazione (Italy: 1983)

Turning to the Source (USA: 1990)

De ongedwongen weg (Netherlands: 1990)

La vía del no apego (Spain: 1991, 1993, 1994, 1998, 2010)

Meditación y eneagrama (Spain: 1992, 1998, 2000, 2007)

Retorno al origen (Spain: 1992)

La vía del despertar (Spain: 1996)

Cómo liberarnos del sufrimiento (Spain: 1998)

Palabras de sabiduría del Buda:
Análisis psicoespiritual del comentario del Dhammapada (Spain: 2000)

La leyenda de Shriton y Manorah. Las pruebas del amor consciente (Spain: 2001)

Una nueva visión del Budismo (Spain: 2005)

El gran río de la conciencia (Spain: 2005)

The Power of Conscious Love:
A Psycho-Spiritual Analysis of a Classic Thai Tale of Shrithon-Manorah (USA: 2006)

Der Weg zum Nicht-Anhaften (Germany: 2006)

Crisis y solución: unión de opuestos (Spain: 2008)

Meditación vipassana y gestalt (Spain: 2008)

Shedding Light on Each Eneatype's Mind:
Enneagram System of Personality/Character (Spain: 2009)

Vipassana and Gestalt Therapy (Thailand: 2009)

Un atajo a la iluminación (Spain: 2009)

Iluminando la mente de cada eneatipo. Edición bilingüe español-inglés (Spain: 2009)

Ο Δρόμος της μη προσκόλλησης:
Η Άσκηση του Ενορατικού Διαλογισμού - Α' Μέρος (Greece: 2007)

Εννεάγραμμα και Αυτομεταμόρφωση:
Με Ενορατικό Διαλογισμό Βιπασσάνα - Τα Εννέα Πρόσωπα της Ψυχής (Greece: 2008)

Медитация, которая Действительно работает, Випассана (Russia: 2010)

Nirvana Upside Down

Dhiravamsa

Wisdom Moon Publishing
2012

Nirvana Upside Down

Copyright © 2012 Vichitr Ratna Dhiravamsa

All rights reserved. Tous droits réservés.

No part of this work may be copied, reproduced, recorded, stored, or translated, in any form, or transmitted by any means electronic, mechanical, or other, whether by photocopy, fax, email, internet group postings, or otherwise, without written permission from the copyright holder, *except for brief quotations* in reviews for a magazine, journal, newspaper, broadcast, podcast, etc., or in scholarly or academic papers, *when quoted with a full citation to this work*.

Published by Wisdom Moon Publishing LLC
San Diego, CA, USA

Wisdom Moon™, the Wisdom Moon logo™, *Wisdom Moon Publishing*™, and *WMP*™ are trademarks of Wisdom Moon Publishing LLC.

www.WisdomMoonPublishing.com

Front cover artwork, *Awake from Confusion*, courtesy of Suttilak Soonghangwa

ISBN 978-1-938459-03-0 (softcover, alk. paper)
ISBN 978-1-938459-07-8 (eBook)

LCCN 2012944140

9 8 7 6 5 4 3 2 1

Table of Contents

Author's Introduction		i
Textual References		iv

Nirvana Upside Down

Chapter 1	Origin of samsāra	1
Chapter 2	The notion of man and his component parts	17
Chapter 3	Karma and rebirth	41
Chapter 4	The constant challenge in samsaric life	93
Chapter 5	In search of immeasurable freedom	119
Chapter 6	Heaven and hell	143
Chapter 7	Nirvana, the ultimate truth	165
Chapter 8	The Buddha's middle path	211

About the Author   235

Dedication

This present work is dedicated to my great parents, Nai Nuan and Nang Indra, my beloved elder brother Boawlin, my deeply connected younger brother Yongyuth, and to my two loving sisters Amkā and Kammā. Also to my two most revered vipassanā and dharma masters: Phra Dharmadhīrarāj Mahāmuni and Ajahn Porn Ratanasuwan.

INTRODUCTION

The theme of this work might sound a bit peculiar to some devoted Buddhists, particularly to those belonging to Theravada School of Buddhism. Since Buddhists in general maintain and stick to the position that samsāra is opposite to nirvana just like the moon to the sun, so it would be extremely difficult for them to bear the tone of voice that the title of this book expresses, let alone to embrace it. This could be compared to the reaction of devout Christians to the saying *"God is the Devil upside down."*

Generally speaking, as all educated Buddhists believe, nirvana is realized here and now in the samsaric life on the planet Earth, and the ending of the *cycle of birth and death* (the main stream of samsāra) is in fact the *emergence of nirvana*. In that case, it shouldn't be so hard to reflect on a new way of understanding "Samsāra is nirvana upside down." Regarding this matter, if we use logical reasoning to examine nirvana and samsāra, we may see that they are ***identical*** or are the one and same thing, depending on how we look at them. When nirvana becomes upside-down, obvious facts turn out to seem to be samsara. Since it has no beginning and therefore no ending, it is only a matter of its appearing and disappearing because of what stands out to the eye of the seer at the moment. If the seer views samsāra as an ongoing cycle of birth and death, he sees it as a truth opposing nirvana (the unborn and the deathless). On the contrary, if he focuses his inner eye on the complete cessation of the cycle of birth and death, then he realizes in his profound wisdom that nirvana ***is,*** exists, right here and right now.

As a matter of fact, such a statement as samsāra being nirvana upside-down is a controversial and debatable one. For this reason, I would like to add to this enormously significant topic. Detailed reflections will be offered in the various chapters of this present work. For example, I will begin by sharing with you the reader what is represented in particular Pali-language texts of great mythological force and significance, describing what happened to those beings that lived on the planet Earth when it was declining and being destroyed by various natural forces. How non-material or spiritual food such as ecstatic joy sustained those original beings but later was not adequate. How human behavior changed their basic requirements for living, the coming to be of male and female humans after the frequent radical changes had taken place in their physical and energetic bodies, and so forth. I will suggest some of the significance of these teachings for our understanding of the great potential present in all human beings, with its implications for human relatedness and universal mutual respect.

In addition, I will continue by dealing at length with the teachings on karma and rebirth, the constant challenge of the samsaric life, the quest for immeasurable freedom, the issue of heaven and hell, and so forth. Furthermore, I will show the reader the existence of the unborn and the uncreated (nirvana), how to view the ultimate truth of nirvana from the standpoint of samsāra, how to live the nirvanic life while still coping with samsaric existence, and what is the right path that one may tread so that the actual living of the nirvanic life in saṃsāra is really practicable and realistic.

As regards the rather complicated issue of karma, I try my best to present the complete picture of it by letting the reader consider the various viewpoints maintained by modern Buddhist scholars and the viewpoints of well-known ancient commentators such as Buddhaghosa, so that this issue may be scrutinized thoroughly. The most significant thing is the accurate presentation of the Buddha's own words translated from the variety of suttas (discourses) that explain this matter of karma. In this case, I feel enormously indebted to my great Dharma master, Ajahn Porn Ratanasuvan, who has made available the Thai version he himself translated beautifully and eloquently from the original Pali text so that I can undertake an easy translation of it all into the English language.

I try to make the issue of heaven and hell simple and practical to the general public so that heaven will not be looked up to as a kingdom of utopia existing somewhere in the sky, and hell will not be imagined as the underworld of the painfully tormented place beneath the earth. I present heaven and hell as proclaimed and expounded by the Buddha in the Pali suttas. As we explore this important issue for the benefit of us all, I will discuss at some length the reason for our not understanding this matter of hell on earth and the existence of heaven and hell, as well as what they actually amount to. Such interesting and frequently asked questions as why the fire in hell burns so powerfully and so painfully, what the reason is for so many people going to hell and what that amounts to, how heaven comes into existence and where it actually is, what the dark corner is that prevents us from seeing this matter of heaven and hell with true understanding, and how one can realize it fully, will all be answered in as much detail as possible.

Nirvana is another complicated issue, especially to those scholars who attempt to explain this concept of nirvana without even having a glimpse of it experientially and, similarly, for common Buddhists and the public. Therefore, I would like first to present it in accordance with what the Buddha himself has said and meant to say. Secondly, we will examine some essential and useful viewpoints presented by some Buddhist scholars and some modern psychologists. Thirdly, I will share with the reader my own inner knowledge and visionary wisdom regarding this wonderful and fascinating subject of nirvana so that it may be more practicable in our daily living.

Since the Buddha used the name Siva (equivalent to Śiva or Shiva in Sanskrit) as the representation of nirvana, I will explore the reasons and the meanings of those two words according to both the Buddha and the philosophy of Brahmanism. Connected with Siva or Shiva is the well known concept of ātman or purusha, which will be explained as precisely as possible referring to various sources in the Pali suttas and the *Yoga Sūtra*. The latter was translated into the Thai language by Swami Satyanandaburi, the author of the *Philosophy of Yoga Sutra*, and I myself translate it into English. In addition, the subject of yoga will be looked into, beginning from the viewpoints of the Upanishads right down to the great yogi named Mahā Patañjali, who re-arranged the order of yoga and the methods of teaching it.

Concerning the practices leading on to the full realization of nirvana, I will present to readers the Pali suttas uttered either by the Buddha himself or by his fully enlightened disciples such as Sāriputta and Moggallāna, the right-hand and the left-hand chief disciples of the Buddha, respectively.

All of the Pali suttas referred to in this work are based on the translations into Thai by my greatly admired dharma master, Ajahn Porn Ratanasuvan, who taught me during my four years of the university studies, at Mahachulalongkorn Rajavidyalaya (University), Bangkok, Thailand. Fortunately, I do not have to search for the Pali texts, but simply translate into English from the Ajahn Porn's Thai text, which he made available in his book entitled *Buddha-Vidaya*, volume 2, for which I feel deeply indebted to him as my my Thai Dharma Master.

Let me elaborate on the nature of Dharma Studies at Mahachulalongkorn University. During that period, the University appointed an ex-monk, Ajahn Porn, to teach us the subject of Applied Dharma Studies. He was a very fine scholar and an eloquent, exquisite speaker on the Dharma, which he made vibrantly alive and extremely interesting subject for us all. In addition, he was training certain selected students (I was one of them) to be good speakers so that they could be dispatched at their invitation to various secondary schools, colleges, and universities in and around the city of Bangkok to teach the Dharma in the modern, progressive way. It was an exceedingly exciting time both for him (Ajahn Porn) and for all of us who participated enthusiastically in such a valuable project. Working on that project diligently and intelligently, I became one of Ajahn Porn's favorite trainees and dharma teachers.

A book of this nature is rarely made available for the general public, so that lovers of reading typically lack this kind of mental and intellectual food for new thinking and for the nourishment of the mind as well as for spiritual inspiration. This is another reason for me to make my utmost attempts of producing this contentious but estimable work. So, let us see what will follow after this book has come out to the world market, about which I am especially curious.

Dhiravamsa
Las Canteras Beach
Las Palmas de Gran Canaria, Spain
March 9, 2012

TEXTUAL REFERENCES

In this book a number of references are made that may not be familiar to the Western reader. These are as follows, briefly explained:

Dhammavicharn
Dhammavicharn is a Thai textbook for Dharma Studies of Naktham Ek, the highest grade in Thai monastery schools, and was written by the Most Venerable Kromvachirañanvaroros, a greatest Buddhist scholar and educator who formulated the Systematic Thai Sangha Education.

Mahachula and Mahamakut (Versions of the Tipiṭaka)
Mahachula and Mahamakut are Buddhist Educational Institutions of the Thai Sangha. When the Tripiṭaka is arranged, some of them are in Mahacula versions, while some others in Mahamakut versions.

All reference numbers follow the Thai arrangements of Suttantas (or Suttas), Abhidhamma, and Vinaya, together with their commentaries, sub-commentaries, and sub-sub-commentaries. Basically, there are 25 volumes of Suttantas, 12 volumes of Abhidhamma, and 8 volumes of Vinaya.

Sangha
This is the Community of Buddhist Monks.

Sangiti
Sangiti is one of the Abhidhamma texts both in Pali and in Thai.

Tipiṭaka
This is Buddhist Canon of Theravada Buddhism, in the Pali language, or as translated from the Pali. The Canon is in three parts: the Suttantas (discourses), the Abhidhamma (theoretical philosophy and depth psychology), and the Vinaya (rules of the sangha). References to texts may also be made citing the text name, followed by the volume and page numbers, in reference to the Pali Text Society's publications unless otherwise indicated.

=1=

ORIGIN OF SAMSĀRA

Since it is commonly accepted among Buddhist scholars that the beginning and the ending of samsāra are inconceivable, how does the present author dare to give this title to this chapter and to discuss the origin of samsara, which has no beginning and no ending. As we know, when there is a beginning, there is an ending; but when the beginning does not exist, then it is not legitimate to talk about the ending. A similar understanding is in the right-to-the-point answer that Huineng (or Hui Neng) gave to Hongren, the Fifth Patriarch of the Ch'an (Zen) Tradition, and consequently became his successor as the Sixth Patriarch. Hui Neng was responding to a claim that **originally, the mirror is clean and clear. Later dust blows in and attaches to it so that the mirror becomes dirty and blurred. How can one make it dirt-free and spotless again?** Hui Neng, who was remarkably sharp and extraordinarily insightful in his inner eye of profound wisdom, after having heard this, replied to this spontaneously and with a great outcry. He clearly declared without hesitation that **fundamentally, the so-called mirror does not exist, so how can there be any dust to make it dirty?**

This reply by Hui Neng, and the consciousness that he is alluding to, can be a guiding light in our investigations here. In this book we will come to a clearer understanding of the mind that is originally and fundamentally dirt-free and spotless, to use the imagery in his reply. And to appreciate the ways in which the mind becomes clouded and confused, with a perspective on all this that allows **the setting upright of what is otherwise nirvana upside down**.

The Aggañña-Sutta

At this time, let us consider the Aggañña-Sutta, a very rich discourse found in the Dīgha Nikāya.[1] As the name of this particular sutta indicates, this is a discourse of the Buddha (sutta; Sanskrit, sūtra) that discusses aggañña: what is recognized or known as (-ñña; Sanskrit -jña) foremost (agga), anterior (agga), primordial (agga), primary (agga), prominent (agga), highest (agga), and best (agga). All of these meanings of this key term agga (Sanskrit, agra) are relevant to the contents and import of this discourse.

The discourse can be understood as a mythological presentation of the world, of humankind, and of society, as these have developed through time. In this teaching, which includes this presentation giving an understanding of people and society, the Buddha also offers an alternative set of values and vision of life. Here we will highlight aspects of the discourse that will be relevant to our overall interests.

---

[1] The Aggañña-Sutta is the twenty-seventh sutta or discourse in the Dīgha Nikāya, part of the Pali Canon (the Pali Tipiṭaka). For more on this, see above, p. iv.

We will use this discourse to begin defining some of the key issues we will address in this book, repeating our invitation to all readers to consider this understanding of the mind that is originally and essentially dirt-free and spotless, to use the imagery in the introductory passage above about Hui Neng.

As with many Buddhist discourses (suttas), this one begins by setting the context of the exchange between the Buddha and his audience. Here, there are two Brahman youths, by name Vāseṭṭha and Bhāradvāja. They have given up their societal position as Brahmans and at the time of this meeting are living as novices, monks for a probationary period (parivāsa) of four months before becoming fully ordained as Buddhist monks. Hoping to hear some teachings by the Buddha, they approach him, show him respect, and walk alongside him.

And, as with many great teaching stories, the concerns that inspire the story are addressed while at the same time additional considerations are introduced that often open up and broaden the perspective of the audience, beyond the initial focus inspiring the story. We will see that this particular teaching story (sutta) operates in this way.

The Buddha remarks that the two young men are Brahmans who have gone forth (as the traditional expression puts it) into homelessness to become monks, with heads shaved, indicating their monk status. He then raises the issue of whether other Brahmans revile them and abuse them in words because of this commitment on their part. Vāseṭṭha replies that that is indeed the case, and that they are criticized for their leaving the highest caste (social group), as the Brahmans see themselves, and going over to the lower, darker groups. In part, they are criticized for abandoning their high social role, with Brahmans seeing themselves as the highest, represented as their coming from the mouth of Brahma, while other castes are deemed inferior, represented as their coming from the feet of Brahma. The Buddha will question this claim.

Here begins the Buddha's critique of the various divisions of society and his own contrasting vision of what is more important, primary, and foremost, over and beyond these divisions.

To give some background information that will make the discourse more easily comprehensible, we may note here that the Buddha refers in his remarks to the four major groups of people into which all of society was divided in the Brahmanic or Hindu culture: the four groups, called castes (or vaṇṇas; Sanskrit, varṇas), are the khattiyas (Sanskrit, kṣatriyas: warriors, administrators, etc.), the brahmans (priests), the vessas (Sanskrit, vaiśyas: cattle-herders, merchants, traders) and the suddas (Sanskrit, śūdras: artisans, laborers, farmers).

The Buddha begins by pointing out the mundane fact that the Brahmans speak of being born from the mouth of Brahma, but in fact Brahman women can be seen to menstruate, to become pregnant, to give birth to babies (who are thereby known to be Brahmans), and then to suckle these same babies. This is birth from mothers, not from the mouth of Brahma. We might say that the Buddha brings the conversation back to earth!

Then, on a moral level, the Buddha points out further that no matter which of these four groups composing society is being considered, there are those in that given group who do good actions and those in that same group who do bad actions. This of course shifts the focus and emphasis from the question of which group any given person belongs to, to the question of how each individual thinks, speaks, and acts. The Buddha returns to this toward the end of this sutta or discourse. The Buddha makes the point that the dhamma — as expressed in the Buddha's teachings — that guides people of all groups is the best (agga) in this world and in the next.

This gentle bridge into the topic of this world and the next brings the discussion to the topic of the Brahmanic cyclic vision of worlds. The Buddha goes on to explain here the way in which the various groups have come to be, a teaching story that contains much implicit advice for all people. He continues after that elaboration of society and its four classes or castes by encouraging the two youths about a proper life path, one that follows the dharma (a harmonious way of acting in the world as presented in the Buddha's teachings), and highlights the goal of life, which, in Buddhist terms, is the elimination of the corruptions and fetters of mind that keep one from complete liberation, through deep insight leading to the highest or best of knowledge and conduct. (We noted that Hui Neng addressed these same issues in other terms.) We will be discussing these interrelated topics in various parts of this book.

Let us look now at the story that the Buddha presents of the development of the world, of humankind, and of society, to see some of the issues that this discourse presents for our consideration. The Buddha describes in that discourse the cycle of worlds that was part of his culture's understanding of the universe and that would also have been easily understood by the two young brahmans listening to him, as with his mention of the four varṇas (above). In this vision of reality, there is a cyclic arising and ending of worlds, measured in what are termed kappas (Sanskrit, kalpas) or world eons. After expanding and developing, each world will contract and end.

At the end of such a cycle-sequence, there are beings born in a brahma (noble) realm called ābhassara (sparkling light). It is said in Buddhist texts that rays of light like flashes of lightning are sent out or emitted through the bodies of those radiant gods (ābhassara brahmas). Upon the world's expansion for the beginning of the next kappa, those beings disappear (die) from the ābhassara plane of life, came back, and are re-born on the earth.

Since at the time of their residing and existing in the brahma world they simply lived on ecstatic joy as their primary food, they obtained their re-existence on earth out of their psychic power (the power of higher meditative absorption). And they were filled with sparkling and brilliant light and moved easily through the skies, features of their earlier lives as ābhassara brahmas.

Let me describe the ābhassara brahma realm more here. Consider these beings that disappeared from the world at the time of its destruction and were then reborn in a special ābhassara brahma realm. While living in that realm, they possessed luminous light of their own with which they used for eliminating darkness and lighting their world, and did not need any external light. (Their precisely accurate name of ābhassara itself means sparklingly bright light.) Timeless time passed by with no day or night, nor did month and year exist, for did seasons. They were sufficient unto themselves for light, and similarly, adequate unto themselves for nourishment. As just mentioned, the primary food that the ābhassara brahmas used for nourishing and sustaining their lives in their higher realm of existence was a non-material and spiritually energetic food: **ecstatic joy**. That is, since those living beings have only an exceptionally refined and vibrantly energetic body without a form, they do not need any material food to live on. Instead, their survival was maintained by a mental-contact food, a will-for-living food, and a consciousness food, all of which are features of ecstatic joy (a category of euphoric feeling known in Pali as attamana). Such a joy in fact permeates these beings, these psychophysical systems, entirely, sustaining and nourishing them with richness and abundance, as this joy is an all-inclusive food in which are contained all essential requirements for a healthy life.

We can be curious about what it was exactly that those beings did while living on earth to lead them on to the ābhassara brahma realm. Certainly, they did not get there by chance, but reached such a higher plane of existence by some very significant deed. What was it, then? Such a deed is not, I am sure, something ordinary that common people do for gaining merit and a good life, but it is a mental training or mental culture that leads to the achievement of a meditative absorption technically known as jhāna.

Here, according to the systems of Buddhist meditation, there are two significant ways of practicing meditation; the first of these is **samatha**, the way of **calm**, aimed at cultivating **tranquility and firmly established mind** in which there is **no distraction** and **no disturbance**. The second way of meditation is entitled **vipassanā**, the way of insight, whose objective is to cultivate and bring to full development **impeccable awareness, firm and imperative attention, and an all-seeing eye of wisdom**.[2] We will say more about this second way of meditation further on in this book.

The highest objective of this first practice is to accomplish both the jhānas with form and the formless jhānas. In this connection, we can suggest that those beings endowed with sparkling light (ābhassara) must have achieved the jhāna with form (rūpa-jhāna); otherwise they would not have possessed such light. Here it is extremely interesting to take note that their sparkling light illuminated their entire realm incessantly, with no need for any other light, including light from the sun and the moon. They became completely self-sufficient regarding light, which is one of the most essential requirements for living and existing. We can recall in this context that the absence of light submerges the world into the dark and murky plane of life in which the living beings cannot continue their existence for very long.

---

[2] See the detailed description of the principle and the practice of this system of Buddhist meditation in the author's book entitled *A New Vision of Buddhism*.

With the resultant outcome of the jhānic states of consciousness (higher concentrative states of consciousness), especially the second jhāna, achieved through the practice of samatha (calm meditation), they are born in the realm of the brahmas that possess brilliantly radiant light. We may see the relationship between this consciousness and the formula of the second jhāna (meditative absorption) of Buddhist concentrative meditation, which is described in the Pali texts as follows: "Through the suppression or elimination of reasoning and reflection, a meditator attains the second jhāna, which consists in internal serenity, the unification or one-pointedness of focused consciousness totally free from reasoning and reflecting, born of the firmly stabilized mind (firm concentration) in which are contained ecstatic joy and happiness."[3]

Out of such attainment, those meditators lifted themselves up and were born in the just-discussed plane of consciousness filled with flashes of radiant light, so that they did not need any external light. In addition, as also mentioned, they lived on *ecstatic joy* alone, since their invisible, refined bodies are full of such eminent light, which they could send out naturally in all directions in the plane of life in which they lived. That is, if we undertake the genuine practice of **calm meditation** (samatha) and accomplish the jhānic states of consciousness, we will certainly be able to get nourished by ecstatic joy since this kind of joy is one of the contents of the jhāna. With such accomplishment, we will be no different from the ābhassara brahmas, but will actually become them ourselves.

All of this is part of a psycho-scientific explanation. We will return to other parts of this and especially the relationship with mental development or meditation just touched upon above, after reviewing the text of Aggañña-Sutta, which refers to the ābhassara brahmas, the radiant beings, just introduced, and talks of the changes that have led to humankind as we know it and the social groups that Vāseṭṭha and Bhāradvāja were concerned with.

The original foods

Let us return to the Aggañña-Sutta, where the Buddha begins discussing the originations of the world with Vāseṭṭha and Bhāradvāja. At first there were only great waters and no light at all. (This beginning might remind us of the text in Genesis 1:1-2.) In the Aggañña-Sutta, the story continues here, bringing in mention of the ābhassara brahmas who were now reborn on earth (quite different from the way Genesis continues, of course).

As noted, the primary food that the ābhassara brahmas used for nourishing and sustaining their lives in their higher realm of existence was a non-material and spiritually energetic food, the special nourishment of **ecstatic joy**. (The story begins here addressing the psychological dimension of existence.) By way of mundane contrast, most of us are not ābhassara brahmas, but just human beings living our lives here, on the earth, and so we might not have a

---

[3] See the detailed discussion on the subject of jhānas in the author's work, in English, *Turning to the Source;* and in Spanish, *Retorno al Origen*.

capacity to get access to ecstatic joy as our food easily since our physical bodies are solidly structured and coarse in their form in comparison with the invisible bodies (energetic, subtle bodies) of those ābhassara brahmas.

Continuing with a mythological representation of our more usual human condition, the Buddha describes a milk-like substance that appeared in those primordial times on the surface of these waters as a thin coating, as the skin that forms on warmed milk as it cools, filled with color, fragrance, and flavor. (This continues the psychological dimension: here, making explicit reference to the senses of sight, smell, and taste. More on this dimension will follow directly.)

Some of the ābhassara brahmas came to an urge to taste this substance, leading to their dipping their fingers into the milk-like film, tasting it and, taken by it, feeling yearning (or thirst, in Buddhist terms) for it. Thus arose strong desire. (Human psychological particulars are slowly introduced here, with their social consequences.) Because of this action taken, they unfortunately lost their luminous light, and due to the disappearance of such light, there came into existence the moon, the sun, and the stars, along with day and night, months and years and seasons. A further consequence was that their bodies began to become more course, more dense (one of the features that earth represents, to be met later in this book as a feature of earthlings as "thick" ones), and with a difference in looks between them (not simply all radiating a similar great light). Some of these individuals then judged themselves to be more beautiful than others, and came to despise the others they saw as less attractive. Thus arose arrogance and conceit. And the ending of the milk-like substance as food.

With this, things continued similarly, with mushrooms next appearing, and still more denseness of body, more differences in looks, more arrogance and conceit. Then there were various sorts of growths for food, such as creepers, ground-hugging vines with their foliage and fruit. With similar results.

And then there was rice that appeared, clean, fragrant, and plentiful. (We may of course see the way in which this story arises from its culture, which was different in these particulars from the situation described in Genesis.) This type of rice, without husk, but filled with fragrance and its white grains, after having been picked (harvested) in the morning, got ripe by the evening without further human effort. Living on this kind of rice, the physical bodies of those beings appeared ever more dense with ever-greater differences in beauty, leading to still greater conceit and despising of others.

Before continuing the story of Aggañña-Sutta, let us focus here on the psychological dimension of this change in density and in the variations of degrees of beauty in various individuals. Mentioned in passing, above, we may focus on the fact that as these changes were taking place, some people began to behave quite inappropriately by creating two forms of mental and psychological reactions: one being self-pride, another, a negative attitude toward their fellow beings, that is, looking down upon the others while holding themselves up as superior. These reactions, put into a religious terminology, may be called a mental and psychological karma (action committed intentionally). In Christianity pride is considered a sin; Buddhism sees pride as a deeply rooted contamination (kilesa) that can be totally transformed only by the achievement of full enlightenment (arahatship). The habit of putting other people down, judging and looking down upon one another is, in a way, a result or by-product of self-pride. In fact, once pride is established, many other unhealthy, negative, or even destructive reactive patterns will inevitably follow. For this reason, we see much more clearly why it is so difficult to overcome pride, let alone to transform it. Moreover, quite a number of people do not really want to get rid of pride since this kilesa (mental contamination) can inflate their ego making them feel self-importance and self-aggrandizement, commonly considered qualities essential for a human person to "survive" in our world.

Now let us discuss in some details the subject matter of the original food or nourishment that those brightly shining beings consumed for their survival after being reborn on the earth. First, in the sutta under discussion, no category of food was mentioned before those beings' death and disappearance from the earth and rebirth in the ābhassara brahma realm, so one has no idea about what they lived on and how they survived before the earth and the cosmos moved toward destruction. So we will begin following the sutta's comments.

How material food affects the human physical body and its light of consciousness

As previously cited above, we understand from the Buddha's discourse that those luminously shining beings from the ābhassara brahma world lost their light because of their consumption of a material food beginning with a tasty milk-like substance that arose unexpectedly on the earth. With the resultant disappearance of the natural light they authentically possessed, they had no choice but became dependent on the external light from the sun and from the moon that fortunately came into existence for their fate at that time; otherwise they would have turned into a complete extinction with no remainder. Instead, they merely declined and decayed physically, mentally, psychologically, and spiritually. Also, with the loss of light, their environment changed utterly, that is to say, day and night appeared and disappeared alternately every twelve hours or so. Following this phenomenal pattern there appeared month and year, and seasons, to complete the cycle of time, light and darkness. Now, their lives exist within the boundary of space and time, whilst timeless time has vanished from their observable reality altogether.

We learn in this sutta about the radical and somewhat mysterious changes that took place to their physical bodies and skin. Mythologically speaking, in the Buddhist discourse there is a major impact in consciousness that comes of what we eat and ingest. (We may consider here the story of the eating in the Garden of Eden and the mythological problems that that created, as described in Genesis 3. We will not go into that in detail here.) Some of us might be wondering how food or what we consume has so great an influence on our body, emotion, and mind. Well, whatever we take in through eating and drinking not only pacifies our hunger, quenches our thirst, and nourishes our psychophysical systems, but also becomes an energy system that carries along with it all the existential qualities of the material food that we consume. Therefore, the solid food eaten by those beings who had just arrived on earth from the ever-shining plane of life, turned their invisible, energetic bodies into a physical human form with the qualities of solidity, hardness, and coarseness, together with at some becoming unattractive (to others). All these changes both in form and in quality are the consequences of the material food with its rough energy consumed by those brightly shining beings. Now their bodies became visible and possessed the definite structure of the human form; and at the same time their luminous light disappeared altogether since they forsook their primary food of ecstatic joy and all other categories of euphoric feeling. From this perspective, we see the truth that a rough energy creates a solid form while a refined energy forms an invisible, energetic, subtle body. A certain kind of form comes into existence as the result of the formation of an energy system with its defining quality or qualities ever-present in that system.

Returning to the influence of thought and behavior on our appearance, we understand that the skin, like other human organs such as livers, kidneys, and lungs, has a function of discharging poison and unhealthy material from inside the body. Further, very rough mental and emotional contaminations, after residing inside the body and the psyche for a while will resurface and affect our appearance, particularly our skin, which is an outlet of the harmful residue. So, we may notice the negative impact on our mind and also on our body of a pessimistic attitude, hurtful thoughts, self-aggrandizement, self-righteousness or pride, greediness, and depressing feelings.

The emergence of male and female sexes

In the Aggañña-Sutta, the Buddha continued discussing with the novice Vāseṭṭha, saying, "Now, it happened that there appeared male and female human beings." When they paid keen attention to the opposite sex, passionate desires were aroused in them and therefore, from great lust they began having sexual intercourse with one another publicly (in front of people around them). Those who did not approve of this behavior threw stones on those making love in public, who, later on, began to build houses or dwelling places for residing and living inside so that their sexual activities could be carried out in an out-of-sight place, so to speak.

The Buddha did not describe exactly how those original human beings created their male and female entities, but simply said that it just happened that the male and female sexes appeared naturally (or through a certain formation, just like an embryo in a mother's womb forming into either a male or a female structure). We may simply note here that the Buddha left this matter of male and female genders unexplained in detail regarding the structural formation of these two genders.

Accumulating food and the emerging of landlords

According to the Aggañña-Sutta it is said that some human beings decided that instead of collecting rice (which was available for all living beings at that time) at one time for breakfast and at another time for dinner, they could gather together more rice, doing so only once a day for both breakfast and dinner. This decision was said to come from an efficient laziness. (Continue watching what all of this leads to!) In any case, such a way of collecting rice didn't work out well since each collection could last only one day, or two days, or four days, or at maximum eight days, and for this reason the act of longer-term storing up food took place. As a result, the white grain[4] of rice changed to being covered with a husk; and in addition, there was no growth of a new rice plant to replace the uprooted one. Gaps in growth and opened spaces between the rice plants were created and spread out throughout the entire rice field. To respond to this situation those primary humans held meetings for discussing such an alarming decline of the rice plants universally provided for them, and they all agreed to divide the rice fields into various boundaries so that each family or each single person could have an ownership of a piece of land for growing rice.

As time passed, some people, in addition to maintaining the ownership of their land, stole rice from other people's fields. Upon being caught and arrested, those thieves were merely instructed not to do such a thing again. Certainly, they promised to obey the instruction, but later they committed the act of stealing once again. Being caught and arrested up to three times they just received the same instruction (without any punishment) and once again they made the same promise; although in some severe cases the thieves got punished by being hit with hands, having lumps of earth thrown upon them, or getting beaten by a rod or a piece of wood. Once again, they called another meeting for consultations and discussions on such matters as stealing, laying blame, telling lies, and beating one another with sticks, which had happened among the people. At the meeting some people proposed an idea of appointing someone to do the job of blaming those who were blameworthy and abandoning those worthy of abandonment; and also suggested that the person holding such responsibility should receive the shared rice from the members of community. For that job, a person endowed with good behavior and dignified quality was chosen and appointed the chief for carrying out the function of leadership. Thus, there arose certain titles for the chief such as mahāsammata (the appointed one), khattiya (landlord), and rājā (the one who satisfies others and brings them happiness). So, the so-called monarch was invented by, and from, those people who were equal and not from other people who were not equal.[5] Such a title and an executive function were created through the dharma or righteousness, and not by adharma (non-righteousness). For this, dharma became first and foremost of all things in terms of respect and guiding light for those people living and sharing their lives together in a community.

Here let us consider **three principal matters**: first, the storing up of food, second, dishonorable deeds based on greed and indolence, and third, leadership. In the Aggañña-Sutta the Buddha pointed out that human laziness caused the accumulation of food in the first place. To review here, to see the development or arising of social roles and then the Buddha's viewpoint on these (including a new perspective on the caste system), those primary humans were quite relaxed about the collection of rice from the shared rice fields that were

---

[4] Originally rice grain was naturally white and without husk. So, there was no need for milling it.
[5] This indicates that originally all people are equal.

naturally provided for all those living there and in the vicinity of those fields. Out of laziness, some people collected a great deal of rice at any one time so that it could last several weeks or months before the next collection would be undertaken. Because of this act of storing up and accumulating rice, the rice-guardian gods, as one might say, got angry and mad with such an unwholesome action taken by those humans. Therefore, they punished all the collective humans by covering the white grain rice with husk in the hope that they would work harder so that their laziness and idleness could be overcome. In addition, nature also punished those humans by not allowing the new rice plants to grow in place of the ones that were uprooted. Getting alarmed by the decline of the rice plants, they held serious discussions over the deteriorating situation and found an unrealistic solution by dividing the original rice fields for all into various individual boundaries so that ownership was created.

Now, with ownership it became inevitable that human greed would come into play. Some wanted to store up more rice in their places so as to have plenty of it without having to feel anxious about the shortage of it at any time in the foreseeable future. Because of greed combined with idleness, they began to commit dishonorable deeds by stealing rice from other people's fields, while maintaining their own fields and their rights of ownership. As the universal law states that an evil action leads to more unwholesome deeds, which strengthen aggressiveness and never-satisfying desires for wealth and pleasure, so the vicious circle goes on and on until it reaches its peak. This kind of event we have already witnessed, with the consequences of the objectionable and nasty actions performed by those primary humans. First, when getting caught and arrested, the thieves only received an instruction in place of punishment, which didn't stop them from doing what they did (stealing), instead, they carried out their stealing activities many more times. Then, secondly, even though they got some very mild punishments such as hitting their hands or a beating with a rod or a staff, they did not care to give up their stealing career since it is still an easier way to get things without undergoing hard work.

The ownership of the land had made people become greedier about land and therefore, they looked for more parcels of land to own. In those days, it was much easier to own the land since it was just there, available for anyone to measure and mark the boundaries of certain parcels and possess them without having to pay a cent. Those who were cleverer than the others could own hundreds and hundreds of acres and became the landlords or khattiyas. Some might own up to a million acres of land and became great khattiyas, so to speak. Usually, one of these property owners was chosen and appointed the chief of the community so that the beginning of a ruling class had been established since the khattiyas, apart from possessing plenty of land, were much more intelligent and better educated than many others in their community. So, they knew how to lead, how to rule, and how to pass judgments on a variety of matters, including the punishments to be imposed on those breaking and breaching the agreements, regulations, and laws of the land. This is the beginning of feudalism and monarchy, which we have seen in our human history both in the East, as here, and in the West.

Regarding absolute monarchy, it is quite interesting to note that in the West it perished much faster than that in the East. The main reason, I think, is because in the West, absolute monarchy was basically involved with power as the principle, whilst the East embraces both power and myth, meaning, a belief system with regard to the concept of monarchy and the power heavily fought for through military means, for instance, the primitive use of elephants and swords. Eastern people, for example, the citizens of Thailand, believe that their kings come from heaven to rule over them and therefore, the monarchs/kings are regarded as putative devas (heavenly beings), and for this reason are put up in the higher throne which the common people can never reach, or where even direct speech is prohibited. For example, a common person like us would speak only to the dust underneath the monarch's feet, but not to the person himself. Furthermore, the king and members of his royal family cannot be criticized even when they behaved badly or did something deadly wrong. This is ridiculous and absolutely primitive.

According to Thai history, the first king of this present dynasty (Chakri-wongs) actually came from the military. He, Thong Duang by name, was a common person, but became a great soldier and fought successfully for independence and stability of the country. Then, he established himself as a king of Siam (now known as Thailand), so he became the first monarch, while the present King Bhumipol is the ninth in the succession of the Chakri dynasty. Therefore, in their blood and flesh they are all common people, and are not putative heavenly beings of any kind at all. The Thai people only make that up and worship them according to their belief system without any corresponding reality. So, with the combination of power and myth, the limited monarchy lasts a bit longer than that of the Western world.

Let us return to the origin of the ruling class, which gives rise to the monarchy and so forth. As we have learnt in the Aggañña-Sutta, the reason for choosing and appointing someone the chief of the community was because of stealing. At first, the number of thieves was relatively small; others could handle collectively the matter of stealing quite easily, without a leader or chief. But when the thieves were on the increase, the others needed someone to take charge and to pass appropriate judgment on those who committed the crime. The person appointed to this kind of job had two principal branches of power, executive power and judicial power, to enable him to rule and to pass judgments on the matters concerned. This chosen person earned different titles as already cited above; and each title implies admirable qualities and good work done for the community and does not, in any way, indicates an egoic power of control and manipulation. We might note here that the authentic power that the chief had was love, respect, and admiration bestowed upon him through his good relationships with the people, and righteousness that he possessed and manifested through the good work carried out for the welfare, prosperity, and happiness of the community members.

Considering what the original society had done and set as an example for us, we may formulate a concept of dhammādhipateyya, which means power and authority of and by the dharma (righteousness). This concept fits in with the message from the Aggañña-Sutta, which stressed that dharma was the most significant thing in their individual and collective lives since dharma is, in truth, first and foremost of all things, meaning, dharma comes first. Even some titles of the ruler such as king or rājā indicate this quality of righteousness. For example, dhammarājā was a ruler's title often found in Buddhist literature from the Buddha's time on — in Western terms, from 543 B.C.E.

This concept of dhammādhipateyya is contrasted with two other forms of governing body, namely, attādhipateyya, the power and authority of a person, which should signify an absolute monarch or a dictator, and pajādhipateyya, the power and authority of the people or democracy, well known to contemporary people. Of these three forms of government, the dhammādhipateyya is the best, while the second best is pajādhipateyya or democracy in the true sense of the word. The dharma that the ruler of dhammādhipateyya must possess and manifest authentically through his relationships with the people around him and with all members of the community as well as through the work to be carried out for all the people, is technically known as **brahmavihāra**, the mental and spiritual virtues for a ruler, a parent, a chief, and for those holding such a similar position in society. There are four categories of the brahmavihāra, namely, **unconditional love or loving-kindness, compassion, empathic joy for the success of others, and equanimity (even-seeing rectitude).** Endowed with these four virtues (which are the noble qualities of heart and mind) the ruler, the parents, the chief, head, or leader of any job, or any position, will be entitled dhammarājā or brahma (noble person). In addition, a measurement of any person's spiritual progress is basically done by referring to the fuller and fuller development of those four virtues of brahmavihāra.

The origination of the caste system

The Aggañña-Sutta went on saying, "There exist those who renounce the world and become mendicants for the sole purpose of purifying and eliminating evil, who are called brahmins (noble)." They build a dwelling place, a leaf-hut, in the forest, and focused their mind with an intense, penetrating and continuous attention, which is technically known as **meditation.** For this reason, they earn the title of **jhāyaka** (meditative absorber), while other brahmins live in simple houses just outside a village or a small town doing some writing and producing textbooks, making comments on the Veda for the purpose of teaching people and letting them chant. The latter do not meditate and therefore are given the title of **ajjhāyaka** (non-meditator/non-absorber). Originally, the ajjhāyaka title was a sort of mocking expression — a negative name, but now it has a positive connotation, which refers to the chanters of sutras and mantras. In addition, there are certain people who live their lives enjoying sexual activities and earning their living by having jobs and trading. Therefore, they are called merchants (vessa, trader/merchant). And further, there are those who live their lives on hunting, or the chase, and for that, earn the title of shudra (Sanskrit) or sudda (Pali), which became the name of a worker or a laborer or a small businessman, the one who carries out small businesses.

(According to the Pali text commentators the word 'sudda' derives from the concept ludda, which means hunter, or from another concept, khudda, that means small business. This seems to indicate that the traders and merchants are those doing the important and bigger jobs while the shudra people perform comparatively unimportant jobs and small businesses.)

Hereupon, the Buddha concluded by saying that the brahmins, the khattiyas, the traders/merchants, and the working class people originated from those who shared their lives equally and had equality in opportunity, and not from any other people who were unequal (who didn't exist in those days). Those four categories of people came into existence naturally and by the nature of their functions or jobs, and not by non-righteousness. This implies that the division of classes does not derive from any other principle or any belief systems, but it is due to the fact that different people hold different positions and perform different jobs and functions according to their skills, qualifications, and abilities that gives rise to the notions of brahmin (religious practitioners), khattiya (land-lord, warrior, ruler), vessa (trader/merchant), and shudra (worker or small businessman). In this way, no one is better or worse, higher or lower, more significant or less dignified, than the other is. They are all equal.

Then, the Buddha continued expounding that upon the passing of time some people within those four categories, namely, land-lord or khattiya, brahmin, vessa, and shudra were not satisfied with the mundane things that they had been carrying out, decided to leave household affairs, and took up a form of reclusion and became homeless ones. Therefore, a circle of recluses was created. This is another proof that the recluses upon whom the brahmins looked down on so much, actually originated from those belonging to the four categories of people, and not from any other classes (because such things did not exist). So, there is no one higher or lower, better or worse; they are all equal by birth, race (only human race existed at that time), and color, and above all no discrimination of any kind ever existed in those days.

According to the explanations made by the Buddha in the Aggañña-Sutta we see clearly that the caste system did not exist in those first days, and that there were only categories of people, four in number, that came to be, based on the performing of different jobs and the carrying out of different functions in society. However, later on, the author believes, the Hindu society developed or transformed those four categories of people into a caste system, starting with Brahmanism that affiliated itself with the ruling or governing people, the khattiya, that developed from being a property owner to a feudalist, to a warrior, and then onto being a monarch). These two classes of people had enormous power over those following their religious practices and working under them as government officials, so they put their heads together and created a definitive caste system. The brahmins maintain their purity of caste by getting married only to those believers and practitioners of Brahmanism and do not mix with any other categories of people, while the ruling class confines themselves to their ruling families only, lifting themselves up and putting others down to the level of "common" people. Then, those who prefer to enjoy their profession of trading and doing various businesses are classified as vessa — traders or merchants; further still, the brahmins and khattiyas classify those laborers with skills and without skills into the fourth class. Later on, there is quite a number of poor people such as slaves, servants, and beggars, since the gap between the richer and the poorer is getting wider and bigger, harsh and ruthless poverty is inevitably created, which gives rise to the lowest class, who are given the awfully unpleasant title of untouchables. All these categories are just human creations out of conceited pride, rigidly opinionated viewpoint, and ignorance of (the act of IGNORing) the simple, historical truth. (All humans are originally and intrinsically equal.)

Equality in the consequences of actions

Finally, the Buddha concluded his discourse stating that all khattiyas, brahmins, vessas, shudras, and samanas (monks/recluses), if anyone of them did a wrong thing either through action, speech, or thought, held a wrong view, performed their activities with such a wrong view, they would suffer the evil consequences of their deeds and would live non-progressive, painful, and emotionally tormented lives with no exception. On the contrary, if anyone of them would do the right things, either through action, speech, or thought, would maintain a right view, perform their activities with such a right view (wisdom), they would equally reap good results of their deeds and would be able to live progressive, happy, and prosperous lives. In case of doing both good and bad things, they would certainly receive both happy and painful consequences. Furthermore, if anyone within those five categories acts, speaks, or thinks rightly, cultivates mental culture, and trains his/her mind properly, and as well also practices mindfully and diligently those seven dharmas pertaining to enlightenment,[6] such a person would realize nirvana in this very lifetime.

Among those four fundamental categories of people, if anyone becomes a bhikkhu (one who sees the danger of samsaric life), transforms all mental contaminations, does all that needs to be done for his/her growth and maturity, lays down the burden (being totally free both in action and in non-action), and becomes completely liberated through profound insight and perfect wisdom, such a person is regarded as the topmost one among them all through his/her own dharma practice, and not by any other means. This is because dharma is the best of all things at all times, and also is timeless (akālika).

At the end of his discourse, the Buddha stressed this teaching, saying, "The khattiya is the best among those holding onto a lineage, but those who possess knowledge and wisdom, and are perfected in good conduct, become the best and topmost persons amidst the devas (shining beings) and humans."

It has been apparent that the Buddha, out of his perfect knowledge and compassion for the novices Vāseṭṭha and Bhāradvāja, explained to them distinctly and without any prejudices, the non-class structure and the caste

---

[6] These, more fully, refer to the thirty-seven dharmas pertaining to Enlightenment, namely, four foundations of mindfulness, four energetic practices, four ways to success, five mental faculties, five spiritual forces, seven factors of enlightenment, and eightfold path (the Buddha's middle way). These thirty-seven dharmas when grouped together become seven groups of dharmas.

system that then originated and evolved throughout the history of humankind. This was because the Buddha did not agree with the then-existing caste system, and he compellingly eliminated it and vigorously prevented it from happening in his Order of Monks (bhikkhu), his Order of Nuns (bhikkhuni), and his circles of male and female devotees. For example, at one time when several Sakyan princes together with their favorite hairdresser, Upali by name, approached the Buddha and asked for ordination, he, with his unmistakable perceptiveness of the Princes' pride, kept them waiting while permitting Upali to become ordained first. After that, he ordained those princes one after another. By so doing, he could subdue the arrogant pride held firmly and rigidly in their psyche as well as in their Sakyan blood before allowing them to enter his caste-free Order. Another, related reason for his compassionately determined action of allowing Upali to receive the ordination before those princes was that in the Buddhist monastic system, the seniority of monks is calculated by their hours, days, weeks, months, and years of joining in with the Order of Bhikkhus starting from the moment of receiving the ordination. One related monastic rule says that a junior monk must obey a senior monk at all costs and above all must walk behind him and be seated on the right hand side of his senior. This is the matter of humbleness (as opposed to pride) and proper respect in accordance with the Eastern culture, which, as a matter of fact, has its root in Buddhism.

Reviewing the issue of equality, we comprehend undoubtedly and precisely that the Buddha, not only respects human rights that offer equality in opportunity and are legitimately and morally free from any restrictions and discriminations regarding race, color of skin, culture, religion, and the birth place of an individual, but recognizes the equality in capacity of men and women to reach full enlightenment and immeasurable freedom, on top of the equality in receiving the consequences of actions done individually or collectively through the body, speech, and thought. This is complete equality, to be seen without any doubt left in the mind of any individual.

Let us now go into the issue of human rights at some length. Being born humans, we are all given various rights such as the right to live, to protect ourselves with a certain measure of security, to believe or not to believe in any religion with respect to any and all dogmatic assertions held by such religions, to embrace any political ideology, to express oneself, and so forth. Each and every person can justifiably claim all those rights since they are natural and also confirmed by both universal and man-made laws.

Since most people do not know many of their human rights due to a lack of education and information, religious organizations should educate them while preaching and carrying out community activities. This is not a political issue. Public education on human rights is a matter of humanity, and we religious and spiritual leaders who are close to people in all occupations should be able to do this very effectively. Keeping this in mind, monks or priests should be fully endowed with knowledge and up-to-date information on the subject of human rights so that they can educate and help people efficiently.

The other thing we can easily do is to cooperate with the United Nations Human Rights Commission, whose mission is to assist peoples all over the globe with respect to human rights. In this connection, we the religious organizations must become globally minded and have open hearts for all kinds of people so as to enable us to work, not only for our religious followers, but also for all humankind without discrimination. As the world becomes globalized, all the organized religions and spiritual institutions should also become globalized, eliminating and transcending our narrow-mindedness and specific interest for our own religions, our own institutions, and our own groups. Although we may act locally, our thoughts and hearts are global, signifying that we open our arms to embrace all humanity using our particular religious organizations as the ways and means for liberating humankind from suffering, social injustice, and hunger not only for food, but also for spiritual realities.

As we are aware, this issue of human rights is rather complicated and not easy to solve. The main reason is that there are different political systems with their distinct ideologies and with leaders who become so egocentric and care only for power and political ideology. In these kinds of situations, human rights suffer. Those who oppose their governments' policies and programs are readily put in jail or even killed with no mercy, which is a kind of barbarism in a civilized world. Due to this power-hunger and aggression, people's rights are undermined and people are oppressed in many parts of the world, and as a result, innocent people and those patriots who have a sincere concern for the well being of their countries and their people suffer tremendously.

In addition to writing about such situations in books, newspapers, or magazines, or discussing them on television or with various groups that care for human rights, we can do one more essential thing. And that is, we all can send out loving, healing energy and good thoughts to those who are oppressed and cut off from their human rights, and in the same instance to those oppressors and dictators, wishing them all to be well, happy, and free from all kinds of oppression, and equally wishing them (oppressors/dictators) wisdom, caring, and compassion for others under their power. This form of meditation or prayer can be done either individually or in groups all over the world so that our planet earth may increasingly gather warm, loving, and healing energy for helping both sides of the spectrum to gain a profound transformation. This contribution can be highly effective since we humans are exceedingly powerful, and meditation or prayer, although invisible, is a very commanding tool.

In conclusion, we all must take refuge in our **awakening nature within,** in the **light of luminous consciousness,** and in the **harmoniously minded community across the globe** because such refuge is **secure,** and it is **supreme** (agga). This means that we must take full charge of ourselves, be creatively present for others, and help one another build up a **world family** with unconditional love in our hearts, mutual understanding in our minds, and peace in all our being.

=2=

THE NOTION OF MAN AND HIS COMPONENT PARTS

It has always been a question frequently asked and for which the right answer has long been sought, not only at the intellectual and philosophical levels, but at the spiritual level as well. This is the question: Who am I? Or, who are we? Although there are many responses to such a difficult-to-answer question, the question still remains unanswered in the convincing way at the level of spirituality, the level of the wholeness of being. A very well-known Hindu Self-Realized and Awakened Brahmin by the name of Ramana Maharshi used this question of "Who am I?" as a mantra meditation, but there is no way to know if anyone practicing that method of meditation ever achieved the definitive answer to our question here, since no one has ever claimed so publicly. Many great religious and spiritual masters such as Gautama, the Buddha, have made enormous efforts and have invested tremendous energy in finding out and explaining as clearly as possible who are we? Who am I? Why are we here at all?

Now the author would like to draw the reader's attention to the Buddha's final analysis of the notion of man, a person, a being, and related ideas. The word "man" is equivalent to the Pali[1] concept of "manussa" or "manushya" in Sanskrit (which is older than Pali). Manussa or manushya signifies "a being whose heart is elevated." Mana = heart or consciousness + ussa = elevated or high-minded = manussa = a being with the elevated heart. Actually, the word "heart" used here refers to consciousness as the **light within** and the **core** of being, so to be considered a manussa, man, or human being, it is absolutely essential that "heart" must be eminent and "consciousness" be raised. Being less than that is not being a human in this sense of manussa, but a tiracchāna (animal) or a peta (ghost) or a vammika (ant), etc.

From merely considering the literal meaning of the word, we can understand the real nature of man as prominently involved with this high-mindedness, the elevation of heart, and the raising of consciousness. Therefore, one may assume man as basically a spiritual being since mind, heart, and consciousness combined in terms of growth and development give rise to the notion of spirituality. For this very reason, we humans need to train our minds, lift up our hearts, and raise or awaken our consciousness in the sense of increasing light to the point of being eternally luminous and vibrantly sparkling so that we will be worthy of the name manussa.

Arriving at this point, we must look into the component parts of a human being, an individual, a being, so as to enable us to encompass a clearly identifiable, analytical knowledge regarding this popularly known notion that is rarely comprehended in its essence.

---

[1] Pali means the language well structured with grammar; it was used by the Buddha in teaching and discussing with others all the essential issues concerning life, birth, and death, and various related subjects.

The aggregates of existence

The analysis that the Buddha makes is as follows: We are *pañcakkhandha,* that is to say, five aggregates (*pañca* means five and *khandha* signifies aggregate or component): *rūpa, vedanā, saññā, sankhāra, and viññāna.* We are a combination of these five constituents and nothing more. Each one of these five things is an aggregate because it is something put together and made up in a group, and not a thing in itself. First, I will present the meaning of each aggregate and later explain them as precisely as possible.

Rūpa is a form, material, or materiality; in another word, the body.

Vedanā are sensations and feelings as the *evaluation* of sense experience.

Saññā is perception and ideation.

Sankhāra refers to the constructive and destructive forces within us, to be precise, inside of our consciousness, which are our virtues and vices, our good and bad characteristics. This is the authentic meaning of sankhāra in the context of the five aggregates, since it has many more meanings depending on where and in what perspective it is used.

Viññāna is *consciousness.*

In our conditioned world there is nothing that exists independently by itself; each thing is a combination of other things, each thing exists depending on another, and each thing exists in relation to the others; and each aggregate (*rūpa, vedanā, saññā, sankhāra, and viññāna*) is also conditioned.

For example, at the moment of my writing it is five and a quarter in the morning. This is the matter of memory of relative time; it is seen to be true through an observation: one knows this because five and a quarter is an hour related to the five o'clock at its point, if there is no five o'clock as this point of time, then there is no five and a quarter. One thing is always related to another.

Another example is that you know your age and this has to be seen relative to the moment at which you were born; otherwise, you would not have an age. Still, another example, we say that we are humans because there are animals, insects, plants, etc. If those living things did not exist, there will not be such a human being as we understand it, with these contrasts to define and distinguish the human being. (Perhaps, we might be called something else, who knows!) This is the theory of interdependence, interrelations. The aggregates are grouped together into a unit as we can see in the rūpa aggregate.

RŪPA: BODY

Rūpa is form, materiality. Take a look at the body! There are plenty of things heaping up: eyes, ears, nose, tongue, physical body, skin, bones, and also an empty space. In all parts of rūpa, there exists space; otherwise, there will be no circulation. There is wind blowing in each part. The wind, in other words, is understood as the element of motion, and it is the movement going through all the material things.

The Buddha talks about the four great elements as follows:

Earth is the first element, which symbolizes solidity and extension. Earth is something extending out in space and having its own boundary since it is a planet. In addition, it is moving itself in rotation. In this way, earth as an element is understood as solidity and extension as within our body. We are in fact only extension in space, to use the terminology of physics. When there is extension, it implies that there is also contraction. If without the extension and contraction of the body, we would not be able to move about.

Fire is the second element, which signifies the heat within the body. Also, this element is essential and indispensable. Without it, we would not survive, especially in winter when we need even more heat. All these things such as clothes, shoes, a house, and so on that we use to cover ourselves and to live in, are basically for protecting the heat inside the body; otherwise the heat would escape and we would get cold. The heat in the body flows up and down, circulating in this way constantly. We all like the fire, or heat, since it gives us a sense of warmth, joy, and pleasant sensation. Also, we love the fire element because it makes us move and act so that we do not remain idle and become inert or lazy. When the sun comes out, we run to it to receive the heat, the light that is arriving at us with a feeling of joy and a sense of opening heart. This element of fire is a very important part of life since it helps keep the body warm and can make breathing more powerful, enabling us use our breathing as a therapeutic technique called fire breath. With this breathing method, more and more heat is generated for cleansing the physical body, energetic body, and for discharging some emotional conditions buried in the psyche as one continues breathing fully and powerfully for a certain period. Some American Indians use the external fire as a form of healing and purification.

Water is the third element. Water here does not mean the liquid in the body, but is the symbol of the physical quality of *cohesion* that is called "water element." The water element keeps things unified and held onto one another without disintegration or falling apart. Without the water element, our fingers will not stay together but will scatter away in different pieces. The water element keeps the form or structure in a solid unit and takes care of maintaining the predetermined form. For example, if one's bone is broken, it remains crooked for a while so that the form still stays together as the body's unit. Therefore, the water element is extremely significant. In fact, water symbolizes immortality since it never dies, but only changes the form: If it is too hot, it becomes steam, if it is too cold, it turns into ice, and when it is normal, it returns to be liquid water again. Water never dies. The steam and the ice are the same thing, that is, water changing its form. Even the clouds are water (when they get dark and come down closer to the earth, then the rains fall.) It is good to think of water as immortal: For we talk about the water of life (the elixir of enlightenment). Life would not exist without water and the water element.

Wind is the fourth element: movement, vibration. The body is always in the movement, in pulsation, like the universe. When one observes the body of a newborn baby, one sees that it is very vibrant and pulsating. Everything around us is in the state of pulsation. If something affects this point over here, it can affect the other point over there because all things are moving, and are connected. In addition, the wind element exists, not only inside us, but also in the world out there.

These four great elements belong to a rūpa. In addition, there are also other aspects that belong to the rūpa such as the male and female sexes, the physical movement in terms of action, and the verbalization in terms of speech, sounds, or voices. All these are the sophisticated aspects of the rūpa, even the faculty of life itself is a rūpa in its subtle, energetic form.

In conclusion, there are 24 categories of the subtle body (upādāya-rūpa), namely:

Five sense organs: *eye, ear, nose, tongue, and body.*

Four corresponding objects: *form (visual objects), sound (audible vibrations), odor/fragrance, and flavor/taste.*

Two genders: *femininity and masculinity.*

One thinking heart.
One life faculty (jīvitindriya).
One alimentary system (food).
One space element (pariccheda-rūpa).
Two movements: *bodily movement and verbalization.*
Three refined physical qualities: *lightness (lahutā), tenderness (mudutā), and workability (kammaññatā).*
Four characteristics: *growth (uccaya), continuity (santati), decay (jaratā), and impermanence (aniccatā).*

What is the difference between action (fire) and movement (wind)? Action is physical. The fire element creates activities and becomes a condition for these activities to exist since it is a great form of energy necessary for making things. Movement is quite distinct from action in the sense that movement is something that happens naturally and flows along unsurprisingly, while action is something intentional.

We say that all forms of energy, including the subtle body or ethereal body, also known as the psychic or energetic body, belong to rūpa. Sometimes when we fall ill, it is not the physical body that becomes sick, but it is the ethereal or energetic body that gets ill. The sick part of the subtle body could end up in affecting the physical body. In another sense, the physical body is not really sick, but is affected by the sickness of the ethereal, energetic body. If the affected part of the energetic body is cured or healed, then the physical body also finds itself in well-being.

The aura comes from the subtle, energetic body. When one observes the aura of a person, one sees if the person is sick or well. The aura of the sick person appears rather dark, or gray, or blue (bruise). Sometimes the illness can be really assessed on the physical body, while on other occasions it is seen only in the aura moving around the person. Once the author knew a certain person who had been ill and very depressed, and that person had done many things to heal the illness and believed that it had been really cured. However, when the author encountered that person the second time, saw that the illness had not been cured because the aura was still unhealthy. In addition, the author still felt the sickness in that person; further still, the energetic, subtle body was not healed. Complete healing implies the total cure of the energetic, subtle body.

When one is meditating, one's subtle, energetic body is also meditating, and therefore the sitting meditation is most important. Let me explain this a bit further: In an intensive meditation a certain illness that once one suffered whether it was a physical illness or a sickness of the subtle, energetic body, or a psychic illness, might reappear. Being seated in meditation is in itself a healing exercise, a natural treatment. We heal our body on the basis of discharging it from physical things, and from emotional, psychological conditions. In this way, we feel much lighter and more spacious. Therefore, when we go out for a walk, we have a feeling that we are able to fly. Do you ever feel that way?

The feeling of lightness is also related to the nourishment that we give to the body. Some people say that they feel rigid in their bodies. That indicates that their bodies are not pure or clean in the sense of being free from the unhealthy physical conditions as well as from emotional and psychological conditioning. The impure body affects the mind and hinders its functioning. Also, it affects awareness. In this case, attention is not clear; it appears as if one were walking through a fog. When the body becomes clean and pure, one's attention is very clear. Also, the author became aware of this in his fasting in which his body was incredibly clean, and consciousness and attention too became exceptionally clear and exceedingly pure. Such is a great benefit achieved through the cleansing and purification of the body.

We cannot go toward the spirit without purifying the body. For that purpose, we do bodywork, clean ourselves, and take care of ourselves in order to be available for receiving the higher energy from the cosmic space or from the higher consciousness within us, or from both energy sources. So, do not forget this. If you do forget this matter of keeping the body clean and pure, you will become ill when the higher and more powerful energy enters your psycho-physical systems. Although the illness is a part of the purification, such a way of cleansing is not a pleasant passageway. In order not to get ill, we must purify ourselves, taking good care of our bodies every moment, every day. We must see that everything we take in is healthy and nutritious for the body, or, on the contrary, we must take a close look at what we take in to see if it is something poisonous. We must try to observe from that perspective what we eat, drink, and put in the body, including the air that we breathe in. The quality of air is utterly important, so please be careful about this!

One must not eat only because one likes to eat it or simply because one knew it well from the viewpoint of familiarity, without a thorough investigation. It can be that some delicious food might not be so good for the body, but instead could contain a great deal of poison. One must choose things mindfully, but not choose them because merely they are delicious; one must learn to assess or make a right judgment about the things one is about to take in. Also, one should not go for good flavor as one's priority of making a choice, but should consider quality first and foremost. By so doing, it is good even though the food is not so agreeable to the tongue and to the palate since we basically eat for sustaining the body, for promoting good health and well-being, and not just for enjoying delicious tastes. So, take good care of the body so that it will become a marvelous vehicle for accomplishing total freedom as the ultimate goal of life.

VEDANĀ: SENSATIONS AND FEELINGS

The Buddha classifies feelings into three categories, although basically we experience just two of them in our everyday living: a pleasant sensation or feeling, which includes the agreeable, the happy, the joyful, etc., and an unpleasant sensation/feeling, which includes the painful, the uncomfortable, the disagreeable, and so forth. These two categories of vedanā we all know well since we experience them incessantly in our lives. The third category is the neutral feeling/sensation that is neither pleasant nor unpleasant, neither painful nor happy. This kind of sensation/feeling we do not experience very often, except perhaps in the fourth stage of the meditative absorption (fourth jhāna) wherein everything is totally balanced and in complete equilibrium.

Those feelings/sensations can be physical, emotional, mental, and spiritual. Spiritual feelings are the most profound and highest one, and one will find it beyond one's physical and mental realms. One does not experience spiritual feelings unless one enters into a deep meditation where the body and mind are suspended or are put to a complete rest for the time being, as when, for example, you enter into an intense and total stillness where you do not really feel any physical form and the mind is absolutely absent. In such a meditation, all mental movements (as we know them) have stopped, although a very subtle movement within this kind of stillness still prevails. As for this, we could say that it is a perfectly balanced pulsation — not a type of perturbing pulsation — that stands out as a kind of feeling. In a certain sense, it is a very agreeable pulsation and therefore, there exists a pleasant feeling in which there is ecstatic joy and a sense of beauty, a beauty surpassing form and yet within a form. This feeling is so balanced that it does not perturb one (meditator or experiencer, figuratively speaking), and so no ups and downs are to be experienced. Its pulsation is exceptionally soft and in a perfect equilibrium.

What do we do with feelings/sensations?

We are now going to talk about the practice regarding sensations and feelings described above. This practice earns the title of vipassana, meaning, Insight based on the cultivation of awareness or mindfulness, which is quite simple. The first step is to *recognize* a feeling or a sensation and see it for what it is. The second step is to *stay with* it, if it is a bad, or negative feeling, try to separate from it in the sense of creating a distance or stepping back in order to have a focus on just looking and simply observing the feeling without trying to eliminate it or put it aside. In the case of a good, positive feeling, one must not get attached to it, let alone become identified with it. Rather, we merely experience it fully, and then let it be.

When staying with a feeling/sensation, just allow yourself to experience it as totally as possible, becoming fully aware of yourself experiencing it and making sure that your experiencing of the feeling/sensation, or even an emotion, is taking place with awareness, since without it you will automatically become it. When you have become the feeling, or the sensation, or the emotion, you inevitably create a "feeler" and therefore, identify yourself with the feeler, even if not consciously. If you become the one who feels, you become completely identified with the new entity of feeler, and then the space between you as an observing self[2] or center of awareness and the energy patterns of feeling/sensation or emotion is not available, let alone any awareness. So, the real you no longer exists but is taken over by the feeler in the sense just mentioned. But if you merely feel whatever you are feeling without becoming it, then there will be space opening up and awareness will be present. With the operation of awareness, you can relate to any feelings, any sensations, or any emotions as they present themselves at the moment. You are completely open to any of them. You *neither withdraw* from, *nor reinforce* the feeling/sensation/emotion being experienced at the given moment. You simply let them come, let them go, or let them stay as they wish. You do not intensify them or try to eliminate them either. I am here referring to the concept "you" only for the purpose of communicating, but you do nothing in terms of ego. The ego must do nothing apart from learning to be attentive and creatively present. When you become the awareness yourself, you are naturally shaking up your ego.

Observe this part of yourselves; it is very important because we always go there (to our ego). The ego must do something and want to do things all the time. It cannot be without doing something. Pay attention to this part that always want to do (ego – the doer), which has a very clear vibration; you must capture it. But if you become identified with it, you will not be able to observe it since the ego does not want to observe itself or to be observed. The ego must become something other than itself, it is always in the front; in this way, one has a sense of being someone, feeling something. However, this kind of feeling is not as strong and powerful as the feeler (ego). It is just a sense of identity. Yet, one may have a different sense of identity, an identity that cannot be named. It is like having a feeling of being you yourself, but this sense does not ask for anything, only being there with awareness. However, the ego is quite important since one has to do something, must feel that there is something to be done. It will not desist from doing and will not shift into just observing or experiencing. Listen to this voice, "Do something. Don't just stand there." Observe this part of you, as it is your ego part.

---

[2] There are several senses of self that are woven into this chapter. They are the following: (1) the ego self, (2) the observing self, (3) the self as sense of identity, (4) the crystal clear self as a form of grounded and non-distorting essence or being, and (5) the self as a sub-personality, an element in a more complex set of sub-personalities described in the psychology of selves.

We are going to differentiate the ego part from the self. (The self is what a moment ago we called a sense of identity.) Inside each of us there is a part that is so clear and free that no form of suffering can reach it; it's just like the diamond that cannot be cut. Within each of us, there exists this pure, beautiful, and crystal-clear part, which is much greater than the ego, is ten thousand times superior to our ego part. We must connect ourselves more often with this hidden part of us. Sometimes we have a glimpse of it. This part does not appear to our ego as having a strong force. When the ego's strength has been exhausted, still the strength of the self (in this sense just introduced) remains intact. So, we can go deeply into the self here and make use of its strength. If the ego is worn out, it does not matter. We may arrange a funeral ceremony for saying good-bye to it. If it returns (the ego is also born and reborn repeatedly in life), just greet it saying, "Hello ego! You have returned!"

The self, which we have just talked about, has a very balanced vibration, whilst the ego's vibration is opposite; and you may notice this since the ego is always looking for something to do, something to entertain itself, a technique for getting rid of pain and suffering, for instance. Try to observe this to see for yourself! Information is made available so that you will be able to observe it better. Open your body and mind to a feeling that you are experiencing at the moment, and you will see how, for example, an unpleasant sensation affects your body and your ego. Do not just say that you are affected by pain or suffering because, if you say it that way, it means you are already become identified with the ego.

We are using this type of language because it is more objective. Truly speaking, it is so since it is opposite to the current, conventional language that we use in our everyday life. The objective language is the dharma language. If we make use of such an objective language, we are actually analyzing ourselves in the sense of separating out bits and pieces (various parts) that assemble our human structure. The real meaning of an analysis is the matter of separating out and putting things in categories. Things are originally separated by their natural formation, but we just need to differentiate them once more so that we will see their reality as they truly are. We differentiate things in terms of saying, "Oh, this is an emotion, that is the physical body, that is the mind, and this is the ego."

Then, perhaps some of us might ask, "Where am I, then?" You are **being** in this space. When you are in the self, you are attentive, conscious, and are able to see how things are occurring. The body is affected, and in a sense, you get affected as well. In what sense? We ask this because this is important: Whatever we have, all that belongs to us – we must not deny it – and at the same time we do not become it either. You can possess a house, a car, clothes, but you are not the house, the car, or the clothes. You have your body, and your body belongs to you, but you are not the body. Your mind belongs to you, but you are not the mind. Your ego (ennea-type of personality) belongs to you, but you are not the ego. You must be absolutely clear that this is the way of seeing the reality without any negation whatsoever. Becoming identified yourself with your body, with your mind, with the positions, is a fact accepted by the society, but it is only a conventional truth.

What happens to the feelings and the sensations when you are in the self with awareness and without becoming identified with them? What occurs is that you see the manifestation of the feeling, of the sensation, that is being experienced, and also see the other things related to it. As a matter of fact, what you are doing is to reinforce your awareness and your attention. If you do it in this way, you are going to have insights, which will be your guide: They are going to guide you so that you may take a course of action, or you may not. You rely on the insights that will lead you on to achieving what you want to achieve.

The sensation being experienced at the given moment receives your total attention, will give you space for a certain period of time, and it can discharge its dramas. It does this naturally by itself. It lets go and releases itself by itself in the same way that our body liberates unhealthy things. The feeling/sensation is an aggregate, so it can discharge its dramas.

For example, you are crying. The weeping is a discharge. The feeling releases its dramas through the body, and you are there being a witness to the discharge. You are witnessing the liberation of your feeling, your emotion. Then, the feeling/emotion leaves you alone and so you have plenty of space within, and the new and healthy energy will come in to replace the bad energy that has been released. In this way, the feeling changes: You experience an agreeable feeling because the new energy has already entered into your psychophysical systems. Another example is when you discharge your anger, the love flows to you and you feel loving and warm. In this process, the release of what is bad and the production of the positive energy go together naturally, hand in hand.

There is someone who has a lot of fear. For example, when someone puts such a question as this, "How am I going to put up with these ten days of the retreat? It's going to be very intense." This means that such an individual has fear. So, if this kind of fear comes to you, simply dialogue with it. It is all right having fear; there is nothing wrong about it. Practically, when we believe that it is not right to have fear, then we have more fear. The fear becomes greater when we believe that one must not have it because it feels rejected. This is as if it were a bad boy that nobody loves, so it continues presenting itself. Therefore, we should say to it, "Hello fear! We are going to meditate together; we are going to pass time together." By so doing, fear will feel better and will leave us more space for relating to one another until it finally gets transformed. One only needs to do this. One does not need any particular techniques for dealing with fear. One simply welcomes it and embraces it without any restrictions.

Such emotions as anger and fear even though becoming transformed still continue living inside us and from time to time return to test us. For example, a person feels hurt and begins undertaking a therapeutic work on this emotion and may clear away the hurt feeling and release the emotions of fear and anger connected to it. Nonetheless, sometimes it came back to your mind. When this happens, just try to observe if the already worked-on feeling is still alive, or it is only a memory. Usually, any energy patterns, after having been worked on, could return as a memory, or as a thought without any emotional power left to be activated, since all the emotional conditioning has lost its potentiality and therefore, has no effect. However, if in the memory or in the thought there is some emotional content that accompanies it, this means that the work of liberation and purification has not been completed. So, it's necessary to bring it to full awareness and feel it once again so that the body and the psyche would liberate all the remaining energy and become totally free and utterly clean from those emotional contents. Then, at last, the issue will be concluded.

The key lies in no reacting negatively. Many people have these kinds of emotions and feelings and react to them in a negative way. Sometimes, the therapists hold a view that one must go back to process them when they appear again; but if one would process all the feelings and emotions constantly, there would be no end to processing. Precisely, in the idea of wanting to process all things until they are totally clean, so that no negativity is kept inside, there is a lack of welcoming, of embracing the feeling and all the particular things at the moment they present themselves. When one concentrates on processing, one forgets the part of welcoming and embracing them. So, give love and hug them since by so doing it is a healing at the very deep level, which processing can never reach. One must carry it through thoroughly after the therapeutic process has been done. In therapeutic work, two processes are brought together (also, in meditation both are done simultaneously): in one, the emotions would be released naturally (this corresponds to the therapeutic process); in the other, one learns to forgive, to embrace, and to accept unconditionally. All this full process is coming together with liberating and accepting. In this way, the complete healing process is achieved.

In reality, we do not have to do anything in particular. Now, we can understand the reason why in those fairly tales the hero, or heroine, or the protagonist does not have to do anything at all, he or she only waits on attention and provides some kind of hospitality only. At this moment in time when you are a hero or a heroine, all the necessary work is done for your benefit by the others. Therefore, it is certain that it occurs in this way in which you are the stream of consciousness, in a sense. (The principal consciousness is the hero or heroine in the fairly tales.) We put it inside of ourselves individually. In this way, we learn to be simple, to experience a feeling as it actually is. Prove it to yourself and see how it goes!

SAÑÑĀ: PERCEPTION

Perception is the recognition of the objects through the six senses. For example, when one sees a flower, one recognizes it, saying, "Oh, a flower!" when one sees a mountain one says, "Oh, a mountain!" Without a perception, one cannot recognize those things. This act of recognizing is the function of perception.

Perception is very important in our lives, and also in meditation practice since perception creates an image or a form for the mind to dwell on. When we perceive something in the ordinary way, we already have a concept, but to capture it, we make an image, something concrete. As a matter of fact, each time we look at it, we see it through that image which we have made.

This is the sequence in ordinary perception: At the moment you see someone, you make an image of the person; then the second time you return to look at that person, you only see the image, unless you are very aware and utterly attentive. Even so, the image, the structure, the form, or the concept that you have created over the person is still there. If your perception is not pure, you create a false, erroneous image because the perception can be conditioned by other forces or factors concealed in your mind. The only way in which the perception could be pure is to have awareness at the moment of perceiving.

There is an Oriental story in which it says that a certain person is walking in a field at night – underneath the Moon's light – and happens to see a rope. The first impression that the person has is that it is a snake, and then this person becomes frightened by it. Later, he turns back to get closer and have another look at it, and then says, "Oh, it's not a snake, but it's a rope!" This is an illusion of perception. The Buddha uttered it in a disturbing way: He said that perception is illusion, referring to the current perception of the people in general, but not to the pure perception. Observe your own life: You make many mistakes with perception because you rush to draw conclusions before examining things thoroughly or before attempting to clarify them.

One of the factors for arriving at enlightenment is that perception must not be distorted or perverted. What do we mean by enlightenment? Enlightenment is when perception and thought are free from any distortion or perversion. Regarding this matter of total freedom from the distortion of perception, from the distortion of thought, and from the distortion of view, the present author explains it especially clearly in the prologue of his book entitled *The Real Way to Awakening*.

We perceive something incessantly in every moment. Now in this moment, sitting here, we are perceiving something because we have the sense-modalities. In meditation, we shut our eyes, but not our ears; we do not shut down the body, and we do not put out or close the mind since it is impossible to do so anyway. When the mind is widely open, there is a perception – at the mental level – which does not even exist in the occidental philosophy or thinking. When the Western people talk about perception, they simply refer exclusively to the five physical senses, but the Buddha said that the sixth sense is the mind itself, in the sense of mental perception. In Pali, it is called *mano-saññā* (mental perception).

Memory is very connected to perception because ordinary perception is indispensably connected to the concepts – since without concepts there is no ordinary perception. Without concepts, perception will be very similar to awareness, which may be called "totally aware perception" (just like a perception of a little child). Perception without any concepts in itself is pretty much like mindfulness. Moreover, when we talk about mindfulness and consciousness we talk about this kind of perception and will make a clear distinction between perception and consciousness in the following pages. What we are attempting to say now is that ordinary perception is always related to concepts and images.

When the mind finds itself in a natural state – when one does not think or imagine anything – mental objects are things of the past. These are many things, such as fantasies, concepts, mental states, contents of consciousness, etc. All that we have done, have thought about in life, has been registered in consciousness. All this is flowing like a river, and because of this flow, the mind is like any one of our five physical senses. The process is as follows: The mind has its own faculty for entering into contact with all those things and in turn, they all enter into contact with the mental faculty. Then, we recognize things due to perception and the sensation associated with it. This function of perception – the recognition of what there is – involves memory in itself. So, that is how we remember things. When something comes along in this flow, we recognize it and therefore, the thought is put in motion.

Thought is a response to making contact with a perception. In the West, you call it "memory." Buddhism has no concept of "memory." There is no Pali word corresponding to this concept of memory since perception is the same as memory in terms of having the function of making contact and of recognizing the things that come into contact with the mental faculty and/or consciousness. For that matter, many people misunderstand it: they understand perception as the same as memory, which is deadly wrong since memory is only recalling something of the past and is not the recognition of objects being perceived at the present moment.

Let us do an exercise of visualization for the purpose of a better understanding of this matter of mental perception under discussion. Think for a moment about something in your house, direct your mind to the house. Try to perceive something, for instance, a shape of your house, the rooms, the kitchen and so forth. Is the kitchen in good order? The contact is very simple since you are already familiar with all those things, and they are all registered in your brain, mind, and consciousness. Now say quietly to yourself what you recognize mentally (or "remember" in the Occidental sense). But in this concept of perception, in reality you did not perceive all the things registered there in your mind. If you actually enter a room, you will see a lot more things with your mind eye – the mental perception – and not with your naked eyes only. Is that clear?

The practice regarding perception

How can we practice perception? Meditation in everyday life has much to do with the perception. It is a place where one must put oneself in the awareness together with perception. At the moment when one sees or feels, there are two main things acting together: One is consciousness; another is perception. The consciousness is more subtle while the perception is more obvious.

Pay attention to how you perceive, how you see things, how you hear sounds/voices, how you smell things, how you taste flavors, how you feel the bodily touch. As we are now sitting on cushions, we are in contact with them and are in contact with the people around us. Our ears hear the noises produced by writing nearby using papers and pens. All is perception, which is taking place from moment to moment unless your senses have been damaged and therefore you can not, for example, have ear perception. When you perceive something, pay attention to *how* you perceive it.

In this atmosphere of silence, with a very soft, very refined, and very subtle vibration, observe how your perception comes into operation. You will see that the quality of perception is changing as you are here meditating, perhaps you do not do any great thing, but you are purifying your senses and these are, in turn, connected with the body and with the mind. For that matter, you put yourself in the energy of meditation more and more, and that meditative energy works in terms of purifying your sense organs, and they are becoming more relaxed and more tranquil. When you go outside, look at things and say, "Oh, everything is seen much more neatly with my eyes, and the sounds resonate much more vibrantly and purely!" Therefore, the quality of things has been changed from the physical viewpoint, and this signifies that your awareness is growing as the sense perceptions become precise and accurate through the purity and tranquility of the sense organs. Doing it in this way, our sense-modalities are improving constantly.

Practice meditation as much as possible in life since there is no way to escape your senses: Look, listen, and sense when you go anywhere; doing anything, do so with vital attention and there will be more efficiency in your senses. In other words, you can be more perceptive. Perceptivity and receptivity go hand in hand. Many people have this gift naturally.

One day I was with a woman friend looking for a taxi. Although both of us were looking together, but she spotted the taxi and stopped it instantly while I had not seen any taxi yet. This friend of mine possesses a great perceptiveness so she does not have to pay much attention really, since her attention is very natural and works with her perception simultaneously. Also, there are other people who have a marked perceptiveness and use it in their lives naturally.

When people are attentive, they show the quality of being awake. For example, it is like a samurai who is just there, being fully attentive. I like very much to see samurai fighting because it is really attention in action; all is momentary. They cannot think about the past because all is happening right there in front of them. It is a good example for carrying out awareness or being fully awake to the perception.

Other examples are football players and referees who have to be very vigilant to enable them to know where the ball goes, and not to make a mistake. I am pleased watching a football match since I see how this thing operates, using my conscious perception how they are perceiving the play and how they perform their movements. The trick is not to take sides because, if you do, you do not feel at ease or very comfortable. If you prefer one team to another, then you already anticipate some kind of suffering, or some anxiety, or the inability to enjoy the match completely. Fencing is another game that necessitates very precise attention for practicing it.

Put yourself into these examples to encourage paying attention. It is quite certain that you observe some changes through the practice of attention. If you do not do this, you would not do anything else apart from repeating your habits. Doing this work of cultivating and enlarging awareness is like swimming against the currents, which are our habits, our habitual way of doing things, and usually, our way of doing things is not very conscious, but is simply a way of conformity. Being aware is staying fully in the present, here and now, without any patterns. Just try to be right here and right now, the question is whether you are doing it or not doing it. That is all there is to it!

SANKHĀRA: THE CONSTRUCTIVE AND DESTRUCTIVE FORCES

The definition given here refers to two forces: On one hand, there are the productive, positive, creative, and constructive forces; on the other hand, there are the dark, negative, and destructive forces. Also, we may call these two forces *Light* and *Darkness*.

These two forces have great influence on our perception and on our consciousness: they are kept in our consciousness and flow with it, while some forces both light and darkness live in the Unconscious. Some of those forces are conscious to us, that is to say, we know them consciously. But many other forces are submerged into our unconscious realm, we do not know them, we do not know all that is flowing in the ocean of the unconscious at a very deep level. We only see things on the periphery, on the surface of the water, but those that do not appear, are much more, perhaps an infinite number of them.

These forces, to put it in another way, are all the things that Dharma characterizes, or in the theistic sense, are given by God. However, God never said, "These are the good things and those are the bad things." It is we human beings that did the classification in the process of creating our culture. So, this cultural process made us classify and divide those forces into two categories: those forces that we denominate "good" are put on the *right* side, while those forces that we call "bad" are put on the *left* side. By so doing, we only want to relate to, and associate us with, the good characteristics and reject the bad ones. All this is sankhāra. Therefore, we have both good sankhāra and bad sankhāra.

It's very simple: A feeling is simply a feeling, but when we do not relate ourselves to it – when we do not face it but negate it outright and bury it in our psychophysical systems - then it creates its own personality, its own energy, and becomes a sankhāra. For example, when you are a child, you get angry, but cannot really express it. Imagine that you were born in a family in which your father does not want you to become angry, and he says to you, "It's bad getting angry! Stop it!" You feel upset and annoyed inside, but being a little person and having no power whatsoever, you become afraid. Therefore, you do not express your annoyance and it is buried within. When you grow up, you feel that you were quite mad with your father. So, you transfer it to other persons who could remind you of your father or to any authoritative figure right there in the world. All that occurs because of this act of burying feelings/emotions, through which the anger and the fear become then the bad Sankhāras, the negative forces.

The practice regarding sankhāra

The sankhāras influence your way of living, of seeing, of feeling, and of perceiving, and so they are enormously important. Working with them, you are open. The practice is very simple: Firstly, you open yourself to your body, to your mind; after that open yourself to all other sankhāras that are arising, and later learn to accept them as they are, without trying to destroy them, change them, or escape from them.

All the sankhāras are right here, in your body and in your mind. They are not over there, in the ceiling or in the sky, in the forest or in the mountains. People are afraid of the mountains and of the demons that are hiding themselves out there, while in reality they are the sankhāras and reside within you. What happens is that there are certain places where perhaps some sankhāras arise and reflect back on you (they are your own reflections), and then you see them as if they were outside.

For example, sometimes in dreams one sees a dreadfully horrible, extremely disturbing figure, which is a manifestation of sankhāra. Each image, each imagination, each dream is a sankhāra. All that one imagines about is a sankhāra. It can be that you have a vision of something very powerful or very sacred, such as a vision of the Virgin Mary, the Christ, or the Buddha. In reality, all that is within you, but appears out there so that it becomes more evident to you. Also, sometimes images would appear to some people while they are meditating. If the images are beautiful, good figures, the meditator becomes attached to them, thinking, "Oh, now I am enlightened with all these marvelous things." On the contrary, when the bad, frightening, terrifying, and destructive images appear, then fear terrifies the meditator and he or she tries to flee or to practice a certain exercise for getting rid of them. In our meditation practice (the Vipassana practice), we do nothing of this kind, but simply open ourselves to them, surrendering and giving ourselves to those dark and destructive forces so as to enable us to see and witness their instantaneous transformation.

Surrendering, or delivering yourself to higher power, in one way, means renouncing the ego totally. In another way, it signifies a total opening up to that which is occurring right in the moment, in front of you. You are with awareness and at the same time have with you an aware and awake ego that will not complicate the matter concerned. Leave the ordinary, heavily conditioned ego alone since it cannot assimilate all this, and in addition may interfere with your experience. If not, instead of experiencing things with the awareness of the awake, aware ego as it operates, you experience them without this awareness but with the deeply conditioned ego that always keeps you away from the actual contact with what is real. But the aware ego will help you be right there, observing, paying attention, and experiencing the occurrence fully. In so doing, the dark forces of sankhāra will have an opportunity to radically change since your energy by being creatively present will generate much more good and creative power.

Therefore, one must pay attention to the dark forces, but be absolutely sure not to become identified with any of them. This is a very significant part of our practice. Then, when these bad parts have been transformed, they will give you tremendous energy and a vast inner space.

Sankhāra and ego

For the conditioned ego it is tremendously difficult to do all that which has been described since it feels shrunk, limited, unable to trust, and then says, "How can anyone have trust in this thing as said above?" As for me, the description of this type is telling me that perhaps it would not work. So, the ego plants this kind of doubt, which is quite normal and therefore, we are not going to curse it. It is reasonably all right for the conditioned ego to feel the way it feels, so do not try to change it. Just accept it and say to the ego, "It's okay, ego, you doubt what ought to be doubted, since it's a doubtful matter, OK!" When you allow the ego to do what it should do, it will think, "Well, perhaps there might be something good in all this." For this reason, one must take into account that this type of ego that we have been talking about cannot do anything, will have no power, unless you become identified with it.

From now on, you are going to have many things to relate to since the aware ego is becoming inseparable from you – it's turning into being one with you - as you will have to function with it in your life. Without the presence of the aware ego, you cannot relate to things, situations, and people objectively. Go ahead working in this way with all sankhāras, both the good ones and the bad ones, embracing them all equally since they are like your children, and they are only asking for your friendly attention. To put it in another way, they want you to spend some considerable time with them, but sometimes they appear to your conditioned ego in a horrible and destructive fashion – all this is their style of requesting an attention.

The ego needs to develop its perception because, normally, the ego's perception is not very good, except for the aware ego's perception, which is quite precise and accurate. The ego in general does not have clear and correct perception, so do not rely on the ordinary, conditioned ego for receiving accurate and faultless information through its perception while working with the sankhāras. Keep in mind that ego is also a sankhāra. So, have compassion for your ordinary ego as well, since it is heavily conditioned by many energy patterns and the patterns of behavior. This ego carries a great burden (it has shouldered all the weight of existence). Have pity and mercy on it; do not condemn or lay blame on it. With awareness, you can approach things anew and freshly, without any necessity for using the old patterns of the ego.

It is equally the same when you are authentically present with another person with full attention and are available for interacting with him or her. In this way, this person will feel very comfortable, relatively at ease (we all need someone to be present with us); and begins to relate himself/herself with you because he/she sees that there is no antagonism whatsoever, and that you are purely there in the present. In this fashion, when you are present, you have love and compassion naturally.

All these qualities are carved into your character: you take care of others, and you are sensitive. Everyone likes it, isn't that true? Well, the sankhāras like it too; although they do not receive much from you since you always try to break into a run and flee from them. Therefore, you just try to liberate yourself from the bad sankhāras or attempt to crush them by saying, "Don't come to disturb me. Get out of here!" However, when you pay genuine attention to them, they are joyful and happy. Put it to yourself this way: Those things that you try to separate from are, in fact, dying of hungry. Why? Because, you have deprived them of nourishment and nutrition. Then, how can you expect them to behave well with you? It is not reasonable, it is not even human.

In the pages ahead, we will return to talk about sankhāra one more time. For now, it is sufficient. Let us now discuss consciousness.

VIÑÑĀNA: CONSCIOUSNESS

Consciousness is something very simple. Think over the consciousness that we experience through the five physical senses and our mental sense (the sixth sense). Consciousness, in this sense, is the act of being conscious of any thing that enters into contact with any of these six senses.

At the moment in which an external object enters into contact, for example, with our faculty of seeing, at that particular moment consciousness appears. Consciousness turns itself into the third factor in set: The first factor is the external object, the second is our eye-faculty, and the third is the consciousness of hearing. To the process of arising together, those three things must be present, and we call it "contact" or "phassa" in Pali. Each time we talk about contact we refer to those three factors in unison.

With respect to the sense of hearing, the sound that we listen to is the external object, the ear-faculty is the second factor, and the third factor is consciousness; they always go together in this fashion. After contact comes the perception; later follow the sensations and feelings, and acting underneath all that is the sankhāra conditioning our way of perceiving, sensing, and encountering emotions. All goes together, but one must see it through how one perceives or how one feels since sometimes it's extremely subtle to see consciousness at the moment in which it becomes present.

The practice concerning consciousness

If one really pays attention at the moment in which one sees something, then one perceives instantaneously that one is aware. But remember that sankhāra is always flowing with a consciousness. In any place where consciousness is, some sankhāras will be right there, present with it. In fact, the manifestation of consciousness is the manifestation of sankhāra.

Consciousness is flowing, flowing, and flowing, and the sankhāras go all along with it.

Therefore, all the forces of light and darkness, all the sankhāras, are contained in the consciousness. For that matter, we have to give them attention, for example, when we get angry, or become irritated, or get bored or sleepy, or feel loving, or have confidence, we must apply attention to any one of them and stay with it fully until it finally fade away. Being sleepy is a sankhāra (sloth and torpor), in the sense of having inertia within, which is the state of lethargy, physical fatigue, or mental laziness. One will inevitably encounter a great deal of sankhāras at the earlier stages of meditation.

Do not try to know it all at once. Only pay attention to what is manifesting at the moment. What is it that is manifesting inside you at this moment? In our practice of Insight Meditation, what we do is recognize the presence of the sankhāras without judging them, simply recognizing them with an attitude of accepting and letting them be. Judging is like putting things in a box, which is negative. We do not need to judge, for instance, when a doubt comes to our mind, we simply recognize it saying, "Oh doubt, you are here!" If we are in doubt, we then think, "Oh, doubt is bad, it should not be here!" By so doing, we reject it and try to put it aside, which is not the correct practice, or not the right way of dealing with doubt. The right thing to do is remember to be aware, to pay vital attention since doubt requires our attention at the given moment it appears in our minds. Perhaps, it is one of our frequent visitors!

Commentary on the five aggregates

The five aggregates are assembled and put in a unit in the same way that different parts of a car are assembled and joined in together in a definitive structure. When these things are put together, the concept of "car" emerges, and then we have a car. When the five aggregates are combined in the structure of a human form, we then have the concept of a person, a man or a woman, a being, or this and that. In reality, it is nothing more than the five aggregates in a certain combination.

If we know ourselves, we simply know the five aggregates, namely, our bodies, our feelings/sensations, our perceptions, our constructive/destructive forces, and our consciousness. If we do not know all this, we then do not know ourselves, we only have a concept, a notion, an image, or a sensation of who we are, but do not really know it. These five aggregates are the objects of Vipassana Meditation. In the practice of vipassana we do one thing at the time, but all things at the same time, for example, our breathing is rūpa (body), and therefore, belongs to the aggregate of body. Also, the movements of the body belong to the subtle, energetic boy (upādāya-rūpa).

In short, the five aggregates are summarized into two:

1) Rūpa: the form, the body.
2) Nāma: the remaining four aggregates.

When a question arises such as: What is the object of Vipassana Meditation? The answer is, nāma-rūpa.

We can meditate on ourselves and on others since all human beings are composed of the five aggregates, no more nor less. You meditate on other persons; observe their manifestations through their bodies, their minds, their activities, and their behavior.

If you go into the city, take a look at people to see how they walk, why they walk in this or that way, why they walk as if they were running, what kinds of sankhāras are manifesting? Or when the people relate to you, observe how they approach you, from which sankhāra they are talking to you? In this manner, you will know the kind of sankhara that is manifesting in that approximation.

It is very good to observe people because you learn to know and to understand them. When you comprehend people, you feel compassion for them. It is not by the way of judging, but by the means of comprehending through observation. In this fashion, you learn at any given moment you encounter something, someone, or a certain situation in any place wherever you are, since your Vipassana will be practiced constantly and everywhere.

It is the matter of just observing people, and not of passing a judgment on them, when you understand, you will be able to help, so your action will be taken correctly. It is fundamental to take into account that people are behaving in a certain way at the moment in which you are observing. Therefore, one must not reach a conclusion that he or she is always like that because the reality is that all things and all kinds of people exist only momentarily and manifest temporarily. The next moment they will manifest something quite different. So, one must go on observing and looking. I believe that this is the best way of establishing the human relationships and of learning to know one another.

Within the categories of nāma (those aggregates that are not rūpa, not the body) are the thoughts, the emotions or mental states, and the feelings and sensations. Thoughts can produce sensations, for example, if you think positively, then you have a positive feeling. Therefore, try to think about the persons positively since there is nothing good coming out of thinking negatively, it only drags you to the negativity and at the same time, you give a bad energy to the others, so neither of those two mental actions is constructive.

Try to think about the people in the positive manner, even though they might manifest something very bad at the time, but they also have something good that is not manifesting at that moment. Make some efforts to find the good things in the people. This is a form of living a healthy life, for example, if a child becomes very bad and behaves quite destructively, what can you do with such a child? Punish him/her? What good can come out of punishments? If that child behaves like that, which is already bad enough for the child, since the child does not know what to do. If besides you punish him/her, you create double badness. So it is better to think about what is manifesting in the child at the particular moment.

If you are teachers and have pupils, try to understand them and see why they are manifesting this way or that way. Then, you will know that all human beings always have many good things. In this case, your duty is to know what you can do to help a child bring out all his/her good things. If you move in this direction, it is very healthy, and you are always growing and progressing.

Differences between viññāna, saññā, and paññā

Consciousness has a function of attracting itself to an object and of knowing the object, but does not necessarily have a concept about the object at this stage; it only has the function of *being conscious*.

From now on, we must make distinctions concerning those three levels of knowing: consciousness (viññāna), perception (saññā), and wisdom or inner knowing (paññā). To understand this better, I will use the example of a child who has a coin of 1 euro in its hands. The consciousness of the very young child appears when it sees the coin as an object, but does not know that it is money or the value that the money has. The perception arises when the bigger child has a concept of this object (the concept that this is exactly the money of 1 euro). Inner knowledge or wisdom comes into play when the grown-up child knows, in addition to the value of the money, that it can be used for buying things, how much it can be exchanged for, and how it can be utilized (knowing all the things concerning the 1 euro).

Our relationships with the five aggregates

There are three ways by which we experience our five aggregates of existence, namely, **satisfaction, dissatisfaction, and liberation**. Those first two types of experience are quite common to all of us, but the last one, liberation, is not very often experienced. This refers to the moment one feels free while experiencing an aggregate, although such a moment might be very brief. Do you experience it often? Do you see yourself satisfactory or dissatisfactory most of the time? Just try to recognize it. Also, try to know what kind of sankhāra is behind or underlies an experience when it is satisfactory. When it is dissatisfactory, notice in what conditions such an experience arises. When you feel liberated regarding your experience of the aggregate, observe in what conditions or circumstances you witness yourself as a free person.

A very significant factor is to see, to know, and to realize experientially; it is not sufficient only experiencing it since the experience without awareness becomes identification. So, it is the matter of practicing being fully conscious. In this way, you can stay in the middle place (the place of awareness), for without understanding and knowing clearly your ego will get inflated or deflated; and then you will lose your presence in the middle place. Well, we have seen the five aggregates through our knowledge and information. Now, we just have to put into practice constant awareness of them all so that we may gain some insights into their realities and unrealities.

Relationships between Consciousness, Perception, and Wisdom
(The Consciousness Process)

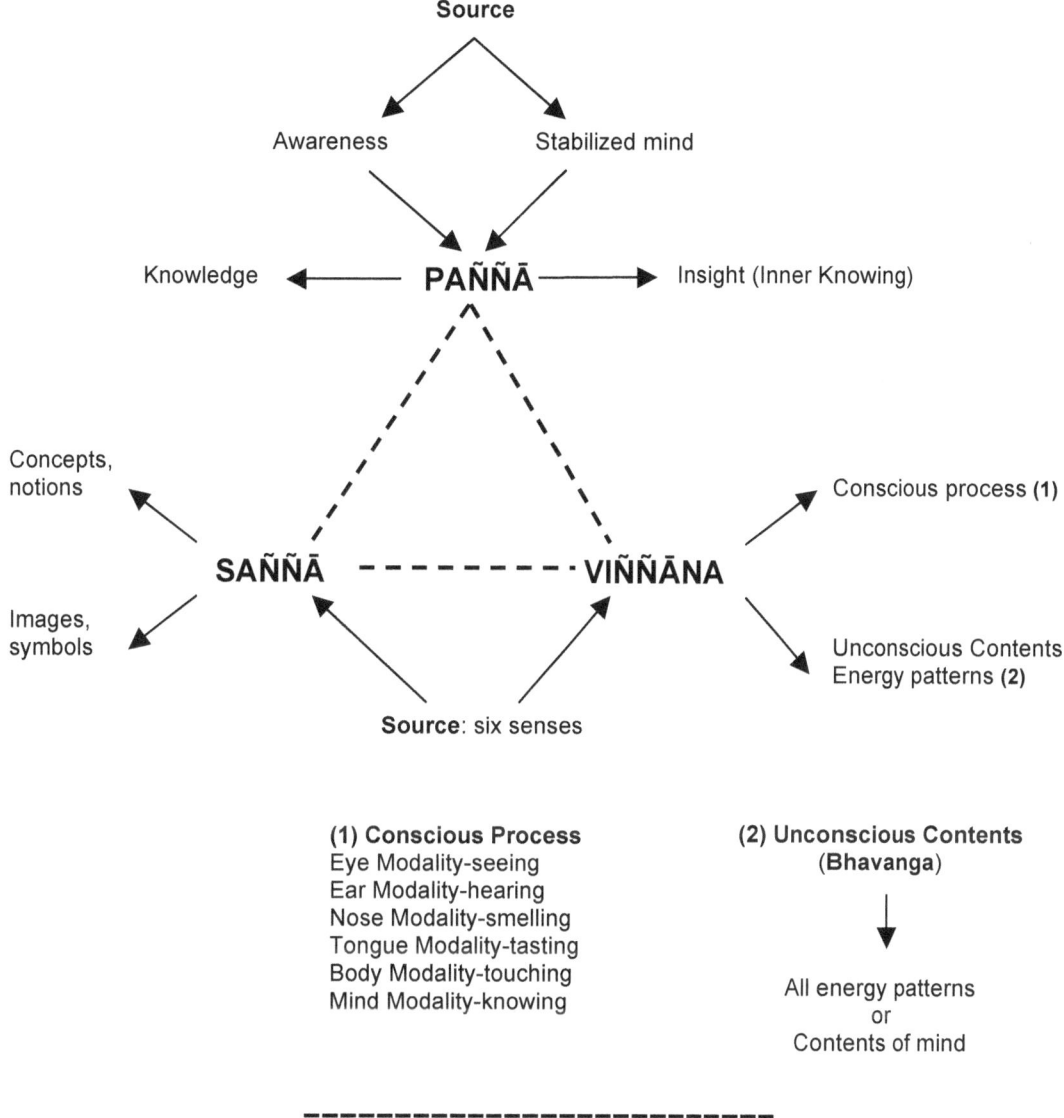

===========================

Consciousness operating in the World of Pleasures (human, deva, animal).

Consciousness operating in the World of Form (Meditative Absorption 1).

Consciousness operating in the Formless World (Meditative Absorption 2).

Consciousness operating in the plane of existence beyond those three worlds (Enlightenment).

The psychology of selves in comparison with the five aggregates

This matter of Psychology of Selves refers basically to the development of the selves (quite an infinite number of them within us.) The fundamental theory of this psychology is that we are a combination of parts or selves, and that we are not a thing in itself. In another word, we exist interdependently and interrelatedly both in the inner world and in the outer one.

What is fascinating to consider, and what is a new idea for most people, is that we have an inner family as well as an outer one. Those who influence this inner family, first of all, are closest to us. It consists of selves that resemble the personality patterns of our family members, friends, teachers, or anyone who has had any kind of influence over us, or conversely, it consists of the personality characteristics (or selves) that represent the exact opposite patterns.

> A) ***Inner family vs. outer family***. The inner family develops when we are indoctrinated with certain ideas about the kind of person we should be, as we grow up in a particular family, and culture. The need to protect our basic vulnerability results in the development of our personality — the development of the primary "selves" that define us to ourselves and to the world. This initial self remains as a vulnerable child, a child of utmost sensitivity, who carries with it the ability to relate intimately to others. This child can be seen as the doorway to our most profound states of being, to our souls. Other selves develop within us early in life to stand between this child and other people so that nobody will ever be able to harm it. This is both natural and necessary.

> B) The first of the protective selves to develop is called the ***protector/controller***. When the protector/controller is in complete charge of our lives, as it so often is, there will be no input that might upset the status quo or lead us to question cherished beliefs and characteristic ways of being. The role of this self is to protect the child and, in so doing, it usually keeps the child from real contact with others.

> The major allies of the protector/controller self are ***pusher, perfectionist, inner critic*** (who works along with the perfectionist to protect the vulnerable child), and ***pleaser*** (who helps to make us acceptable to others). When they take over completely, they can prevent us from experimentation and keep us from bringing the totality of our imperfect, complex, contradictory, and exciting selves into our relationships. They may prevent us from realizing the possibilities that exist beyond the known and the familiar.

The primary selves

In the process of the development of personality, we observe that the primary selves represent our value structure of our original protector/ controller and the parts that he or she has helped bring into the world in order to protect us. The parts that represent the opposite value structure, that which had to be rejected in the growing-up process, are *disowned selves*. Each of us has a surprising array of disowned selves. Learning about these selves is an important part of personal growth.

The disowned selves

Each of the primary selves has a complementary disowned self that is equal and opposite in content and power.

Projection

The disowned selves that are unconscious in us are automatically projected onto another person or another thing; our inner pictures are literally projected upon the other person as though the other person were a screen. These projections act like a bridge that extends out from us to meet that other person. It is one of the significant ways in which we make contact with other people in the world. Consider the following presentation:

"Falling in love is, to a large extent, the projection of our unconscious selves onto another person. All of the softness and sensitivity that lies within John as disowned selves are projected onto those women in his life. Sally, his latest love, has an additional feature; she is spiritual, an area of life that John has never touched and about which he has considerably negative feelings. Although John finds himself arguing with Sally for hours at a time about her spiritual viewpoint, he loves her deeply and is at some level fascinated by her unfamiliar way of looking at life. It is his unconscious self, then, that draws him into the relationship to Sally, via the mechanism of projection. By projecting those unconscious contents onto Sally, John has the chance to realize them in himself, if he uses their relationship as an opportunity to grow.

"Sally's primary selves were loving, pleasing, and caring. Her disowned selves were her rational and analytic mind, and her drive for professional achievement. We can easily see how these qualities in her unconscious would be projected onto John, while his opposite selves would be projected onto her. This kind of mutual projection is the natural start of many relationships, but it can become damaging when we do not understand how it works.

"These mutual projections can bring with them much richness when we see that they represent a natural tendency toward growth, a direct and exciting path for our evolution of consciousness, a chance to integrate unconscious material into our own lives."[3]

From these viewpoints lucidly presented by Drs. Hal and Sidra Stone, we can see the similarities and a connection between the five aggregates that make us up as human beings and the Psychology of Selves which lays an emphasis on the combination of parts or selves that form our human structure and together reveal to us convincingly that we are not a single, independent being, but an assemblage of aggregates or parts. While this branch of modern psychology creates and explains the concept of selves in an indefinitely large number of parts or selves, the Buddha analyses human beings into five

---

[3] See the detailed description of this matter in Drs. Hal and Sidra Stone's book entitled *Embracing Each Other*.

aggregates of existence, which actually covers the whole structure of the physical and mental formation that we consider to be an individual human being. In another word, we can say that the Psychology of Selves only discuss the psychological aspects of the human beings (as it's appropriate for a psychology to do within its field), the Buddha goes several steps further to include the three categories of the rūpa (body)[4], feelings, perceptions, and consciousness with the additional sankhāra in which are included those concepts of various selves talked about in the Psychology of Selves.

Since the aggregate of sankhāra is pretty large and comprehensive in the sense of dealing inclusively and extensively with the constructive and destructive forces within human consciousness and in the projected images and psychological material thrown out to the world and to other human beings, we hereby accommodate the Psychology of Selves in this aggregate of sankhāra. As we are aware, the concept of a self or infinite number of selves is quite proper here since each self has a definite character and fixated patterns of personality (ego-type) together with its feelings, perceptions, and certain conditions for being conscious of things (meaning, each consciousness is conditioned by the aggregate of sankhāra). Therefore, the use of such concepts is very helpful for a clearer comprehension of human phenomena and human manifestations. Adopting it with an open attitude we appreciate the new idea put forth by the Psychology of Selves since it elaborates the Buddhist concept of sankhāra and simplifies our ego or personality structure. As a matter of fact, those selves presented earlier are actually the sub-personalities relative to what each of us has as our identified primary selves. With the thorough understanding of the variety of selves existing within us as our inner family we will be able to practice more effectively the impeccable awareness regarding various sankhāras as they appear with each consciousness through which are appropriately manifested our inner family members.

---

[4] Please go back to the section on Rūpa and review it all carefully.

=3=

KARMA AND REBIRTH

Karma is a most significant thing in Buddhism and it is closely connected with death and rebirth. In order to comprehend precisely these issues of death and rebirth it is absolutely essential to understand the Buddha's teaching of karma profoundly, and in turn, to understand thoroughly the issue of karma is equally important in order to discern deeply the questions of death and rebirth.

Considering the basis of the Buddha's self-enlightenment, we will see that after he achieved the impeccable insight into the death and birth of all sentient beings, he then totally realized the law of karma and so formulated all those matters into the law of conditioned genesis or dependent origination (paticcasamuppāda). Soon after his attainment of full enlightenment, he spent a full seven days contemplating and reviewing it, accomplishing the third category of irreversible *insight* into *the total transformation of all the mental, physical, and psychic contaminations* (āsavakkhaya-ñāna), destroying utterly, in other words, ending definitively, *ignorance* (absence of awareness and wisdom)*, craving/thirst, and attachment/clinging.*

Following the Buddha's example, the author of this work tries to deal with the issue of karma before getting into the question of rebirth. A crystal-clear and precise knowledge of rebirth (death and birth) and a thorough comprehension of the very profound and all-inclusive law of karma go hand in hand.

This matter of karma it as appears in Buddhist texts and as the general people understand it, is rather complicated, to the point of becoming a very confused issue; what is really the correct Buddhist principle regarding this law of karma? To cut off these complications and confusions the author will divide this matter of karma into two views: the view indisputably accepted as the authentic teaching of the Buddha, and another view of karma, that of the Buddhist commentators. For this reason, the Buddha's wise words will be introduced and explained first; then we will reflect on the commentaries made by various commentators. In this way, you, the reader, will see for yourself the truth that the Buddha's own words are straightforward, and not complicated in any ways.

The authentic Buddhist teaching of karma

This real teaching of karma that the Buddha himself proclaims is found in the law of dependent origination in the very concise formula: "***Viññāna or consciousness is conditioned by, or arises through, sankhāra.***" Since this matter of karma is incredibly profound and there are many wise words spoken by the Buddha in many places, it is quite essential to deal with it scrupulously. It is said that *we all commit karma both during sleep and in waking time, and actually do so from the moment of conception onward.* In order to discern this statement properly let us consider in all its details this formula of paticcasamuppāda: ***Consciousness is conditioned by sankhāra or arises by way of sankhāra***. Here it means that consciousness will arise depending on ***sankhāra*** as ***volition*** (cetanā, in Pali) — sometimes termed sankhāra-cetanā — without it, consciousness cannot come into play, although the six sense-modalities, namely, eye-modality, ear-modality, nose-modality, tongue-modality, body-modality, and mind-modality or brain are all in good condition and ready to function. For instance, in the case of entering and abiding unwaveringly in the jhānic meditation (deep meditative absorption) as the Buddha was at one time, there was a powerful thunderstorm and the thunder came down and destroyed several trees very near to where he was, but he didn't hear anything.

Please keep in mind that when one first studies this matter of consciousness, one must be very aware of how it operates since the arising of consciousness does not depend only on the six sense-modalities, but on volition as the most significant factor. This shows that the sense of consciousness here is slightly different from the usual sense in the West. Here it is a particular consciousness, with its own particular conditioning, particular volition, and so forth. One particular consciousness can thus be appreciated as different from other particular consciousnesses (here in the plural); the way one particular karma (an action performed intentionally) is different from some other karmas (actions; also, similarly, in the plural). This is the way the karma (and the karmas) and the consciousness (and the consciousnesses) are understood in Buddhist texts and teachings.

Each consciousness arises depending on volition, as just said, and volition is one of the mental properties (cetasika) or the aggregates of sankhāra. We must emphasize very strongly that each of the feelings, sensations, emotions, and all mental states arise under the direction of volition, since volition is a coordinating factor: volition coordinates with all the energy patterns and thoughts, including the consciousness, in the way that each operates exactly in the fashion that volition wants it to, each playing its part in the particular manifestation. To put it in the language of abhidharma (higher teachings of the Buddha that deal specifically with the philosophical and psychological aspects of human beings), each consciousness is associated with volition or will and in turn, the will or volition becomes an approximate condition for the manifestation of consciousness. With this understanding, we will find it much easier to discern the truth that volition/will is an inseparable condition for the arising of a consciousness, and that without this indispensable condition of will/volition, there will be no consciousness arising. This implies that if will/ volition is not prepared to receive any external or internal objects awaiting at or coming through the doors of sense-modalities, no consciousness can arise.

Since volition or will is a cetasika (mental property) appearing and disappearing together with a consciousness every moment, the Buddha said, "Monks! I declare that volition or will is karma." According to this, it becomes quite obvious that we humans perform a karma at any given moment when a consciousness is in operation, both at time of sleep and at waking time, apparently from the period of embryo onward, and not only at the time of keeping awake as the majority of people comprehend.

As a matter of fact, there is not any action taken without volition, although it is said that someone does something with no volition, which simply means that some certain volition for taking an action at the given moment is not there. Nonetheless, there is another volition associating with the action itself, for example, in case of intending to shoot a bird, the bullet misses it and goes to kill a person who happens to be nearby. This does not mean that such an action of shooting is done without any volition, since the shooter has the volition for shooting. Factually speaking, a kind of volition is always underlying an action performed at the moment since in principle consciousness is a condition for the coming into existence of the four great elements that shape up the physical body and of the subtle, energetic body belonging to the aggregate of rūpa. But the arising of consciousness depends on a sankhāra (here, referring to mano-sankhāra – volition); and without the sankhāra there will be no consciousness. The volition pertaining to mano-sankhāra is present in consciousness right from the very moment of conception.

We humans perform a karma (an action performed intentionally), be it good or bad, in each moment, particularly a mental karma, in the process of becoming something or someone doing something. Normally, while staying awake we think about something, either good or bad, and from the thinking, we either speak or act physically, even though during sleep we undergo dreaming. Do not misunderstand that a dream takes place with no volition since all dreams have their reasons or volitions backing them up all the time. For instance, each dream that appears within us, has an intention to get our attention one way or the other. A person who has a beautiful consciousness, has a good volition deeply rooted in his or her inner character, and so doesn't encounter a bad dream or nightmare. But those who meet with bad dreams simply have the bad volitions contained in their consciousness stream (in the unconscious), which manifest in violent, or frightening dreams.

So long as one has inner contaminations (kilesas) flowing along together with one's consciousness, one always encounters dreams during sleep. The only category of people who can sleep without a dream is the fully enlightened ones (arahats), since those arahats have transformed all contaminations and cleaned out their unconscious (bhavanga) without any remainder whatsoever. Such fully enlightened people can control their minds spontaneously and naturally, unlike unenlightened folk (puthujjhana – thick people, people who are thick, that is, with kilesas), who are under the control of their conditioned minds most of the time (ninety-nine point ninety-nine per cent perhaps). For example, one part of their minds wants to do something, while another part desires something else, and eventually they end up doing something improper or bad in spite of knowing it intellectually. This kind of incident is often found in the actual lives of the puthujjhanas.

However, when thinking further about a human birth, we realize that the consciousness that enters the womb at the moment of conception has the complicated volitions for forming and structuring a human being, although at that moment it is still extremely feeble and unconscious. But because all the organs and organism shaped up in the human structure have a meaning and significance, we can appreciate that the consciousness that directs the formation and the growth of embryo has as its coordinating factor the intent or will to perform these particular intentional actions (karmas).

There is a popular view held by educated Buddhists, following the Buddhist teaching. This view states that the qualities of the body born into life, whether good or bad, are partly the results of the karma done in the previous life, and partly due to the influence of the biological genes coming from the mother and the father or from the ancestors. As we already know, any karma performed in life is stored up in consciousness and becomes its energy patterns influencing it incessantly, so too this consciousness will use those qualities of karma to build the new body, brain, and mind; therefore, all these new things with their appropriate qualities are largely predetermined by the qualities of karmic energy contained in the rebirth-consciousness (the one that descends into the mother's womb at the moment of conception). In this way, we see precisely and unmistakably that the karmic force in each instance has been deeply rooted in consciousness from the very first moment of this process, which is in a complete accord with the Buddhist principle as follows:

Consciousness gives rise to the body and to various behavior patterns, but the qualities of the physical and energetic bodies together with the behavior patterns depend partly on those qualities of karma performed through bodily action (kāya-sankhāra), speech (vacī-sankhāra), and thought (mano-sankhāra). Those three forms of karma all must have volition or will underlying their performance, otherwise consciousness will be unable to manifest. Also, such properties of consciousness as feelings (evaluation of experience), perceptions (recognition of objects), and the mental and psychic forces of sankhāra, both dark and light, are fundamental to the rebirth-consciousness. Please keep in mind that volition or will (cetanā) is one of the many sankhāra aggregates.

With a thorough examination of the statements presented just above, we will see that volition or will gives rise to an action and the action will produce results, which become properties of consciousness; then the results give rise to volition/will. If it is a good result, the volition/will is also good; and the action taken or performed with the good volition/will is certainly good. On the contrary, bad volition/will will cause a bad action, which will produce a bad result. This is because a karma is volition itself, which appears and disappears together with a consciousness. A consciousness, too, has the nature of appearing and disappearing momentarily, having the same nature of coming into being and passing away moment to moment.

Please give deep consideration and examination on this matter of a volition and a consciousness as appearing and disappearing continually from one moment to the next. The one that disappears really vanishes altogether, just like the disappearing of the flames after they have arisen. But so long as there is fuel feeding the fire, the flames will continue the process of appearing and disappearing. This is certainly applied to the nature of consciousness and that of volition. In the case of an action (karma), we will see that if it's not done every moment, it will certainly disappear for good with no continuation, and then a consciousness will be unable to manifest and to carry on its work of shaping the body and forming the mind. For this very reason, we declare, "we humans perform karmas (actions) in every moment starting from the moment of conception."

How can the embryo create karma?

Such a question as that posed above arises, requiring an answer or response, especially since the embryo has no capacity to think, to speak, or to act, because of having just a very tiny spot of the body-to-be without a brain, without a mouth (tongue), and without a completely formed physical body. The answer: a consciousness can arise and provide the appropriate conditions for the formation of the psychophysical systems without the awareness of the embryo (since at this stage of development the embryo has no awareness). This is not surprising, after all, since we, too – grown-up people – can create karma (perform an action) without our knowledge of doing it: it is a natural process of creation carried out by a consciousness and volition/will. This is because the environment, the circumstances of living, and the way of life are all in general the approximate conditions for creating a karma. If we consider the twelve topics of the law of dependent origination starting from ignorance right through birth, decay, old age, and death, we see that each topic can become a condition for creating karma. This is clearly stated in the Vibhanga, a text in the Abhidhamma-piṭaka (part of the Pali Canon or Tipiṭaka), in the section dealing with conditionality.

The law of karma, according to the law of dependent origination, has the concise principle as briefly explained above, which we may summarize as follows: "Whatever karma one creates, so is the result one reaps," or "In whatever field of studies or practices one is trained, so one becomes endowed with knowledge or mastery and is perhaps specialized in that field." Confirming this statement the Buddha declares: "Whatever seed is planted, so the fruition will ripen; doing good, receiving good; doing evil, receiving evil."

The Buddha's standard on how to do good and how not to do so

The principle of "doing good, receiving good," is the basic teaching of the Buddha at the moral level, but many people misunderstand this fundamental thing and therefore, misrepresent Buddhism in the sense of interpreting it quite mistakenly. In this connection, people in general understand this teaching in a material way, that is, they take "doing good, receiving good" to signify that they must gain more money, more wealth, more power, and more reputation or fame. This is the measurement of "doing good, receiving good" that the majority of people maintain, which is in opposition to the real meaning conveyed by the teaching. Here is the Buddha's standard of measuring this teaching: "Any action taken or performed does harm oneself and/or others as its consequences, such an action (karma) is considered ***not*** good. On the contrary, any action taken or performed does not, in any way, harm oneself and others as its consequences, such an action (karma) is indeed a ***good*** one."

Now, it has become quite obvious that the Buddha measures a good or bad action by its consequences and not by the action in itself. If trouble or any harm, whether physical, emotional, psychological, mental, or spiritual, is received as a result of the action (karma), either by oneself (doer) or by the other (receiver or affected person), it is considered **bad** by the Buddha's standard. But if the result of the action is harmless and trouble-free, then such an action is indeed a **good** one. In short, we may put it this way, which is in accord with the Buddha's teachings: "***Whatever action (karma) taken or performed is conducive to the increase of mental, psychological, and spiritual contaminations, impurities, and pathologies (kilesas), such an action is considered bad. But any action taken or performed does lead on to the transformation, the utter extinction of those contaminations, impurities, and pathologies, whether mental, psychological, or spiritual, such an action is indeed a good one.***"

What is actually meant by "doing good, receiving good" and "doing evil, receiving evil"?

The principle is this: Doing good signifies an action done with such virtues as the basic five precepts,[1] the five basic dharmas,[2] the four spiritual faculties (brahmavihāra-dharma),[3] the seven dharmas[4] for the wise, and the eightfold path.[5] Hence, receiving good means the well-trained mind, the elevated heart, and the increase of virtues (in terms of fuller and fuller development). Those who possess a highly cultivated mind and elevated heart are not necessarily going to have plenty of money, but the opposite, that is, such people are materially not rich, or rather, are poor, since they do not focus their attention on, or invest their basic energy in, becoming wealthy or having fame and name spread out all over places near and far.

As for doing evil, it refers to any action performed with such vices or unskillful mental states as greed, hate, delusion, envy, jealousy, anger, fear, and selfish desires, etc. Receiving evil implies the increase of bad habits and the deepening of the uncreative, destructive qualities of mind and heart. Considering here the principle "Whatever seed is sowed, so one reaps the fruit thereof," we understand that any seed of karma or volitional action is planted through a physical action, verbal activity, and thought or mental activity, and that we will certainly receive its consequences sooner or later, without any exceptions. Let us cite some examples: when one is trained to be a thief or robber, one will develop skill in robbing and stealing. If when trains oneself to tell a lie, one will definitely learn the arts of speaking lies skillfully. On the contrary, if one receives a proper training to be good, kind, loving, and compassionate, one will unquestionably possess and increase those wonderful qualities of the heart. This is the true principle of karma. Once again, keep in

---

[1] These five precepts are: not killing, not stealing, not committing sexual misconduct, not speaking a lie, and not taking intoxicating drinks and drugs.

[2] These five basic dharmas refer to unconditional love (mettā) and compassion, right livelihood, responsibility and control over sexual activities, honesty, non-negligence and mindfulness.

[3] These four spiritual faculties are: mettā, karuṇā (compassion), muditā (sympathetic joy over the success of others), and upekkhā (equanimity and rectitude).

[4] These seven dharmas for the wise are: self-confidence or trust, healthy shame regarding evil things, healthy fear of doing evil, much learning, energy, mindfulness, and wisdom

[5] These eight parts of the path are: right understanding, right thinking, right action, right speech, right livelihood, right effort, right mindfulness, and right concentration (stabilized mind).

mind that we create karma in every single moment, both in sleeping time and in the waking life. During waking hours, we create karma through the conscious process of mind; in the hours of sleep we create karma by way of the unconscious process (bhavanga-citta). So, volition/will vitally operates together with both the conscious and the unconscious processes of mind; karma done by way of the conscious process is physical action, speech, and thought, while karma created and manifested through the unconscious process refers to the physical behavior patterns such as the heart beating, the functioning of lungs, and so forth. Since karma is created through both the conscious process (vithī-citta) and the unconscious process (bhavanga-citta), it will naturally produce the consequences in one way or another just like the law of action and reaction. The consequence of karma (vipāka) means many different things such as the ability and capacity of the brain and/or of both the physical body and the psychic (energetic) body. This matter of vipāka will continue operating in cycle: Karma produces the outcome (vipāka), in turn vipāka becomes a cause of karma; when karma turns into **A**, vipāka also becomes **A** as its outcome, when karma becomes **B**, vipāka also turns into **B** as the outcome of the karma **B**.

Since we humans are fully equipped with the sense modalities, namely, eye-modality, ear-modality, nose-modality, tongue-modality, body-modality, and mind-modality, through which consciousness can be in contact with both the internal world and the external world at all times. When there is contact, there will arise feelings/sensations and desires. Through the arising of desire/thirst/craving, there will come into operation attachment or clinging. When attachment or clinging is actively present, karma will be created. When there is karma in vital existence, consciousness is also there in full operation. When consciousness takes complete charge of the creation, physical and mental phenomena will emerge as our human psychosomatic systems so as to enable life to function more efficiently.

Taking the above-described formula into thorough consideration, we will comprehend that the capacity of life or the potentiality of consciousness will be able to continue from this present life time to the next, equally the same as the capacity of life and the potentiality of consciousness of the present life are the consequences of those existing in the past life transferred through the energetic process of consciousness that carries the karmic energy through mysteriously. For this reason, those wishing to become someone important or something significant and training themselves in accord with their wishes, will certainly one day succeed in fulfilling those realistic wishes.

Since the law of karma is so simple and straightforward as briefly explained above, the Buddha declares: "*All sentient beings have karma of their own, are inheritors of their karma, and have karma as origination and kinship or species. They all depend on their karma since it classifies them into the good and the bad.*"

Normally, most of us maintain the view that the physical body and the material wealth earned and gained righteously are our real properties, but the Buddha has the opposite view and makes it known that those things are, in truth, not ours, since eventually the body will break up and die, and material wealth cannot accompany us in the case of death. Whoever does any karma will have to reap its fruits until they are all exhausted and become ineffective, and because of this, the Buddha declares: "**All sentient beings have karma of their own.**"

Parents keep their wealth for their children, and so those children who inherit the wealth from their parents are called "inheritors." In this connection, the children might not receive such wealth since it might get lost or perish before they could get it, or in case of their inappropriate behavior, the parents might cut them off from the inheritance or those children might have died before their parents and therefore, would not be able to inherit their wealth. But as to the karma, it never goes that way since for any karma committed, whether good or bad, black or white, the doer of the karma will inevitably reap its consequences and therefore, will always become the inheritor of his/her karma. For this reason, the Buddha declares: "**All sentient beings are the inheritors of their own karma.**"

Generally speaking, parents give birth to their children and become their generators and their origin. If the parents are humans, their children will become humans as well, or if the parents are animals, their children will certainly be animals. In spite of the fact the Buddha makes a declaration that karma gives birth to all sentient beings or they are all born of their own karma, this doesn't mean that he denies the fact that the parents are the origin of their children, meaning, they do give birth to them so that they can be here on the planet Earth. Therefore, we can affirm for certain that both the parents and the karma give birth to, and are origin of, their children. Of these two factors, karma is the important thing because all sentient beings have their personal karma as their origin and without it, the predetermination of their fate is impossible. Those who perform good karmas will be born of good parents and a healthy environment; on the contrary, those performing bad karmas will be born of bad parents and an unhealthy environment. So long as the residue of karmic energy remains intact, all sentient beings will be reborn time and again until the karma becomes exhausted and ineffective.

There are those who are close to us, such as our brothers, sisters, and relatives of both the father's side and the mother's side, and whom we call our kin because of their intimate relationships with us. However, all these people may sometimes become quarrelsome or get into conflict with us, or they might become separated from us or might even abandon us. But the karma already performed will be like a shadow that never leaves; on the contrary, it will follow us wherever we go and literally anywhere we are. For this reason, karma earns the title of The Most Intimate Kin, and so the Buddha declares: "**All sentient beings have karma as their intimate kin.**"

As far as we humans are concerned, after having been born into life we, first of all, depend on our parents, and later on, we are also under care and support of our relatives from time to time. However, all these people including our parents cannot remain our refuge or safe haven forever since they might be unable to give us love constantly, let alone living with us for the rest of our lives; but the karma already done through action, speech, or thought will be our secure refuge and safe sanctuary both in this life time and in the life to come: For this reason, the Buddha declares: "**All sentient beings have karma as their refuge,**" which also implies that the good karma becomes the most significant factor for supporting and helping us climb to the top of whatever we do either in the worldly life or in the spiritual realm of consciousness; while the bad karma will do us in the opposite direction.

According to theistic religions, the followers of such religions as Hinduism and Christianity believe that God creates heaven and earth and all living beings, and that people and animals are born into their lives, whether good or bad, high or low, noble or ignoble, depending on the will of God. But the fact that the Buddha could recall his various past lives, and was able to possess impeccable insights into birth and death (or decease and conception) of all beings, which helped him know precisely and directly the truth of the matter that in actual fact all living beings, with no exception, will become despicable or elegantly refined depending entirely on their own karma, and not on anyone or anything else, including the One Being or God. For this reason, the Buddha declares: "**Karma divides and classifies all sentient beings into the appalling or refined, inferior or superior categories.**" This implies that it is the karma that creates, arranges, and categorizes all the humans, animals, insects, reptiles, living things, and non-living things into pairs of opposites: Good-bad, high-low, noble-ignoble, beautiful-ugly, intelligent-stupid, wise-ignorant, liberated-thick (with kilesas), and so on and so forth.

The frequently misunderstood concept of karma

One matter which the Buddhists and the students of Buddhism often misunderstand is when they maintain the view that karma is separated from consciousness. For example, they say that at the final moment of death, the consciousness becomes extinguished while the karma remains intact, and this remaining karma will makes up a new consciousness for a new life. This kind of understanding is quite wrong since in considering the word "karma" which literally means "action or doing," an action or a doing can become karma only if it has been done with volition or will. So, without the will or volition as the coordinating factor actively present with the action or the doing, there will be no karma; this covers all three categories of karma, namely, to repeat, physical karma, verbal karma, and mental karma. These three forms of karma depend on volition or will for their coming into existence; and volition or will is a cetasika, which means a mental state that arises together with a consciousness, and is inextricably associated with a consciousness. It appears and disappears together with that consciousness, and exists implicitly within the aggregates of sankhāra. In this way, we can affirm the truth of the matter under discussion that karma cannot exist independently without consciousness or outside of it and therefore, it is absolutely impossible for a karma to be separated from consciousness at any moment in time.

Even the arahats, who have been totally liberated from good and evil, or virtue and sin (which means that they are above the good karma and the bad karma), still carry out daily activities and perform certain karma. This interesting third kind of karma is neither good nor bad, is neither karmically wholesome nor unwholesome; thus it is considered to be "indeterminate" or avyākata). It is an act with no volition that would bring forth a result in terms of good or bad. In Pali it is termed ahosi-karma (karma that was), referring here to action that is lapsed, that produces no additional effect in the karmic life of the arahat.

These actions of an arahat, performed without a self-interested aim or egocentricity, arise out of a karmically inoperative state of consciousness called kiriya-citta (in short, kiriya), which is totally free of the three unwholesome roots of greed, hate, and delusion (lobha, dosa, and moha). Here, to say this differently, the action (karma) of an arahat is merely a *function* with no effectiveness in the sense of not becoming a condition for rebirth and of not being able to cause the rebirth-consciousness to take place.

What we must examine thoroughly in this context is the formula that says, "Sankhāra-cetanā is a condition for the arising of viññāna or consciousness." Here, sankhāra is taken specifically as volition (cetanā). Do not misunderstand that cetanā (sankhāra as volition) and viññāna arise separately in different moments since in actual fact cetanā or volition becomes the indispensable condition for the origination of the conscious process of consciousness (vithī-citta), the process of the unconscious (bhavanga-citta), and the rebirth-consciousness (patisandhi-viññāna). The volition must arise together with each of the three types of consciousness, which, according to abhidharma, is called consciousness associated with volition. To put it in another way, volition is the associating condition of consciousness: this is because every form of action manifesting through physical expression, verbal expression, or mental expression, all this is connected with volition of one kind or another at all time. Volition, in turn, cannot come into play without the presence of consciousness since the latter is the foundation of all cetasikas (mental contents). As it is often quoted, "Consciousness is the condition for the arising of nāma-rūpa; without consciousness, the nāma-rūpa (psychophysical systems) cannot come into existence and into operation." Or, "consciousness is the basis of all the dharmas (things) and is far better than all things (dharmas) since all the things are made up through consciousness." Such a principle as "karma and consciousness are inseparable" (as already explained at some length) is a most important issue, which most people miscomprehend. So, keep in mind that *wherever the current of karma exists, the current of consciousness is also found there*, and *wherever the stream of consciousness exists, the stream of karma is found there also*.

According to the law of dependent origination, we understand that karma is taking place in every single moment since the concept of "karma" used in this context simply refers to the behavior patterns of both the body and the mind. Let us think about this matter of karma that operates from the time of the embryo (kalala in Pali) on, in which sankhāra, or in other words, karma, is the condition or provision of consciousness. Or, in reverse, that the particular consciousness at that time becomes a further condition for the karma manifestations in the embryo's growth process.

Some people mistakenly maintain that the growth and development of life depend on the potentiality and creative energy of previous karma, which actually means the capacity and potentiality of consciousness, which carries with it all the energetic material stored up within its systems. This mistaken thinking takes out of context (and misconstrues) the idea that at the moment of conception no karma can be created due to the lack of the physical body with all its basic equipment for carrying out any physical action, the lack of the mouth organ for making speech, and the lack of the brain for initiating the thinking process. All this is a miscomprehension of some people!

Now, with a profound and total comprehension of sankhāra as the condition for the arising of consciousness and consciousness as the condition for the appearing and manifesting of nāma-rūpa or psychophysical phenomena, we will see clearly that we humans perform karma in every consciousness, and karma at this stage is the manifestation of the physical behavior patterns. The potentiality and capacity of consciousness transferred from the previous existence, still continues operating effectively in this present life. If the physical behavior patterns together with their underlying or on-feeding conditions are cut off for some inconceivable reasons, the capacity and potentiality of consciousness will come to an end entirely. Please give vital attention and deep thought to this matter since it is enormously significant!

In fact, we may state simply and briefly that when there is action (karma), there will be capacity, the consequence (vipāka) of the action. In this way, we see karma as a cause or a condition of vipāka and in turn, vipāka becomes a cause of karma. However, karma will be the condition of vipāka and vipāka will turn into the cause of the rebirth-consciousness when the rebirth-consciousness is in full operation there will be reproduction of karma, and the underlying cause of all this is kilesa (mental contamination/defilement/destructive forces) such as ignorance *et cetera*. At this point, let us understand that various kilesas are all related and associated with one another. For instance, when ignorance is in operation, craving/thirst, attachment, and some other kilesas are also present, giving support to the ignorance so that karma can continue to reproduce. Therefore, do not miscomprehend that at the moment ignorance is providing itself as a condition for the arising of another sankhāra, it is only that sankhāra alone with no presence of any other kilesas, because the truth of the matter is that ignorance is not there alone, since its associates and team workers are right there together. In this fashion, we may summarize the law of karma as follows: "***kilesa causes karma, the karma becomes a condition for producing vipāka, and in turn vipāka turns itself into a cause of karma***," continuing its cycle one after another endlessly, and this is denominated samsāra. So long as the kilesas have not been transformed and cleaned out of the character and of the unconscious, the stream of karma, the stream of consciousness, and the stream of life will keep on flowing incessantly. In accordance with this, if death comes to any form of life in any place and at any time, birth (or rather rebirth) will be found right there at the given moment. Such a sequence of events will be found throughout the entire universe since those streams of karma, vipāka, and consciousness will go forward and come backward in their endless, complicated cycles with no limitations, although they rotate in their orbits according to the universal law of order (niyāma).

There is an issue of karma which some people find rather mysterious and hard to comprehend, due to a confused view holding that the karma, after having been performed, exists outside of those performing it, and appears like many other superstitious things and supernatural powers to be operating out there in the world, and in the universe. This kind of wrong view and miscomprehension is quite pitiful and harmful in the sense of self-growth since it complicates the simple issue of karma. If we study the law of dependent origination properly, we will see that this matter of karma is quite simple and easy to grasp with our intellect and intelligence without any complications. So, the teaching of karma according to the law of dependent origination, which comes directly from the Buddha, is the real and trustworthy one. Therefore, we can conclude that *any principle of karma that is in conflict with the principle of dependent origination is to be considered not the authentic Buddha's teaching.* All these explanations on the issue of karma are in accord with the law of dependent origination, and so the author will bring in much more such law.

Why is karma called sankhāra?

It is interesting to note that in the teaching of dependent origination, the Buddha calls karma by the name of sankhāra (here it means *creation, or conditioning, or the process of making or composing things*). The Buddha's reason for naming it so is that karma becomes a condition for creating and increasing the capacity and potentiality of consciousness. When consciousness has more capacity and more potentiality or power of creation, consciousness will be able to form the body efficiently, to shape up the human structure and any other structures of existence, and to cause the variety of cetasikas (states of consciousness or mental contents) to arise and to operate fully.

The main principle of karma is this: Karma if performed with good states of mind and beautiful feelings will produce desirable results (vipāka); on the contrary, karma if performed with bad states of mind and negative feelings will produce undesirable and even harmful and destructive results. The desirable results here refer to all the virtues of good dharmas, while the harmful and destructives consequences signify the vices of bad dharmas. Therefore, karma will become skillful (kusala) or unskillful (akusala) depending specifically on the states of consciousness and feelings that cause it to be taken or performed. In this connection, the Buddha declares: "*Karma performed with the skillful volition will become skillful karma, but if it's performed with the unskillful volition, will inevitably become unskillful karma.*"

In this case of considering karma as skillful or unskillful, it is normally meant to include physical action, speech, and thought committed by way of the conscious process only, and not through the unconscious process. But, in fact, unskillful karma performed through the conscious process is also related to unconscious process since in unconscious process there exist negative, bad feelings and destructive forces, which, when stimulated or instigated, will emerge and manifest through the conscious process. Therefore, the unskillfunness of karma has already existed in the unconscious process (bhavanga). This will mean that those who still have kilesas covert in their character, that is, in the unconscious (bhavanga), will certainly have to express their psychophysical behavior patterns in their daily living. As for the arahats (those who have been fully enlightened and completely liberated from all kilesas), although they stay above and far beyond the reach of any unskillful karma (and skillful karma as well), they still need to manifest their behavior patterns in their everyday life just as the thick people (puthujjhana, thick, that is, with kilesas) do. But such manifestations are merely natural functions, whether physical, verbal, or mental, and are totally free from the dominance of any categories of karma.

In thinking about karma, first of all, let us think for ourselves and think in such a way that it can be proved: *Karma is volitional action, and vipāka is its consequence, which includes the capacity and potentiality of virtues and vices.* This is the most significant criterion, which must be embraced fully, and not neglected by any means. If this formula is not firmly maintained, there will be a great deal of difficulties and confusion concerning this issue of karma.

When and how karma bears fruits

Up till now, we have discussed what karma is, what kinds of effects it produces, and how it is able to continue to the so-called next life. However, there are still some problems about karma that many people find hard to comprehend, for example, the questions of what the indisputable criterion is that helps us know for certain that karma after having been performed will bear its fruits in this very life time and the next, what the means are that will bear the results, whether there are any conditions attached to the means whereby the consequences of karma will be received, and if the good and bad karmas already performed can be redeemed or not. All these questions are a great concern for many people and therefore the author will bring in some quotations from the Buddha's wise words for our careful examination and thorough scrutiny, to clarify these matters.

These quotations will come from the Tipiṭaka (Pali Buddhist Canon), volume 20, at page 130 (Mahachula Version), page 171 (Mahamakut Version), and page 172 (Sangīti of Abhidhamma). They are most worthy for studies and are the sources of the twelve categories of karma of which many educated Buddhists have good knowledge. Please keep in mind that the twelve categories of karma are actually classified by the great Buddhist commentator named Buddhaghosa, and not by the Buddha himself. Those twelve karmas have been explained at some length in the Commentary Text of Anguttara-Nikāya, volume 2, pages 116-117, and in the Paññā-Nidesa of Buddhaghosa's Visuddhimagga, page 223. Nonetheless, first, let us study the Buddha's words, and after that, examine the commentator's views.

Here, first, are the Buddha's own words, which demonstrate whether karma already performed will yield the result at an appropriate time, and how it could be redeemed:

"Monks, these three roots of evil, namely, *greed, hate, and delusion*, are the root causes of all kinds of karma. Monks, any karma done with greed and has greed as its root cause and condition, any karma done with hate and has hate as its root cause and condition; any karma done with delusion and has delusion as its root cause and condition, will yield the fruit to the person who has performed it, wherever he or she is. When his/her karma has yielded its fruit, he/she will reap its consequences in such a place where he/she lives, which may be in the present life, or in the next life, or in many other lives to come."

According to those words uttered by the Buddha we understand that karma performed with the influence of any kilesa, if such a kilesa hasn't been transformed and cleaned out of one's character, will always give the result, if not today, it could be tomorrow, or if not in this life time, it could be in the life to come. Normally, every form of karma will produce its consequence when the appropriate occasion is presented. If such an occasion presents itself in this very life, it (karma) will yield the result right away, but if the appropriate occasion hasn't arrived in this lifetime, it will yield the result in the next lifetime, or in any other lifetimes to come, so long as greed, hate, and delusion still exist in one's character and continue influencing and dominating the course of action. Any karma performed with the power and influence of any one of those three kilesas will never disappear or become devoid (ineffective), but will yield its fruit in any suitable occasion and, therefore, the Buddha declares once more:

"Monks, just like any unbroken, unrotten, seed free from any damages, abundant in quality, fertile, and ready to grow, when it's planted in well-prepared soil and with the rain falling down at a suitable time in accord with its seasons, will certainly grow and reach maturity in due course. Monks, the karma done with greed, born of greed, and has greed as its root cause and condition, the karma done with hate, born of hate, and has hate as its root cause and condition, the karma done with delusion, born of delusion, and has delusion as its root cause and condition, each will yield the result to the doer or performer wherever such a person will be. When the karma yields its fruition, the doer or performer of the karma will reap its consequences, if not in the present lifetime, in any other lifetimes ahead."

Please observe and examine carefully the Buddha's words quoted above. He said that *greed, hate, and delusion* are the root causes of karma, which pointed out precisely that any action done with those three root causes of evil (kilesa-akusalamūla), will yield its fruition at all times so long as those kilesas are still in operation. So karma performed with greed, hate, or delusion is compared with the seed, abundant in potentiality of growing, and will yield its result at an appropriate occasion, with no exception whatsoever. But in case of those three kilesas having been transformed and cleaned out of the character completely, the karma already performed, although it has the potentiality to yield its fruition but has lost the suitable opportunity to do so, will then become ineffective (ahosi-karma). Nonetheless, do not forget that the karma performed with the kilesa, its vipāka will become the kilesa as well, since it will further turn into the cause of karma. So, any kind of karma performed with the kilesa(s) will inevitably yield the results in one way or another. But when the kilesas no longer exist in the consciousness (included here is the unconscious), the opportunity of performing karma will not be found. When no karma can be performed, there will be no vipāka, and no condition for carrying out karma either. In conclusion at this point we emphasize that karma can yield its result because of the kilesas that then exist, and any action to be considered karma is because it is performed with the kilesa(s).

Let us continue examining some more of the Buddha's words:

"Monks, non-greed or generosity (alobha), non-hate or love (adosa), and non-delusion or wisdom (amoha) are the root causes of all good karmas. Monks, the karma performed with alobha (generosity), originates by way of generosity, and has the generosity as its cause/condition; the karma performed with adosa (love), originates by way of love, and has love as its cause/condition; and the karma performed with amoha (wisdom), originates by way of wisdom, and has wisdom as its cause/condition; such karmas as these will be able to transform, redeem, and uproot all the remaining kilesas, as well as to bring the utter mutation of them all in the individual concerned, whose greed, hate, and delusion are no longer in operation. This is like a palm tree with its top cut off entirely! Monks, it's also like the seeds with all their good conditions and potentialities to grow, but if those seeds are put on fire, and then are crushed up until they turn into powder; and after that someone will gather their powder and scatter it all in the swift current, then certainly those seeds cannot grow again. Monks, the karma performed with alobha, or adosa, or amoha in such a condition that greed, hate, and delusion no longer exist in the character of the performer/doer will yield their fruits/consequences in exactly the same way as previously described. Monks, these three root causes of the skillful karma are the conditions for the origination of all good karmas."

Once again reconsidering those words uttered by the Buddha we understand that there are two categories of karma, namely, skillful karma and unskillful karma: The karma performed with non-greed, non-hate, and non-delusion is called skillful karma – kusalakamma, while the karma performed with greed, hate, and delusion is called unskillful karma – akusalakamma. Those two forms of karma are in opposition to one another, that is to say, when the karma is increasingly performed with non-greed, non-hate, and non-delusion, the consequences (vipāka) of the unskillful karma performed with greed, hate, and delusion will become decreasingly effective (in the sense of yielding its fruition/ dividend). In the same fashion, when the unskillful karma is more and more performed, the consequences of the skillful karma will become less and less effective (in the sense of yielding its fruition/profit). However, the skillful karma eventually will utterly defeat the unskillful karma. In order to overcome the unskillful karma it is essential to perform the skillful karma constantly, and not just waiting idly for the unskillful karma to get worn out. Take a look at the Buddha's words quoted just above one more time: Non-greed, non-hate, and non-delusion are the conditions for performing the skillful karma, so when such karma is on the increase, greed, hate, and delusion will gradually diminish from the character until it eventually becomes extinguished without remainder. At the utter extinction of the unskillful karma, the skillful karma will be transcended as well."

In this connection, the Buddha made another declaration. "The arahats are those who have transcended both good and sin[6] (skillful and unskillful karma)." This is because when all the mental and spiritual contaminations or diseases (kilesas) no longer exist in the character of an arahat, any action performed by that person, although it is good and skillful karma, will not be able to yield any result, but will become ineffective naturally. This is in accord with what we have been saying all along: Any karma which is done with no support or influence of any kilesas will not become a condition for the arising of the rebirth-consciousness. For this reason, the Buddha compares the karma performed with non-greed, non-hate, and non-delusion to the productive seed put on fire and burned entirely, which will have no potentiality to grow.

The twelve karmas of Buddhaghosa

Up until now, we have discussed the principle of karma as the Buddha himself taught, which is quite straightforward and without any complications. He did not determine which karma will produce its consequence in this life time, and which will yield its fruition in the life to come, but simply stated that so long as there exist the kilesas in the character, the karma already performed will give its results definitely either in this very life or in the next; and all this depends on the appropriate occasion. But the Buddhist commentators, especially Buddhaghosa, adhere to the Sutra and continue by classifying karma into twelve categories as follows:

1. Ditthavedaniya-kamma: this refers to that kind of karma that will yield its fruition in this present life. Buddhaghosa explains that either skillful karma or unskillful karma performed at the first *potent operation (javana) of consciousness* is called *ditthavedaniya-kamma*. This category of karma will yield its fruition only in this life on earth, and if there is no suitable occasion for giving its yield, then it will become automatically ineffective, meaning, not being able to produce any result. It's comparable to the hunter shooting an animal or a bird with his arrow. If the arrow pierces the animal or the bird, such a poor living being falls down dead in that very place where it was before; but in case of the arrow missing it, the animal or the bird would have fled and would not be hurt by that arrow.

2. Uppajjavedaniya-kamma: that karma which yields its fruition in the life next to this present one. The commentator's explanation is this: Either skillful karma or unskillful karma performed at the *seventh potent operation* of consciousness is denominated *uppajjavedaniya-kamma*. As for skillful karma, this refers to the *eight attainments*,[7] while unskillful karma is any of the *five gravest karmas*[8] *(anantariya-kammas)*. Furthermore, the commentators went on expounding it this way: As for those who accomplish the eight attainments, after

---

[6] Puññapāpappahīnassa in Pali.

[7] These eight are the same as the four meditative absorptions regarding form (Rūpa-jhāna) and the four formless meditative absorptions. See the details in *Turning to the Source,* and in Spanish version, *Retorno al Origen.*

[8] These five are: killing a mother, killing a father, killing an arahat, hurting the Buddha's body to the point of causing his blood to explode, and causing schism in the Sangha (Community of Monks and Nuns).

death they will be born in the realm of Brahma as the result of any one of the eight attainments, while the rest of those attainments will become ineffective. In the case of committing the five gravest karmas, if after death, the performer of such karma would be born in the most tormented hell called *avecī* as the consequence of such karma, the remaining anantariya-kammas will also become ineffective. The comparison is the same as the action of the hunter as previously referred to.

3. Aparāparavedaniya-kamma: that karma which yields its fruition in any of the lives after the present one. Buddhaghosa explains that as skillful karma or unskillful karma performed between the *second* potent, swift-running operation (javana) and the *sixth javana* is called aparāparavedaniya-kamma. When the suitable occasion is presented in any of the next lives to come, this aparāparavedaniya-kamma will yield its fruition in such lifetimes. As long as the cycle of birth-life-death is not broken, but continues its cyclical process, this karma under discussion will always yield its result. There is no way for it to become ineffective; it is just like a hunter's hunting dog chasing a prey: at the moment of arriving at it, it will attack the prey immediately so that the prey will fall down and remain immovable or dead. Like that, indeed, is this aparāpara-vedaniya-kamma.

4. Ahosi-kamma: This refers to that karma which abandons its rights to yield its dividend and therefore becomes ineffective.

5. Garu-kamma: This category of karma is a heavy or grave one. In terms of skillful karma it refers to the great kamma, which is eight jhānas (four rūpa-jhāna and four arūpa-jhāna), and in terms of unskillful karma it covers the five gravest karmas or anantariya-kamma (see again, footnote 7 above). The commentator explains further, stating that so long as the garu-kamma is in existence, the other karma, whether skillful one or unskillful one, may not be able to yield its result, and the garu-kamma will lead on to the conception before any other karmas. This is compared to, according to Buddhaghosa, a tiny piece of gravel with its size as big as a lettuce seed, or to a small piece of metal. When either of them is thrown into the water, it will be unable to float up on the water's surface but will only sink down into the bottom. Just like that, indeed, is this (heavy) garu-kamma, which will yield the result before any other karma.

6. Bahula-kamma: Literally *bahula* signifies much (many), but here it is meant to say "*very often.*" So bahula-kamma is that karma which is performed very often, repeatedly, or habitually. In other words, the skillful bahula-kamma indicates the skillful karma, which, after having been done, brings about peace, happiness, and joy, while the unskillful bahula-kamma causes a great deal of troubles and remorse. Therefore, the bahula-kamma with greater strength and much more force will yield its result before any other karma that is weaker and less powerful. Buddhaghosa compares it to two wrestlers in the fighting ring: the one who is stronger and cleverer will manage to throw the weaker and less clever down to the floor. Just like those two wrestlers, indeed, are the bahula-kammas. This also means that the karma performed frequently and for a long while and with much more strength will bring a great deal of joy and happiness, or cause much less trouble and remorse, depending on whether it is the skillful bahula-kamma or the unskillful bahula-kamma.

7. Āsanna-kamma: this refers to that karma which is performed at the moment close to death, or is recalled at the time of dying process. As for this āsanna-kamma, if the garu-kamma or bahula-kamma does not exist or is not in operation, it will be able to yield its result. Buddhaghosa makes a comparison to a herd of cattle in a barn: when the gate is open, the one that is standing by the gate, although it might be an old or weak one, will have a chance to get out first. Similar to this, indeed, is the matter of karma; although there may exist other skillful or unskillful karma, the karma performed and/or recalled at the moment of dying will produce its result before all other karmas.

8. Katattā-kamma: this is that kind of karma that is merely an action or a doing, with no intent to perform. For example, a parent would punish a child with a rod just for the reason of teaching, but unfortunately the rod hit an inappropriate, sensitive point and the child lost its life. This type of karma will be able to yield its result only when the garu-kamma, bahula-kamma, or āsanna-kamma does not exist or is not in operation. Therefore, the production of results by this katattā-kamma is not quite definite, and is compared to an arrow shot by a crazy, amateurish person, that will fall down totally missing the target.

9. Janaka-kamma: It is that karma which causes the conception in the mother's womb. Here, while certain karma causes the conception and gives rise to existence, another kind of karma produces vipāka or consequence at the time when life continues to live. Janaka-Kamma is compared to a mother who is pregnant with a child, and the karma that yields the result after the conception is like a nanny providing milk for the child.

10. Upathumbhaka-kamma: this is the supportive karma, which can be both skillful and unskillful karmas. Its example is: Someone has done a lot of skillful karma and, after death, is born in a happy plane of life; and during the life in such a plane of existence carries on performing skillful karma more often. Therefore, that karma will be supportive of and maintain such a person so that he/she will be able to continue living the happy and good life in the happy plane of existence for quite a long time. On the contrary, some other person has done a great deal of the unskillful karma and, after death, is born is the unhappy, painful plane of life. During the period of living such an unpleasant, disagreeable life in that plane of existence, he or she carries on performing the unskillful karma more often. Therefore, that karma will become supportive of and maintaining him/her so that such a person will continue living an undesirable, miserable life in such a hellish place for quite a long time.

Furthermore, the janaka-kamma, whether skillful or unskillful, can cause the aggregate of vipāka regarding form and the formless to come into existence both at the moment of conception and in the period right after that. However, the upathumbhapa-kamma will be unable to give rise to the vipāka (consequence), but will remain supportive in the sense of increasing happiness or suffering as the consequences of the janaka-kamma, as that may be.

11. Upapīlaka-kamma: That karma which oppresses and makes trouble for the other karmas, not allowing them to yield their results fully, is called upapīlaka-kamma. For example, when skillful karma is yielding its result, unskillful karma comes in to interfere and cut it off in the middle so as not to let it produce its consequences completely. Alternatively, when unskillful karma is yielding its result, skillful karma interrupts it and obstructs it so that it cannot produce its consequences totally. This is compared to a plant or a tree that has been growing steadily and beautifully, then someone comes along and destroys it, cutting it down with a knife or and axe so that the plant or the tree cannot continue growing, but will die instead. Skillful and unskillful karmas are opposing each other in exactly the same way.

12. Upaghātaka-kamma: That karma which kills or brings to a halt the other karmas in the sense of cutting them off from the opportunities to produce their results to the full scale is denominated upaghātaka-kamma or upacchedaka-kamma. This indicates that either skillful unskillful karma may destroy utterly the other karma that is weaker and less powerful, preventing the consequences of that karma from being produced or yielded. But the upaghātaka-kamma itself can yield its result with no obstruction. For example, King Ajātasattu, after having listened to the Buddha's Discourse, became very happy and therefore, had complete trust and confidence in the Buddha, which, normally, would have helped him achieve the dhamma-cakkhu, the eye of the dharma, or enter the stream of nirvana. However, because of his crime committed with respect to killing his own father (King Bimbisāra) he was prevented from attaining such achievement, which means that his extremely grave unskillful karma interrupted and cut him off absolutely from reaching the most desirable goal of the entry into the nirvanic stream.

Another example is about the skillful upaghātaka-kamma interrupting the unskillful karma, that is to say, at the time the unskillful karma is yielding its result, the skillful karma comes in and cut off exclusively the power of the unskillful karma so that it becomes totally powerless in producing its results. This is like the monk, Angulimāla by name, who had been a fierce robber, killing many people (nine hundred ninety-nine in number), and who then had the opportunity to meet with the Buddha, listened to his convincing discourse, became converted, and attained to full enlightenment (arahatship). Therefore, his grave unskillful karma was interrupted and cut off thoroughly, and, as a result, became ineffective. (Certainly, by accomplishing arahatship or complete enlightenment, all karmas, if having not yet yielded their results, will lose their power completely so that they cannot produce or yield any more consequences, since the power of the arahatship is most forceful of all the powers.)

A full investigation of the twelve karmas

As mentioned earlier, all the twelve above-explained karmas are the arrangements and viewpoints of the well-known Buddhist commentator, Buddhaghosa, the author of the most respected commentary, Visuddhimagga. His arrangements and explanations of those categories of karma are, on one hand, useful and helpful in bringing about some clearer comprehension of karma, on the other hand, some of his interpretations on this issue of karma, instead of helping us understand it easier, turn into creating a great deal of complications and some conflict with the Buddha's original words. For example, Buddhaghosa said, "karma done in the early swift movements of the potent operation of consciousness yield its result on in this life on earth. If it misses the opportunity to do so, it will become ineffective."

I do not understand at all the reason why he uses the swift movements of potent operation of consciousness to determine which kind of karma would produce its consequence, and when to do so. In fact, if we read the suttas carefully, we will find that the Buddha considers the kilesas as the predominant factors for determining if the karma would give its result and when it would do so, since so long as there is kilesa, karma always yields its result, depending on the appropriate opportunity. The concept of "opportunity" used in the context of karma, refers to the environment or the circumstance that provides a suitable condition for such and such karma to produce the results. It is like the seeds with great potentiality to grow, when they are planted in good soil and having the help of the sun, the rain or moisture, and the proper season, will certainly grow. Therefore, the opportunity under discussion means four things, namely, the plane of life (gati), the proper condition (upadhi), the occasion or time (kāla), and the adequate performance (payoga). Relevant evidence supporting this appears in the Buddhist Tipiṭaka, volume 35, pages 412-413 (Mahachula version), page 458 (Mahamakut version), and page 471 (Sangīti Text).

Let us return to the principle of dependent origination once more. The formula goes thus: "**Karma is the proximate condition for the arising of consciousness.**" The consciousness employed in this context signifies, not only the rebirth-consciousness (consciousness present at the moment of conception), but all types of consciousness both at the conscious process level and at the unconscious process level. As is its nature, consciousness arises, passes away, and continues its process of manifestation incessantly, so that karma which is associated with consciousness goes on appearing, disappearing, and manifesting together with consciousness at all times. The factors that keep consciousness and karma operating in this fashion are the internal six sense modalities and their corresponding external objects, also six in number (visual objects, sounds, smell, flavor, body touch, and mental things). These sense modalities and their corresponding objects keep the wheels of consciousness and karma turning round and round continually, from birth to death; even after death the energetic karma residing in the six internal sense modalities will become a further condition for the arising of the rebirth consciousness. *However, karma can continue providing such a condition only if the kilesas still remain operative and forceful. This is the very basic principle and therefore is the fundamental standard regarding the issue of karma.*

Furthermore, the criteria of javana-citta (the swift, powerful movement of consciousness during its operation process) which Buddhaghosa uses for determining when the karma would yield its result, is in conflict with the Buddha's foremost view. Buddhaghosa's criterion that the karma performed during the early javana-citta, if it does not yield its result in this life, will become ineffective (ahosi-kamma), is conflicting itself. The simple reason is that to be able to perform the karma, whether good or bad, the first javana-citta must be based on a very strong intent to perform it. This implies that the person performing the skillful karma (at the first javana-citta) must be endowed with many high virtues. In the case of performing the unskillful karma he or she must have an utterly destructive intent and must be completely thick (with kilesas) and filled enormously with the dark forces so that the karma will get done quite early, meaning, at the very first moment of the javana-citta. In this connection, one of the examples given by Buddhaghosa is the monk named Devadatta who committed two gravest karmas (anantariya-kamma) of causing schism in the Sangha and attempting to kill the Buddha by hurting his foot with a huge rock rolling down from the mountaintop. Those two categories of the anantariya-kammas are classified as the garu-kamma (heavy karma) and as the uppajjavedaniya-kamma (the karma that will yield its result in the life next the present one). Let us consider this matter carefully: Suppose that the monk Devadatta performed the gravest karma during the first javana-citta, which, according to the Buddhaghosa's criteria, must yield its result in this present life. If there is no chance for such karma to produce the result, will it yield its result in the life to come? The answer is NO, since it will become ineffective when it misses the chance to do so. However, according to the Buddha, any karma, with no exception, will always yield its result and will never become ineffective so long as the kilesas still exist and dominate the human character. In addition, the Buddha never uses the javana-citta as a criterion for classifying karma with regard to the occasions for yielding the consequences.

Since Buddhaghosa himself said that anantariya-kamma is classified as uppajjavedaniya-kamma as well, this implies that those two anantariya-kammas performed by Devadatta at his first javana-citta must be classified as ditthavedaniya-kamma (the karma that yield its result in the present life), as uppajjavedaniya-kamma, and as aparāparavedaniya-kamma. This is supported by the Dhammapada text, according to which Devadatta was first devoured by the earth, and after that, would be reborn in the avecī hell, and further still, would continue to pay off his gravest karmas in various hells during many lifetimes. Therefore, Buddhaghosa's classification of the karmas by using the javana-citta as the criterion is unnecessary and is of little meaning. The fact of the matter is that whether or not the karma will yield its result depends entirely on the kilesas that are the causes and conditions giving rise to it; it does not depend on time, how long or how short the period of time may be. As long as such kilesas are still in operation, the karma will certainly produce its consequence, and will never turn ineffective. Therefore, the best criterion is that of the Buddha as previously quoted quite repeatedly.

However, talking about the javana-citta, we may put it in this way: When we humans think about doing something at the first javana-citta, we will certainly carry the same thought throughout in the following moments of the javana-citta up to the seventh one. According to the Abhidharma, those seven javana-cittas normally have one and same object all the way through, although there may be some differences only during a few moments of attaining the path (magga) and the fruition (phala), just before entering the stream of nirvana. In this respect, it is said that in the earlier javana-cittas the mind has the meditative device as its object, while on the fifth, the sixth, and the seventh javana-cittas, the pure consciousness grasps nirvana as its object. This implies that in the conscious processes by way of the sense modalities, the mind of the meditator who is preparing himself/herself for the attainment of the path and the fruition may change its object, but for the people in general their minds will find it difficult to do so. When the first javana-citta has anything as its object, the following javana-cittas right up to the seventh one will have the same object, which ordinary people cannot change. Nonetheless, common people may change the objects for their javana-cittas when consciousness has descended into the bhavanga (the unconscious). This explanation is found in Buddhaghosa's work, Visuddhimagga, in the Section on Knowledge and Wisdom, page 324, and in Paramatthadīpanī (one of the Abhidhamma books), in the section dealing with the conditions for associating acts (āsevana-paccaya). Considering this issue of karma attentively according to these books, we see that any kind of karma, if it belongs to the category of ditthavedaniya-kamma, will become both the uppajjavedaniya-kamma and the aparāpara-vedaniya-kamma and therefore, Buddhaghosa's classification of karma by the use of the javana-citta as criterion is unnecessary and pointless.

As a matter of fact, someone may perform some sort of karma during the first javana-citta only, but later may change his/her mind while arriving at the second javana-citta. In this case, the intent to perform the karma lasts merely one javana-citta and does not continue there through all seven javanas. In this way, such karma is definitely classified ditthavedaniya-kamma.

However, let us continue with further considerations: For anyone who intends to perform either a good karma or a bad karma for just one javana-citta, if it is a good karma, it would have a very little strength, and the same is applied to a bad karma. Therefore, it would be possible that such weak karma would yield its result only in this present life, and, if it cannot find the suitable occasion to produce the consequences, it may become the ineffective karma because of its limited strength or the lack of force.

Arriving at this point, we may speculate that Buddhaghosa's classification of karma by using the javana-citta as a criterion could be interpreted in the way we have just discussed. However, the example given by him is not in accord with reality since the ditthavedaniya-kamma points to the strongly definitive intent to perform so that it can yield its result right here in this very life on earth. It seems to me that Buddhaghosa might have attempted to point out that the karma that will yield its result in the present life must be a very strong, forceful karma, which is intended to be performed right from the first javana-citta onward. However, his fashion of using the javana-citta as the criterion for classifying karma and for determining the time frame of yielding its outstanding consequences is quite confusing and complicated indeed.

It might be possible that Buddhaghosa misunderstood what the Buddha has actually said about this matter of karma since he said that these three categories of karma, namely, the ditthavedaniya-kamma, the uppajjavedaniya-kamma, and the aparāparavedaniya-kamma, do not interfere with one another in any way. If any of them would be in position to yield the result in any lifetime, it would do so in that lifetime only; and when the occasion for producing the result was over, it would automatically become ineffective. It is not possible for the ditthavedaniya-kamma to turn itself into either the uppajjavedaniya-kamma or the aparāparavedaniya-kamma. Any kind of karma that belongs either to the aparāparavedaniya-kamma or to uppajjavedaniya-kamma cannot become the ditthavedaniya-kamma or any other karma for that matter. Buddhaghosa's reasoned that if all those karmas would be able to interfere with one another, the Buddha would not have said and classified karmas the way he did. In fact, the Buddha did so because he just meant to say that if the karma did not yield its result in this life, it would do so in the next life or in the lives to come. Moreover, the karma performed by Devadatta, which Buddhaghosa regards as ditthavedaniya-kamma, he classifies as belonging to both the uppajjavedaniya-kamma and the aparāparavedaniya-kamma, which is contradictory to his own view concerning the non-interference between those already mentioned karmas.

The categories of karma from number one to number four are classified in accordance to time or occasion for yielding their consequences, but the next four karmas that we are going to discuss are classified by considering which karma will yield its result before and which one will do so afterward. In this type of classification, Buddhaghosa said that garu-kamma would yield its result prior to any other karma, in case of non-existence of the garu-kamma; the bahula-kamma will have a chance to produce its result; if the bahula-kamma does not exist, the āsanna-kamma will do it, and if the āsanna-Kamma does not exist, the katattā-kamma will produce its consequence. In my view, it is not necessary at all to classify karma in that fashion since his classification is done in such a way that the karmas will yield their results in the lives after this present one. Therefore, what he meant to say is this: If there exists the garu-kamma, it will become a proximate cause for the conception through the rebirth consciousness in the life to come. But in case of non-existence of the garu-kamma, the bahula-kamma will do its duty of causing the conception in this fashion respectively. In this connection, Buddhaghosa does not seem to care to clarify that every kind of karma, whether a heavy karma or a light karma, after having been performed will produce the proper consequences, and those consequences will definitely affect the life in such and such birth, all this depends on the four conditions, namely, the plane of life or the place where life exists (gati), the bodily conditions (upadhi), time (kāla), and the adequate performance regarding the karma. For example, an act of studying a certain subject or receiving an education in a certain field is considered a kind of karma, and the result will be knowledge, ability, and skill. Then, the knowledge, ability, and skill will produce a profit, whether much or little, at which time or on which occasion depending on the variety of situations and circumstances such as having a regular job, or receiving the valuable support from someone, or any other things.

However, it is not necessary to maintain the view that the garu-kamma will yield the result before any other karma, and then the next lighter karma will follow suit, since even the bahula-kamma or āsanna-kamma may be able to yield its result in this lifetime even if the garu-kamma is still in existence. Moreover, every type of karma that will become a condition for the conception in the life to come will appear at the moment when the last breath breaks up in the dying process. By āsanna-kamma, Buddhaghosa refers to the karma that is recalled at such a moment of dying and therefore, the garu-kamma and the bahula-kamma will always become the āsanna-kamma. In this manner, the classification of the karmas into various categories is quite fatal since eventually all kinds of karma will end up being the āsanna-kamma. Nonetheless, there is some value resulting from this form of the classification, for example, the garu-kamma is quite significant in the sense of a strong impression and has a lot of weight on the performer's mind. Therefore, at the near-death moment, this karma will occupy the dying individual's feelings and mind particularly just before the disappearance of the death consciousness, and for this reason it will surely yield its result by laying the solid foundation for the next life. For that matter, Buddhaghosa emphasizes that when the garu-kamma still exists, it will yield its result before any other karmas. But as for the karma that has been performed a long while ago, or has been done repeatedly, which weighs a great deal of the impressive force over the mind, nonetheless would not imprint the greater emotional conditioning or impose more forceful power over the mind than the garu-kamma would. For this very reason, he said that without the existence of the garu-kamma, the bahula-kamma would produce the consequence by way of providing a condition for the conception.

Furthermore, the classification of the other four karmas, namely, the janaka-kamma (originator), the upathumbhaka-kamma (supporter), the upapīlaka-kamma (interrupting/interfering one), and the upaghātaka-kamma (killer) is based on their distinct functions. In this connection, it is said, "That karma which carries out the function of laying the solid base for the conception earns the title of **janaka-kamma**, which is, in fact, the āsanna-kamma. The janaka-kamma is compared to a mother giving birth to her baby, but there is something quite suspicious regarding the Buddhaghosa's explanation on this issue. He said, "The karma that causes the conception will terminate its function right after that. Then, the other karma will come in to render its service by way of providing a supportive system, which is the manner of yielding its result." As a matter of fact, speaking about the mother we understand that she not only conceives us, but does nurture us, and does care for us, so that this analogy suggests that the janaka-kamma would not terminate its duty entirely after causing the conception, but instead would continue yielding its result and teaming up with the upathumbhaka-kamma. Certainly, all karmas are indispensably associated with consciousness and the nature of consciousness is involved with the phenomena of appearing and disappearing. Therefore, keep this in mind: the consciousness which disappears, really disappears completely just like the extinction of flame; extinguished, it is not stored up anywhere else. The rebirth consciousness, although it is not totally the former, has these characteristics, as well, provided the condition of attachment in the previous consciousness has not changed. This is like a new coconut that is the product of the old one that was planted and that grew up as a coconut tree. Equal to this analogy indeed is the matter of karma that, after causing the conception the janaka-kamma, does not disappear from the operation process; this is because the new karma, which continues its conditioning process from the previous karma, will performs its function of supporting the growing process. For this reason, there is no need to build up any new theory regarding the janaka-kamma that it would terminate its function completely after laying down the firm foundation for the conception.

In the case of maintaining the view that all skillful karmas will support one another, this implies that the skillful and the unskillful karmas will oppose and/or kill each other with no mercy. This explanation undertaken by Buddhaghosa is quite interesting since it is in accord with all the facts concerning the karma. Examining our own feelings, we see that the bad feelings will subside and fade away when the good feelings arise and take over; on the contrary, the good feelings diminish as the bad feelings come in and play the dominant role. However, either the good or the bad feelings will get stronger and become more powerful because of the support received from their own allies. This is a very significant point to be kept in mind since generally people hold the view that it is impossible to do good for overcoming evil. But that very important observation described above indicates quite precisely that the evil or even sin can be cleansed off by the good, noble, and meritorious deeds performed increasingly with compelling intent. As we know, good and evil, sin and purity, are opposing one another, if the one is on the increase, the other is on the decrease. The word "puñña" often used in Buddhism refers to the variety of virtues, while the concept of "pāpa" signifies all the evil things including what in Christianity is popularly called sin. Puñña literally means that which purifies the mind.[9] In this connection, we observe that for those who possess abundant virtues, their minds become purer and wide open, and puñña will come into existence when these persons perform more good deeds. In this respect, doing good for overcoming evil simply points to performing all possible good things in order to cleanse off the negative, bad feelings and thoughts of that nature, which is the right thing to do.

However, some people might think in the conventional way that the pāpa or evil things already committed in life cannot be altered or purified. Moreover, these people believe that even they do plenty of good things, but their evil deeds or pāpa will yield the consequences one day undoubtedly. This kind of comprehension stems from a sort of attachment to the idea or belief system that pāpa is a superstitious, magical power existing outside of the human systems. In fact, the pāpa is not any kind of external power, but a form of unskillful karma within each of us human beings; relatedly, all kinds of papa performed in one way or another turn into the vipāka (consequences) buried inside our consciousness and those consequences will materialize when the suitable occasion presents itself. However, all sorts of vipāka are in the constant state of change and alteration just like everything else that is made up and put together in a form or structure. As such, they will be on the decrease if something opposite to them takes place in the consciousness. Therefore, let us listen to the Buddha's wise words as follows:

"Monks, just as that pot filled with water which gets turned upside down will let the water out and will not let it flow back in to fill it up. So, a monk who receives a proper training, develops or makes much of the Noble Eightfold Path, lives in solitude (within), will relinquish once and for all the pāpa or the unskillful karmas and the unskillful dharmas. In addition he will not allow such things to return to him again because his mind and his consciousness are firmly

---

[9] This is the traditional analysis and explanation of the term; in Pali: punāti sodhetīti puññam.

and wholly associated with freedom from lust (virāga), and with extinction of all fires (nirodha), which are the path (magga) leading on to the utter relinquishment of all kilesas."[10]

Now, you, the reader, should keep in mind that both puñña and pāpa, upon yielding their consequences, will predictably conform to the existential vipāka dormant in the consciousness. Since the vipāka is changeable and transformable, the vipāka of the bad, evil deeds, although they might have been done quite a long time in the past, will certainly decrease when the good things are increasingly cultivated. Take another look at the Angulimala's story since it showed undoubtedly that all his evil deeds of killing so many innocent people turned into the ineffective karma (ahosi-kamma) upon reaching arahatship (full enlightenment).

Let us pose this question: if the pāpa could not be cleansed off by the good karma, how would it reach its extinction, then? Once again, the author would like to remind his reader of the Buddha's authentic teaching that **karma will continue yielding the result and influencing the flow of life so long as kilesa exists and is in full operation**. Accordingly, the pāpa or unskillful karma will be relinquished from the character and human consciousness when it has exhausted all its energetic vipāka and therefore has nothing more to yield. This might be like a certain person who committed a crime or simply did something unlawful and was sentenced to imprisonment, and after having served the terms of punishment in the prison, he or she would be liberated and released and became a free person in the world. Now, the question arises: can the pāpa and all the unskillful karmas be relinquished in that fashion? To respond to this question properly we need to remind ourselves of the basic principle of karma that says, "The suffering resulted from the vipāka of the pāpa-kamma could cause the kilesa to arise and in turn the kilesa would become a cause for performing the karma." It is really a vicious circle!

Let us now listen to the specific formula of the dependent origination which is related to what we have just discussed: "Decay, old age, death, sorrow, lamentation, pain, grief, and despair are the conditions for the arising of Ignorance (avijjā), and then avijjā becomes a definitive condition for the arising of sankhāra (action, speech, and thought) et cetera. To put it in another way, those things listed here, beginning with decay and continuing through despair, are in fact vedanā (feelings or sensations in terms of evaluating experience). Now, when the vedanā exists, craving, desire, or thirst (taṇhā) will come into existence. When craving, desire, or thirst is operating, there will be attachment (upādāna). With the operation of attachment, the karma (kamma-bhava) will come into force. With the influence of the karma, consciousness will arise. With the arising and manifesting of the consciousness, the psychophysical systems (nāma-rūpa) will be created, and so on."[11]

Although some people maintain the view that when one has sufficiently reaped the consequences of the karma, it will disappear from one's character,

---

[10] Samyutta-Nikāya, Mahavagga, 19/45 (Mahachula), /72-73 (Mahamakut), /69 (Sangīti).
[11] See the detailed explanation on the teaching of dependent origination in the author's book entitled *A New Vision of Buddhism*.

but the fact of the matter indicates that such view is partly correct and partly incorrect. It is correct in the sense that on the surface the karma appears to be inactive like a dead volcano, while deep inside it still holds the explosive power. As to the incorrect aspect of the mentioned view, the karma will not diminish from the character only through the adequate reaping of its vipāka, but will fade away totally, when the kilesa that causes it has been eliminated or transformed completely. Therefore, the significance of redeeming and transforming the karma lies in increasing the virtuous characteristics and in burning away the fires of karma so that it could become powerless and ineffective.

The criterion for determining the ahosi-kamma

Considering the ineffectiveness and the effectiveness of the karma in accordance with the teaching of dependent origination we see quite clearly that the most important thing involved with this issue is **kilesa**. So long as the kilesa causing the karma to be performed still exists, the karma will continue playing a significant role in the performer's life. With the continuation of the karma's active role, the consequences of it will be definitely produced eventually. Therefore, the ahosi-kamma will materialize only when all the kilesas causing those karmas to be activated are no longer in operation. This is the key criterion for determining whether the karma will become ineffective (ahosi). In this connection, the Buddha said:

"Oh, the Noble One! The stream-enterer (sotāpanna) is the one perfected with the three qualifications, namely, (1) unwavering confidence in the Buddha, in the dharma, and in the Sangha (an enlightened person/monk and the Community of such noble individuals), (2) perfection in the five precepts, and (3) experiential realization of the dependent origination. Such a person could do so, if he or she would like to determine by himself/herself whether he/she has transcended the *hell*, the *animal kingdom*, the plane of *hungry ghost*, the *unprogressive* plane of existence, the *unhappy, painful, and troublesome* plane of living. In addition, such a noble person may determine if he/she is a *stream-enterer* who will never fall down once again to those lower planes of life by any means, and who is completely sure for achieving the full enlightenment."

According to those words uttered by the Buddha, the sotāpanna or stream-enterer (the person who has entered the stream of nirvana) is the noble one who has permanently shut the doors to all the unprogressive planes of life, including hell. This is like the robber with a red beard that Buddhaghosa told us about in the Dhammapada Commentary. The story reads as follows: Some times ago, there was a fierce robber. Later, he was caught and arrested by the security police, and then was appointed to be an executor. Serving in such a position, he executed all his follower robbers, continued his service until he reached the retirement age and therefore abandoned his job. After that, one day he offered food to the Venerable Sariputta, (the right-hand disciple of the Buddha), and then listened to his dharma talk and attained to the stream-entry. From this story, Buddhaghosa explained that the pāpa-karma that the red-bearded robber had done, by the standard of karma, would conduce him to hell, but it did not happen that way according to Buddhaghosa; instead, he was freed from entering hell. From this example, it is said that those who have eliminated the first three shackles, namely, (1) the view concerning the permanency self or soul, (2) doubt or indecisiveness, and (3) the superstitious beliefs, will turn their unskillful karmas into ineffectiveness (ahosi-kamma).

For this reason, Buddhaghosa's criterion of fixing the time or the occasion for yielding the consequences of the karma as in case of ditthavedaniya-kamma and uppajjavedaniya-kamma is not valid since the kilesas that are present in any given instance is the vital factor for determining if the karma will yield its result. The same is applied to the issue of the ahosi-kamma.

As a matter of fact, this matter of ahosi-kamma is found in the Buddhist text entitled, Patisambhidā-magga, the author of which was Sariputta. His explanations are as follows:

"There is the karma done in the past, and its vipāka has already been yielded. There is the karma done in the past, but its vipāka has not been yielded. There is the karma done in the past, and its vipāka is yielding the result in the present. There is the karma done in the past, but its vipāka has not been yielded in the present life. There is the karma done in the past, and its vipāka will be yielded in the future. There is the karma done in the past, but its vipāka will not be yielded in the future. There is the karma being performed in the present, and its vipāka is being yielded in the present. There is the karma being performed in the present, but its vipāka is not yielded in the present. There is the karma performed in the present, and its vipāka will be yielded in the future. There is the karma performed in the present, but its vipāka will not be yielded in the future. There is the karma to be performed in the future, and its vipāka will be yielded in the future. There is the karma to be performed in the future, but its vipāka will not be yielded in the future."

From the twelve categories of karma described by Sariputta in Patisambhidā-magga we grasp the meaning of the ahosi-kamma conveyed to us that there exists a kind of karma performed in the past, or being done in the present, or to be done in the future, which does not produce any results. Nonetheless, Sariputta did not point out precisely which kind of karma already done does not yield its result and why it will not. But Buddhaghosa did explain that the karma that does not yield its result is the kind that does not find the suitable occasion to do it, according to the categories of the karma that are supposed to produce their consequences at the appropriate times. For example, the karma performed at the first javana-citta, if it does not find the suitable occasion to produce its result in the present life, will automatically become ineffective (ahosi-kamma). What he actually means by "the karma yielding its result" is that it creates the proper conditions for the conception to take place and for the embryo to take a definitive form. As previously explained repeatedly, certain karmas may not produce their results either in the past, at present, or in the future; but they can become ineffective only because of missing the appropriate opportunity for doing so both in the past and at the present time. The opportunity refers to these four conditions, namely, (1) the plane of life or the place where the doers live, (2) bodily conditions, (3) suitable occasion, and (4) the adequate performance. If not so, there is another condition, which is that the kilesa causing such karma to be performed in the past was already eliminated before the karma could produce its consequence (vipāka) and therefore, this kind of karma will also become ineffective.

The appropriate opportunity for karma to yield its result

All kinds of karma will produce their consequences depending on the four earlier mentioned conditions expounded by the Buddha himself in the Tipiṭaka volume 35, section 810 (Mahachula), section 840 (Mahamakut), and section 810 (Sangīti) as follows:

1. There is certain unskillful karma, upon being obstructed by ***gati-sampatti*** (suitable place of living or the proper plane of life), will not yield its result.
2. There is certain unskillful karma, upon being obstructed by ***upadhi-sampatti*** (appropriate bodily conditions), will not yield its result.
3. There is certain unskillful karma, upon being obstructed by ***kāla-sampatti*** (right time), will not yield its result.
4. There is certain unskillful karma, upon being obstructed by ***payoga-sampatti*** (adequate or perfect performance), will not yield its result.
5. There is certain unskillful karma that will yield its result because of ***gati-vipatti*** (improper place of living or unfortunate plane of life).
6. There is certain unskillful karma that will yield its result because of ***upadhi-vipatti*** (inappropriate, unhealthy bodily conditions).
7. There is certain unskillful karma that will yield its result because of ***kāla-vipatti*** (wrong time).
8. There is certain unskillful karma that will yield its result because of ***payoga-vipatti*** (inadequate, imperfect performance).
9. There is certain skillful karma, being obstructed by ***gati-vipatti*** (unsuitable place of living/improper life plane), will not yield its result.
10. There is certain skillful karma, being obstructed by ***upadhi-vipatti*** (inappropriate, unhealthy bodily conditions), will not yield its result.
11. There is certain skillful karma, being obstructed by ***kāla-vipatti*** (wrong time), will not yield its result.
12. There is certain skillful karma, being obstructed by ***payoga-vipatti*** (the inadequate, imperfect performance), will not yield its result.
13. There is certain skillful karma that will yield its result because of ***gati-sampatti*** (suitable place of living or the proper plane of life).
14. There is certain skillful karma that will yield its result because of ***upadhi-sampatti*** (appropriate, healthy bodily conditions).
15. There is certain skillful karma that will yield its result because of ***kāla-sampatti*** (appropriate, right time).
16. There is certain skillful karma that will yield its result because of ***payoga-sampatti*** (adequate, perfect performance).

According the Manopūraṇī, a derivative commentarial work (pakaraṇa) on the Tipiṭaka (Pali Canon), there are explanations given as follows; consider each of these examples:

"When there exists a kind of karma to yield the disagreeable, undesirable result, but the doer of such karma went to take a birth in the happy plane of life. In this way, it is said, "the unskillful karma is obstructed by the gati-sampatti (perfection of the life's plane)" and therefore, it has not yielded its result yet.

"[Consider] whosoever who was born of the slave mother or of the housemate mother because of his/her unskillful karma, but has the healthy body with a pretty shape. When the master of the slave woman or the middle class woman has beheld her beautiful and pleasantly formed body, he thinks to himself that such an attractive woman should not do a low job, and therefore appoints her to a higher rank of guarding his wealth and property. In addition, the master or boss takes good care of, and nourishes her as if she were his own daughter. So, the unskillful karma of the above-mentioned woman is said to be obstructed by the upadhi-sampatti (perfection of the physical body) and therefore, has not yielded its result yet.

"[Consider] whoever was born at the prosperous time abundant with good taste and plentiful food easily found anywhere such as in the first kappa (eon of time), although such a person still has some unskillful karma. Since the kāla-sampatti (perfection of the appropriate time) obstructs the chance for such karma to produce its result, therefore it has not yielded its result yet.

"[Consider] whoever knows so well how to get the work done, how to render the services, or to carry out any activity assigned on him or her. For example, he or she knows exactly when to keep a distance, when to leave the work, when to give tips or to present rewards, when even to do a robbery, he or she does it in accordance with the situation and circumstance, time and place required for such an action. The person who knows precisely how to do things at the right time and in the proper place as the situation and circumstance are required of him or her, in this fashion his or her action is called payoga-sampatti (perfection of performance). Even though, such a person may still have some unskillful karma in his or her character, but since it is obstructed by the payoga-sampatti, such karma has not yielded its result yet.

"[Consider] the person whose unskillful karma brings him/her to be born in the unhappy, painful plane of life, who suffers its consequences tremendously. This is called an unskillful karma yielding its results because of the gati-vipatti.

"[Consider] whoever was born of the slave mother or of the housemate mother, after having been born has a bad physical body with an ugly skin and hideous shape, and appears to the people as if he/she were a giant or an unsightly human being. If being a man, he would get a job of caring for the cattle; in case of being a woman, she would get such a low job as sweeping the street, dealing with garbage, or any other revolting work. This kind of result produced such unskillful karma that comes into effect is called an unskillful karma yielding it consequence because of the upadhi-vipatti.

"[Consider] whoever was born at the time of war and of drought or at the time when the world was crammed with such troubles as flooding, fire burning forests and houses, etc., in this way he/she suffers the consequences of his/her unskillful karma. This is called an unskillful karma yielding its result because of the kāla-vipatti.

"[Consider] whoever lacks knowledge or skill regarding the job or the labor so that he/she does not know how to get things done and how to perform his/her duties and how to relate properly to their bosses or to the people working under them. In this way, such a person reaps the consequences of his/her unskillful karma, and this is called an unskillful karma yielding its result because of the payoga-vipatti.

"[Consider] on the contrary, when there exists a skillful karma that would yield its pleasant and desirable results, but the performer of such karma went to be born in the unhappy, painful plane of life. In this way, his/her skillful karma is obstructed by the gati-vipatti and therefore has not yielded its results yet.

"[Consider] whoever, out of his/her skillful karma, was born in a good, happy, and wealthy family, or in the family of well known, highly respected, or advanced spiritual people, but his/her physical body is deformed and unfitting for doing anything proper. For this reason, he/she will not be appointed to such respectable jobs as the Government Minister or the Treasurer at the King's Court. In this way, it signifies that the skillful karma of such a person is obstructed by the upadhi-vipatti and has not yielded its result yet.

"[Consider] whoever was born in wartime and during a hard, long period of drought, or in the time of so many troublesome situations and highly risky, insecure circumstances of living, although he/she has done a great deal of the skillful karma and it is still dormant in his/her character. But because of being obstructed by the kāla-vipatti, his/her skillful karma has not yielded its result yet.

"[Consider] whoever, out of his/her skillful karma, was fortunate to be born in the happy and prosperous plane of life. This is called a skillful karma yielding its result because of the gati-sampatti.

"[Consider] whoever was born in the good, loving, happy, and wealthy family or in the family that holds so much power over the people and the nation, and his/her physical body is in a perfect form with good-looking appearance and charming, appealing personality. Therefore, he/she would be appointed to the higher ranks and to the respectable positions in the country, which is the consequence of his/her skillful karma that yields the desirable result because of the upadhi-sampatti.

"[Consider] whoever, out of his/her skillful karma, was born at the time of economic prosperity such as in the first kappa. Therefore, his/her skillful karma yields its result because of the kāla-sampatti.

"[Consider] whoever knows how to behave properly and how to perform his/her job effectively as the consequence of his/her skillful karma. Therefore, we say his/her skillful karma yields its result because of the payoga-sampatti." [Here ends the passages from the commentary being quoted.]

The author has done his best to translate these explanations made in the Manopūraṇī commentary,[12] in order that his reader would be able to comprehend this commentator's viewpoints on the four conditions by which the karmas would or would not yield their consequences. Here, those who object, considering that the idea of *"doing good receiving good, doing evil receiving evil"* is not always true, will perhaps reconsider their position and probably make a proper change through the new teachings from the Manopūraṇī. The truth of the matter is this: **Only the power of the karma alone, whether skillful or unskillful, will be able to produce its fruit**, but each karma depends largely on the four above-described conditions appropriate to it at the moment to determine if it would yield its result or not. For this reason, it is not unusual that a good person might be born in a bad place under an unhealthy, vicious environment, or a bad person might be born in a good place under a wonderful, healthy environment. To put it in another way, a good-natured person might associate himself or herself with a bad, destructive individual, and a bad-natured person might make an association with a good, creative, and progressive individual. This is because the proximate cause of karma is the ***intent*** or ***volition***, and the vipāka of karma is the capacity and potentiality as well as the feelings that arise together with the consciousness. Therefore, anyone would be born anywhere depending solely on the mental picture and the feeling that appear during the last few moments of the disappearing of consciousness in the dying process. For example, the meditator who has achieved the jhānic state of the absorptive meditation, upon the dying moments his consciousness disappears during his firm stay in the jhāna, is determined to be born in the realm of brahma in accord with the stage of jhāna attained by him or her. The similar reason may be applied to the unskillful karma. Therefore, we may emphasize that *the dead will be reborn in accordance with their own karmas*.

Furthermore, bear in mind that the vipāka of karma contained in the consciousness will lay the foundation of the life to come. With this definitive foundation, as we observe it closely, the individual's present characteristics are identical with the mentality manifested by the dying consciousness just before the rebirth consciousness take over. In this connection, the specialist in Abhidharma, the Venerable Anuruddha commented as follows:

The rebirth consciousness, the unconscious, and the death consciousness[13] are identical and have the same object (atītārammana, object of the past) as the basis for defining the specifics of their next birth (the birth of the next moment of consciousness or of the next lifetime).

However, because of the fact that the body shape and its conditions are consequences of the rebirth consciousness (in addition to genes), it has become obvious that the human personality and bodily manifestations originate in the consciousness together with the karmic energy carried along with it. For

---

[12] The Manopūraṇī can be distinguished from Manoratthapūraṇī, the commentary by Buddhaghosa on the Aṅguttara-nikāya.

[13] In Pali they are paṭisandhi-citta, bhavaṅga-citta, and cuti-citta respectively. From *Abhidhammattha-Sangaha*, page 28.

example, the physical form and the character of the Buddha are the results of the ten perfections[14] that he has completed, which are contained in his consciousness. Certainly, those who have a negative, aggressive, or even violent character in the present life would have done some evil things under the influences of hate, anger, resentment, and delusion (specifically in the sense of self-deception). Nonetheless, we must classify the causes of the individual's life qualities into three categories:

1. *the influence of genes transferring from earlier generations*
2. *the environment both during the stay in the mother's womb and afterward*
3. *the qualities of karmic energy containing and transferring through the rebirth consciousness process*

Arriving at this point, let us look into the detailed explanations of the four conditions present for any karma to yield its result:

1. **gati** - referring to the birthplace and the place where one lives
2. **upadhi** - signifying the bodily qualities (conditions)
3. **kāla** - meaning time and period of time
4. **payoga** - referring to the perfect or imperfect performance of the karma

Concerning the gati, we explain that the condition for the yielding of the skillful karma depends on the place and the environment where the doer of such karma lives. For example, the honesty will become effective when such an honest individual lives in the community or in the place where honesty is respected and honored. On the contrary, if the honest person lives his/her life among dishonest, evil people, his/her honesty (as a consequence) of the skillful karma has not yielded its result yet. This is the meaning of ***gati-sampatti.***

As for ***gati-vipatti***, it refers to a unhealthy, destructive environment and place of living. An individual who possesses a bad, aggressive, and hateful character happens to be born in a good family and therefore living in a happy, healthy place with all desirable environment, such an individual, although he/she has such unwelcoming character, is not always bad since within his/her consciousness there are good things as well, which he/she can manifest in life and at work from time to time. In this way, the unskillful karma will be delayed to yield its result, but if the individual would be born in the bad family and live in the destructive environment, his/her unskillful karma will certainly yield its result with no delay. This is the meaning of the ***gati-vipatti.***

With regard to either ***upadhi-sampatti*** or ***upadhi-vipatti,*** we may explain it in this way: A good person with many appealing and desirable qualities, who lacks a handsome or beautiful physical shape and charming or attractive personality, will be unable to receive the consequences of his/her skillful karma. This is because of the upadhi-vipatti (lacking the perfect bodily

---

[14] Giving (dāna), moral discipline (sīla), renunciation of the world (kekkhamma), wisdom (paññā), energy (viriya), patience (khati), truth (sacca), determination (adhitthāna), unconditional love (mettā), and equanimity (upekkhā).

conditions). On the contrary, a good person with such lovely bodily qualities as above described will certainly receive the consequences of his/her skillful karma. This is the meaning of the upadhi-sampatti.

Now, a bad person with an unwelcoming character who is relatively perfect in the physical form, meaning, handsome, beautiful, attractive, charming and appealing to the eyes of others, may get a great deal of attention, or even get a good job, and may be placed in a high, respectable position. In this way, it implies that his or her unskillful karma has not yielded its result yet because of being obstructed by the upadhi-sampatti. On the contrary, if such a bad person with an evil character has an imperfect physical form such as an ugly body, his/her unskillful karma will be able to yield its result quite quickly because of the upadhi-vipatti.

As for the kāla-sampatti and the kāla-vipatti, the indication is this: A good person endowed with desirable, admirable, and beautiful qualities of heart and mind, who happens to live in a time when noble people are needed and highly admired, will be able to receive the consequences of his or her skillful karma without delay. This is called "the skillful karma yielding its result because of the kāla-sampatti." If the time were not quite appropriate, then the skillful karma of such a good, noble person would not yield its result because of the kāla-vipatti.

In the case of a bad person who has done many evil things, but whose good deeds still guard and protect him/her, the right time for unskillful karma to yield its result has not arrived yet. In this way, we say that the unskillful karma does not yield its result because of being obstructed by the kāla-sampatti. However, when the appropriate time has come and the influences of his/her good deeds have faded away, the evil things will appear and therefore such an evil person will receive the consequences of his/her unskillful karma right away. This is called the unskillful karma produces its result because of the kāla-vipatti.

Regarding payoga-sampatti and payoga-vipatti, the commentators simply point out that the performer of the karma either knows or does not know the suitable time and the proper place for carrying out his/her actions. In fact, the meaning of "payoga" is the perfect action or the just-right performance; for example, if someone would practice the eight factors of the Buddha's middle path, and the practitioner will do all of them completely without leaving out any single factor, this way of performing the action is called payoga-sampatti. On the contrary, if only one or more, but not all, of the eight factors are chosen to practice, such a manner of carrying out the action is called payoga-vipatti. Therefore, the authentic meaning of the payoga-sampatti refers to doing good things completely, while payoga-vipatti signifies doing good things partially. The skillful karma of the person who does things with the payoga-sampatti will yield its result quite immediately provided it be not obstructed by the payoga-vipatti. But the unskillful karma of someone who carries out the duties or functions with intelligence, prudence, and good knowledge of the proper ways and means for getting things done, will not yield its result because of being obstructed by the payoga-sampatti. On the contrary, if the bad person does things unwisely and without a good knowledge of how to get things done properly, his/her unskillful karma will surely yield its result straight away because of the payoga-vipatti.

The issue of karma is difficult to prove

All the explanations of the karma made until now are carried out in accordance with the law of dependent origination. Therefore, the issue of karma and its explanations are not so complicated, with the exception of thinking along the line of the twelve karmas, which are rather confusing, complex, and problematical. Nonetheless, some sutras in the Buddhist Tipiṭaka give us a headache with regard to the relationships and the interconnectedness between the karma and its vipāka or cause and effect. However, if we use our common sense to grasp the real meaning, we will realize the unsuitability or incompatibility of the karma and the vipāka or cause and effect. For example, in Buddhism there is a popular belief system regarding the matter of *giving* (dāna) that giving the material things either to the monks and nuns or to the poor and the needy will produce wealth and prosperity, particularly in the life after death. This kind of belief is not quite compatible with the actual fact in our world today since wealth and prosperity depend on knowledge, skill, and prudence in managing businesses, and certainly not on giving away, although it might help with writing off taxes if such donations are done in accord with the law of the land. Nonetheless, the Buddha gives a clue for getting rich and becoming prosperous economically as follows:

1. *endowment of efforts (utthāna-sampadā)*: This simply means putting the right proportion of energy into earning the living or carrying out careers/professions, into the businesses, into studies, and so on.
2. *perfection of guarding or protection (ārakkha-sampadā)*: This refers to guarding and maintaining the wealth and property won through the hard work and enormous perseverance.
3. *kalyanamittatā*: This signifies association with good people, forming friendships with all possible persons involved with work, life, and businesses, and at the same time disassociating oneself from the bad and unwelcoming people.
4. *samajīvita*: This implies earning a living by righteous means and spending the money in such an appropriate way that the income and expenses are kept even at least, as well as distributing wealth proportionately and wisely. In addition, do not commit oneself to any means that is unprogressive and seemingly inclining to get rich or to win the money easily, which may cause disaster and danger to the loss of money, business, and property.

If anyone would put into practice those four requirements for creating richness and becoming wealthy, it is quite certain that the success will be his or hers. Try it! Forget about the sayings such as giving or dāna will bring about wealth or make one a millionaire, since in reality there is no correspondence to such a belief system.

Cūlakammavibhanga-Sutta, the discourse on why people are not born equal materially

At one time, the Buddha was staying in the Jetavana Monastery built for him by the billionaire, Anāthapindika, located in a quiet and peaceful area just outside of the city of Sāvatthī. At that time a good, young man, son of the Brahmin Todeyya, approached him and after exchanges of the courteous greetings with him seated himself in a proper place, and then asked him this question: "Blessed Gotama! What is it that causes all the human beings to be born into the various, unequal lives? That is to say, some live short lives, some live quite a long while on the planet, Earth, some have just a few diseases while some others suffer so many illnesses? Further still, some humans were born with bad, ugly skin, while others are endowed with lovely, pretty skin? Some are much less dignified, while others are quite noble and very dignified; some are poor or less wealthy, while others are so rich with enormous wealth. Some were born in low families, while others were born in highly respectable families; still, some are rather ignorant and possess quite low intelligence, while others are very knowledgeable and wise? What is it that causes the humans either to be low or to be high, either to be bad or to be good?"

Here is the Buddha's response: "Oh, good, young man! All sentient beings have their own karma, they are inheritors of their karma, have karma as their originator, have karma as their associate, and have karma as their refuge. It is the karma that divides all the sentient beings into good and bad categories."

"Blessed Gotama! What you have just said is rather brief and lacks any detailed explanation. I do not quite grasp the full meanings of those statements made by you, Most Venerable Sir! Would you please expound them at some length so as to enable me to understand what you meant by those words?"

"Oh, good, young man! If so, be attentive, and I will speak." After having received the good, young man's agreement and consent, the Buddha explained his statements as follows: "Good, young man! People in this world, whether men or women, kill living beings on a regular basis, are aggressive and hateful, have their hands full of blood, earn their living by execution, and are without mercy. Such people, after their bodies break up and die, will enter into the unprogressive, painful, disastrous, and hellish plane of existence because of such unskillful karma performed regularly. If not so, they will be born humans and will live short lives.

"Good, young man! People in this world, whether men or women, refrain from killing, put away the beating wood and the dangerous weapons, possess healthy shame, are kind, compassionate, and generous to others by helping them in all possible ways and means. Such people, after their bodies break up and die, will enter into the happy, heavenly plane of existence because of such skillful karma performed regularly. If not so, they will be born humans and live long lives.

"Good, young man! People in this world, whether men or women, possess the character of harming the living beings by their hands, by beating sticks, or by dangerous weapons such as knife, sword, and so forth. Such people, after their bodies break up and die, will enter into the unhappy, unprogressive, disastrous, painful, tormented, and hellish plane of existence because of their unskillful karma performed regularly. If not so, they will be born humans and suffer a great deal of diseases.

"Good, young man! People in this world, whether men or women, possess the good character filled with love and caring for the living beings, and without harming or tormenting them by any means, whether by the hands, by the beating wood, or by dangerous weapons such as knife or sword. Such persons, after their bodies break up and die, will enter the happy, heavenly plane of existence. If not so, they will be born humans and will experience only a few illnesses.

"Good, young man! Some people in this world, whether men or women, are habitually angry, full of resentment and ill-will, and possess the habitual tendency to scorn and curse those who may just behave improperly toward them, whose hearts are filled with hatred, black dots, and unreasonable anger. Such people, after their bodies break up and die, will enter the unhappy, unprogressive, painful, disastrous, and hellish plane of existence because of their unskillful karma. If not so, they will be born humans who will have the bad, ugly skin.

"Good, young man! Some people in this world, whether men or women, are hardly angry, have just little resentment and ill-will, do not tend to scorn or curse in response to those who behave very badly and very aggressively toward them, and instead they respond to them with loving-kindness, good thoughts, and compassionate hearts. Such people, after their break up and die, will enter the happy, heavenly plane of existence because of their skillful, good karma. If not so, they will be born humans who will possess the beautiful, charismatic bodies with pretty, attractive skin.

"Good, young man! Some people in this world, whether men or women, envy quite easily those who are successful in building up wealth, in obtaining prosperity, whether material or spiritual, in gaining respect and admiration of others, whose minds and hearts are full of revenge, greed, and evil wishes. Such people, after their bodies break up and die, will enter the unhappy, unprogressive, painful, disastrous, and hellish plane of existence because of their unskillful, bad karma. If not so, they will be born humans who will have just very little dignity.

"Good, young man! Some people in this world, whether men or women, whose minds and hearts are free from envy, but filled with appreciation and sympathetic joy over the successes of others, whether big or small, in all possible ways and means. Such people, after their bodies break up and die, will enter the happy, prosperous, and heavenly plane of existence because of their good, skillful karma. If not so, they will be born humans who will enjoy great dignity.

"Good, young man! Some people in this world, whether men or women, do not offer rice, water, flowers, incense, beddings, candles or lamps, or transportation to those monks and nuns who are in need of them. Such people, after their bodies break up and die, they will enter the unhappy, unprogressive, painful, disastrous, and hellish plane of existence because of such karma that they have carried along with them. If not so, they will be born humans who will possess very little wealth, but will suffer much poverty. On the contrary, those who offer all the things mentioned above will enter the happy, prosperous, and heavenly plane of existence because of such good, skillful karma that they have performed. If not so, they will be born humans who will possess enormous wealth and enjoy their economic prosperity.

"Good, young man! Some people in this world, whether men or women, are obstinate, arrogant, prideful, do not respect those worthy respecting, do not return courteous greetings to those greeting them courteously, do not provide the seats for those worthy or needing them, do not offer things to the recluses, or give some things to the needy, etc. Such people, after their bodies break up and die, will enter the unhappy, unprogressive, painful, disastrous, and hellish plane of existence because of such unskillful karma habitually performed in their lives. If not so, they will be born humans in the low and bad families. On the contrary, those who do not behave themselves in such a way as described above, but do exactly opposite, will enter the happy, prosperous, and heavenly plane of life after the breaking up of their bodies, because of such skillful karma constantly performed in their lives. If not so, they will be born humans in the high and good families.

"Good, young man! Some people in this world, whether men or women, do not approach monks and nuns, do not ask any questions about skillful or unskillful karma, about what to do regarding self-growth, spiritual development, about suffering, the cause of suffering, the cessation of suffering, and the path that leads to the ending of suffering, etc. Such people, after their bodies break up and die, will enter the unhappy, unprogressive, painful, disastrous, and hellish plane of existence because of such unskillful behavior patterns. If not so, they will be born humans who will possess very little wisdom, but will suffer a great deal of stupidity and ignorance. On the contrary, those who do the opposite, that is to say, always approach monks and nuns, the scholars, the wise, and the highly respected people, asking them all the significant questions concerning life, birth, and death, including the techniques for achieving material prosperity, the methods for carrying out self-growth work and spiritual fulfillment, etc. Such people will enter the happy, prosperous, and heavenly plane of existence after the breaking up of their bodies and death of consciousness because of the skillful behavior patterns. If not so, they will be born humans who will be endowed with great wisdom and plenty of knowledge.

"Good, young man! The practice conducive to a short age produces human beings who live a short life. The practice conducive to a long age produces persons who live a long life. The practice conducive to many diseases produces people who suffer many diseases. The practice conducive to a few diseases produces people who suffer just a few illnesses. The practice conducive to bad, ugly skin produces individuals who possess such skin. The practice conducive to pretty, lovely skin produces individuals with such skin. The practice conducive to just little dignity produces individuals with little dignity. The practice conducive to great dignity produces individuals with great dignity. The practice conducive to less wealth and poverty produces individuals with little wealth and poverty. The practice conducive to huge wealth and richness produces individuals with massive wealth and richness. The practice conducive to being born in the low, poor, and/or bad families produces individuals of such low, poor, and/or bad families. The practice conducive to being born in the high, wealthy, and good families produces individuals of such high, wealthy, and good families. The practice conducive to poor wisdom and little knowledge produces individuals with such poor wisdom and little knowledge. The practice conducive to great, perfect wisdom and incredible knowledge produces individuals with such great, perfect wisdom and tremendous knowledge.

"Good, young man! All sentient beings have karma of their own, are inheritors of their karma, originate through their karma, have their karma as associates, and have their karma as refuge. In this fashion, the karma divides the sentient beings into good and bad categories."[15]

In addition to the Cūlakammavibhanga-Sutta there is another sutra with the name of Nidhikaṇḍa-Sutta (concerning the **well of treasure**) popularly accepted as the Buddha's Discourse, which will be translated as follows:

"Whoever, be a man or a woman, buries his/her (inner) treasure in the pagoda, in an individual monk or in the whole community of Sangha, in the parents, in the brothers and sisters, or in the visitors by giving, by observing precepts, by practicing restraint, and by the practice of patience and tolerance. Such treasure buried in such a place for worship and in those honorable people is regarded as the good and secure well of treasure, which no one can steal or take away from one, but will follow one wherever one goes just like the shadow that never leaves.

Such a well of treasure is just for an individual and by the individual, and it is not a public property, which any robber or thief can never steal. Those endowed with wisdom and intelligence should do all possible good things that actually belong to them forever, whether alive or dead. Such good deeds will produce the desirable consequences which all human beings and devas alike love to have in their lives, here and hereafter.

This well of treasure includes the pretty, lovely, and attractive skin, the loving, beautiful voice, the properly and beautifully build shape of the physical body, the greatness of being a person, the popularity among those close to one and those who know about one. All these things are obtained through the foundation of puñña (literally, meritorious deeds)

In addition, this well of treasure will help one achieve the highest position in the nation such as a king, an emperor, a president, a prime minister, who can enjoy power, happiness, wealth, and love or respect from the people under his/her rule or governing body. Either the material wealth in the human world or the divine wealth in heaven is achieved through this well of treasure.

Whoever, with the genuine help and assistance of a good friend (a teacher or an adviser/counselor), makes good efforts of doing things earnestly,

---

[15] This is Majjhima Nikaya, Sutta/Discourse 135 (M.iii.202-206); M.U. 14/261 (Mahachula), 14/376 (Mahamakut) 14/342 (Sangīti).

using intelligence, knowledge, skill, and wisdom in the performance of his/her activities, such an individual will be able to gain the mastery over knowledge, wisdom, and freedom.

Such dharmas as the four ***patisambhidās***, namely, ***penetrating wisdom and sharp knowledge regarding the meanings*** (attha-patisambhidā), ***penetrating wisdom and incredible knowledge of the dharma*** (dhamma-patisambhidā), ***penetrating wisdom and enormous knowledge of languages*** (nirutti-patisambhidā), and ***penetrating wisdom and illimitable knowledge regarding wittiness and intelligence*** (patibhāna-patisambhidā), the eight ***deliverances (vimokkha[16]), the perfections of followers (listeners), the firm ground of silent Buddhas, the unshakable foundation of the Buddha*** are all accomplished through this well of treasure.

Since the treasure or wealth of puñña (merit, goodness) has so much benefit and vast power as described above, the wise praise it at all times.[17]

In the above sutta there is something interesting worth noticing, which is the matter of pagoda (cetiya). In the Buddha's time, no one was ever taught to worship the pagoda or to present the offerings to it. However, the ancient Thai Buddhists loved to bury their treasures in the pagoda, believing that by so doing they have buried their wealth in their religion, which is in accordance with the Nidhikanda-Sutta as we have seen it. In fact, the Buddha used to instruct his followers to construct the pagodas only for the purpose of containing the relics of arahats, and he did teach them to worship and to present offerings to such pagodas. This is because such devotional acts of worshipping will remind them of the practice that will lead to the attainment of arahatship, the ultimate goal of the Buddhist religion.

Nonetheless, what we find hard to understand is about *giving, observing precepts, controlling the sense faculties, mental training, etc.* How can those things become the conditions for having pretty skin, sweet voices, beautiful physical bodies, and so forth? We do not see the reason and the connection between practicing these things and the consequences to be yielded by them. Normally, we understand that the genes transferred from the parents, grand-parents, and ancestors influence the form and quality of the human physical body. This is quite evident to all of us human beings.

However, this becomes clearer if we understand that consciousness knows exactly which place is suitable to it and its karmic energy. The high, advanced consciousness will take rebirth in the high plane of life, while the lower and less developed consciousness with do the opposite. Therefore, it

---

[16] The eight vimokkhas or deliverances are (1) the person who has the body sees it (as it is), (2) the person who perceives things as having no body sees the external body, (3) the person has the inclination toward what is beautiful, (4) the person who conceives of infinite space attains ākāsānañcāyatana, (5) the person who conceives of infinite consciousness attains viññāṇañcāyatana, (6) the person who conceives of "nothing whatsoever" attains ākiñcaññāyatana, (7) the person who surpasses the ākiñcaññāyatana attains the jhānic state of "neither perception nor non-perception" (meaning, perception exists but is so extremely refined that it does not function as it normally does), (8) the person who surpasses the neva-saññānāsaññāyatana attains the extinction of perception and feeling/sensation (saññāvedayitanirodha).

[17] Khuddaka-Nikāya, Khuddakapātha, 25/12.

could be possible that those children born of the beautiful parents are because the beautiful consciousness causes them to be born of such parents, which is quite reasonable since it is in accord with the Buddhist principle. Nonetheless, the fact of the matter is that the child born of beautiful parents is in some cases beautiful, but in other cases is not so, or even opposite to the parents. For this reason, adding the rebirth consciousness to the genes would be more perfect regarding the physical shape, whether pretty or not so pretty. Moreover, such practices as the mental training, giving things away to the needy and to the noble people, and observing precepts for training the physical body and speech will certainly contribute such good and desirable qualities to the physical body, to the voices, and to the skin as well, since the vibrantly good energy, delighted/uplifted mind, and joyful heart gained in the course of those practices can shine forth through these channels.

The dark corner in the issue of karma

The most significant thing in Buddhism for common people is karma and at the same time this matter of karma becomes quite complicated and complex for them. In this connection, we see that the force that encourages people to do good and to refrain from evil due to fear of its destructive consequences is this idea of karma. As for Thai Buddhists, in some cases the issue of karma obstructs and discourages them from doing good since it has become a kind of dogma by conforming to the idea that this matter of karma rules over their entire lives. For example, some people complain that doing a small bad thing is considered "pāpa" or unskillful karma, so people feel too much responsibility regarding their movements and actions in lives because of the karma's ruling force over them.

In addition, it is rather disturbing to note that those Buddhists who blindly believe in the law of karma always want the results of their actions to be produced in the next life. Therefore, they lack eagerness and enthusiasm in improving themselves with regard to earning a living prosperously and in making good efforts for becoming wealthy and happy in this life on Earth. Because of fear of committing the pāpa or unskillful karma some people do not dare even to rear the cattle and to create the large vegetable gardens, which could imply tormenting or killing (or letting others kill) living beings unintentionally. This way of thinking and believing is an extreme approach to the matter of karma, which is far beyond the authentic, actual teaching on karma under discussion.

In the Girimānanda-Sutta, the Buddha was talking about various diseases caused by many different viruses including karma. He said, "Not all illnesses and diseases originate in, and derive from karma, but there are many illnesses and disease that are caused by the variety of viruses and infections such as poison in the blood, the crisis of wind element, the lack of balance of the inner organs, or the breaking down of the control system over maintaining the physical body equilibrium." In that sutra he cited as many as ninety-two types of diseases, and then emphasizes that only one type is caused by karma. Apart from this, he opposed many contemporary masters who grasped the view that everything comes from karma and has karma as its origin. In addition to this, he gave a clear warning to his followers regarding this issue of karma and instructed them to hurry up in liberating themselves from suffering or at least building themselves up for all possible successes both in the material things and in the spiritual development in this present life on earth.

Let us now study another significant sutta (sutra) on this issue of karma in which the Buddha made it absolutely clear that those doing demeritorious deeds do not always go to hell, and that those performing meritorious deeds do not always go to heaven. The title of this sutra is Mahākammavibhanga-Sutta in which the Buddha explained this matter of karma to Ānanda, his attendant monk, thus:

"Ānanda, there are four categories of people living in the world, there are (1) *those who do killing, stealing, committing misconduct in sexuality, speaking lies, using nasty, improper language, making slandering and non-sensical talks. In addition, these people's minds are filled with greed, ill-will or destructive, violent thoughts, and erroneous, heretic views regarding the truth. These people, after the breaking up of their physical and energetic bodies and the death of consciousness, will be born in the unhappy, unprogressive, painful, and hellish plane of existence. However, there are (2) those doing exactly those same things as previously described, and holding a heretic, erroneous view, after the breaking up of the physical and energetic bodies and the death of consciousness enter the happy, prosperous, and heavenly plane of existence. Then there are (3) some people who refrain from killing, from stealing, from committing sexual misconduct, from speaking lies, from using nasty, improper language, from carrying out slandering and non-sensical talks. In addition, their minds are full of generosity, loving-kindness, compassion, and consist of the right view regarding the truth. These people, after the breaking up of their physical and energetic bodies and the death of consciousness, go to the happy, prosperous, heavenly plane of existence. However, there (4) some other people who do exactly those same things as previously described, who enter the unhappy, unprogressive, painful, and hellish plane of existence after the breaking of their physical and energetic bodies and the death of consciousness.*

"Ānanda, as for those doing the killing, stealing, and all the rest as described in the category 1, go to the unhappy, unprogressive, etc. because they had accumulated the unskillful karma or pāpa filled with painful feelings either in their previous lives or in the past of this present life. And later on, they commit a great deal of the unskillful karma in their present lives. Or, even on the death bed, they still hold firmly a heretic, erroneous view; they certainly reap the vipāka (consequences) of their unskillful karma, if not in this life, in the life to come.

"Ānanda, as for those who kill, steal; etcetera go to the happy and heavenly plane of life because in their previous lives or in the some distant past of this life they had accumulated the skillful karma filled with happy and joyful feelings before committing the unskillful karma. Later on, they carry out performing more and more skillful karma full of such happy and joyful feelings or on the death bed they hold quite firmly the right view, therefore they enter the happy and heavenly plane of life (a level of consciousness) here and hereafter.

"Ānanda, as for those refraining from killing, stealing, etcetera and holding the right view throughout, after the breaking up of their physical and energetic bodies and the death of consciousness, enter the happy and heavenly plane of life. This is because of their skillful karma filled with the happy and joyful feelings performed either in their previous lives or in some distant past of this life, or because later on they perform more and more skillful karma full of such happy and joyful feelings, or on the death bed they maintain firmly their right view. As a result, they reap the vipāka of their skillful karma here and hereafter.

"Ānanda, as for those practicing those same self-restraint and maintaining the right view throughout, after the breaking up of their physical and energetic bodies and the death of consciousness, enter the unhappy, unprogressive, etc. plane of life. This is because of their unskillful karma filled with the unhappy and painful feelings performed either in their previous lives or in some distant past of this life, or because later on they perform more unskillful karma full of the unhappy and painful feelings, or on the death bed, they still grip the heretic, erroneous view tightly. As a result, they suffer the vipāka of their unskillful karma here and hereafter.[18]

The Mahākammavibhanga-Sutta has shown us that those performing the skillful karma or meritorious deeds may go to hell and those performing the unskillful karma or demeritorious deeds may go to heaven. The reason is that the significant factor for determining the plane of existence and the type of life into which to be born is the almost final moment of death. If at such moment the consciousness is associated with the skillful karma, the happy plane of life will be the destination, but in case of the dying consciousness associated with the unskillful karma, certainly, the unhappy, unprogressive, and painful plane of life is expected. In this connection, the Buddha said:

"Monks, if the consciousness of the dying individual is delighted in and tied up to certain appearing images or to the definitive aspects of the body (anubayañjana) at the dying moment, it is possible that the individual concerned will be born either in hell or in the animal kingdom."[19]

That example was showing us the consequence of the unskillful karma, but in the similar fashion, we should be able to know the consequence of the skillful karma based on the dying consciousness associated with that which is good and skillful to determine the destination of the happy plane of life for the dying person. For more explicit clarity on this matter of the final moment of dying as the significant factor for determining where to be born and the kind of life into which to be born, let us read the following sutra of the Anguttara-Nikāya, Tikanipāta:

"Monks, some people in this world have done a little unskillful karma and they will enter hell because of such karma. But some other people who have done just the same quantity of the unskillful karma only reap the fruition of such

---

[18] M.U. 14/271 (Mahachula), /289 (Mahamakut), /354 (Sangīti).
[19] Samyutta-Nikāya, salayatana-vagga.

karma in this present life on earth, and after that their unskillful karma no longer yields any result.

"Monks, what kind of people who have performed just a little unskillful karma enter hell? Monks, certain people in this world do not train their bodies, do not train themselves in moral discipline, do not train their minds nor do they raise their consciousness, do not cultivate wisdom, possess a little virtue, and have a low mind. As for this kind of people, although they might perform just a little unskillful karma, such karma would lead them to hell.

"Monks, what kind of people who perform just a little unskillful karma, will reap its fruition only in this present life, and after that such unskillful karma ceases to yield its result? Monks, certain people in this world, train their bodies diligently and intelligently, train themselves in moral discipline, train their minds and raise their consciousness constantly, cultivate wisdom regularly, possess a great deal of virtues, have a high mind, and live the righteous (dharmic) life: Monks, as for this kind of people, although they might have performed a small quantity of the unskillful karma, such karma yields its result only in this present life, and after that ceases to produce any consequence."

"Monks, it is like someone pouring some salt in a small jug filled with water, what would you say about that? Will just little water in the small jug become salty because of the little quantity of salt?"
"That is correct, Sir!"
"What is the reason for that?"
"Blessed One, because the water in the small jug is very little, therefore it becomes salty."

"Monks, if someone would throw that same amount of salt in the Ganges River, what would you say about that? Will the water in such big river become salty because of that quantity of salt?"
"No, Sir!"
"Why not so?"
"Blessed One, since the quantity of water in the Ganges River is enormous, so it will not become salty because of just little amount of salt."
"Just like that, indeed, monks, certain people have performed just a little unskillful karma, but such karma leads them to hell. However, some other people have done exactly the same thing, but their unskillful karma yields its result only in this present life, and after that ceases to produce any consequence."

Is it possible to eliminate evil with good?

The issue that preoccupies many people is whether it is possible or not to cleanse off evil with doing good, noble, skillful deeds. Some hold an opinion that if it is possible, then a great number of people will have no fear of doing bad, evil, and destructive things, and that it is not fair, either. For example, if someone gets corrupted, or cheats someone else, or commits a murder, or causes pain and suffering to another person, such an individual would then do such good deeds as giving, practicing precepts, entering monkhood or becoming a nun, and so forth, since he or she believes it to be the way for cleansing off and eliminating the evil things already done. In this way, it is not fair at all since the individual under discussion is not punished and does not reap the consequences of his or her evil, unskillful actions. To put it another way, we can see that in the case of poor people, if doing good can really eliminate evil, they would all go to hell because they do not have the ways and means, or even the time to perform such good deeds as previously described. But wealthy people and those having power, in spite of committing a great deal of crime and carrying out a lot of evil deeds, may cleanse off their horrible, violent, and highly dangerous actions by performing good deeds since they truly can afford to do so by any means that appeals to them. In this fashion, we see more clearly that in this view there is no justice whatsoever.

Further still, some people maintain the view that the idea of eliminating evil by doing good is, in fact, not the Buddhist teaching since Buddhism teaches, embraces, and respects this matter of justice with all its heart and mind. This religion maintains this position: "Whoever performs any kind of karma must reap its consequences unavoidably." Therefore, some people hold the very strong and firm opinion that it is totally impossible to cleanse offs the evil deeds with doing good deeds.

Nonetheless, we must keep in mind at all times that so long as the kilesa (defilement, impurity, contamination, corruption, fetter, shatter, and things of such a nature) exists in the human consciousness and exercises its influences over action, speech, and thought, the elimination of evil through doing good deeds is impossible. However, those who have transformed all the kilesas completely and put them to the utter extinction stay above the law of karma. Therefore, we may reach a conclusion at this point that as long as there is the kilesa which can cause any bad karma to be performed, the doer or performer of such karma will reap its vipāka (consequence) to be yielded in one way or another and at the appropriate time.

In spite of those opinions and views cited above there is some authentic evidence to support the principle of cleansing off evil by doing good. For example, the Buddha himself stated in one of his discourses as follows:

"Monks, just as a pot that turns upside down will let the water flow out and does not allow it to flow back in, a monk who cultivates and makes much of the eight factors of the noble path will be able to cleanse off and to purify his pāpa (evil), his unskillful karma, and will not let the pāpa and the unskillful things to enter his inner world any more."[20]

Another of the Buddha's statement is: "*The person who is pure, perfect in purity, namely, purity of action, purity of speech, and purity of thought, and is without any contaminations, him or her the wise call the one that has cleansed off the pāpa.*"[21]

---

[20] Sam. Mahā. 14/45 (Mahachula), 14/72 (Mahamakut), 14/69 (Sangīti).
[21] Kāyasucim, vācāsucim, cetosucimanāsavam; sucim soceyyasampannam, āhu ninhātapāpakam. This verse the Buddha uttered with reference to the monk Angulimāla, and its details may be found in the

All in all, once again, let us examine carefully and thoroughly those encouraging statements made by the Buddha regarding the ways and means for cleansing off all evil and destructive things within each of us so that we will comprehend unmistakably *who* is the person who can do that.

Pāpa is the kilesa Itself

Some people think that pāpa and unskillful things are two different things and are not identical. However, in reality, pāpa is the same as the unskillful dharma (thing); the evidence for supporting this is as follows:

> *Greed is pāpa.*
> *Atilobho hi pāpako.*[22]

> *Whoever pacifies all the small and big pāpas entirely,*
> *him the wise call a samana because of bringing the pāpas*
>   *into total tranquility.*
> *Yo ca sameti pāpānam anumthūlāni sabbaso*
> *samitattā hi pāpānum samano'ti pavuccati.*[23]

> *Any Brahmin who has eliminated the pāpa and is without*
> *the threatening kilesa, without any shatter, has the self*
> *fully developed, reaches the end of the Veda, and has completed*
> *the practice of the Holy Life; him indeed the wise call Genuine*
>   *Brahmin.*
> *Yo brahmano bāhitapāpadhammo*
> *nihumhuko nikkasāvo yatatto*
> *vedantagū vusitabrahmacariyo*
> *dhammena so brahmavādam vadeyya.*[24]

> *All the unskilful dharmas (pāpa-dhamma) are the blemishes*
> *both in this world and in the world to come.*
> *Malāve pāpakā dhammā asmim loke paramhi ca.*[25]

In the commentary those words "pāpakā dhammā" refer to the *unskilful dharmas* (pāpakā dhammāti akusalā dhammā). Therefore, the pāpa and the unskilful dharma are identical or one and same things. By unskillful dharma we mean the kilesas; an action called "pāpa karma" signifies an intentional action done with the kilesas, and an action called "puñña karma" is one that is done with the virtues. However, the real puñña karma means the skillful action that yields its result depending on the kilesa in operation. The virtue that causes the puñña (meritorious thing) to come into force or to become effective is normally one which is associated with ignorance, craving, and clinging. Good intentional

---

Angulimāla-Sutta in the Majjhima-Nikāya, Majjhima-Pannāsaka, volume 13, page 330 (Majjhima-Nikāya Sutta/Discourse 86, M.ii.97)

[22] Vi. Bhikkhuni, 3/78 (Mahachula).
[23] Khuddaka-Nikāya, Dh. 25/62.
[24] Vi. Mahā. 4/4 (Mahachula).
[25] Khu, Dh. 25/59 (MCR).

action of those who are free from those three kilesas is not regarded as skillful karma because of its not yielding a further result in the next life. Such karma performed without the influence of any kilesas is, according to the Abhidharma, simply called "*kiriyā*" for the simple reason that it is neither skillful nor unskillful. In this connection, the Buddha denominates all arahats as the ones totally liberated from puñña and pāpa of all kinds. Therefore, all good actions performed by the Arahats are merely "functions" or "kiriyā" since they do not have any kilesas remaining in their consciousness and their actions are not fitted in with either the skilful karma or the unskilful karma.

Now, let us study attentively the following sutra that demonstrates the true meaning of the various karmas:

1. ***Black or dark karma with a black or dark result***
2. ***White karma with a white result***
3. ***Both black and white karma with both black and white results***
4. ***Neither black nor white karma with neither black nor white results***

"Monks, what kind of karma is black with its black result? Monks, some people in this world perform action (kāya-sankhāra), speech (vacī-sankhāra), and thought (mano-sankhāra) that ***are*** conducive to harming other living beings; such persons will enter the harmful world. When they live in such a harmful world, they will be in contact with harm and danger; and with such harmful contact, they will experience the painful and harmful feelings as those beings in hell do. Monks, this is called the black karma with the black result.

"Monks, what kind of the karma is white with its white result? Monks, some people in this world who perform action, speech, and thought that are ***not*** conducive to causing any harm to other living beings will enter the world where there is no existential harm. When they live in such a world free from any harm, they will be in contact with the harmless situations; and with such harmless contact they will experience only the happy and liberating feelings just like the subhakinha[26] brahmas do. Monks, this is called the white karma with white result.

"Monks, what kind of karma is both black and white with its black and white result? Monks, some people in this world who perform action, speech, and thought that are sometimes conducive to harming other living beings and other times are not conducive to causing any harm to anyone will enter the world that is both harmful and the harmless. When carrying out their lives in such both harmful and harmless world their contact through the six sense modalities is both harmful and harmless. With such contact they will experience both the painful, harmful feelings and the happy, liberating feelings (mixed feelings which are sometimes painful and other times happy) just as all the human beings, some devas (shining beings), and some disastrous beings do. Monks, this is called the black and white karma with its black and white result.

---

[26] Subhakinha symbolizes the person who has achieved the third stage of jhānic meditation. This word means "good light" and refers to the Brahma who radiates brilliant light out of his body naturally.

"Monks, what is the kind of the neither black karma nor white karma with the neither back nor white result and is conducive to the cessation of karma? Monks, whatever black karma produces the black result, whatever white karma produces the white result, whatever both black and white karma produces both black and white result. That karma which consists of the intention to relinquish all those three categories of karma is the neither black nor white karma with the neither black nor white result and is conducive to the extinction of all the karmas.

"Monks, these four categories of the karma I myself have fully realized and totally comprehended with the profound wisdom of my own."[27]

According to the Manopuranī Commentary, mentioned and discussed above, the concept of black karma refers to the ten akusalakammapathas[28] (the ten bases on which unskillful karma can be performed), while the black result means the reason for being born in the unhappy, painful, and unprogressive plane of existence. (Such plane of life does not necessarily mean a certain place outside of our planet earth to be reached after death, but it is within our human consciousness in this very life.)

The white karma refers to the ten kusalakammapathas[29] (the ten bases on which the skillful karma can be performed), while the white result means the reason for being born in the happy, heavenly plane of existence. (This concept of such a plane refers to the healthy and happy state of consciousness and also to the beautiful place somewhere on earth.)

The kind of karma that is both black and white with both black and white result refers to the mixed skillful karma and unskillful karma performed on the different occasions as the case may be. Such mixed karma yields both happy and painful results respectively.

Now, the neither-black-nor-white karma with the neither-black-nor-white result means the **four kinds of the visionary, inner wisdom of the path**, namely, the visionary, inner wisdom of sotāpatti-magga (the path of the nirvanic-stream entry), of sakadāgāmi-magga (the path of once-returning), of anāgāmi-magga (the path of non-returning), and of arahatta-magga (the path of full enlightenment). These four kinds of visionary, inner wisdom leads to the relinquishment of all karmas. In addition, on attaining the first path of sotāpatti-magga, all the unskillful karmas will become ineffective (ahosi-kamma) while the skillful karmas may yield their results in various lives up to seven lifetimes since the nirvanic stream-entrant will take a maximum of seven lifetimes to reach final, full enlightenment.

---

[27] Anguttara-Nikāya, Catukavagga, 21/258 (Mahachula), 21/314 (Mahamakut), 21/330 (Sangīti).

[28] They are killing, stealing, committing sexual misconduct, speaking a lie, talking by way of causing division and disharmony, using rough and nasty words, talking non-sensical matters, greed, ill-will, and holding the heretic, erroneous view.

[29] They are refraining from killing, from stealing, from committing sexual misconduct, from speaking a lie, from talking by way of causing division and disharmony, from using rough and nasty language, from talking non-sensical matters, freedom from greed, freedom from ill-will, and holding the right view.

Please bear in mind that the fourth and final category of the karma that is neither black nor white with its neither black nor white result is considered the most significant of all kinds of karma since it is the karma to be performed by noble, enlightened people (ariya-puggala) or by those walking on the noble eightfold path constantly and sincerely on their way to enlightenment. Unfortunately, the people thick with kilesas (puthujjana) are incapable of performing such karma yet since whatever they do is done under the influences of craving (including greed) and attachment, and they always expect something in return (some result). Therefore, their karma (action/activity) continues yielding its result until the kilesas of craving, greed, and attachment have been utterly eliminated and totally transformed. As for the noble enlightened persons, whatever karma they do is done for the clear purpose of transforming and relinquishing all the remaining kilesas and with no expectation of any result or of anything in return. For this reason, their action, speech, and thought always lead to lessening and reducing those remaining kilesas until eventually they become completely extinguished with no ashes remaining.

However, keep in mind that skillful karma, although it may yield a happy result, might yield a painful consequence because the skillful karma performed under the influence of the kilesas such as craving and greed will provide a condition of rebirth (being born again). When there is rebirth, old age, illness, and death, the mass of suffering will necessarily follow.

Nonetheless, those who realize fully the four noble truths, namely, seeing birth as dukkha, seeing craving as the cause of dukkha, seeing nirvana as the cessation of dukkha, and seeing the middle path as the ways and means for ending all forms of dukkha, will only think of performing karmas for transcending skillful karma and for transforming and eliminating unskillful karma. These people belong to the noble, initial enlightened ones.

For the purpose of understanding the sutra under discussion easily and precisely the author is introducing here the short form of paticcasamuppāda (the law of dependent origination), as follows:

The kilesa is the approximate cause of karma. The karma yields its vipāka (result). Then, the vipāka causes the kilesa to arise and to operate once again. Therefore, these three things: **kilesa, karma, and vipāka**, always go on in cycles exactly in the described fashion. Nonetheless, only the arahats do not follow these cycles because their kilesas have been totally eliminated and completely transformed. When kilesas do not exist, the cause of karma is cut off once and for all and therefore, no karma will be performed, and with the absence of karma, there will no vipāka. So, the full cycle stops.

Based on the Mahākammavibhanga-Sutta we formulate this law:

Consciousness knows precisely the place suitable for itself. A high consciousness leads to a higher plane of life, while a low consciousness leads to a lower plane of life.

In addition to the above-mentioned sutra let us study the following text:

"Monks, just as a piece of wood thrown up to the sky, sometimes falls down with the bottom heading down, other times with the top end heading down, still other times (laterally) with the middle part heading down. Monks, the living beings under the enormous obstruction of ignorance and overwhelmed by the binding force of craving will go on repeating the cycles of birth and death, sometimes from this world to another world, other times from the other world to this world.

"What is the reason for that, monks?

"Because they have not realized fully and experientially the Four Noble Truths."[30]

In Apannaka-Sutta the Buddha said:

"Life on the other planets may come to be born on this planet, Earth, or life on the planet, Earth may be born on the other planets. Those who do not have faith in this matter are called the heretics.

There are such messages as the above-cited ones that appear in the Buddhist scriptures, which many of us tend not to believe them to be true because they are not reasonable and cannot be proved scientifically. But now several things such as in the universe there exist the sun, the moon, and many other planets.[31] The Buddha knew all these things before his achievement of full enlightenment since he studied all of the eighteen sciences and liberal arts, including astronomy or the studies of the various planets and stars, and certainly his total enlightenment illumines his knowledge of the entire universe.

The issue or the law of karma is the most important matter in everyone's life, which the Buddha undoubtedly wishes all of us to understand correctly and clearly. He definitely does not want anyone to believe blindly and superstitiously in phenomena and events, whether physical or psychic, that take place in the world and in the individuals' and collective lives. However, since the world consists of an infinite number of illusory things perceived through our distorted perceptions, those who are weak and shallow in wisdom and knowledge may fall victims to such miraculous events and mysterious, psychic phenomena until the consciousness totally free from ignorance and delusion comes into full operation. In addition, the careful and thorough studies of the issue and law of karma are carried out realistically and in accord with what the Buddha truly taught and authentically said in the Buddhist Tipiṭaka will surely help us penetrate profoundly and cut through utterly this enormously big and complicated matter of karma. Then, the ever-shining light of wisdom regarding the issue of karma will manifest constantly in our daily living.

A concise description of rebirth

As you are probably aware, all along in my writing about karma this matter of rebirth pops up here and there, particularly the rebirth consciousness

---

[30] Samyutta-Nikāya, Mahavagga 19/382 Mahachula, 19/550 Mahamakut, 19/538 Sangīti.
[31] As found in the Buddhist Tipiṭaka, volume 20, page 221, volume 25, page 47, and volume 14, page 150, Mahachula version.

(patisandhi-citta). So, we understand the position of Buddhism maintaining that when a certain person dies, not only the physical body and the breath stop functioning completely, but the consciousness deceases as well. Concerning this dying process, we observe that at first the verbal activity (vacī-sankhāra) or speech ceases to function, secondly the physical body dies and the breath breaks up, and thirdly (finally) the consciousness disappears (is dead). But the death of consciousness becomes a condition for the rebirth consciousness to take place so long as the karmic energy has not been exhausted. This signifies that so long as the three principal factors of life are still active in the sense of having the full potentiality to operate, another form of life will be created and come into existence. Those three things are *kilesa (impurity/contamination), karma (volitional action performed through physical action, speech, and thought), and vipāka (consequences of karma)*. They are actually inseparable in their functioning and operating since they are absolutely interdependent, which implies that one is an approximate condition for another. For example, a kilesa of greed becomes a cause for a greedy action, and then such an action produces a consequence of winning money or gaining some material wealth and at the same time greed is on the increase as the result of the mobilization and the use of greed in action or performance. This is a sheer samsara, the cycle of kilesa > karma > vipāka and vice versa! This cycle or samsara will not end unless full enlightenment is attained and nirvana is fully realized experientially.

Rebirth, then, takes place after each death, which forms another cycle of samsara: *birth > life > death*, or in short we say that *birth and death* continue ceaselessly so long as the fuel of kilesa still feeds the fire of karma and does not become extinguished. As a result, vipāka or a consequence of karma is naturally and inevitably produced; and then each vipāka turns into a cause of kilesa and therefore, the vicious circle, the circle of the good and the bad, goes on and on. Nonetheless, this circle as the indispensable part of samsara will eventually end in the nirvana (the complete extinction or cooling off of all the fires of kilesa, karma, and vipāka, and of birth, death, and rebirth).

To respond to the frequently asked question of how rebirth actually takes place, I would like to use this metaphoric illustration for an easy comprehensible grasping of the rebirth process. In a certain forest there is a lovely and beautiful river with its clear and evenly flowing water. Unfortunately one side of the river got burned by a big fire, and the burning spread out far and wide rapidly because of the drought and a strong wind. Approaching the bank of the river, there is an enormous heat coming out of the fire and therefore, the trees, bushes, and shrubs on the other side are on fire almost instantly, and the burning turns out to be as powerful as the previous one due to wind and drought conditions.

Now, the question arises: Does the fire on one side of the river jump over to the other side? Or, is the fire on one side of the river the same as the fire that burns the forest situated on the other side of that river? Truthfully speaking, the proper answer is "No" since there is no jumping over of the fire from one side to the other side of the river, and the fire that burns the forest on one side of the river is *neither the same nor different* fire, but is just fire. But as the burning produces tremendous, unbearable heat on one side of the river, so such heat becomes an approximate condition for the burning on the other side. This is what actually happens in this case of fire burning both sides of the river.

In exactly the same way, we say about the rebirth process that there is no coming and no going of the consciousness from the dead to the new-born person. Ultimately speaking, there is no "person" or "individual" or "being" to be taken as the authentic reality since what we denominate as a person, an individual, or a being, is nothing but a notion, a concept, a word, or an idea to represent the existential reality within the clothes of the concept, the notion, the word, in which the idea contains certain features created for certain purposes in our human world. For this reason, we say this: the death consciousness that contains and carries the kilesas and the karmic energetic forces becomes an approximate condition for the rebirth consciousness to take place and to receive the transference of those kilesas and karmic energy so that a new form of life appropriate for such conditions may be created. Therefore, the dead person is neither the same nor different from the new-born person, which means there are both uniqueness and difference (the paradoxical reality) in the new-born individual. At this point, the author would suggest that his reader goes back to take a closer look into the issue of karma once more so that the understanding of rebirth will become clearer. Karma and rebirth are totally interdependent and absolutely inter-related or inter-conditioned.

= 4 =

THE CONSTANT CHALLENGE IN SAMSARIC LIFE

Our constant challenge in the samsaric life is **dukkha** or conflict, the details of which will be discussed beginning with the following introduction:

In the course of existing and living we find a constant struggle between opposing forces, not only in human life, but also in all living things. This is because there are the pairs of opposites such as day/night, light/dark, life/death, good/evil, right/wrong, true/false, constructive/destructive, yin/yang, pleasure/ pain, sorrow/joy, etc. Those opposing forces not only struggle to take charge or run the show of all the existences but to survive themselves. As the result of this struggle, all forms of existence are put into motion and manifestation. Each pair of opposites, when they manage to find a gesture of balance and harmony between them, may take a break from playing out the conflict, and then dance together for a while. As a matter of fact, all natures have a similar ultimate goal of their existence and functioning; and that is the creation of a dynamic equilibrium or some kind of right proportions in existing and manifesting. This indicates that in any form of life, conflict is inevitable and becomes an indispensable characteristic of existence. If there would be no existential conflict in all things (*sankhāra*), the struggle between opposing forces would not exist; and for that matter, it would be unnecessary at all to endeavor to create harmony and dynamic balance. But because conflict does exist, there comes into operation the work of bringing about the right proportions of manifesting and the harmony of existing together.

As for human existence, it's quite obvious to all of us that conflict is part and parcel of life. When in pain, we struggle to get rid of it or to do something about it so that we can find a relief and have a pleasant experience. Getting confused, feeling sick emotionally, or facing some crisis, whether psychological or spiritual, we resort to health professionals or spiritual mentors in order for our confusion, our sickness, and our internal crisis to be therapeutized and healed. Being unhappy or dissatisfactory, we look for happiness and satisfaction. When confronting death, we fight as hard as possible to secure our existence, attempting to make sure that we do not die in an inappropriate time, or perhaps do not lose life at all. The reason for doing all these things is that there is an opposite of everything in our existence and therefore, we look for it and work hard to get it. If there would be no opposite and we could not have choice, then our existence would just go on existing without conflict and we would have to live with all that we are exposed to, however painful or pleasurable it might be. But in reality there are pairs of opposites, and opposing forces do exist and operate as experiential facts within us and in our external lives. So, we are tempted to search for the opposite when the negative experience overwhelms us, or to go on seeking something better and more satisfying even when we are experiencing times of happiness and good life.

In addition, because conflict exists as an underlying force in our existence, we very often confront conflicting desires. For example, first we have a desire for doing some obligatory work at home or in the office, then up comes another desire for going out and having fun with friends since the weather is good and the day inviting. What shall we do? Do we have to go against one desire and fulfill another? Which one, if we must choose? Or, must we try to accomplish both desires? Work and pleasure/fun are a pair of opposites. Because of their existence, we get into conflict, we fall into a pushing-pulling situation, and are put under the influences of the compelling desire to get something done and the driving force to enjoy the pleasures of life. This might appear like having a hot charcoal in the throat to some people. (It cannot be swallowed, nor can it be thrown up!) Or to others it might be similar to sitting on a hot seat where one must face all kinds of anxiety, discomfort, and suffering caused by opposing forces struggling inside us. If we have faith in fate or trust in the free flow of life, we will not get very upset by such a life situation, for it is quite normal in living and we can always find the way out. Sooner or later a practical solution will be discovered and we will be able to move on with life as it unfolds. On the contrary, if we go against fate and lack the trusting willingness to experience fully whatever life brings to us, certainly we will be in more troubles, or may have to struggle much harder. As a result, in this case we allow conflict to victimize us because we do not understand how to live with it.

Learning to live with all kinds of conflict, whether internal or external, is the key to living, because it is an art that one must utilize constantly. Utilizing wisely the art of living with conflict, one reduces stress and minimizes suffering since, by so acting, one will find inner calm and mental clarity. In this way, the struggle between the opposing forces will be immediately checked by alert attention and, therefore, kept under control. This significant issue of conflict or suffering will be discussed at length in the following pages."[1]

Now, let us look into the ***most significant issue*** of ***suffering*** more deeply:

On the section on conflict in the previous chapter we have discussed, to some extent, the implication of dukkha as an indispensable characteristic of existence. In this chapter, we will elaborate the broader and more complete meaning of this truth in order to grasp the whole significance of dukkha and understand it fully, beyond reasonable doubt, beyond any doubt for that matter. This is because suffering (dukkha) plays a very significant part of our lives. We must possess complete and clear knowledge of it, in order to enable ourselves to relate to it and to manage it efficiently in the course of our daily living. If we fail to achieve such abilities, we will dip ourselves into suffering intensely, and will be unable to get out of it without leaving a deep wound in our psyche.

Generally speaking, suffering means *something that happens* and therefore, anything and everything that occurs in life, in the world, and indeed in the entire universe belongs to suffering. This meaning is, in fact, in complete agreement with what the Buddha said in the Dhammapada: *All conditioned and*

---

[1] From the author's unpublished English manuscript *A New Vision of Buddhism*.

made-up (constructed) things are dukkha (sabbē sankhārā dukkhā). For this reason, we understand that suffering is not just an unpleasant, painful, dissatisfactory, or disagreeable feeling/sensation, but includes all physical, mental, psychological, and spiritual phenomena. Indeed, all conditioned states and on-going things in existence belong to suffering because they are all *something happening*. The physical body is something happening and going on for a certain period of time, feeling or sensation is something happening, perception is something happening, activities are something happening, and consciousness is something happening. In brief, all occurrences and manifestations, whether internal or external, are something happening and going on right here in life, in the world, and in the whole universe. All the happenings affect us in one way or another, so we cannot avoid them but must deal with them, whether we like them or not. Hence, it's utterly obvious that suffering is part and parcel of life, and no one can deny its existence and its involvement with life.

The three categories of suffering (dukkha)

According to the Buddha the noble truth of dukkha is divided into three categories, namely, *ordinary dukkha, dukkha as produced by change, and dukkha as conditioned things (sankhāra-dukkha)*. Let us consider their implications as broadly as possible.

(1) Ordinary dukkha (suffering)

This category is quite simple and familiar to everyone, since each of us experiences some negative feelings, uncomfortable sensations, bad mood, and so forth. From the physical part, we occasionally feel aches, pains, discomfort, fatigue, exhaustion, uneasiness, itchiness, etc. All these physical sensations belong to the category of ordinary suffering or dukkha since they are common to all human beings that walk on earth. We all, to some extent, experience them; the only difference lies in the degrees of those sensations. That is to say, some sensations might be more acute, more intense, more severe, or more deeply hurting and more biting, while some others might be less painful and more bearable. Nevertheless, for all of us the most common feeling in the experience of suffering is that it is hard to bear, or sometimes is *un*bearable.

With regard to the emotional, mental, and psychological experience of pain and suffering, we from time to time are exposed to, and encounter, feelings of despair, depression, sorrow, grief, agony, mourning, resentment, hate, anger, and so on. Name it what you will! There is an almost endless number of those negative, bitterly torturous, and destructive feelings or emotions that enter our lives, very often to some, while to others *just* occasionally.

From the psychological standpoint, we may state that those having a very difficult childhood caused either by abandonment in one form or another, or by lack of love and intense internal insecurity, will suffer much more severely than those who have a relatively happy childhood. Nonetheless, we all encounter and, at one point in life, must live through our psychological suffering because we are unable to choose where to be born and what kind of parents to grow up with. You are fortunate if loving, caring, and understanding parents raise you, for you will suffer less psychologically. This is because such a happy upbringing provides for you a sound basis of flowing and flowering with life as well as of meeting the world more positively.

As for spiritual suffering, basically those seeking spiritual development quite often suffer from a desire to achieve high consciousness, and, once such achievement might be accomplished, they suffer another desire to maintain it. Or they suffer the greed for beautiful experiences and the drive for repeating or returning to them when those desirable experiences have faded away. Encountering certain frightening images discharged from psychic centers, some spiritual people undergo enduring much fear, anxiety, and pain because of lacking information required for understanding them and for dealing with them efficiently. When worse comes to worse, their suffering will surpass what they are at ease to deal with and will lead to a *spiritual crisis* that is hardly bearable because such a crisis affects not only one's psychic instability, but may lead to an emotional or mental distortion, and probably to a physical illness as well. On the contrary, at good times in spiritual experience, one clings to, and gets lost in, the spiritual world, turning one's back to the ordinary, daily life. In this case, one suffers an *attachment and delusive consciousness*.

It seems impossible to escape suffering, wherever we go and whatever we do. It's just there as if waiting for us. This might sound a little pessimistic. But, in fact, it is a *realistic* experience in our existence and in the course of our living. Although suffering is part and parcel of life, we are not entirely deprived of fleeting pleasure, transient joy, and short-lived happiness. It appears that our existence provides us with both sides of experience, and it's up to our wisdom (or the lack of it) either to bring about the dynamic balance or to create the unbridgeable extremes between them (or not). We are the creators of our own problems; meanwhile we are the ones who will find the real solution.

(2) Suffering or dukkha as produced by change

We have already discussed the matter of change and impermanence in the previous chapter. Any changes in life or in the world, to some extent, affect us in the negative way. For instance, deprivation from a good, healthy environment costs us, if not an illness, at least a physical discomfort and/or an emotional and mental agitation, a form of suffering. Certainly, separation from loved ones and dear things, brings about pain of loneliness and insecurity. Leaving an old life condition and entering a new one causes some anxiety and fear to us since we are unable to let go of the old and embrace the new totally. We suffer when the life situation changes from the smooth, happy, and comfortable lifestyle to the uncertain, painful, and disharmonious one. When the waves of change rock the boat of life, we cannot help but suffer apprehension and worry about our safety and security as we resist change and do not want to accept it as it comes, but wish to remain in our well-established lifestyle.

(3) Suffering as conditioned things (energy patterns)

It is this category of dukkha that most people, including Buddhists, do not take into serious consideration since they think of dukkha only as something unpleasant or painful, which pertains to those two previous categories that we have discussed. Only seldom, do we take sankhāra dukkha (suffering as conditioned things) as the most significant matter to put an end to. The other two types of suffering are natural responses arising from sense-contact through any one of six sense-doors with their corresponding objects. (These are eyes in contact with visual object, ears in contact with audible sound or vibration, nose in contact with smell, tongue in contact with taste, physical body in contact with tangible things, and mind in contact with the internal world of idea, thought, fantasy, dream, and imagination, etc.) No one can ever prevent a sensation or feeling from arising when there is contact between the six sense modalities, their corresponding objects, and consciousness, except a paralyzed or mentally benumbed person. The sensation or feeling may be pleasant, unpleasant, or neither pleasant nor unpleasant, depending on the quality of the contact and the sense of evaluation. Therefore, suffering in the form of unpleasant sensation/feeling must be produced as the result of an impoverished contact with a disagreeable object. No individual person, whether enlightened or unenlightened, can stop such a sensation/feeling or avert its course. The only thing some more self-developed people and enlightened beings can do, is suffer less, or not at all, depending on their abilities to rise above the unpleasant or even painful sensation with the virtue of non-attachment and dis-identification.

Now, let us consider more specifically this matter of suffering as conditioned things or as something happening. Looking thoroughly into our physical body, our feelings/sensations, our perceptions, our psychophysical activities, and our consciousness, as well as the physical world, environmental world, and phenomenal world, we don't see anything *unconditioned* since all things are mutually dependent and conditioned by one another. That is to say, the whole existence of breathing beings, non-breathing but living beings, and non-living things (such as rocks and stones) is inclusively interdependent, interconnected, and mutually conditioned and for that matter, there is no single thing that exists independently on its own.

What do we actually mean when we talk about putting an end to suffering? Do we have to destroy all conditioned things, including our existence, so that suffering may end? Certainly, we do not destroy anything whatsoever, but what we must do is *de*condition and *transform* the constituent components of existence as well as constantly *renew* the authentic relationship to our varying parts, to our inner and outer environment, and to ourselves both as who we really are and as what we appear to be. The authentic relationship refers to the genuine, bona fide way by which we relate to our various realities and those of others, the relationship that is based on, and guided by, *mindfulness and insight* (inward light and inner knowing), or in brief, by *the inwardly directed relationship.* With this kind of relationship in operation we will not dance with the dances of illusion unconsciously, but manage to rise skillfully on the waves in the ocean of life and to live artfully with the entire *on-going rhythmic dance* both within our existence and in the world around us. This is because the inwardly directed relationship is formed through, and maintained by, impeccable awareness, unbroken attention, lively wakefulness, and vital alertness.

How can we decondition ourselves and our states of existence? First of all, we must realize through awareness and insight that both our external states of existence and the infinite number of selves or beings living within us are all relatively conditioned things. On top of that reality, each and every one of them struggles constantly to run the show of our lives according to their conditions. In this context we can never *be* free to live and to go about in life without their dominance, partly insofar as we conform to their influences and partly insofar as we identify with whatever self or part that directs our lives at the time. We are in this way *un*able to be ourselves as we truly are. For this reason, it is absolutely essential that we *decondition* ourselves by *separating* ourselves from whatever arises and goes on both inside and outside, by *not identifying* with all the occurrences, and by *listening deeply to the still voice.* This voice is a silently pronouncing sound that springs up from the free and unconditioned state of being filled with wisdom and genuine caring.

With respect to *separation*, we pull ourselves out and create a distance in order to enable ourselves to have our own space and to be who we really are. For example, when experiencing a physical discomfort or an emotional pain, we do not get involved with, or engage ourselves in the sensation in such a way that we become authoritarian experiencers of discomfort and/or pain. We think, "it's my pain, it's my discomfort," instead of saying simply, "discomfort arises in me, pain arises in me." By such an act of separating, we are not in the sensation of discomfort or pain, but are out of it. We have a clear distance and space for being and functioning so that we can relate to the sensation genuinely. We can let it be and watch its manifestation together with our own reactions. We do not attempt to dominate or exercise any authority over the sensation by making efforts either to overcome it or to get id of it. We simply relate to it and may take an appropriate action or non-action as the insight guides us at the moment.

As a matter of fact, we have no authority over any sensations, whether pleasant or unpleasant, agreeable or disagreeable, happy or painful, or over any physical, mental, and spiritual phenomena, for that matter. Ultimately speaking, we are not experiencers either since there is no "we," in the first place, apart from a concept or an idea with no tangible reality corresponding to it. When in the ultimate truth "we" does not exist, how can there be experiencers? Some people might argue that there is "we" in relation to "they" or "we" exists as an expansion of "I," But this is *merely* the pattern of language and a manner of speaking. In the final analysis, in the separating out of the constituent components of our human existence, we find only the psycho-physical structures. They are the physical body grouped together with its energy systems and material structure, the assemblage of sensation/feeling, the assemblage of perception, the assemblage or structuring of mental, psychological, and spiritual realities, and the consciousness process. To this combination or assemblage we give a label "person," "being," "self," "I," "you," "we," "they," etc. Obviously these are only words, concepts, or labels, and there is no concrete entity standing out independently within or outside of the psychophysical assemblages. In short, the factual representation of the "person," the "being," the "self," the "I," the "you," the "we," the "they," etc. cannot be found. We invent many concepts and varying notions for the purpose of clarifying things and phenomena, but we end up confusing ourselves with what is real and what is unreal. Eventually, we submerge ourselves more profoundly in a delusive consciousness, dancing indefinitely with the dances of illusion until we wake up or suffering awakens us.

As for *disidentification,* the majority of us find it extremely hard *not* to identify with something that enters our experience or comes into contact with our sense-modalities. In addition, it's impossible not to become an identified subject such as "I," because in life we must have an identity and have to function. Since our functioning self or part is *ego* (a sense of "I" that makes me experience myself as who I am), every one of us definitely needs this ego-self for becoming and operating; otherwise there will be no movement and no activity. As soon as the executive part of our total being traditionally known as "ego" comes into existence and operation, we identify with it immediately so that we can become someone or something in our existence and in our functioning. From then on, everyone can exist and is able to function *only* through the acts of identifying with ego, and then the identification takes root in human personality and, as time passes, becomes a deeply rooted habit in every human being. Therefore, the act of identifying with ego brings about the *primary* separation and then follows instantly the creation of "self" and "other". Hence the work of identification leads us to inventing an infinite number of parts within us, and the roles we play in the external world. In accordance with this invention, it appears to our traditional ego's eye as if we were basically schizoid or a one-two man and a one-two woman. But this is not so, because we are not really split in half, but only become fragmented by identifying with varying parts (one part at a time, of course). By *schizoid* we mean a kind of illness that is pertaining to or affected by a personality disorder marked by coldness and inability to form social relations. It resembles or tends toward schizophrenia, but with milder or less developed symptoms. Nevertheless, identification with a major part – for instance, with the mind with its extremely one-sided idea or belief – may probably cause a severe mental illness and a personality crisis so that one could become schizophrenic.

In summing up, *dis*-identification keeps us *away* from any identified parts and functions and therefore, we can become ourselves as who we truly are and can make *real* choices in our lives. Normally, choices in life are made by parts in charge of functioning with which we identify. Very rarely, it is the real *we* that makes choices, although we make-believe that we do. More importantly, disidentification creates *space* for being, allowing us to relate genuinely to the parts, the roles, and the people around us, including the rest of the world in which we live. Certainly, with disidentification we will be able to *de*condition ourselves successfully so that, instead of operating from the ego-personality center, we manifest and carry out our activities and functions from the *liberated, aware ego* and *essence* level. In other words, we live our lives and go about doing our things from the *middle place (the place of wholeness or equilibrium)* instead of either from the right (*light side*) or from the left (*dark side*). To be able to operate ourselves that way we need *impeccable awareness or insightful mindfulness (sati) and clarity of consciousness (paññā - the knowing and see-ing directly together with the unfailing ability to be).* These are the highly effective tools with which we use constantly in our functioning and manifesting with ***disidentification***.

Listening to the small, still voice

There is something very precious but hidden within us that the majority of us tend to overlook. This inestimable, priceless thing has a tremendous loving care and genuine concern for us, and tries its best to communicate and to let us know of what is the right thing to do at the moment. Those believing in God state convincingly that it is *the will* of God or *doing God's will,* while many others who are independently minded prefer to use the terminology of "*small, still voice.*" This type of voice is so gentle and almost imperceptible that our conscious mind or ego mind does not take it into account seriously but rather rationalizes it as something *unimportant or unworthy of our listening to*. But the small, still voice has enormous weight in helping us *do* the right thing at the appropriate time because it is an unconditioned thing and comes from the place of unconditional love. It doesn't want from us anything in return and its gifts to us are totally free. Since our ego mind has been trained in a give-and-take thinking, in reasoning, and in rationalization, it's extremely hard to accept that which is seemingly *un*reasonable and freely given (the gift that doesn't come from common interests or shared benefits). For this reason, the ego mind will reject, ignore, or brush aside such a voice almost instantly, for it absolutely doesn't have any confidence in the irrational (beyond rationality), still voice. Instead, the ego mind prefers to set up definite plans and clear directions to follow and therefore, we lose the capacity of a deep listening to the precious, still voice, or of following *slender threads* that show us the way at the moment. In other words, we fall into disharmony from the universe and become slaves to our ego mind because of our great loss of the capacity and the opportunities to connect with the slender threads or to listen to the small, still voice.

Getting wiser, we learn to listen and to pay close attention to something that appears irrational and insignificant. With sufficient experience of such a thing as the small, still voice, we miss less and less the opportunity to do the right thing either for ourselves or for other people, including the world at large. We know for certain how to derive benefit from the presentation of the small, still voice and the revelation of the slender threads. In this way, we gradually decondition ourselves and therefore have more authentic freedom to ensue our birthrights of a deep, wise listening, direct knowing, and can abide in the inner solitude wherefrom we look out and connect with both the internal world and external world. By so doing, we become more and more enlightened and are able to conduct our lives more happily and more successfully.

Suffering is that which we *must* discern totally and experientially

Now we arrive at the point where we will answer the question of what to do with suffering. First of all, we must make it clear beyond reasonable doubt that all three categories of suffering or dukkha should be comprehended not only intellectually but also through experiential realization and in profound wisdom. There is not much more to do, although a great deal of energy, focused attention, and considerable time are required to be invested in studying, observing, examining, contemplating, and analyzing all aspects of suffering (something that is happening) with keen intellect, sharp intelligence, and profoundly penetrating wisdom. This is because the *real* solution of suffering lies in the complete understanding of it all, and such a wise and complete understanding can only be achieved through properly exercising *pointed* intellect and the creative presence of *total, impeccable* awareness. With accomplishment of full and wise discernment of suffering and all its related features, the real solution is right there *within* such discernment and comprehension. On the contrary, if we attempt to solve the issue of suffering merely through trying to find the answer or solution without making good efforts to understand it thoroughly, we may end up complicating and creating much more confusion concerning the matter at hand. In short, one might state that the *right answer* to the question is to be found in the complete understanding of the question itself."[2]

The entanglement of life and how to solve it

First of all, let us listen to what the Buddha says about this matter of entanglement:

"This teaching of dependent origination is very profound in all its aspects. Because of not knowing, not understanding, and not realizing this most essential teaching, the mind gets tangled up, complicated, and confused, just like a ball of threads making themselves tangled all over and leaving no easy way out of the entanglement. Indeed, such an entangled mind finds it extremely difficult to reach the real solution of problems, let alone to free itself from the cycles of birth, death, and suffering."

Now, it is essential that we take a closer look at the formula of this law of dependent origination (this formula continues onto the next page):

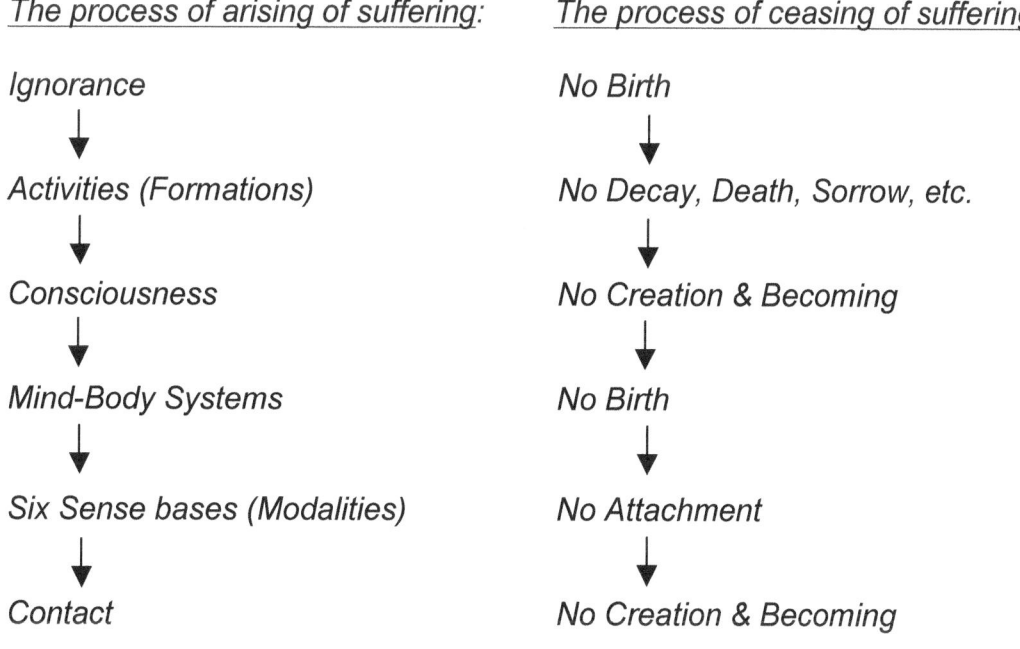

The process of arising of suffering:

Ignorance
↓
Activities (Formations)
↓
Consciousness
↓
Mind-Body Systems
↓
Six Sense bases (Modalities)
↓
Contact

The process of ceasing of suffering:

No Birth
↓
No Decay, Death, Sorrow, etc.
↓
No Creation & Becoming
↓
No Birth
↓
No Attachment
↓
No Creation & Becoming

---

[2] From the author's unpublished English manuscript *A New Vision of Buddhism*.

↓ Sensation/Feeling
↓ Craving/Thirst
↓ Attachment
↓ Creation & Becoming
↓ Birth
↓ Decay, death, sorrow, lamentation, pain, grief, and despair/tribulation.

Thus arises the mass of suffering and fleeting pleasure.

↓ No Craving/Thirst
↓ No Attachment
↓ No Sensation/Feeling
↓ No Craving/Thirst
↓ No Contact
↓ No Sensation/Feeling
↓ No Six Sense Bases
↓ No Contact
↓ No Mind-Body Systems
↓ No Six Sense Bases
↓ No Consciousness
↓ No Physical & Mental Phenomena
↓ No Activities/Formations
↓ No Consciousness
↓ No Ignorance
↓ No Activities/Formations

Thus ceases the entire process of suffering.

Some detailed studies of dependent origination

We may note here an important pair of phenomena: conditioned by such activities of ignorance, a consciousness is brewed up which, in turn, influences and strengthens further those activities expressed through physical action, speech, and thought. By consciousness here we mean the acts of seeing, of hearing, of smelling, of tasting, of touching, and of knowing or sensing. Generally speaking, how we see, what we hear, and how we think, are clearly conditioned by our limited personal experience, knowledge, education, training, and cultural or religious background. We only see what we want to see and see it in the way that fits in with our conditioning. In other words, we normally see things and people through our colored glasses, and believe them to be true with no wavering doubt, or try to become convinced that such is the only truth. It is hard, if not impossible, to allow ourselves to see the way other people see because that kind of permission will be in severe conflict with our ideology, philosophy, and belief system. Therefore we nail ourselves down to fixated, unbendable ways and means of seeing, hearing, thinking, and believing. Such a human phenomenon as this is rather unfortunate, to say the least.

It is quite obvious that the consciousness that we have in our daily life is made up not only by our personal conditioning, but also by varying influences and archetypal energies. And such archetypal energies prevail in our environment, in the land we walk on, in the group of people we associate with, in our community, in the society that we belong to, and in the world in which we live. We then manifest such consciousnesses in all our functions and activities in life, at work, and in all the relationships with ourselves individually and with the rest of the world. This means that we have definitive, predictable patterns of acting, reacting, and responding to life situations, social situations, and world situations. With this heavily conditioned consciousness we are trapped in a very narrow, limited whirlpool of existence, which we have become rather familiar with through personal experience. Trapped and spinning, we become aggressive, punitive, and violent, especially toward those living on the other side of the fence. In this way, individual defense mechanisms get stronger and more deeply rooted in our psychological reality, calling for territorial defense systems to be built up more and more so that our security can be guaranteed. The longer we live under the dictates of this kind of consciousness, the more fears and suspicions dominate our lives; and as a result, we cling even more tightly to our superficial existence.

With this consciousness, we create a definite condition of our body and mind befitting for containing and accommodating such consciousness. To put it in another way, whatever consciousness we have at the moment will drive us into automatic modulations or transformations so that a certain form of our physical body and mental state suitable for the manifestation of the consciousness will be created. For example, when confronting fear, the physical body gets contracted and the mind becomes rigid, terrified, or even paralyzed; and then it projects the idea that all sorts of imagined bad things might happen. On experiencing a pain, whether physical, emotional, or psychological, the body tenses up and the mind screams and agonizes itself. In this context, we observe the variety of body language, definitive bodily posture, and distorted physical structure, manifested in the individuals as the consequence of the presence or the invasion of a certain type of consciousness with its energy patterns. Therefore, we can understand how blocks or blockages are created in our psychophysical systems. These have a natural rhythm, which the physical body loses due to the arising of a new consciousness. (When talking about consciousness we also include the energy patterns pertaining to it, for without the presence of each such energy pattern there can be no consciousness). A new inner form of the body is made up in order to contain such a new consciousness with a specific energy pattern operating with it at that particular moment. Not only that, the mind or rather mental properties such as feeling, perception, intention, impression, and attention are also formed in such a way that they become appropriate partners and coordinators of the consciousness.

Here we see that consciousness works closely and indispensably with perception, feeling, and the quality of contact (impression). For example, on the arising of angry or hateful consciousness, the perception will form an ugly, disgusting image of the object perceived through the particular consciousness so that the mind can dwell on such an object. In this situation, one can imagine what kind of feeling will come into play; and the quality of contact will certainly be a rough and unpleasant one. This process goes on and on so long as the different types of consciousness arise endlessly, one after the other; and each consciousness is categorized according to the energy pattern that arises or associates with it. To mention just a few, we have a delusive consciousness, a depressive consciousness, a sad consciousness, a loving consciousness, a compassionate consciousness, a balanced consciousness, a harmonious consciousness, and so forth. This is like fire: when the fire burns with wood it is called a wood fire, the fire which burns through electricity is called an electric fire, the fire that burns by the gas is called a gas fire, and so forth.

Now, let us be more specific about the creation of blocks in the body. In its normal state, the body has a proportionate rhythm of contraction and expansion just like our breathing, which has its rhythmic movement of arising (inhalation) and falling (exhalation). When the normal rhythm is disturbed due to changes taking place in the world of consciousness, which operates through our senses, there is a shift (a gap or a vaccum) created out of the fact that either the contraction or the expansion loses its momentum. That is to say, the contraction cannot contract in its own rhythm, or the expansion is unable to expand according to its normal rhythm. Then, the energy patterns operating with the consciousness at the moment get buried or locked-in, in that particular gap or vacuum and, therefore, a block is created, which is filled with whatever is appropriate at the moment. Consequently, we discover anger is buried in the jaws, in the ankles, in the lower back and mid-back. Fear is hidden in the knees, in the shoulders, and in the upper chest. Sadness and grief are submersed in the middle of the chest. Anxiety is immersed and locked up in the belly and around the rib cage. Primal pain is buried in the stomach. And so on.

Here it is interesting to mention that in each location of the block there is a story or an incident, in addition to the energy pattern itself. The story or the incident reveals itself to the subject and his/her therapist when such a specific energy pattern is released and becomes dissipated through the therapeutic process. Sometimes this happens to some meditators during a silent meditation, which gives great surprise not only to the meditator, but also to all those present in the meditation session. It is a surprise because one never thinks that there is such a thing as anger or fear or grief buried in such a particular part of the body. Certainly, in our journey through the consciousness process we will encounter many surprises or things that we never anticipate. That is why we call it the journey of discovery.

Up until this point, I hope I have made it clear how the body and mind (the mental and physical phenomena) are conditioned by consciousness. Please bear in mind that this process occurs in the course of your everyday living. To see this fact for yourself, you only need to pay attention and observe what actually happens to your physical body and mental realm when you experience a certain feeling or emotion in your life. Also, remember that whenever a feeling, an emotion, or a state of mind is experienced, a certain consciousness is present, as it is the main stream of natural flow. In this respect, this consciousness is like a river, which runs on and on continuously; while the feeling, the emotion, and the states of mind are equal to the things carried along by the water in the river.

Continuing along here (you may refer back to the formula of the law of dependent origination, above, at pp. 101-102), next is the question of how the body and mind condition the sense faculties. We are equipped with six senses, five physical and one mental, which enable us to communicate and get in touch with both the internal world and the external world. Through the eyes, we can see form or shape and visual objects. Through the ears, we can hear sounds and all audible vibrations. Through the nose, we can smell all the olfactory things. Through the tongue, we can taste all kinds of flavors, including the flavor of spiritual energy (delicious!). Through the body or sense of touch, we can experience all the tangible objects and sensations. Through the mind or inner sense, we come into contact with thoughts, ideas, concepts, fantasies, dreams, daydreaming, and all the mental and spiritual phenomena.

All the qualities of the sense-faculties depend on the conditions of the body and mind. If the body and mind are in good, clear, and clean states, the senses become sharp, smooth, and shining, able to process all information accurately. On the contrary, in case of the body and mind existing and functioning in poor or even destructive states, the senses will possess such poor conditions that they are unable to give us accurate reports. In this way, realities and facts may be distorted; and then we see the real as unreal, the unreal as real, the true as false, and the false as true, and so forth.

This is temporary and momentary, of course, because all things exist momentarily. In order to make real changes to our sense faculties, or at least to improve them, we must go to the root, which is to develop our body and mind by training, changing, and transforming them. When the body and mind are properly trained and increasingly developed, there will be no problem about the qualities of the senses; for they will get better, smoother, and more shining in accordance with the present states of the body and mind. With regard to those working on their particular sense-organs, for instance, improving eye sight by practicing certain selected exercises or learning to listen deeply according to the definitive method of listening, they are in fact training their bodies and developing their minds indirectly. Bear in mind that consciousness is present in all sense-contacts without exception, particularly when they are in their actual operation. The training and the improvement of any physical senses necessarily include the development and the betterment of the related consciousness. Thus by the body and mind are conditioned the six senses and vice versa.

Here we come to the inter-relationships between the six senses and contact. Once again, the quality of contact through the senses, whether good or bad, pleasant or unpleasant, agreeable or disagreeable, depends on the properties of the senses. Through clear, unclouded, and penetrative eyes, for instance, contact with the visual objects is excellent and therefore, we are able to have an impeccable, flawless seeing as well as perfect, faultless vision. The same can be applied to other senses such as hearing, knowing or sensing, smelling, tasting, and touching. With respect to touching, many of us make use of this sense contact as an effective healing technique called "loving touch or therapeutic touch." Such capacity of successful healing comes about not only because of the high, free energy and universal life force flowing through the hands unimpeded, but because the body sense-faculty incorporating with the inner (mind) sense provides an excellent channel for such powerful flow. This is one of the greatest contacts we can ever experience through our sense modalities. Furthermore, we can imagine the possibility of other powerful human capacities such as clairvoyance, psychic power, and the ability to recall one's past life. All these phenomena are produced through our sense-contacts; although some individuals might be gifted to possess such special power and to express it almost naturally.

Nevertheless, what can actually be taken into account here is the innate property of the sense-faculty, whether systematically developed in this lifetime, or present with certain individuals from the moment of conception onward. With respect to the inner (mind) sense-contact, very often the experience is not obvious or is perhaps even unconscious to the majority of us. An example is called for here. When two people meet, the psyche (a deeper mind which covers its spiritual, emotional, and motivational aspects) of one person has its effect upon the other. This includes all its desires, fantasies, feelings and emotions, its consciousness and unconsciousness; although much of what happens in the psyche is neither stated nor directly expressed. For at such a meeting the totality of the two psyches encounters each other — conscious and unconscious, spoken and unspoken — and all have their effect upon the other. This is what the Buddha calls "contact through the inner (mind) sense-modality," which takes place in the internal worlds of the two persons. This fact can be observed time and again because the inter-exchange between two individuals at the level of energies or energy patterns operates naturally through the network of inter-connectedness, even if this contact-flow or inner (mind) exchange is not known precisely by the individuals concerned.

From the sense-contact, there arises a sensation or a feeling of the quality of any experience, an evaluating our experience, in which the feeling or sensation could be pleasurable, unpleasurable or painful, or neither agreeable nor disagreeable, or neutral. Obviously there will be no sensation or feeling if there is no sense-contact; and the contact is only possible if the sense-faculty is alive and functional. In case of paralysis or mental numbness, there is no contact because the body sense-faculty and the mental sense are permanently or temporarily dead and non-functioning, as the case may be. For the sense-contact to come into operation all three factors must be present: a sense-faculty (any one of the six senses), a corresponding object, and a consciousness. If any one of those three requisites is absent, then there is no contact in this context, in our discussion here.

Up to this point, we see clearly that any kind of sensation or feeling is determined by the conditions of the sense-contact at the moment when those three factors gather together. For example, an undesirable object enters the visual field of the eye-faculty and seeing arises, which produces an unpleasant or even painful feeling. On the contrary, contact with a desirable thing gives rise to a pleasant and agreeable feeling. Regarding the inner sense or the mind-faculty, the objects corresponding to this comprehensive sense are memories, ideas, thoughts, fantasies, dreams, or, in short, energy patterns. Certainly, each mental content or the definitive energy pattern of consciousness will determine the category of feeling when it enters the mental field and therefore, takes charge of the mental realm at the moment. Many times we are not aware of the actual contact in the world of the mind or at the psychic center, but we simply experience various feelings ranging from good to bad, from positive to negative, from destructive to constructive, from the emotional level to the psychological level, and from the mental plane to the spiritual field. At this point, some of you might raise the question of why sometimes you just feel sad or fearful with no reason and without any awareness of any sense-contacts, whether physical or mental. The answer is simple. In the internal world of the human mental realm, including our psychological and spiritual realities, there is a constant movement or incessant flow, which indicates an endless contact. Such a contact is largely unconscious to us since the conscious mind exists and operates only in a very small, limited, known world in comparison with the unconscious, our largest realm of existence. Hence, whenever there is a contact, there arises a feeling, and any categories of feeling (*vedanā*, this being an evaluation of the experience) depend on the quality of the sense contact. This is a natural law of our interdependent existence.

Here is the practice of awareness regarding sensation or feeling: whatever sensation or feeling is present just experience it *without attachment*. Then it does not lead to suffering. In this respect, there is no limit or restriction concerning our experience of the emotion, feeling, or sensation; the only thing to do is to bring attention to bear on it with a complete freedom from attachment. After a while, all the sensations, feelings, and emotions will become peaceful just like the flame of the lamp when the oil and the oil burner have been consumed. Hence our safeguard! In this connection, the Buddha said: "Seeing things as they are, without the deluded views of consciousness, or ignorance, constitutes both the extinction of greed or thirst and the cessation of suffering (dukkha). The person endowed with such noble, absolute wisdom, the insight-born knowledge of the total extinction of dukkha, realizes the Truth (in this special, specific sense) and achieves full liberation. His freedom founded in the Truth is indestructible and immeasurable."

We may now come to the issue of the interdependence between feeling and craving or thirst. Feeling good about something or somebody, one craves for it or for that person. The wanting or desire arises to drive one into taking an appropriate action since the craving is the drive to get. In contrast, a bad or negative feeling gives rise to the opposite desire, that is, the drive to run away or to move against, depending on the particular case. Furthermore, the neutral feeling (neither agreeable nor disagreeable) will cause another kind of desire or thirst to come into operation, that is, the craving for non-becoming. In each of these cases, there is no need for an action to be taken; and therefore one just lets it be, or simply lets it pass by. It is an attitude of non-doing. If one does some things, one inevitably becomes somebody or something, because the doing implies an identification, which creates a doer, and as a result, the doer becomes somebody according to the function carried out for a definite period of time. Here we've got a notion of what we psychologically call "ego," the functioning entity (or to put it in an objective expression: the process of functioning), which constantly becomes something or somebody so long as the function is in operation.

There are in general here three categories of craving: the craving and thirst for sensual pleasures; the craving and thirst for becoming; and the thirst and craving for non-becoming or non-existing. All these cravings are conditioned by feelings/sensations as previously described. In turn they energize and heighten those sensations and feelings that initiate them. This is interdependence. Here is a short formula: Depending on A, B arises; when B ceases, A also comes to a stop. Or when B is affected, A is so also.

Now, craving instigates clinging or attachment. The more one craves, the deeper and stronger one becomes attached to the object of craving. This is similar to fire and fuel. The burning will go on so long as there is fuel to feed the fire. In this case, the fuel is like the craving and the fire is equal to attachment; or, in completing this loop, the fire represents the craving and the fuel symbolizes the attachment. As long as the craving takes charge of the life situation, there will always be an attachment to bolster it in one form or another.

Attachment may be classified into four types: attachment to the pleasures of the senses, attachment to opinions and views, attachment to rites and rituals for self-transformation, and attachment to the notion of self as a separate reality. (This reflects our human primary division into self and otherness, with each retaining its separate, unique reality). The first category is quite obvious to everyone, and there is no need for an explanation. As for the second type of attachment, it also includes knowledge, information, ideology, insights or visions, and so forth. This is also within the grasp of everyone, because we all cling to our views and opinions and all the rest of that category. As a result of this clinging, we become narrow-minded and self-restricted, unable to open up to compromise or to make any concessions, or even to examine those ideas and points of view that are held by the others.

Certainly, underlying attachment is fear, particularly the fear of not getting what we want or of losing that which we are attached to. The obvious example is the fear of death, which results from our clinging to existence. Furthermore, ignorance (in the sense of lacking inner knowing with regard to what is real or unreal) becomes a principal cause of attachment and fear. Once the clear light of wisdom and impeccable awareness replaces this ignorance, there will be no need for attachment and, therefore, no fear will creep in. But so long as there is attachment, there will be fear or anxiety (a milder form of fear); and when fear enters our conscious experience, it implies the operation of attachment and/or ignorance underneath, although it might be unconscious or unknown to us most of the time. For this reason, we could easily deceive ourselves or become beguiled by our life experiences. The only way to be really safe and psychologically secure is to maintain vital awareness, wakefulness, and clarity of consciousness constantly, so that we will be able to recognize the network of this subtle, deeply seated ignorance and attachment before they can take grip on us.

As the chain of our interdependence goes on, we have the ongoing process of becoming; this is due to the active presence of attachment, which itself resulted from craving or thirst. What is actually meant here is that we create a sense of "I" which makes us experience ourselves as who we are, when attachment is in charge of our life manifestations. Not only does the sense of "I" or "I am ..." come into our conscious mind, but the notion of many "I"s or "I am ..."s looms up in the conscious process, which make us become infinite selves in our day-to-day functioning: I am a father, I am a mother, I am a secretary, I am a teacher, I am a meditator, I am a spiritual person, I am a skeptic, I am a believer, I am this or that. This goes on and on infinitely so long as the process of becoming continues to operate and we carry on living our lives on this planet, earth. Nevertheless, there will be some moments of having no sense of "I" or "I am ..." when we reach the nirvanic state in which the "I" gets blown away with no trace, since in accord with the ultimate truth, there is no "I" or "I am ..." in the first place.

The process of becoming or the sense of "I" and "I am ..." operates in three planes of existence. They are the plane of sensuality and sexuality, the plane of form (the first four stages of *jhāna* or meditative absorption), and the plane of the formless (the higher, second four stages of *jhāna*). It is quite apparent that in our experience of pleasures or of displeasures through the senses, the sensation of "I" or the feeling of "I am ..." becomes predominant, giving us an articulate experience of who we are and consequently being able to make choices in life. This plane of sensuality and sexuality is obviously our human world in which we live and enjoy the pleasures of the senses, or suffer the lack of them or their displeasures when our desire for them cannot be fulfilled. At this point, if you wish to ask a question, "Who is it that suffers?" you will surely get a very distinct, basic answer; "it is the I that suffers." For this reason, we say "I am suffering;" or simply "I suffer." So the sense of "I" as the choice-maker becomes here, specifically, a sufferer. The same may be applied to our desirable, positive experience of life. Without this feeling of "I," who is it, then, going to suffer or to enjoy a sense-experience? There is none. Only an experience exists with no experiencer to be found. To be more precise we may say there is only an *experiencing*.

When we transcend the pleasures of our physical senses, we enter the higher world of experience through meditation or other practices of spiritual discipline. In this plane of life, we talk about joy, ecstasy, inner peace, tranquillity, harmony or oneness with the universe, beauty, light, colours, et cetera; or in one comprehensive expression, a *peak* experience. In this connection, in the Buddhist texts we have found the following descriptions: "Aloof from sense-desires, aloof from unwholesome thoughts, one attains to the first *jhāna*, which is born of quietude, stillness, and non-attachment, and which has innerthinking,[3] reflection/investigation, joy, and bliss."

The formula describing the second *jhāna* is: "By the suppression or transcendence of reasoning and reflection, one attains to the second *jhāna* which is inner serenity, which is unification of consciousness, and which has greater joy and fuller bliss."

As for the third *jhāna*, the formula or description reads as follows: "By detachment also from joy, one dwells in equanimity (a sense of balance or equilibrium), mindful and aware. One enjoys happiness in (subtle) body, and attains to the third *jhāna* which the noble ones call dwelling in equanimity, mindfulness, and bliss."

The passage that describes the fourth *jhāna* is as follows: "By the abandonment of happiness and suffering, by the disappearance already of joy and sorrow, one attains to the fourth meditative absorption, which is neither happiness nor suffering." (It is an altered state of consciousness that has a complete equanimity with pure mindfulness.) When we develop ourselves and evolve further, we reach the other four planes of the formless worlds. Here Buddhists maintain that there are realms of existence where consciousness alone exists without form or matter. For in the formless plane of existence, matter or physical body doesn't exist. In this connection, Kassapa Thera stated: "Just as it is possible for an iron bar to be suspended in the air because it has been flung there – it remains so long as it retains any unexpended momentum – even so the formless being appears through being flung into that state by powerful mind-force, and there it remains till that momentum is expended. This is a temporary separation of mind and matter, which normally coexist." In this context, the formless plane is divided into four realms, as follows:

1. The sphere of the conception of infinite space
2. The sphere of the conception of infinite consciousness
3. The sphere of the conception of nothingness
4. The sphere of the conception of neither perception/ideation nor non-perception/non-ideation.

---

[3] This term 'innerthinking' derives from the quantum physics terminology of David Bohm, where 'innerthink' is contrasted with 'autothink'; innerthink is thinking done with mindfulness/awareness as an observer observing the thinking.

In all these planes of existence, the sense of "I" still operates as the process of becoming or as the identity that actualizes and recognizes the experience. This sense of "I" that makes me experience myself as who I am, and who makes the choices of either continuing to stay on and/or to move forward or of stopping and coming out of the experience, is called "ego" according to the traditional psychology. This concept of ego is nothing but the process of becoming in the Buddha's teaching on the conditioned genesis (paticcasamuppāda).

Now, being conditioned by and dependent upon attachment, the ego or the process of becoming develops itself further to the point of being born fully into a personality that carries with it all the compulsive patterns of conditioning. Hence we call it birth, the birth of the ego-personality or character. Together with this birth, all the passions, virtues, psychological defects, chief features, and the high, noble ideas, which had already been built in, come into effect fully and are prepared to take charge of an individual's life. For example, the character of *ego-indolence* is born of spiritual inertia or sloth and torpor (as its passion), and similarly for essential action (as its virtue), unconditional love (as its high idea), narcotization (as its psychological defect), and going with the stream or lacking one's own priority (as its chief feature).

Bear in mind that the concept of birth used here in the doctrine of dependent origination simply refers to the actual, full operation of the human ego-personality in the present moment, and does not, by any means, indicate the birth of an individual in this lifetime. From this teaching, we understand that our human personality is unique but not totally fixed since it only operates in the moment and undergoes changing, modifying, and even transforming in the course of living. Nevertheless, the moment continues its existence and becomes many changing moments infinitely; and therefore our ego or character does not cease to function and to dominate our lives until we do something about it. As change or impermanence is one of the innate characteristics of existence, it is always within our power and empowerment to make some changes for the better, not only to our personal selves, but also to many others, to the society and to the world at large. This is in accordance with our psychological reality, which reflects the fact that we all have at our disposal the archetypal energy of *finding the way out* of any problems or challenges.

Hence, our ego is no exception! It can be changed, developed, and transformed into *aware ego* so that each one of us may be able to carry out our functions with full awareness. In this case, the aware ego becomes the *executive* branch of our human personality, which monitors life situations and makes decisions on all matters concerning selves and others, just as the chief executive of the Government performs his or her duties in the nation and in international relations. What will happen after the birth of the ego-personality? It repeats and deepens its patterns in the course of existing and becoming; it eventually becomes destructively insensitive to the inner life and actual living; in short, it becomes entangled in self-forgetfulness in terms of personal growth and transformation. (In our common language, we say that old age and death follow birth with no exception. That is, the endless cycle of birth/life/death and death/birth/life/death continues unless nirvana is reached and all the compulsive conditioning becomes extinguished (or the ego patterns finally cease to be effective, due to a full human development).

During the lifetime between birth and death we encounter pain and pleasure, sorrow and joy, distress and happiness, agony and bliss, et cetera. Once again, bear in mind that all the fleeting pleasures, passing happinesses, transitory joys, and impermanent bliss belong to what the Buddha calls dukkha or suffering in the broad and original sense of the English word suffer (to *allow*). To be able to bring an end to suffering, first we must recognize, understand, and accept it for what it is. Second, we must look into the cause, to find the root, and to transform it completely. Third, we must keep in mind that whatever arises will come to a stop at one point, and that nothing in life and in the world can remain in its own existence forever. Fourth, we must embark upon the genuine path (Insight Meditation, for instance) that leads to the ending of suffering. As we know conceptually, at the end of suffering we will find the eternal enlightened being in whom all the fires that had previously been burning (have now been blown out completely) and are thus permanently extinguished. That which emerges at present is the *ever-new state of being*, total, immeasurable freedom and the infinite spaciousness of consciousness.

For working effectively with the teaching of dependent origination (paticcasamuppāda) both in everyday life and in the formal setting of meditation practice, there are important contexts in which one must establish an impeccable awareness and clear mindfulness. The establishing of this awareness and clarity will enable one to see precisely and to attend immediately to that which arises at the very moment of its arising. Those contexts are *where consciousness brews up the definitive mental and physical phenomena* for containing and carrying out its energy patterns. By so doing, it can manifest fully through the six sense-bases *and at each point of contact*. There are six particular points of contact: eyes, ears, nose, tongue, body, and mind — where the six sense-modalities, their corresponding objects, and consciousness are all present so that a sense-contact may operate and give rise to a feeling or a sensation which could trigger a desire or a thirst to come into play.

It is absolutely essential to observe closely how a consciousness forms a certain condition of the body and the mind (psyche). Such formation is prone either to burying an energy pattern pertaining to the consciousness or to carrying out the full-scale manifestation of the consciousness that brews up such an appropriate physical and/or mental phenomenon. This is good both for preventing any blocks to take place and for processing, healing therapeutically, and transforming emotional and psychological wounds. With the presence of awareness, one is able to stop the consciousness from creating any ill health or unhealthy condition to the body and/or the mind. This simply means that one deals directly with the consciousness itself, together with its energy patterns, of course, since they accompany it from the moment the consciousness is brewed up by the physical, verbal, and mental functions (sankhāra.) So, watch your consciousness and its manifestation at any one of the six doors of senses so that you may cut it off (not allowing it to create a block) or transform it in such a way that your body and mind can remain clean, clear, and healthy. This is a very delicate point! So, be fully awake and vitally attentive to it.

As for the point of contact, one must establish simple, clear, and unattached awareness on the faculty of seeing, on the faculty of hearing, on the faculty of smelling, on the faculty of tasting, on the faculty of body impression, and on the inner sense of thinking and direct knowing. To use a metaphor, this energy of awareness is like a *doorkeeper* who checks everyone thoroughly before allowing anybody to enter as well as watches everything with full attention. In this way, security is guaranteed and information is processed correctly. With the eyes we see, with the ears we hear, with the nose we smell, with the tongue we taste, with the body contact we feel, and with the mind-sense we know directly what actually happens at the moment. All the qualities of the experience through the senses can be improved and brought to perfection when awareness is present at each point of contact. Remember that we have six points at which the contact can be made both with the external world and the internal world. For example, color and shape come into contact with the eyes; and then seeing arises. Sound and audible vibration come into contact with the ears; and then hearing arises. Tangible objects come into contact with the body; and then a sensation (feeling) arises. And, at the sixth point, ideas, thoughts, fantasies, and all mental, psychic, and spiritual phenomena come into contact with the mind; and then we know and become fully conscious of them. For such mindful action and clarity of consciousness to be achieved, it is essential that awareness as the door keeper must be precisely positioned at each point of contact wherefrom something always happens and one must be able to know it for what it really is, moment by moment. With this alive awareness present at all six points of contact, one will be able to check any fetters[4] that may bind one to an object or an experience as well as to acknowledge immediately any sensations or feelings at the moment of their arising. In this way one can exercise one's empowerment on making a *real choice* without being influenced either by a fetter or by a sensation/feeling. At this point, instead of allowing the process of conditioned genesis to continue all the way through, it will be cut off; and one is fully in charge of all one's sense-experiences.

We may exercise this capacity to make a real choice at any point in our ongoing process. In terms of the links of dependent origination or conditioned genesis, which are presented as a specific sequence, each of these links is a point at which this choice may be made. Here is the formula defining this sequence:

(1) Conditioned by ignorance, physical, verbal, and mental activities or functions arise.
(2) Conditioned by these activities or concoctions, consciousness arises.
(3) Conditioned by consciousness, physical and mental phenomena arise.
(4) Conditioned by physical and mental phenomena, the six sense bases arise.

---

[4] There are ten fetters that may bind one to what one sees, hears, touches, tastes, smells, or thinks. They are: idea of self, indecisiveness or doubt, attachment to rules and rituals, sensual desires, ill-will or hating feeling, attachment to the world of form (fine arts and/or meditative states), attachment to the formless world (higher meditative achievements), restlessness, pride, and ignorance (absence of awareness).

(5) Conditioned by the six sense bases, contact/impression arises.
(6) Conditioned by contact/impression, sensation/feeling arises.
(7) Conditioned by sensation/feeling, craving/thirst arises.
(8) Conditioned by craving/thirst, attachment arises.
(9) Conditioned by attachment, creation & becoming arises.
(10) Conditioned by creation & becoming, birth arises.
(11) Conditioned by birth, old age, decay, death, sorrow, lamentation, pain, grief, and despair or tribulation comes into play.

Thus arises the mass of suffering and fleeting pleasure.

This teaching supplies us with an analysis of this long process of the genesis of suffering, and with it, an understanding of the end of suffering, expressed by this complementary formula:

With the cessation of birth — old age, death, sorrow, lamentation, pain, grief, and despair or tribulation cease.
With the cessation of creation & becoming — birth ceases.
With the cessation of attachment — creation & becoming cease.
With the cessation of craving/thirst — attachment ceases.
With the cessation of sensation/feeling — craving/thirst ceases.
With the cessation of contact/impression — sensation/feeling ceases.
With the cessation of the six sense bases — contact/impression ceases.
With the cessation of the physical and mental phenomena (nāma-rūpa) — the six sense bases cease.
With the cessation of consciousness — the physical and mental phenomena (nāma-rūpa) cease.
With the cessation of the activities (physical, verbal, and mental) — consciousness ceases.
With the cessation of ignorance — the physical, verbal, and mental activities cease (to function in the old way of conditioning with contaminations).

Thus ceases the entire process of suffering.

The goal of accomplishing our human liberation from our human character traits and arriving at full enlightenment cannot be reached unless the entire *dark side* of the unconscious is brought into *light* and thereby is totally transformed. Here we have powerful tools to accomplish precisely this goal.[5]

When we take a closer look at those two processes of the conditioned genesis or dependent origination, we see clearly that the process of the arising of the mass of suffering represents **samsara** while the second process that shows us how the entire suffering may come to a complete cessation, is in fact the **nirvanic** process. Therefore, both samsara and nirvana are just the two sides of the same coin: One shows how the relative things operate within the relative truth of samsara, while the other demonstrates the path that leads to the arrival at the absolute truth of nirvana. For this reason, the Zen Buddhists

---

[5] From the author's unpublished manuscript, *A New Vision of Buddhism*.

affirm this paradoxical reality that samsara and nirvana are *identical* since they belong to the same coin and the same ground (the foundation from which spring the two aspects of the truth: *relative and absolute.* (We will discuss this matter later on in this book.)

Let us view another process of the paticcasamuppāda teaching, which shows exactly the same path of samsara, but quite a distinct path to nirvana as follows:

THE TWENTY-FOUR FACTORS OF PATICCASMUPPADA

How to achieve immeasurable freedom while still living under this law of dependent origination

Certainly, the law of dependent origination will go on, no matter what happens, and whether anyone likes it or not, since it is the law. But, if one is wise, one will be able to break its continuity and enforcement. In this connection, one can begin anywhere in this process of conditioned genesis. For example, one may start at the point of contact where the sense modality and its corresponding object meet, which provides the opportunity for consciousness to be present and operate. Or one may commence at the feeling point where a desire or a thirst for something is likely to appear and to team up with attachment and with the becoming process in order to take charge of life. And one may begin with focusing attention on the process of becoming that creates the sense of "I" and allows the ego-personality to come into operation. All these three points are very obvious and each one of us experiences them all the time, whether or not one is aware of the experience that arises from one of those points.

Let us first look into the point of contact. Since there are six points through which one gets in touch with the external world of physical phenomena and also the internal world of ideas, thoughts, dreams, fantasy, and imagination, as well as the psychic and spiritual phenomena, one will have to be well prepared at all times. One never knows in advance which point is going to claim one's attention first. It could be the eye point (seeing), or the ear point (hearing), or the nose point (smelling), or the tongue point (tasting), or the physical body point (sense of touch), or the mind point (contacting the inner world). For this reason, one must be on the alert as if one would have to meet with a challenge such as a thief or a danger that might be coming on to one. Certainly, the external objects corresponding to the internal sense organs can enter any one of the six senses and give rise to impressions, literally at any moment, even in sleep. It's not so easy to be fully conscious of what actually happens at each point of contact, especially when many things appear at two or three points of contact all at the same time, let alone during sleep.

Concerning eye contact, for example, there might be a nice, beautiful, and pleasant visual object that could give one a lovely experience. On the contrary, one might encounter an ugly, threatening, or frightening visual object that could impose a nightmare on one. Similar things could happen to one at other remaining points of contact, because our sense experience can be good or bad, positive or negative, pleasant or painful. It all depends on these three factors: on the conditions of the internal sense organs (healthy or unhealthy, sharp or dull, tranquil or turbulent), on the types of external corresponding objects, and on the energy patterns of the consciousness that is present. One cannot do much to help oneself at the moment of experiencing the contact or impression unless one has been working on oneself regularly and has awareness available at hand. Therefore, absolutely essential is the inner work of improving and developing the senses constantly to be carried on side by side with the work of raising consciousness. The sense organs must be clean, clear, and sharp so that they will be able to perceive things, be they external or internal, without any distortions, and to process all the information accurately. In order to achieve this, it becomes greatly important that *impeccable awareness* must be in full operation at the point of contact, because such awareness has an enormous capacity to select and to feed the correct information into the *aware ego*. Then, it is the aware ego that has the function of making changes to enrich life and to illuminate the world; otherwise there will be no uplifting and forward movement toward the immeasurable freedom and complete enlightenment.

With the presence of awareness at the point of contact at any given moment, one will have a high quality of perception, the quality that helps perception recognize the perceived objects with no error or misprint on the mind. When perception is pure, accurate, and total through the assistance of awareness, one will be certain to receive precise information and an undistorted mental picture for the mind to utilize and dwell on.

In this way, the mind will be safe and can remain clear, firm, and healthful so that it will be capable of handling a sensation and/or a feeling that is bound to arise right after the assemblage, the coming together, of those three factors at the point of contact. The sensation or feeling could be pleasant or unpleasant, agreeable or disagreeable, welcoming or unwelcoming, depending on the quality and characteristic of that which enters the sense modality, including a certain attribute of the energy pattern that dominates the present consciousness. Nevertheless, awareness must be present and take full charge of the whole situation so that no mistake will be made, so that illusion or deception will have no place in the decision-making process; or these will not simply be there to exercise their influence whatsoever. The fact is that when awareness is absent, illusion and deception will be present to run the show in full scale; and the only thing that can stop them is awareness.

Now, with awareness in charge of the sensation or feeling, whatever kind it may be, one will certainly be able to make a real choice since one has a clear space to be because of dis-identifying from the sensation or feeling being experienced at the moment. At this point one is in the position to relate realistically to the sensation or the feeling and therefore is able to prevent desire, thirst, or craving from arising in the sense of influencing or dominating one's choice-making process. In this manner, one can really make a real choice by and for oneself; otherwise the choice will be made by the energy pattern, possibly desire in this case, which is in charge of the life situation at the moment. This is because desire is due to arise immediately after the sensation or feeling according to the law of dependent origination. But when the sensation or feeling is checked by awareness, the aware ego can stop the operation of desire, and for this reason the dependent origination process or the law of conditionality will be cut off. If this is not done, the process will run right through the law of conditionality, that is, attachment and the ego-centric personality will come into operation, strengthening and manipulating the desire, which is extremely difficult to handle.

It has been quite clear that the conditioned genesis process can be stopped by placing awareness and wakefulness at each point of contact. That is, one must learn to be fully attentive and totally vigilant in regard to one's experience through the six senses. With respect to this, there are only three ways whereby one can manifest in life. One way is to conform to the habitual patterns and the establishments widely accepted by most people and society. The second way is to apply awareness constantly and to be fully awake at all times. The third way is to do nothing but become a victim to illusion and pathological indifference. But for enrichment of life and immeasurable freedom, I am certain that all of us will choose the middle way, the path of awareness and insight that is naturally awaiting us to embark upon in our journey through life and through total consciousness.

As for the other two points (the point of feeling or sensation and the point of becoming or the process of the arising of a sense of ego): the method to be used is exactly the same as has been described with regard to finding real solution concerning the point of contact. The only difference will be that it might be harder to start at the point of becoming since the I-consciousness or the sense of "I" that makes up one's ego is rather complicated, and the driving force behind it has already gained tremendous strength and power. Even so, one can still be successful if one is wholeheartedly willing to carry out with total commitment the work of cultivating awareness and developing insight. As is always the case, the real solution lies in making use of insightful, energetic awareness continually and in staying long enough with whatever appears to be a problem so that a crystal-clear insight will arise. With such ongoing insight, the problem will be solved, since the real solution grows out of the unique situation that one is facing, which can be seen into by such an ongoing awareness. And thus, the dependent origination process will be shattered. In this connection, the Buddha admonishes:

> *Be steadily aware and sharply observant as always,*
> *reflecting the world as a fertile void and reviewing it*
> *constantly so that nothing is left unattended.*
> *By so doing the real solution is found.*[6]

---

[6] From the author's unpublished English manuscript, *A New Vision of Buddhism*.

=5=

IN SEARCH OF IMMEASURABLE FREEDOM

The Vammika-Sutta, the Buddha's Discourse on the Comparison of an Anthill, is the only sutra, so far as we know, that reveals the meaning of things or teaches the dharma by way of using symbols.[1] Those symbols came through the monk, Kumāra-Kassapa by name, who was by himself practicing the solitary meditation in the forest called andhavana, which literally means "the forest of darkness or the dark forest." This concept itself refers to the dark side of our inner world or psyche since "forest" symbolizes "inner world" and "andha" signifies "dark or blind"; the Buddha himself once used these words "andhako loko" to refers to the dark side or the destructive force of our aggregates of existence and reminded us of looking for the "light" of consciousness.

Before getting into the detailed analysis of the sutra I would like you, my reader, to read the full text of what the monk Kumāra-Kassapa had heard from a certain deva (angel, a divine, radiant being) and of the significant clarification that the Buddha made in response to Kumāra-Kassapa's questions. The sutra reads as follows:

"At one time the Buddha was staying at the Jetavana Monastery, located in the City of Sāvatthī, and at that same time the monk Kumāra-Kassapa was dwelling in the Andhavana forest. By that time at night a certain deva illuminating the forest by his own beaming light approached him, and after exchanging greetings with him, stood right there in a proper place. Then he said to the monk thus: Oh, monk! There is an anthill that sends out smoke at night time and becomes flames during the day. A Brahmin tells a seeker after truth, saying, "Oh, Sumedha (intelligent one), bring the tool and dig this anthill!"

So, Sumedha obeys him, and while digging finds a bolt or iron bar, saying, "Oh! It is a bolt, sir!"

In response the Brahmin says, "Take it out (let it be), and go on digging, bringing your tool."

Sumedha carried on digging and finds a frog, and then says, "Oh! It is a frog, sir!"

The Brahmin gives him the same advice by saying, "Take it out (let it be), carry on digging, bringing your tool."

Sumedha carries on digging with his tool and finds a forked road, saying, "Oh! It's the forked road, sir!"

---

[1] The Vammika-Sutta is Sutta/Discourse 23 in the Majjhima-Nikāya (M.i.142-145).

The Brahmin responds exactly the same way with the exact same advice, saying, "Take it out (just let it be!) Carry on digging, bringing your tool."

Therefore, Sumedha keeps on digging and then finds a strainer, saying, "Oh! It's a strainer, sir!"

The Brahmin advises him to throw away the strainer and to carry on the digging work, which Sumedha takes to heart and carries on doing his job, and then finds a turtle, saying, "Oh, It's a turtle, sir!"

Upon receiving the same advice from the Brahmin Sumedha carries on digging with his tool and finds a slaughterhouse, saying, "Oh! It's a slaughterhouse, sir!"

The Brahmin tells him to go on digging, which he does with diligence and then finds a lump of meat, saying, "Oh! It's a lump of meat, sir!"

The Brahmin responds, saying, "Throw it away! Carry on digging, bringing your tool!"

So, Sumedha digs on and finds a serpent (cobra), saying, "Oh! It's a serpent, sir!"

Now, the Brahmin responds, saying "Let the serpent be where he is! Do not kill him! Pay respect to him!"

After that, the deva (shining being from heaven) tells the monk Kumāra-Kassapa what he should do, saying "Monk, now you must go to the Buddha and asks him to clarify all of these questions, since in this world and in the whole universe I do not see anyone else, be they brahmas, devas, recluses, or other human masters, who is better, wiser, and more capable of expounding all these matters concerned than he. Whatever he says, you must take it to your heart and hold it firmly in your mind." Having said so, the deva vanishes then and there.

Then, as the night has passed and the dawn of the day arises the monk Kumāra-Kassapa was heading toward where the Buddha was staying (the Jetavana Monastery). Upon his arrival, he approached the Great Master without delay, and after having exchanged the appropriate greetings, he seated himself at the proper place and then related his story to him, mentioning all of the things that had happened to him during his night-time meditation. (There is no need to repeat that entire sequence here, of course; the reader may review it, above.)

After that, the monk Kumāra-Kassapa asked the Buddha to elucidate those symbols, such as the anthill, the smoking at night, the burning in flames by day, the Brahmin, the intelligent one, the tool, the bolt (iron bar), the frog, the forked road, the strainer, the turtle, the slaughterhouse, the lump of meat, and the serpent. The Buddha then responded by illuminating and simplifying those significant symbols as follows:

"Kumāra-Kassapa, what is meant by the anthill is the physical body composed of the four Great Elements, nurtured by the mother, and nourished by food and milk, which is breakable, impermanent, and subject to change.

"The significance of the smoking at night is that people carry out their activities during the day and then at night become preoccupied (by what they have done, what has been left to do, how they should have done things differently, and the things to be done in the near future, et cetera.

"Burning in flames during the day means people perform their functions, activities, and businesses through action, speech, (and thought) after having planned them out during the night.

"The Brahmin represents the Tathāgata (another title of the Buddha, meaning the One who has gone thus), the Fully Enlightened One.

"Sumedha (the intelligent one) refers to the monk (or any person) who is still in the process of learning and attempting to accomplish his ultimate goal of the experiential, complete realization of Nirvana.

"The tool refers to perfect, noble wisdom, while the act of digging implies putting energy into the practice or persevering with ongoing attempts to work through the process in order to achieve the set goal.

"The iron bar or bolt represents ignorance in the sense of not fully realizing the four Noble Truths. For that matter, it is absolutely essential to remove ignorance by making use of this tool of perfect, insightful wisdom.

"The frog symbolizes anger and resentment, which must be transformed through the sharp and highly effective tool of the wisdom just mentioned.

"The forked road symbolizes doubt and indecisiveness, which only perfect wisdom can overcome by uprooting fully.

"The strainer represents the five spiritual obstacles or hindrances, namely, sensual desire, destructive thought, revenge or hate, sloth and torpor, restlessness, and indecisiveness or skeptical doubt that delays the proper pace of the meditative progress. Only the tool of impeccable awareness and perfect wisdom can remove them utterly.

"The symbolic turtle refers to attachment to the five aggregates of existence, namely, attachment to the physical body, attachment to feelings and sensations, attachment to perceptions, attachment to the mental formations, and attachment to consciousness. Make use of these tools so that all kinds of attachment will be transcended and transmuted.

"The symbolic slaughterhouse signifies the five sensual objects, namely, the visual objects entering the eye-consciousness, which are desirable, agreeable, likeable, appealing to the mind, attractive, lust-stirring, and linked with sexual desire, the sounds entering the ear-consciousness, which are desirable and so on (the rest is the same as the visual objects), the different kinds of smell entering the nose-consciousness, which are desirable et cetera, the variety of flavor enter the tongue-consciousness, which is desirable et cetera, all forms of bodily contact entering the body-consciousness, which are desirable, agreeable, likeable, appealing to the mind, attractive, lust-stirring, and linked with sexual desire. Awareness and insightful wisdom are the tools for nailing them down, keeping them under spontaneous control, and transforming them.

"The symbolic lump of meat refers to the lustful desire, which can be dealt with effectively by the use of the tools mentioned here.

"Finally, the symbolic serpent (nāga in Pali) represents the enlightened being, who is completely free from all kinds of contaminations and therefore has a completely pure and spotlessly clean psyche. So, let the nāga be. Do not kill him. Pay respect to him.

"After the Buddha has concluded his clarification, the monk Kumāra-Kassapa's mind is totally delighted, deeply appreciated, and his heart is filled with joy."

The author's commentaries

Now let me elaborate those meanings expounded by the Buddha in order that some more light may shine forth within our human consciousness.

The anthill of our human psychophysical dystems

Certainly, it is not only the physical body that can break up, is transitory by its nature, and goes on changing constantly under the natural law of impermanence and temporary existence of all things. The energetic, subtle body, psyche, and all the psychological and mental realities within us also all fall operate as described by this same law. They are all impermanent, in conflict with one another, and eventually end up in death. In addition, it is because of being driven by the force of conflict that all of the bodily components and mental, psychological, and spiritual conditioned states make constant attempts to keep their systems function in harmony as much as possible. If such efforts fail, there would be a breakdown, a neurological illness, psychotics, and schizophrenia, which we often find in our fellow human beings. Please contemplate for a moment the reality and characteristics of an anthill to see how fragile and easily exposed to breakability it is. (The author would like to draw his reader's attention to Chapter 2, *The Notion of Man and His Component Parts*, starting at page 17, above, for detailed studies of the five aggregates.)

Tathāgata

It is interesting to note that the Buddha refers to himself as a Tathāgata quite often, particularly in delivering his discourses on the Dharma, while in speaking to his monks and nuns about the disciplinary rules he uses the authoritarian word "I." So, the Tathāgata has become a familiar name or title bestowed upon him not only by his followers and those admiring and respecting him, but by the Buddha himself. This is because, as I understand it, he does not want to become egocentric in his functioning since the concept of "I" represents an ego that carries out the executive function in the ordinary persons as most of us are. The Buddha is the Extraordinary, Fully Enlightened Human Being, who always centers his gravity in the Self, if I may use this modern psychological terminology here, and therefore he uses an objective language to keep his executive function clear of contaminating his mind. In this connection, some of us might raise a question as to what kind of the executive function he uses in his daily manifestation and in functioning as a master. The simple, but not very easy answer is: He carries out his activities and his mission using the *transcendental function*, which stands above the law of cause and effect or the law of karma. This simply means that the Buddha does not expect anything in return from his actions, his speeches, and his services rendered to humanity since all his activities are done out of compassion and with perfect wisdom, which fits in with the fourth category of karma (the karma that is neither black nor white with the neither black nor white result; see details in the chapter on karma and rebirth).

As the Buddha realizes and teaches the doctrine of suchness (tathatā) in which everything is such and such, arises and passes away with such and such conditions, et cetera. There is nothing existing independently of its own, everything exists in relation to such and such things and so forth. Therefore, suchness becomes something-ness that cannot be explained in words of any languages adequately. For this reason, the word "Tathāgata" (the One who has reached or arrived at suchness) is employed to represent the Buddha since he himself cannot really be described in words, but can only be seen through his being and manifesting at the moment. In other words, the Buddha is perceived as a perfect human structure through which all the pure, wise, enlightened, and compassionate energy systems come to operate for the great benefit, happiness, peace, and the complete release from suffering of all sentient beings without discrimination.

Let us learn from his own words recorded in the Buddhist Canon, in Itivuttaka, 25/314:

"Monks, the world[2] that the Tathāgata fully comprehended, he has utterly left behind; the cause giving rise to the world that the Tathāgata fully comprehended, he has eradicated completely; the cessation of the world that the Tathāgata fully comprehended, he has made totally clear to himself; and the practice leading to the cessation of the world that the Tathāgata fully comprehended, he has brought to full cultivation. Whatever seen, heard, sensed, sought for, contemplated on, discerned, and comprehended by humans, devas, brahmas, recluses, and brahmins, all that the Tathāgata himself has fully and experientially fully comprehended. Therefore, he earns the title Tathāgata.

"Monks, the Tathāgata reached total enlightenment that particular night, entered the parinibbāna without any elements remaining (final passing away)

---

[2] This terminology ("the world") often used by the Buddha includes specifically the aggregates of human existence.

that night, all the things that the Tathāgata has said, spoken about, and preached during those nights (meaning, from the time of his full enlightenment to the time of his final passing away) are as such and such, are not other than such and such. Therefore, he earns the title of Tathāgata.

Monks, whatever is uttered by the Tathāgata, all that he does and acts on; whatever he has put in action, all that he speaks out. It is because he speaks as he does, and does as he speaks. For this reason, he earns the title Tathāgata.

Monks, the Tathāgata is the Greatest One (with all good things — gunadharma) and no one can exceed him (in terms of the gunadharma). He directly knows things as they truly are, and is the Most Powerful One (with the gunadharma). For this reason, he earns the title Tathāgata.

Sumedha

The person who carries out the work of digging is called Sumedha, which is not a personal name, but a title. Sumedha means the intelligent one. According to Buddhism, this kind of person refers to the noble ones (sekha ariya-puggala) who have achieved the earlier stages of enlightenment: They are the stream-enterer (sotāpanna), the once-returner (sakadāgāmi), the non-returner (anāgāmi), and the noble one who has just attained the arahatta-magga (the path to arahatship or full enlightenment), and who, not long after that will surely accomplish the final stage of enlightenment. By sekha we mean the noble person who is still in the process of learning or who has some more work to do for completing the full enlightenment or arahatship. The word sekha derives from the root sikha, signifying *seeking, training, or educating*, in the sense of bringing out that which is within, and technically refers to undergoing the training in natural moral discipline (sīla-sikkhā), the training in meditation (samādhi-sikkhā), and the training in perfect wisdom (paññā-sikkhā). Actually, the noble sekha is unquestionably assured that arahatship is within his or her reach so that he or she may cross his or her fingers.

The tool used in digging

According to the sutra, the Buddha simply points to the noble wisdom as the tool for digging, which actually specifies the kind of wisdom that leads to enlightenment technically known as ariya paññā or noble, enlightened wisdom. Although the Buddha did not mention awareness or mindfulness (sati), nonetheless this essentially required factor of the path is inseparable from wisdom, that is to say, wherever wisdom is found, awareness or mindfulness is also there. The two indispensable factors work hand in hand and co-exist at all times, whether before or after the attainment of full enlightenment.

Let us look here into some more details of how wisdom works and how it is cultivated: First of all, let me give you a definition of wisdom. It has two meanings: One is a deep understanding and a total seeing of things as they are, and not as we think, suppose, or imagine they are. The second meaning refers to the capacity to be what we know, and the ability to translate idea and/or knowledge into action. Although the former sounds rather intellectual, it is not an intellectualization, since wisdom springs from a profound vision and a penetrating insight into what *is*, while intellect is merely a mental exercise of knowing in accordance with one's intellectual training and systematic thinking or education. In wisdom there is power of transcending and liberating whatever it is that obstructs or hinders the way and/or the natural, free flow of life. That is to say, with possession of authentic wisdom, one naturally becomes enlightened in the sense of throwing light upon things and eliminating darkness. In this connection, the enlightened person is filled with the unsurpassed light of wisdom and shines forth with it luminously, and also transforms all the dark forces so as to achieve genuine wholeness. In the unified whole both our light side and transformed dark side become so completely integrated that there is no room for non-equilibrium or lack of balance. In such wholeness of being and becoming our executive function, *aware ego*, can perform its duties perfectly well, including managing our inner and outer lives in full capacity so that we will be able to act, speak, and think in accordance with the guidance of inner knowing or wisdom. In this way, "we are a king outside and are a sage inside."[3]

There are three principal ways whereby wisdom arises. First is by way of *listening*, meaning that one listens attentively and silently to anything and everything that enters one's ear-modality or ear consciousness. For example, Siddhartha listens to the sound of the river and obtains very useful information and clear insight into the unexpected. One may listen to the *still* voice within and find an answer or solution to the problem that concerns one, or one discovers a direction, a way forward, or a way out, if lost inwardly. The point is that when one listens, one *hears*. Without proper listening or not wanting to hear, there is no hearing. Hearing is a consciousness arising through sense contact between ear modality and sound, voice, or vibration, and at that moment, consciousness is present. That is why wisdom, insight, illumination of knowledge, or a piece of helpful information can spring up and becomes relevant to one.

The second way or means whereby wisdom can be obtained is *thinking with the heart* or *objective thinking*. This includes the scientific way of obtaining information or assumptions for formulating a theory or finding a solution to, and a clarification of the obscuration. In this way of thinking, one allows a subject or an issue to stay on the mind as long as it takes while one is contemplating silently and observing thoroughly everything that is going on without adding any opinion or making any comments. After a while, a flash of insight or the light of wisdom arises just like the dawn of a new day disperses darkness and gives light to the world simultaneously. As each day is new, so is life. It becomes new, is renewed every moment so that one can be fresh, and refresh oneself as life continues to flow and the moments of living pass from one to the next without end.

The third and most significant way of gaining wisdom is through *insight meditation* or vipassanā practice. This practice is based on making perpetual use of *non-verbal, non-judgmental, and non-attached awareness* of what is

---

[3] Compare this with a teaching from Daoism: "Also in the *Zhuangzi* is a teaching about being inwardly a sage, outwardly a king, nei sheng wai wang." The Chinese characters of nèi shèng wài wáng are given in a note: 內聖 外王. From Mitchell Ginsberg, *Calm, Clear, and Loving* (2012), p. 195.

happening or going on at the given moment. In this type of awareness, *disidentification and choicelessness* play the key role in obtaining wisdom and providing space for insight to arise as well as for unsurpassed light of knowing directly and experientially to shine forth. Through insight meditation, flashes of insight and inner knowing emerge to the meditator in two ways: One by way of the constant application of the above-defined awareness and objective observation of all phenomena, be they physical, mental, emotional, psychological, psychical, or spiritual; another through a prolonged period of silence in a deep meditation where words and images no longer exist. Traditionally speaking, when samādhi (symbolic: clear and still water) or stabilized mind becomes firmly established and all conditioned states rest in stillness, insightful wisdom comes into view naturally, just like the rising of the sun giving light and dispersing darkness.

Now, let us talk about the *body and its wisdom*. The term "body" refers to the corporeal nature of a human and the whole material organism in which are composed the four basic elements of earth (extension and solidity), water (cohesiveness), fire (heat and activeness) and wind (motion and vibration) together with the energetic or bio-energy body, including respiration or breath. The energetic body is sometimes referred to as psychic, subtle, or ethereal body, which occupies various energy fields, or stores up emotional and psychic energy patterns accumulated through personal experience of negative, painful feelings and disagreeable/unpleasant sensations.

Before going into the details of the energetic body and its creations, let us look briefly into consciousness as the first and foremost condition for creating the physical and mental phenomena. It is quite obvious that the consciousness that we have in our daily life is made up not only by our personal conditioning, but also by varying influences and archetypal energies. In addition, such archetypal energies prevail in our environment, in the land we walk on, in the groups of people we associate with, in our community, in the society that we belong to, and in the world in which we live. We then manifest such consciousness in all our functions and activities in life, at work, and in all the relationships with ourselves individually and with the rest of the world. This means that we have definitive, predictable patterns of acting, reacting, and responding to life situations, social situations, and world situations. With this heavily conditioned consciousness we are trapped in a very narrow, limited whirlpool of existence, with which we have become rather familiar through personal experience. Trapped and spinning, we become aggressive, punitive, and violent especially toward those living on the other side of the fence. In this way, individual defense mechanisms get stronger and more deeply rooted in our psychological reality, calling for territorial defense systems to be built up more and more so that our security can be guaranteed. The longer we live under the dictates of this kind of consciousness, the more fears and suspicions dominate our lives; and as a result, we cling even more tightly to our superficial existence.

With this consciousness, we create a definite condition of our body and mind befitting for containing and accommodating such consciousness. To put it in another way, whatever consciousness we have at a certain moment will drive us into automatic modulations or transformations so that a certain form of our physical body and mental state suitable for the manifestation of the consciousness will be created.

For example: When one is confronting fear, the physical body gets contracted and the mind becomes rigid, terrified, or even paralyzed; and then it projects the idea that all sorts of imagined bad things might happen. On experiencing a pain, whether physical, emotional, or psychological, the body tenses up and the mind screams and becomes agonized. In this context, we observe the varieties of body language, definitive bodily postures, and distorted physical structures, manifested in individuals as the consequence of the presence, or the invasion, of a certain type of consciousness with its energy patterns. From this, we can understand how blocks or blockages are created in our psychophysical systems. These systems have a natural rhythm, which the physical body loses due to the arising of a new consciousness. (When talking about consciousness, we also include the energy patterns pertaining to it, for without the presence of each such energy pattern there can be no consciousness). A new inner form of the body is made up in order to contain such a new consciousness with a specific energy pattern operating with it at that particular moment. Not only that, the mind or rather mental properties such as feeling, perception, intention, impression, and attention are also formed in such a way that they become appropriate partners and coordinators of the consciousness.

In its normal state, the body has a proportionate rhythm of contraction and expansion just like our breathing, which has its rhythmic movement of arising (inhalation) and falling (exhalation). When the normal rhythm is disturbed due to the changes taking place in the world of consciousness, which operates through our senses, there is a gap created out of the fact that either the contraction or the expansion loses its momentum. That is to say, the contraction cannot contract in its own rhythm, or the expansion is unable to expand according to its normal rhythm. Then, energy patterns operating with the consciousness at the moment, whether they are sensations or feelings (negative ones), get buried or locked-in, in that particular gap or vacuum and, therefore, a block is created. Nature, which does not want to have a vacuum left empty, fills it with whatever is appropriate at the moment. Consequently, we discover that anger is buried in the jaws, in the ankles, in the lower back and mid-back. Fear is hidden in the knees, in the shoulders, and in the upper chest. Sadness and grief are submersed in the middle of the chest. Anxiety is immersed and locked up in the belly and around the rib cage. The primal pain is buried in the stomach, and so on.

Here it is interesting to mention that in each location of the blockage there is a story or information together with an incident linked to it, in addition to the energy pattern itself. The story or the incident reveals itself to the subject and his/her therapist when such a specific energy pattern is released and becomes dissipated through the therapeutic process. Sometimes this happens to some meditators during a silent meditation, which gives a great surprise not only to the meditator, but also to all those present in the meditation session. It is a surprise because one never thinks that there is such a thing as anger or fear or grief buried in such a particular part of the body. Certainly, in our journey through the consciousness process we will encounter many surprises or things that we never anticipate. That is why we call it "the journey of discovery."

Up till now, I hope I have made it clear how the body or the system of corporeal nature and bio-energy is conditioned by consciousness. Please bear in mind that this process occurs in the course of your everyday living. To see this fact for yourself, you only need to pay attention and observe what actually happens to your physical body and mental realm when you experience a certain feeling or emotion in your life. Also, remember that whenever a feeling, an emotion, or a state of mind is experienced, a certain consciousness is present, as it is the main stream of natural flow. In this respect, this consciousness is like a river, which runs on and on continuously; while the feeling, the emotion, and the states of mind are equal to the things carried along by the water in the river.

Although the body is primarily conditioned and greatly influenced by consciousness, it has its unique way of giving a hint or an implication to the Aware Ego, particularly when it wants, to a great extent, that the block or the locked-in energy be removed so that there will be no more pain or no development of a life-threatening illness. The most general implication or insinuation is *pain*, through which the body tries to let the individual know that there is something wrong in the part of the body that is suffering the pain. Being an energy pattern itself, pain has helpful information, as all energy patterns have, for that matter, so as to urge the individual to take positive action in order for the unhealthy buried energy to be released and set free. But we in general do not see it as the way the bodily pain is attempting to convey to us such useful information. Instead, we try to eliminate the pain by all possible techniques available to us at present. *We do not understand that the removal of pain without liberating or transforming the energy underneath it is not a permanent cure or total healing, but only a temporary relief.* Usually the energy underneath the pain is an emotional conditioning unless it's purely a physical injury or merely a physical tension that gives rise to pain. In order to know this for certain, *awareness* plays an essential role since awareness has a function of feeding information into an *aware ego*. With the aware ego present and taking charge of the life situation the *real* solution to any troubles or challenges will be found. This is because each type of energy or energy pattern has information and is always willing to share it with the aware ego (the individual with awareness).

Another way the body tries to communicate to us is what is technically known as "body language." Realistically speaking, it is the energy that moves and shapes up the body; for example, when one loses right posture (erect, upright, and harmoniously aligned position) the body will have to find a compensation by holding it in a crooked, out-of-balance position, which develops with the passage of time some form of pain or acute tension. The manner of one's walking, the way one stands and holds oneself publicly or in private indicates the presence and the maneuvering of a certain energy in charge or running the show of one's life at the time. Bear in mind that when talking about energy I also mean a consciousness operating with it, although its movement is invisible on the surface. In fact, consciousness underlies the presence and the operation of all energy patterns that manifest in our lives through the six senses.

In general, the body expresses its wisdom in telling us what is right and what is wrong for it, not in terms of morality of course, but in the sense of health and harmony, or harm and grave poison. For example, when eating, drinking, or taking something into the body, it knows exactly whether or not what we eat, drink, or take in, is right or wrong, harmful or healthy. But most of us, instead of listening to the body, adhere and conform to the mouth or the preference of the mind (meaning, flavor or an agreeable sensation to the palate). Therefore, we don't hear the wisdom of the body and as a result, we end up in poisoning it and/or abusing it seriously sometimes, although without intention, while at the conscious level we mean to enjoy life or take all possible pleasure to its fullness from that which we consume.

If we pay attention to the body, certainly we will be able to know what it wants and what its needs are since the body tries very hard to communicate to us what it actually desires, so that what is lacking and deficient in its corporeal system will be fulfilled and therefore, will enable it to take pleasure in good health and to remain in harmony with all its energy systems. The caring for harmonious existence and health is undoubtedly the expression of wisdom, whether it comes from the body or from the mind (a mind that is associated with wisdom or a wise consciousness). The reason why the body has wisdom is because the entire body is one of the six sense modalities, such as eye, ear, nose, tongue, and mind; this indicates clearly that the body is a source or starting place from which a consciousness arises. The consciousness that manifests through the sense modality of the body is, in Buddhist terminology, "body consciousness." Likewise, we have the eye consciousness, the ear consciousness, the nose consciousness, the tongue consciousness, and the mind-consciousness (a consciousness arising through the sense modality of mind). Operating with consciousness in the above-described context is wisdom; here the term "consciousness" in the broad, modern use refers to discernment, a form of wisdom.

There is a story of a Buddhist monk in the time of the Buddha, Cakkhupāla by name. It was said that the monk was meditating with the eyes lightly opened for a period of three months without sleep. He took a vow of using only three postures (sitting, walking, and standing) for his austere practice of meditation, and he didn't lie down for those three months. As a result, he went blind and could not see insects, ants, or living beings on the ground where he was doing mindful, walking meditation. Consequently, he stepped over them and hurt or even killed them with no intention to do so. As many monks-friends advised him not to do any walking meditation, he said to them that he would consult his body, and so he did. The message he got from his body was that he could go on doing the walking meditation as he has no intention to harm, kill, or step over the living beings, and that it is perfectly a right action for him. Soon afterwards he attained to full enlightenment.

From this story, we learn that the body wisdom draws a thin, but distinct line between *essence* and superficiality, or between the essential action and the so-called moral action. The morally-oriented mind will be driven forcefully or even painfully by guilt if an immoral action is taken, or it would not be able to take an essential action against the precept laid down by an organized religion. This is because guilt, although a milder form of fear, has a powerful authority over the mind, which very often paralyzes the morally minded person(s).

Regarding *processing*, the body knows so well what to do exactly, how far to go, and how much time to spend on each session of processing. For example, when an individual has made contact with a buried energy pattern within the psychophysical systems, then a kind of expression is taking place, either by way of spontaneous, sudden outburst of sound, noise or physical movement, or by sobbing or crying for a certain period of time. This incident is called "processing," and it will continue until the locked-in energy pattern is discharged, released, and cleaned out properly. In such a situation the body is able to facilitate the work efficiently, provided that the mind does not interfere and the ego stays away from complicating the processing. Sometimes the body wakes the individual up in the middle of the night, if it sees that the processing work needs to be done at a particular time, so it has its own timing, while the conscious mind or ego does not know and therefore, will resist the work programmed by the body. Furthermore, the body understands quite well how to create a dynamic balance between the release of the blocked energy and the production of the new, healthy energy to fill the vacuum, in a way that the release does not overwhelm, exceeding the appropriate proportion of the release of this blocked energy and the production of this new, healthy energy; in this way, the harmony within the various energy systems can prevail.

In this connection, let us keep in mind that, like nature's work in general, the body is very much concerned with maintaining some kind of equilibrium, and it does so by keeping its eye of wisdom on the harmonious flow of different energy systems within its life form or organism. Therefore, we need to open ourselves to the body more energetically in order to be able to approach an illness, or the lack of equilibrium, with a creative attitude and to learn more about healing, health, and integrated wholeness.

Back to the iron bar or bolt

In digging into ourselves and exploring our inner world, according to this process, the first thing Sumedha found is an iron bar or a bolt for locking the gate or door so that no one can enter to discover the things hidden or stored up in the internal, mysterious world of our human psyche. The iron bar represents ignorance, the absence of awareness and the lack of full realization of the Four Noble Truths. These truths are the noble truth of dukkha (suffering, psychological and/or spiritual crises, and the conditioned states of existence), the noble truth of the cause of dukkha, the noble truth of the cessation of dukkha, and the noble truth of the path leading to the cessation of dukkha.[4] In the story told to Kumāra-Kassapa by the deva, the Tathāgata symbolized by the Brahmin told Sumedha, the Intelligent One, to pull out the bolt and unlock it so that he could enter the anthill of our psychophysical world in order to experience directly both the treasures and the frightening, destructive things kept in there.

---

[4] See details of these four truths in the author's book: *A New Vision of Buddhism*, English version, or in its Spanish version: *Una Nueva Visión del Budismo*.

The frog

It's quite amazing that upon entering and looking around with vital attention and alertness, Sumedha discovered the symbolic frog, vibrantly alive and vigilant, looking for a way to act and awaiting the prey of a stimulating (irritating) incident. This frog, according to the Buddha, represents our human anger, resentment, and hate, which is either circulating round and round close to the periphery or lying dormant in the psyche ready to wake up and to emerge. Nonetheless, inside the frog, or its other side, is a treasure of love and transformation. Once the negative side represented by the hot and destructive emotions of anger, resentment, and hate is transmuted, genuine transformation will take place with the flow of love, caring, and kindness.

The forked road

After encountering and dealing with the frog of the common human emotion, Sumedha surprisingly arrived at the forked road where he felt totally perplexed and confused, not knowing which way to go. This is our doubt or indecisiveness, which can occur during our inner journey of discovery. The effective way to deal with doubt or indecisiveness is stay with it, to experience it completely with full awareness and dis-identification until clarity appears (without expecting it, of course). In addition, it's important to maintain an open, positive attitude of welcoming such mental states as doubt and indecisiveness since they play a necessary part of investigating, examining, and penetrating things deeply and thoroughly in the course of affirming what is real or right and of denying what is not real or wrong. Imagine for a moment that upon arriving at the forked road one just sits or stands there, waiting with attention, calmly, quietly, and vigilantly, and after a while some kind of clarity or a signal of insight arises — then one takes action accordingly with no hesitation. In the case of being driven by worry and/or anxiety, one merely has some more work to do, and that is, apart from waiting with attention, one observes and watches closely how the worry or anxiety appears and disappears momentarily but continuously. Simply do just that until eventually such a mental state subsides and fades away, leaving a clear space within one's head and giving clarity to one's mind, and then the right action will be taken and the correct road will be followed.

The strainer of hindrances

It's very natural and normal, whether in the external journey or in the internal journey, that one will encounter some obstacles that can delay the journey. However, one wisely has a firm and strong determination to go on journeying for the sole purpose of reaching the final goal, and one puts all the necessarily required energy, attention, and intelligence into mobilizing and energizing oneself constantly, no matter what happens. In this manner, all obstacles will be overcome and the journey will continue until it is completed.

As for spiritual practice, we talk about five hindrances that obstruct the mind, discouraging it, weakening it, and preventing it from going further with the inner journey. These hindrances are (1) sensual desire, (2) violent, destructive thought, including revenge and hate or the drive to destroy, (3) sloth and torpor,

(4) restlessness and anxiety/worry, and (5) doubt or indecisiveness. For obtaining some more details and practical knowledge regarding those hindrances, we need to study their detailed implications as follows:

Beginning with the first hindrance, we can ask: How does the desire for sensual gratification hinder spiritual growth? Perhaps it is just a long-standing tradition in Eastern religious practice to achieve detachment from sensuality. We can best approach an understanding of the meaning of this hindrance by viewing it from an unexpected angle. To shed light on this issue, let us see it at this time as a hindrance when we associate spiritual development with high goals and rarified states and identify sensual gratification as lowly and inappropriate to spiritual attainment. This mode of thinking can become an obstacle, putting us into conflict with our natural tendencies and attachments. Conflict over desires creates a negative attachment to the senses, and ties us to the sensual world, the empty village.

In all the Buddha's discourses, he admonishes monks to stay clear of sensual distractions. He impressed the monks with the disgusting nature of sensuality in order to keep their full attention on the practice and devotion of the holy life. This was a clever technique on his part for creating single-mindedness of attitude. *But it became an obstacle when it was followed blindly, when it was taken literally to mean that sex and sensuality were inherently evil.* This idea leads to obsessive patterns of thoughts, all centering on sensual objects and their rejection, and to lack of mental clarity.

When we talk about sensuality, we refer to the five physical senses. When our experiences come through the eyes, ears, nose, tongue, and touch, and mingle with desire, they become hindrances, rather than passing phenomena. But in the vipassanā practice, we are taught not to shut off the senses, but, rather, to be open to every one of them with full attention. In this way, we work through our obstacles by putting ourselves in their world, rather than shutting them out and leaving them like a hidden menace. It would be easier to retire to a forest or a cave, and see nothing but rocks and birds. But living in the world is harder, more exciting, and valuable for learning insight. This is, of course, a matter of personal choice. It puts us in an awkward position to deny the very senses that we rely on for experiencing our lives. Living with an acceptance of them leads to insight about how we are ruled by the need for gratification. We can use our senses to deepen our perceptions of ourselves and of others, while strengthening our wisdom and watchfulness. In this way, we take sensual desire as a challenge, with the possibility of converting an obstacle into a tool. We must learn to enjoy our sense faculties without being victimized by them. This is why in vipassanā practice we observe clearly how sensual desire arises and how much power it holds over our consciousness. Then, too, we can notice if our attachments are weakening, and when we are becoming free. *That is the way to use our potential obstacles as tools.* It is a more effective technique than suppression, which only submerges the effect. If something is not dealt with, it will emerge at some later point with explosive energy behind it. We can see the effect of this in people who have been politically oppressed, or sexually repressed exploding into violence and aggression.

Allowing sensual pleasure to become an available object of awareness leads us to insight into how compulsive we are in relation to it. The best attitude to develop is freedom in relation to desire, sex, and sensuality. In other words, having the freedom to act out needs without being compelled to do so — freedom of real choice. Sometimes, when people become involved with one another, they fixate on their sexual relationship and forget to attend to the work they need to accomplish. This can become compulsive behavior in an effort to avoid losing a pleasurable experience. Even in meditation practice, we can struggle to achieve pleasant states of mind, and then become addicted to maintaining them, or recovering them. The mind is very often restless, and compulsion is a manifestation of restlessness.

Not only blissful states of mind and body but also overwhelming states of consciousness can become obstacles. We might cling to the experience of being overwhelmed, without proceeding further in the process. Perhaps, when we release strong body blocks, we experience a surge of sexual energy. In this case, rather than becoming fixated on the feeling, we can accept being in the momentum of the energy, arriving at a centered place in that energy, to be able to proceed onward in our work. It is important to differentiate between sexual *energy* and sexual *desire*, lust. Desire arises from the mind, it is thinking without necessarily any biological needs being expressed. This could be an instance of simply reaching out for pleasure and distracting entertainment. By simply looking at this process as it presents itself, we achieve a simple attitude in relation to it, and hence quietness of mind.

There is no reason to obstruct sexual energy, or feel guilty if it arises in our practice. It is an understandable experience at the human level of reality. Most people, in fact, are not familiar with this energy. Often, they experience sexual frustration, arising from not being able to feel because of too much blockage in the body. This becomes a problem of rigidity. Rigidity operates on both the physical and mental levels. When sexual energy is blocked, the personality is blocked. Then, the mind becomes rigid with rules, manners, and fixed modes of communication. Physically, we become controlled and restricted. This presents dangers to the well being of our physical system. Even high meditative states will not help if this rigidity is not broken through.

The tendency in some situations is to become cut off from the world and to confine ourselves to a narrow and narrow reality in which we feel safe from threat. We experience conflict because of our need to come out and to relate to others. This is prevented by our little but quite potent ego, tied into rules and restrictions, like a frog living in a small pond who has never experienced the ocean. This conflict arises in the context of our biological urge to connect and relate, it pushes and pulls at us, creating distortions of free flow energy. In this state we experience no freedom.

Rigidity also includes attitudes of stubbornness, annoyance, and irritation. It signifies a lack of a free flow of energy, leading to tight, restrictive responses. When this energy can flow freely, it unifies and softens one's relationship to oneself and everything around. It can lead to a completely expansive state of loving energy, without interfering in others' space or being in disharmony with whatever may be around. Sometimes, when the energy is released, its power causes the body to shake; especially if it is the energy that has been blocked at the sexual level. When this happens, it is important to be open to this pelvic expression without a striving attitude. Striving is connected, again, with sensual desire, the longing to experience. Instead, we can look at the experience in the moment, without anticipating future needs. In this way, any state of experience becomes an object of awareness rather than a dilemma. This is the open path of seeing through applying intelligence.

The second hindrance is violent, destructive thought, including revenge and hate or the drive to destroy. This is a deeply rooted trait, sometimes called a sleeping dog because only when it is aroused does one notice its existence, and then it jumps up and bites. It is the kind of attribute that needs stimulation to bring it to the surface. In pleasant states of consciousness it hides, but with arousal, anger, hating feeling, mental dis-ease (=lacking ease), physical discomfort, and frustration will manifest themselves. Ill will[5] is the deepest manifestation of this attribute, leading to hatred, as the root of a tree pushes to the surface. When anger is suppressed, we experience resentment, a manifestation of avoidance. Resentment is the result of holding on to feelings that we do not feel free to acknowledge or express. In this case, we are held back by some image, or idea, of what is proper, and some desire to be seen as good. This leads in turn to irritability and short temper, and an increasing need to avoid situations that will arouse the suppressed feelings. The standard of peacefulness has become an obstacle, hiding a deeper layer of intense agitation. This includes the attempt to achieve tranquil states of mind through chanting and other meditative techniques. Avoidance and non-acceptance of negativity is the root of the second hindrance.

We can see through the process of understanding ill will, and the negative states associated with it, how it obstructs spiritual growth through creating suppression, loss of energy, and despair. In vipassanā practice, the objective is to uncover this process by looking at every level of manifestation of this hindrance, and to its point of arising. We can see how a feeling or idea came about by uncovering every detail of its arising. Penetrating in this way leads to the dissolution of the feeling at its core. This is a natural process of cleaning rather than a plan arising from ego's image and intentions.

The third hindrance is sloth and torpor, a theme familiar to all of us. Physical sleep is a common sign of just being fatigued and readily relieved compared to mental lethargy and dullness, the fetters of mental and psychological sleepiness. This sensation arises from encountering a difficulty, and wanting to avoid going through a full experiencing of it by escaping into drowsiness and mental inertia/inactivity. Then the mind becomes slackened and weak, sluggish rather than pursuing the work of meditation or spiritual development. This can become a very dreamy state, dull and heavy, without focus or attention, with a meandering mind. Focusing on this dullness, with extended

---

[5] Ill-will is the translation of Pali word paṭigha, which underlies vyāpāda — violent, destructive thought — that manifests on the periphery of the mind and the energetic body. Actually, as a hindrance to the meditative and spiritual progress we talk of vyāpāda, which in fact includes paṭigha as well.

attention, while sitting through this state, will produce more energy, burning away the dullness. The longer and deeper we allow the process of looking, observing, and sitting to penetrate our dullness, the more energy is produced. Then the obstacles are eradicated and cleared away. This is no excuse to stop.

Whether dullness leaves completely, or uncovers more resistance, discouragement or slackening off effort is simply further slothfulness. We cannot rest on achievement. We can progress only by carrying on with perseverance and patience. Staying fully open and alert to energy, we will experience its pouring forth into our process, providing strength and clarity. With full attention, there comes a strong vibratory energy at the center of awareness, unifying the field of consciousness. In that state, nothing matters, although we are still hearing, seeing, tasting. The body adjusts to a natural posture for its well being, and we are free of agitation and restlessness. That is when peacefulness comes: All this comes about without intention or willful pushing, but with loving attention and easefulness. For a time, we are free of dullness.

The fourth hindrance is worry, anxiety, and restlessness. This hindrance arises from unhappiness deep within the mind. We might express it as turmoil, frustration, and paranoia in the psychic world. We become restless, easily distracted, and are always looking for diversions. We move endlessly from thing to thing, object to object, pointlessly. Being dominated by this hindrance is like dust being scattered by the wind. The movement depends on the force of the wind. We lose concentration and focus, and must yield to the wanderings of the mind. Instead of insisting on another mental state, we can allow this one to remain; we wait and see how long the storm will last, and watch ego suffering through it. We just wait with attention. There will be some urge to take action, to change things by our intervention. However, if we merely become passive and inert, without executing vital attention and clear awareness, then this itself turns into another subtle form of the hindrance, continuing to manifest restless action out of despair. The task is to continue watching until the storm naturally subsides, and with this extended mindfulness comes renewed energy. Struggling against this natural process will lead to a great waste of energy and additional waves of restlessness and anxiety. Non-action is the best attitude in this situation. This is what we mean by "waiting with attention." It will not feed the flame of scattered energy. Non-action becomes the most powerful weapon in this case. The vipassanā approach is to *allow* and to let things calm down through awareness, rather than denying or trying to alter the situations egotistically.

The last hindrance is doubt and indecisiveness. Doubt is a passion of fear, while indecisiveness is a characteristic of doubt. One cannot decide whether or not there is such a thing as enlightenment, or, if there is, one is doubtful that one can achieve it. One becomes tied up in uncertainty and feels insecure about continuing to do the work one has started. At the same time, one is driven toward some goal and is anxious to proceed. Therefore, one cannot leave the situation as it is, and one cannot go forward either. One is in conflict. That is doubt. One can neither let it go, nor can one stay with it.

There is nothing to be done in this situation, as with all the other hindrances. Action can only complicate the situation. One must reside in a quiet, watchful space and attend to the noises of doubt and uncertainty, to that inner dialogue. Trying to weigh everything and come to a conclusion is not effective since it arises out of the confusion, rather than stillness. Attempting to work it out will only increase the doubt. Instead, one can watch the doubting game with interest and healthy detachment until some true feeling arises. When that feeling comes, some clarity will arise and will provide guidance to the next action. It may be a very brief moment, but the impulse will arise from a source of alertness and bring about authentic action, sureness and precision in movement. It is not constant and will subside to doubt once again. Instead of struggling against this sequence, one can settle back and surrender to the reality of change, and benefit from the moments of clear seeing, when all the phenomena of doubt disappear like an illusion.

Hindrances are not to be taken as excuses for ceasing to work, or for avoiding the practice. Instead, as described above; they can become objects of our awareness as they manifest challenges to our practice and objects to strengthen our focusing. They can help bring about wisdom and discovery of the capacities and strengths within us. In any case, one has nothing else to work with. One must work creatively with them, accepting their companionship without self-blame; otherwise, one suffers the loss of energy and the positive attitudes that help one move forward toward progress on the path.

Everything that arises passes away, like the wind and the rainstorm. The end is in our understanding of any situation as it is, rather than the situation itself. Things will constantly arise since such is the nature of phenomenal reality. One can relate to this fact with an attitude of conservation of energy. When one finds oneself in the midst of a particular situation, one applies one's understanding as a basis from which to be in a helpful relationship toward it. Then, one dwells in the realm of freedom; one lets things be, without conflict, and accepts whatever arises, confident in one's attitude of awareness. Then and only then does wisdom arise and flow through whatever one's particular reality may be, creating a reality of freedom.

The turtle of attachment

Imagine a turtle that has four legs, one head with a long neck, a very short, tiny tail, and with a strong, hard shell covering its total physical form. When it draws in those things, it's quite difficult to pull them out. Therefore, I think, the Buddha uses the turtle as a symbol of attachment since this deeply rooted passion of attachment is the most difficult thing to give up and let go of. Everyone loves it as it makes one feel secure, safe, and comfortable when one has grasped it tightly, even if the other person might feel entirely opposite in terms of relationships.

Here the Buddha talks about four categories of attachment, namely, (1) attachment to sensual pleasures, (2) attachment to view/opinion, (3) attachment to rites and rituals as the means and ways to achieving the liberation and/or enlightenment, and (4) attachment to the notion of attā or atman (a permanent and ever-lasting entity existing within or outside of the humans). However, in his response to Kumāra-Kassapa's question on the turtle, the Buddha simply refers to the attachment to the five aggregates of our human existence. They are the attachment to (1) the physical body, (2) feeling/sensation, (3) perception, (4) the conditioned mental states, including various emotions, or to the mental and psychological formation, and (5) one's consciousness process. All these are quite obvious to us and therefore, there is no need for elaboration.

The slaughterhouse

It is interesting to know that the Buddha relates sensuality to the slaughterhouse. First of all, we must keep in mind that he was talking to his monk who has already taken a vow of celibacy or has undergone living the holy life (brahmacariya), the way of life that has its definite objective of putting an end to suffering. Therefore, the Buddha uses a powerfully destructive and life-threatening symbol of a slaughterhouse to represent the pleasures of the senses so the monk would feel much more reassured in leading the pure, clean, and flawless life as the right thing to do.

All sensual objects such as beautiful, desirable, agreeable, inviting, and attractive to the mind experienced through the five physical sense modalities (eyes, ears, nose, tongue, and body touch) are actually things that bind and tie up human beings (especially the thick people) and animals alike to their pleasures, whether imagined or realistic/actual. Therefore, the sensual pleasures (with attachment and blind consciousness, of course) are like a slaughterhouse where our true, free spirit and uncontaminated soul are killed in the sense of being deeply buried and condemned to live in the unconscious as we humans waste our valuable time and vital energy by living basically on the periphery or side-line of life. Unfortunately, some even have gone too far by ignoring and putting aside completely the existential reality of spiritual, inner life.

The lump of meat

For those non-vegetarian people who enjoy eating meat, this symbol must be a great delight, an enormous joy when it just appears to their naked eyes. On the contrary, vegetarian advocates will feel awful, repulsive, and disgusted when perceiving a piece of fresh meat lying there underneath the symbolic anthill. The Buddha points out that it is nandhi-rāga, lustful desire that appears like a sleeping dog living in the dark corner of our human consciousness. On the surface sensual desire (in form of passionate, vital energy for sensuality) might appear null sometimes, but make sure if the sleeping dog of the dormant, lustful desire is still lying latent in the depths of our psyche. This nandhi-rāga needs the explosive enlightened bomb to blow it up with no remainder.

The nāga or serpent

According to the Buddha, a nāga represents the being whose fermented conditions have reached a complete cessation (knīnāsava: khīna = cessation + āsava = fermented conditions), which signifies the fully enlightened person. It's another title for an arahat. The nāga is actually an imagined animal, which does not actually exist, but is believed to be very powerful, to live in the vast stretch of water in the underworld, and able to disguise itself as a human being at will. However, the arahat is a real human being who has achieved full enlightenment through his perseverance, fully cultivated awareness, and firmly stabilized mind.

It's quite amazing that this concept of the enlightened being existing within is in accordance with the Zen saying, "We are already enlightened." Therefore, the only thing remains to be done is *uncover the covered and manifest the unmanifested.* In this context, let us elaborate the actual meaning of enlightenment as popularly accepted in Buddhism as follows:

"After giving up the opportunity for becoming a great emperor, the Buddha-to-be prince left the royal palace, his wife, his newly born child, and his parents, at night; and took on being a form of monk at dawn. After that he searched for the right teacher and discovered the two distinguished spiritual masters: Kalama and Rāmaputta. He industriously studied and practiced all their teachings and methods of practice for achieving enlightenment and freedom until those great masters recognized him as equal to themselves. Realizing that what he was actually looking for had not been accomplished, he took leave of them and continued seeking after the truth by himself. At this point in time, he experimented with the practice of fasting and he did it to his utmost until he almost died. As the story said, during that period of severe fasting, one day he could not move his body and therefore, lay down completely still under a tree and went through a near-death experience. Fortunately, a young boy who took care of cattle discovered him and out of his compassion for the Monk Gotama (the Buddha's name known at the time of his monkhood) he decided to help him. The young cowherd went to milk his cow and brought a full bottle to pour into the monk's mouth. (The Monk Gotama must have been in a state of semi-unconscious, for he knew nothing until he came back to his senses and opened his eyes.) After swallowing the milk and assimilating it fully, he looked around and saw a young boy standing at a near distance. He then asked who the boy was and what he did to bring him back from his exhausted fasting. When he was informed of the fact that the boy gave him the bottle of milk by pouring it in his mouth, he then realized what was happening. He thanked the boy for his good deed and great help; whilst the boy apologized for touching a holy man like him since he was born from an untouchable family (the untouchable people have no rights to touch the holy people). The Monk Gotama simply told him that there was nothing to apologize for because he did nothing wrong, and then he went on saying, "One is not noble or ignoble because of his birth from a noble family or from a poor family. But the good deeds or bad ones make people good or evil."

That late afternoon, the Monk Gotama happened to hear a song sung by the country girls in a forest nearby as they were collecting firewood. The content of the song was that in playing a violin if the strings are too loose, they would not produce a good music; on the contrary, if they are too tight, they might break. But good music can be produced from a violin whose strings are just right, that is, neither too tight nor too loose. Through grasping the meaning of the song, the Monk Gotama woke up from his lack of awareness or ignorance and realized that his practice of fasting was too severe and was absolutely to no avail. So he gave it up right there, and returned to his normal eating. He thanked the girls with all his heart for helping him receive such invaluable vision, at a distance, of course!

From then on, he followed the middle way, cultivating right mindfulness and visionary insights up to the point where his mind was clear and his body relaxed and clean. In the eve of the full moon day of May, after having made a strong determination that he would not get up from his meditation seat until full enlightenment was accomplished, although his bones might be broken into pieces, his blood dry up, and his flesh get rotten, he sat there under the bodhi tree (the tree of knowledge) in front of the River Nerañjarā, facing the east. As he was sinking deeply into the meditative state, he encountered two overwhelming passions: attachment and fear manifested to him in form of seductive young women and a scene of a battlefield.

The first images that appeared to him were the pictures of the three beautiful, young women whose names are Taṇhā (craving or thirst), Rāga (passionate desire), and Arati (aversion). They manipulated him and seduced him by showing various parts of their bodies together with saying to him that enjoying the pleasures of senses in life is much better than sitting still and doing nothing but hoping for the best. They asked him to give up such useless practices and return to the ordinary life in the world. At first he was slightly tempted by their performance, but later realized that it was the manifestation of his delusive consciousness in which are contained the inseparable passions of attachment, craving, and fear. So he let them be, and continued deepening his meditation. This time he saw himself in great danger since the images of warships, bombing aircraft, and armed forces appear in such way that they were all pointing their destructive weapons toward him. At this point, he become so frightened that one of his hands suddenly slips out of the meditation posture and his eyes open up slightly. Realizing that it is simply a mental picture symbolizing his fear, particularly the fear of death, he then returned to his meditation and continued his profound inner journey until the dawn of the day. At the moment of the rising of the sun and the disappearing of darkness, he reaches full enlightenment and therefore becomes the Buddha, the Awakened One.

The Buddha's enlightenment consists of three principal factors. The first factor is the vivid memory of his detailed past lives, which explode to him at the first watch of the night (around 10 p.m.). The second factor involves the visionary insights into birth, death and rebirth of all beings in the universe arising in him at the second watch of the night (around 2 a.m.). The third factor is inner knowledge and insightful wisdom concerning all the defilements and contaminations within his consciousness that have been fully purified and totally transformed with no destructive elements left unfinished, arising in him at the last watch of the night (around 6 a.m.).

It is interesting to note that this kind of enlightenment, the Oriental type one may say, is actually very different from enlightenment popularly understood in the West. According to *The New Shorter Oxford English Dictionary*, enlightenment means *the action of mentally or spiritually enlightening; the state of being so enlightened.* To enlighten means to make luminous, give spiritual knowledge or insight, shed light on, or illuminate, including removing the blindness from one's eyes. *The Western idea of enlightenment does not include cosmological or religious beliefs such as rebirth or omniscient perception. The word "enlightened" is used as a broad description for an open-minded, humane, ethical person (in a secular sense). Today when Western people talk about someone being an enlightened person, usually they mean that the person is open-minded, forward-looking, and free from prejudicial thinking.* These meanings do not actually cover the illuminating knowledge of one's past lives (for traditionally speaking, the Western world does not have such a concept of a past life), the vision and understanding of how human beings are born, die, and are reborn in accordance with their karmic energies contained in their personal consciousness, let alone the knowledge and insight into the complete eradication and total transformation of one's own dark forces, an indispensable condition for achieving *wholeness* and *enlightenment* in the oriental sense.

If we put it in the psychological sense, the concept of a past life may be applied to the past incidents in the present life with all the minds (mind-states), emotions, and feelings buried in certain parts of the physical body and in the psychic center within human consciousness. Certainly, these matters must be worked out through psychological and therapeutic processes in order to bring about healing, health, and wholeness on the way of growth; otherwise there will be no psychological freedom, nor will there be enlightenment (in the Western sense, of course). I am certain that Siddhartha (the personal name of the Buddha) had completed all his psychological, therapeutic, and spiritual processes through his method of meditation in those six years of his intensive practices before he obtained such knowledge of his past lives.

Now, the question of whether enlightenment is permanent or subject to change like everything else in the phenomenal world, arises in many people who undergo searching for it. With respect to this question, my own understanding is that *enlightenment is*. It cannot be stated definitely if it is permanent or subject to change because it arises in the moment of shedding light on something, or of intending to know something specifically. Even so, the fundamental state of being enlightened remains a stable ground for being and becoming or actualizing in daily living; that is to say, immeasurable freedom and clarity of consciousness prevail no matter whether the enlightened person is in action or in non-action. This is because in full enlightenment there are three forms of freedom: *freedom from distortion of perception, freedom from distortion of view and thought, and freedom from delusion of consciousness*. This implies the dynamic balance and stability of emotional tones in the enlightened being as well. All these three freedoms determine if enlightenment *is* or is *not*.

How can we judge who is enlightened? The answer simply is: *do not judge*. One must exercise one's keen awareness and stillness of mind during one's association with such a person so that one may know this is an enlightened being. Taking face value as a criterion by judging appearances and certain behavior patterns manifested on different occasions and in various places will not help one know for certain that a given individual is enlightened.

By and large, the enlightened person is quite ordinary and does not indicate any signs of enlightenment, except being natural and unhesitatingly doing what needs to be done. For this reason, just learn to be fully awake and constantly aware in every moment of living and interacting with people and life situations, and to be totally present. When you become enlightened, or when enlightenment hits you by surprise, you will certainly know for certain that *this is it.*

Nevertheless, in the Buddha Dharma criteria for deciding if a person is enlightened or not are provided. These criteria are as follows: *first, freedom from the lower bondages of self-delusion, doubt and indecisiveness, attachment toward rituals and ceremonies, attachment regarding sensual pleasures, and ill-will or destructive, negative thinking. And second, freedom from the higher bondages of attachment to the meditative states associated with form and formlessness, pride on all levels, anxiety and restlessness, and avijjā (ignorance as ignoring the truth, an absence of pure awareness or the highest knowing).*

MENTAL CONTAMINATIONS TO BE COMPLETELY ERADICATED and TOTALLY TRANSFORMED

FULLY DEVELOPED FACTORS

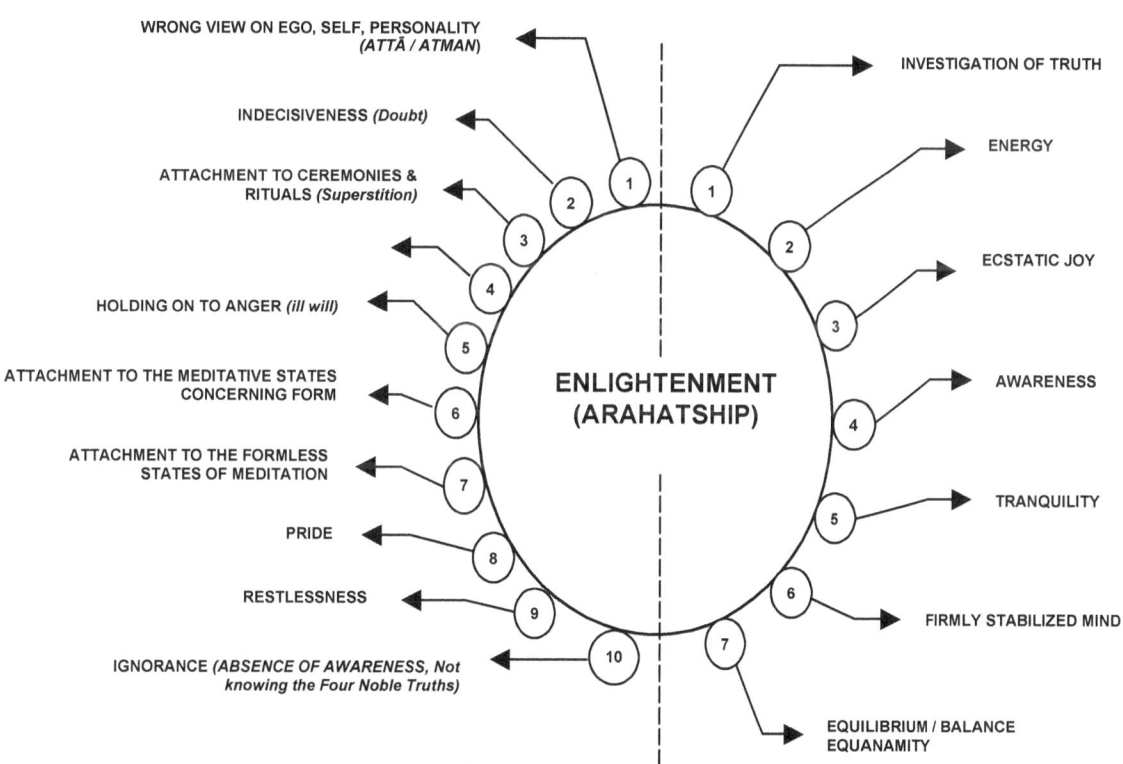

Defining Features of Enlightenment

10 SAMYOJANAS (things that dominate and bind the mind to both the lower and the higher realms of consciousness)
7 BOJJHANGAS (with awareness (4) operating evenly between the 3 investigative (1-3) and 3 concentrative (5-7) factors of enlightenment)[6]

---

[6] From the author's unpublished manuscript, *A New Vision of Buddhism.*

All in all we see that the digging process shown in the fully described Vammika-Sutta is, in fact, a process of reaching enlightenment. However, we must bear in mind that such is not the *only* process since there would be various distinct processes through which different individuals would undergo working. Nonetheless, each one of us would take a similar journey to enlightenment or to meet with the enlightened being (the nāga) who is awaiting our arrival patiently.

= 6 =

HEAVEN AND HELL

It is quite important to understand the issue of heaven and hell so that one may deepen one's comprehension of the law of karma since the Buddha has mentioned very often the words of heaven and hell in various places where he was talking about karma. However, it is rather difficult either to affirm or to deny if he would like us to believe in the existence of heaven and hell, or to maintain the view that this matter of heaven and hell has nothing to do with *real* Buddhism since it lacks a strong, logical reason to support its existence.

In fact, the reason for not believing in this issue of heaven and hell for so many people is that it appears as if it were a legend invented for the purpose of deceiving unintelligent and unwise people, and also this matter is extremely hard to believe considering how it's presented. Some people even go so far as to say that heaven and hell are tools created by the Order of monks and the Church to frighten their followers regarding doing evil and/or non-believing in the religious teachings, and at the same time to encourage the devotees to do good both for themselves and for society, so that the Church and the religious institutions can go on flourishing and maintaining their stability.

In spite of the reasons cited above, the author would like to affirm the existence of heaven and hell, which, he believes, is in accordance with the Buddha's wishes regarding the spiritual welfare and happiness of the believers and the seers. The convincing reason for supporting this affirmation is that this matter of heaven and hell is one of the principal teachings of the Buddha, and that it is the issue fully realized by the enlightened people according to the Buddha's dialogue as follows:

"Who clearly comprehends this earth? Who fully realizes the yama-loka, this world and the worlds of heaven and hell? And who understands how to choose the dharma well taught by me, just as a flower-arrangement person knows precisely which flowers to choose for making beautiful garlands?

"The noble, enlightened persons with the title of Sekha clearly comprehend this planet earth, realizes fully the yama-loka and this world together with the worlds of heaven and hell. They are the Sekha people that understand perfectly how to choose the dharma well taught by me, just as flower-makers know precisely what kinds of flowers to choose for arranging beautiful garlands."[1]

In the commentary to this sutra, it is explained thus:

This earth means the psychophysical systems. By "comprehends clearly" is meant the "thorough discernment with one's own profound insight."

---

[1] Khuddaka-Nikāya, Dhamma-Vagga, Mahachula edition, 25/24.

The concept "yama-loka" refers to the four progressive planes of existence, namely, hell, animal kingdom, hungry ghosts, and the low grade, fearful devas (asurakāya).

This **world** signifies *the human world,* and *the world of heaven* refers to all levels of the heavenly world, including the heaven of sensual pleasures, the realm of form *(rūpa-jhānic consciousness) and the realm of the formless world (arūpa-jhānic consciousness).*

The concept of "topics of dharma" refers especially to the thirty-seven factors required for the attainment to enlightenment. The meaning of "knowing to choose" is understanding the method of the dharma investigation and the means whereby the complete realization can be achieved.

The "Sekha" refers to those who still undergo training in the higher moral discipline, in the deeper and higher meditation, and in the more profound and higher wisdom. They are classified into seven categories as follows:

1. Those firmly established in the path of stream entry
2. Those firmly established in the fruition of stream entry
3. Those firmly established in the path of once-returning
4. Those firmly established in the fruition of once-returning
5. Those firmly established in the path of non-returning
6. Those firmly established in the fruition of non-returning
7. Those firmly established in the path of arahat

Literally, the word "Sekha" means *self-educator*, but it has a specific meaning which is confined to self-education concerning the matter of higher moral discipline, self-education concerning the matter of deeper meditation, and self-education concerning the matter of the more profound wisdom. Such self-education or self-cultivation must lead on to the achievement of the noble enlightenment starting with stream entry (entering the stream of nirvana). As for the arahat (one who has fully accomplished all levels of self-education or self-cultivation — full enlightenment) he or she earns the title of Asekha, meaning No more self-education.

Please keep in mind that those who can realize fully and experientially the matter of heaven and hell are the noble enlightened people, and that they realize this issue through their own insights and not by believing in, or being convicted by, other people such as the Buddha. Therefore, this issue of heaven and hell is not non-sensical or superstitious. Let us now take a look at the criterion that the Sekha people use for affirming their comprehension of heaven and hell. In this connection, the commentator simply makes this statement without providing any explanations. The statement is this:

"The Sekha people realized fully and experientially this world of human psychophysical aggregates, and discern thoroughly the world of heaven and the world of hell because of the total transformation of their attachment to the existence."

The means whereby the heaven and hell become realized

It is essentially important to keep in mind that the realization of heaven can be achieved *only when* our life or existence has been realized. However, to be able to realize (to make undoubtedly clear to oneself) this matter of life/existence only when the complete transformation of clinging to the physical body and to the mind together with all its mental states including feelings and emotions has been accomplished. The reason for this is that being attached to the physical body and to the mind causes a dimness or lesser light to one's wisdom, while the wisdom of those who have transcended attachment to body and mind realities shines forth luminously day and night.

As a matter of fact, stream-enterers (sotāpanna) have not yet transformed the body and mind systems completely, only the arahat has done so. Nonetheless, the love that the stream-enterers have for their bodies and their minds is the one associated with proper reasoning and the clarity of consciousness, and so becomes a *conscious love*. It is that love which exceeds the egocentricity and personal pride unlike the thick people or puthujjhanas whose love is egocentric and prideful.

Another thing to be noticed is the fact that not all noble people starting with the stream-enterer can possess supernatural powers such as clairvoyance, for example, a seven-year old child attains to the sotāpanna merely through listening to the Buddha's dharma talk without achieving any meditative absorptions or any attainment to the higher samādhi before. Therefore, the realization of heaven and hell does not depend on the achievement of any supernatural powers, but it does require personal *impeccable insight* for obtaining such realization.

Bear in mind that this issue of heaven and hell, which we are going to discuss at some length, is actually in accordance with the Buddha's teachings, and is not the kind of dharmic legend that most people consider to be. Such a belief system regarding heaven existing somewhere in the sky and hell hidden underneath the earth belongs to primitive, uneducated people both in ancient times and at present. In spite of that, if we take some considerable time to examine objectively the heaven and hell legends together with their implications, we would find some interesting meanings of the dharma and of religious practices concealed between the lines.

The Buddha's words on heaven and hell

"Monks, it is your great benefit and your enormous fortune that you have the opportunity to live the holy life. Monks, I have already seen heaven and hell existing in and manifesting through the six sense modalities, namely, eye, ear, nose, tongue, body, and mind. Whenever one experiences visual objects, sounds, smell, flavor, tactile sensations, and mental objects that are undesirable disagreeable, uninviting, unpleasant, and unlikable, at such a time one is in hell. On the contrary, whenever one experiences those external objects corresponding to the six sense modalities, which are desirable, agreeable, pleasant, likable, loving, inviting, and delightful, at such a time one is in heaven."[2]

In the Buddhist Tipiṭaka there are two words used for representing "hell": **niraya** and **naraka**. The former refers to the plane or level of life that is without happiness but full of pain and suffering, while the latter signifies a cliff or canyon. As for the word for heaven, it implies the plane or level of life that is filled with joy and happiness.

Therefore, our lives on earth could be either a heaven or a hell, and the world in which we live could be exactly the same since heaven and hell exist here within our personal and/or collective experience of life through our senses. In this way, some of us might have gone to heaven many times while some others go to hell quite frequently. Actually, going to hell means entering the steep and deep cliff of pain and suffering, while ascending to heaven simply refers to experiencing happiness, peace, and joy both physically and mentally. However, the most significant thing for determining our daily destiny is the *mind*. If the mind is uncultivated, undeveloped, and not properly trained in natural discipline, in meditation (in raising consciousness), and in wisdom, it will direct us to take a certain action, speaking, and/or thinking in such a way that can bring about trouble, difficulty, physical and mental pain, emotional and psychological suffering, or even spiritual crisis, et cetera. As for the well-cultivated, methodically developed, and appropriately trained mind, it will lead us to doing the right thing, speaking fittingly and aptly, and thinking positively, creatively, and skillfully, which will bring peace, happiness, and joy. For this reason, the Buddha declares in the Dhammapada (Khuddaka-Nikāya):

> *Mind is first and foremost of all things.*
> *Everything is invented and made by mind.*
> *Mind is also the best and most significant of all.*
> *If one acts, speaks, or thinks with the troubled mind,*
> *suffering will follow one just like the wheels do the oxen's footprints.*
> *Instead, if one acts, speaks, and thinks with the clear mind,*
> *happiness will follow one just as the shadow that never leaves.*

The fire of hell

"Monks, eyes, ears, nose, tongue, body, and mind are burned by the fires. What are these fires? They are lust, hate, and delusion, and also birth, decay, death, sorrow, lamentation, pain, grief, and depression are fires."[3]

From these words it becomes quite clear that "hell" is right here in daily life and that the fires of hell exist in the mind. And, similarly, in Dhammapada:

> *There is no fire equal to lust.*
> *There is no destructive force equal to hate.*
> *There is no snare equal to delusion.*

---

[2] Samyutta-Nikāya, Salāyatana-Vagga, 18/118 Mahachula. These words are from the Buddha.
[3] Vibhanga, maha., 4/49 Mahachula.

The Buddha has made it quite plain that "hell" in this life on the planet earth is really a very steep, deep cliff of suffering where so many people thickened by lustful desire, hating feeling, and delusive mental/psychological traps are getting burning and putting themselves in those emotional fires without acknowledging the fact that they are in hell. On the contrary, they dream daily that they live in a heaven of sensual pleasures, revenges, and a sensorial panoramic world.

Nonetheless, although the noble ones who have begun the focused transformation to enlightenment — the "initial enlightened people" such as the stream-enterers and other, slightly more developed individuals — still have those fires lying latent in their psyche, they are under the control of awareness so that there is no way for them to fall into hell. This is because awareness is self-protection (real self-security) and, for that matter, is secure protection for other people, other living beings, and things.

In the Samyutta-Nikāya, Tika-Vagga, the Buddha was talking to the monk, Anuruddha by name, about women in connection with the fires of hell:

"Anuruddha, women in the world are preoccupied with the blemish of being average in the morning, while in the afternoon they become obsessive of the fire of envy and jealousy, and in the evening they are overcome by the fire of lustful desire. Listen, Anuruddha, all these women thickened with such fires of hell suffer so much in this life, while in the life to come they will enter the non-progressing, painful, disastrous, hellish plane of existence."

To illustrate sensuality as hell let us listen to the short story of the Novice Sānu as follows: As far as the story goes, the Novice Sānu wanted to give up the robe and told this to his mother. Then, she said, "Sānu, my dear son, I have helped with lifting you up from "hell." Do you still want to fall back into it?" The Pali text of the Samyutta-Nikāya, Sagātha-Vagga, reads as follows:

Narakā ubbhato tāta narakam patitumicchasi.

While in the Dhammapada (in the Khuddaka-Nikāya), the Buddha said:

"Monk, you must contemplate the Dharma, must not be negligent, must not turn your mind back to sensuality. Do not deceive yourself swallowing the burning charcoal, do not get burned by the fires of hell, and do not lament about pain and suffering."

In the Anguttara-Nikāya, the Venerable Sariputta was once sharing with the Buddha his view on this matter of sensuality as hell thus:

"Blessed One, the fully enlightened monks (khīnāsava) see things as they are, very clearly and totally in their profound wisdom, that sensual pleasures are indeed compared to the large and deep ditch of charcoals burning powerfully."

Why do we not see hell?

It is because hell is hard to be seen, our ancestors taught us that the kingdom of hell is right there beneath the earth, although it in fact exists within each of us humans. Symbolically speaking, our existence is symbolized by earth as a great element shaping up our physical bodies; therefore our ancestors have the reason to say that "hell" is located underneath the earth (the symbolic physical form).

Generally speaking, when ordinary, common people become rigidly attached to their physical bodies, their minds get burned worrying and preoccupying themselves with its physical shape, its beauty and its health, etc. In this way, they are in the fires of kilesa (defilement, impurity, contamination, and dark, destructive forces) and therefore will find it difficult to encounter peace of mind and tranquillity of mental states so that they may abide in such peace and tranquillity for a considerable period. Actually, this matter of peace and tranquillity is pretty much like clear and evenly flowing water in which people bathe themselves on a warm, hot day, and feel tremendously satisfied and vibrantly alive.

Unlike the unenlightened folk as the majority of us are, the initial enlightened people such as the stream-enterers (mentioned above) do not cling to the physical body since they have eliminated utterly the wrong view concerning the concept of self and ego, have overcome doubt and indecisiveness totally, and have transcended all the superstitious belief systems. Their consciousness is cuddling the nirvanic state of flow, which is a deep and complete peace prevailing in the energy field of dynamic stillness. In addition, while abiding in such state of nirvana those initial enlightened people are able to transform the remaining kilesas to the final stage and, therefore, they can see more precisely that sensual pleasures yield little joy and happiness but produce more dangerous and painful consequences. However, the joy and happiness derived from sensual pleasures, if they are not based on the Dharma (light of wisdom and righteousness); really belong to those living in hell in spite of much difficulty in seeing this truth. For this reason the Buddha declared in the Dhammapada:

> *The world is dark, which very few can realize,*
> *just like the birds caught in the net, very few indeed*
> *can escape. Those fleeing into heaven are quite few.*

Since the realm of hell is so hard to see, although it is within us human beings, the Buddha made another declaration in the Samyutta-Nikāya:

"Monks, there exists the burning hell, which refers to visual objects, sounds, smell, flavor, tactile objects, and mental things. By experiencing those things that are undesirable, disagreeable, and unloving (repulsive), they are actually a fire burning hell.

Monks, still there is another kind of hell that is much hotter, more powerfully burning, and more frightening; which refers to those who do not realize the four noble truths, namely, the noble truth of suffering, the noble truth of the arising of suffering, the noble truth of the ceasing of suffering, and the noble truth of the path leading to the cessation of suffering. These people will get caught in all the conditioned things (sankhāra), being caught in the snare of sankhāra they will go on repeating the cycle of birth-life-death and the rest of suffering including sorrow, lamentation, grief, pain, and despair since when birth comes into existence it will be followed by decay, illness, and death. Here, monks, is the place where the most powerfully burning hell lies."

Heaven in hell

The pleasure of senses that most people enjoy and take to their mind as the goal of life is, according to the Buddha's viewpoint, considered a kind of hell. Let us listen to what he said:

At one time, the Buddha was staying in the Veluvana Monastery in the city of Rājagaha, and then the dance master, Tālaputta by name, approached him, and after exchanging greetings, seated himself at a proper place. He then said to the Buddha that he had learned that many ancient dance masters had taught all their entertainment professionals to do their best regarding entertaining people so that their audiences (fans) could be extremely happy and filled with exceeding joy; although what they tell or perform might be real or unreal. They further indicated that those entertainers, after their physical bodies had broken up and died, would be born in heaven enjoying friendship with the heavenly, shining beings there. Now, the question is whether the above-mentioned matter is true or not according to the Blessed One's opinion?

The Buddha was very reluctant to give any answer to Tālaputta's inquiry and therefore asked for excuses for not responding: Even so, Tālaputta persisted in getting the Buddha to reply by asking him the same question three times. Eventually, the Buddha responded to that question saying that usually all sentient beings have lustful desire and are fastened (tied) to the samsāra by the chain of the lustful desire, possess hate and are fastened to samsāra by the chain of hatred, and have delusion and are fastened to the samsāra by the chain of delusion. Whatever is based on lustful desire, hatred, and delusion, the dance entertainers unintentionally increase those three roots of evil in their audience by attempting to make them feel artificially joyful and unrealistically happy. In fact, the entertainers themselves are still overcome by, and satiated in, lustful desire, hatred, and delusion; their entertainments can only enhance and boost the passionate energy of the roots of unskillfunness and evil. The Buddha ended his speech by stressing that such a thing as entertainment is "pahāsa-naraka", meaning the "entertaining hell." Therefore, the viewpoint maintained by those ancient dance masters are indisputably erroneous, and those who believe in it will go either to the realm of hell or to the animal kingdom after death."

Having heard such an unexpected teaching of the Buddha, Tālaputta burst out crying, and so the Buddha said to him that he had warned him not to seek the answer to his question. Then, Tālaputta responded by saying this: "Oh, Blessed One! I do not cry because of your statement of the truth, but the reason for my crying is the realization of being deceived for a long while by the ancient dance masters. Blessed One! Your discourse is so beautiful, which is pretty much like uncovering the covered, like turning back up what was upside down, like pointing out the right path to those getting lost, or like lighting the oil lamp for shining forth so that those having the eyes will be able to see things as they are.

"Blessed One! May I go to the Buddha for refuge, may I go to the Dharma for refuge, and may I go to the Sangha for refuge? May I obtain the ordination to become a bhikkhu (monk) in your Order?"

Out of compassion for the dance master, Tālaputta, the Buddha admitted him into the Order of Monks. Soon after that, he attained full enlightenment or arahatship through his earnest and sincere practices of meditation and his monastic discipline.[4]

It might be rather surprising or at least unpleasant to many people to hear that the pahāsa-naraka, which the Buddha was talking about, implies the cinema theatre, the opera hall, and places of similar entertainments.

Why do so many people go to hell?

Up till now, all the explanations on the subject of hell have been made in accordance with what the Buddha said to a variety of people at various places, which are all in accord with one another and without any conflicting elements. We now know that those going to hell are much more than the people who go to heaven. This is because those who are thickened with the mental contaminations and driven by craving, attachment, and ignorance (in the sense of not knowing what should be known, such as the four noble truths) are easily prone to falling into hell as their eyes, ears, nose, tongue, touch, and mind are looking for and anticipating new sensations and pleasures of the senses, which potentially beget pain and suffering. It seems that for those who are not wise and whose minds are not elevated with the dharma, almost all pleasurable things contain the poison of dukkha (sorrow and pain, grief and despair, agony and suffering, etc.), which can affect them at any time. For this reason, they often go to hell in their everyday living. Let us consider the Buddha's following words:

The story recorded in Samyutta-Nikāya, Mahavagga goes like this: At one time the Buddha picked up certain amount of dust with his hand and asked his monks, "the dust in my palm and the dust on earth, which one is more?" It's quite obvious that the dust on earth is much more than that in his palm, so the monks responded accordingly. Then the Buddha said to them, "Monks, those going to hell and to the spiritually non-progressive plane of existence are pretty much like the enormous dust on the planet earth."

Arriving at this point, we need to examine such often-used concepts such as *apāya, dugati, and vinipāta* in addition to the concept of naraka as previously explained.

---

[4] Samyutta-Nikāya, Salāyatana-Vagga, 18/277 Mahachula.

The Devadūta-Sutta:
The source of heaven in the sky and hell underneath the earth

Since this sutta is quite long and repetitious the author will summarize it for general information about heaven in the sky and hell beneath the earth as follows: At one time the Buddha was staying at the Jetavana Monastery in the City of Sāvatthī and there he said to the monks: "Suppose, monks, there are two houses situated opposite each other, a person with the good eye-sight standing between them will be able to see quite clearly the people coming in and going out of those two houses. Monks, just like that indeed the Tathāgata can perceive deaths and rebirths of all sentient beings with his pure divine eye that is a very special one which many human beings do not possess. Monks, some sentient beings are born low while some others are born in elegance, with beautiful skin or with poor, ugly skin, with a prosperous and good life or with a bad life of poverty in accordance with their own karmas. Those performing good deeds through action, speech, and thought, not insulting those who are enlightened, and holding the right view firmly will certainly go to heaven or at least stay on in the human plane of life. But those performing bad, evil deeds through action, speech, and thought, insulting the enlightened persons, and hold tightly the wrong, erroneous view will go to hell, or to the plane of hungry ghosts, or to the animal kingdom, living the hard, non-progressive, and miserable lives.

"Monks, as for those going to hell, the hell guards (niraya-pāla) would bring them to the king of hell (yama) and inform him of all the evil things and various crimes they have committed. Then, King Yama would ask them the five significant questions whether they have encountered a variety of common signs indicating birth (for instance, a newly born baby), decay or old age, sickness and diseases, robbers and prisoners, and death and corpses, and what they thought about those things. In responding to their negative answers, King Yama would say to them that they were negligent, unaware, inattentive, and did not do good works either for themselves or for other fellow beings on earth. In addition, Yama, the king of hell, would convince them of all the bad, unskilful, and evil karmas performed by themselves and not by anyone else, and that therefore they would reap the consequences with no exception.

"Monks, after that the hell guards would punish them with many distinct methods such as crucifying them with extremely hot iron bars placed over their hands, legs, feet, and chests; in this way, they would suffer tremendously, but would not lose their lives since their evil karmas would keep them going until the suitable punishments are done."

The Buddha carried on telling his monks about the variety of hells, small and big, fiercely tormented and lightly tortured, just like the various ways and means used for punishing and torturing our human prisoners, be they crime-committing prisoners, political prisoners, or terrorist prisoners. He even spoke about certain thoughts that occurred to Yama, the king of hell, such as sympathetic thoughts concerning the pain and suffering experienced by the performers of the evil karmas and the thought about his wishes to see and to be near the supremely enlightened Buddha so that he would hear his Dharma talk and would absorb his wonderful energy.

Finally, the Buddha concluded his discourse by uttering the following stanzas:

*Those who are negligent, although warned by common signs,
will enter the realm of lower birth and will suffer a long time.
Those who are good and serene, on receiving subtle warnings
become attentive, vigilant, and aware at all times.*

*Those seeing the danger of attachment, a cause of birth and death,
reach freedom through becoming unattached as well as through realizing
nirvana, the cessation of birth and death. They attain genuine security
and become totally peaceful in this life overcoming obstacles, hazards,
and all forms of suffering.*

Some criticism and feedback on the subject of hell by a great Thai Buddhist scholar, Krompraya Vachirañanavaroros

"The concept of Niraya exists not only in Buddhism but in all doctrines and belief systems that recognize the cycle of birth and death or samsara. Here I would like to make a comparison with Brahmanism only since it is very close to us the Buddhists. Niraya is a Pali word while the Brahmins call it Naraka in Sanskrit, and in Thai language we use the word "Narok." In addition, they call it *pātāla* while we Thai people say *bādāl* and understand it as the realm of nāga. The Naraka of the Brahmins is used for punishing the *atman*[5] that commits evil acts at the time of living a life in this world. They divide the Naraka into seven main parts without giving names and classifying who would go into which Naraka according to the evil things committed in life. Yama is the king of this realm of Naraka and become the supreme judge himself, and Yama's messengers guard the entire realm and survey the whole human world. As soon as someone dies, his messengers will bring the dead to him."

We don't really know what name or title those messengers have since it is not provided in Sanskrit, but I read the English version, which is re-written much later and is not the original text. So, I find it exactly the same as the concept we use in Buddhism and that is Niraya-pāla. The road to naraka or niraya is cut through the Fire River (without a bridge for crossing over) and therefore, there is tradition that when a terminally-ill person is dying the relatives are instructed to give a cow or an ox to a Brahmin for using it as a vehicle to cross over the Fire River. Upon that individual's arrival, King Yama does not have to interrogate the dead since there is a full report already written in the dead's book, he merely opens it up and reads it, and then passes his judgment over the dead who has done bad karmas (actions). As for the dead who have done both good and bad karmas, he might just balance them out and send such a person up to heaven or to be reborn in the human world depending on the degrees of the karma that has been evaluated. For those who have done heavy, bad karmas, the proper punishment will be assigned, for example, putting them in the dark jail or in the pond filled with dogs' feces and urine and

---

[5] This Sanskrit word "ātman" according to Hinduism refers to a soul that goes from life to life until it has purified all its bad karmas, and then becomes one with the Permanent Supreme Soul (paramātman).

human mucus, or punishing them with burning fire, with a hotly heated iron bar, with the poisonous animals/reptiles, or letting fierce animals eat up their flesh and blood, et cetera. Even with such heavily brutal punishments the beings in hell do not die since they must bear the consequences of their evil karmas until those karmas get exhausted and balanced out. After that they could be released and would be born in the lower grade of the animal kingdom before they could find an opportunity to do good deeds.

All these stories that I have related the author of the English text said that he got them from the scripture called *Padamapurāna*. So, it seems to me that the name of such a naraka might be *Padama-Naraka*, which is in agreement with the concept used in our Buddhist tradition, *Paduma-Niraya*.

Krompraya Vachirañanavaroros came to a conclusion that the stories of Naraka might have been written in connection with prison and jail used in all the countries of the world to-day for punishing those committing crime or prisoners of all kinds. For example, the thirty-two methods of punishing the criminals (dvattimsakarmakarana) are said to be the heavily brutal punishments, which are later on believed to be true because of not knowing the reality about them.[6]

On pages 83-85 of that same book, *Dhammavicharn — Investigation of the Dharma*, he continues investigating this matter of naraka and saying "The view on Naraka maintained by the Brahmins and the view on Niraya in our Buddhist scripture are quite in agreement. So, it seems to me that the origin of both sources (Brahmanism and Buddhism) would be the same, or this issue of hell had been handed down through both religions from the same original source. The difference lies only in the adjustability to suit the belief systems of each religion, for example, we Buddhists place our trust in justice and therefore want to translate Devadūta (common signs) into decay, suffering, and natural cessation, we make up the idea that Yama, the king of Niraya ask certain questions, and since we are a bit nervous about punishment we let Yama remain silent after his interrogations so that the hell guards (Niraya-pāla) would know what to do next. We worship our religion, so we try to make Yama have faith in Buddhism. Similarly, the Brahmins want the external source of power to dissolve for people the problems in order that those committing evil acts would turn to God for their refuge. For this reason, they make believe that Vishnu and Shiva have the authority to let their messengers take away by force from King Yama's messengers the atman of those who place their faith in them so that those hell-beings would be released from hell and go to the heavenly world of Vishnu and Shiva. It is also said that Vishnu himself have the authority to liberate the beings in hell from the hellish punishments, so the Brahmins believe that there are existential evidents supporting their view in the human world at the point in time as we will consider the following issues:

1. How much is the Buddhist recognition of hell? Does Buddhism recognize the matter of hell as merely recorded in the previously mentioned Pali texts or does it also recognize all the details described in the Devadūta-Sutta?

---

[6] Translated from Dhammavicharn, pages 79-80 (2536).

"2. If Buddhism doesn't recognize the latter, we may understand that the Buddha was describing the matter of hell in order to point out the hell in our human world. The questions would be whether the original text is authentic, or it has been modified to make believe this matter of hell, or is it the matter of the Dharmic comparison or a false morality rewritten in much later epoch?

"3. The investigation of those two queries would indicate that Buddhism recognizes the hearsays without seeing in profound vision as we all maintain the "seeing for oneself – Sanditthiko". Or apart from seeing for oneself there is no recognition of that thing which is not true?"

Of those three topics for investigation, I would prefer to begin with the third one, and then would investigate the remaining two issues to see if they would be in agreement with one another. If those having faith in the other religion would criticize the religion that they do not believe in, such a way of criticism would not elevate their own religion too high. So, they might come to a conclusion that our religion (Buddhism) recognizes hearsay, which has not been penetrated by profound inner knowledge. In this way, they would not feel so bad that Buddhism recognizes hearsay since the detailed description of hell appears in the Buddhist scripture. However, we naturally put high value on our religion, but when we encounter the matter of hell described at length in the Devadūta-Sutta, we feel a bit awkward. We are in a position of being ashamed to recognize it, and denying it would not help us feel at ease, either. Therefore, it's quite hard for me to pin it down and reach a comfortable conclusion, so I would rather leave it for now to the reader to answer this individually.

Not to be deceived by scriptures

It is quite understandable that Krompayā Vachirañanavaroros does not make a definite decision on this issue of hell simply because many Thai Buddhists strongly believe in the Devadūta-Sutta and the distinguished Buddhist commentators seem to have faith in it as well. However, if we would believe in the matter of hell as described in the Devadūta-Sutta, we have plenty of evidence in the Tipiṭaka and in some later texts such as Milindapañha to support our belief. Nonetheless, the Buddha taught us "Not to believe in scriptures and not to believe in hearsay." I think that we should do some studies on the Tipiṭaka for the simple reason of not being deceived by the scriptures. In addition, we will see some clarity of the investigation and positive criticism done by Krompraya Vachirañanavaroros regarding this issue of hell. So, let us listen a bit further to his investigation into the Buddhist history of preserving and handing down the Buddha's Doctrine and Discipline as follows:

"In our Pali texts it is said that the existing Arahats had convened a special meeting for discussing, collecting, and synchronizing the Buddha's teachings together with various views on the Dharma. At that meeting Ānanda, the Buddha's attendant monk, was appointed the key speaker, since he heard everything and learned all the teachings directly from the Buddha both at public places and in privacy. At the first Buddhist Council those fully enlightened monks merely put certain questions to one another and listened to each other's comprehension of, and commentaries on, the Dharma, and then established as evident those selectively agreed-upon teachings through memory, inscribing, and learning by mouth from those enlightened monks. Later on, the memory or the scriptures became different, or the understanding of certain aspects of the Dharma was not agreed to by all, and so the chief monk at that time called another meeting for counselling and establishing the authentic teachings after having found mutual agreement and clarified the absurd subjects of the Dharma and having cleared away all the doubtful matters related to the true Dharma proclaimed and taught by the Buddha.

"Soon after the Buddha's final passing away (parinibbāna), the principal disciples who had been with him when he was still living, it seems to me, did not deem it necessary to put the teachings in writing since they all had known them and practiced them under his guidance. So, they merely brought the teachings together through learning and practicing them as living realities, following the Master's model of how he lived and carried on the Dharma. This tradition of conserving and handing down the Dharma (Doctrine) and Vinaya (Monastic Discipline) has been practiced all the way throughout the history of Buddhism. However, around the sixth century, counting from the year of the Buddha's parinibbāna, his teachings were inscribed or written down, in Sri Lanka. Nonetheless, earlier, during the reign of Ashoka the Great (from the 200s B.C.E.), there was a Great Council of investigating and clarifying the Dharma and Vinaya, which was counted as the third council, under the patronage of the Emperor Ashoka who held Buddhism in his heart. During that period the writing had been officially used, that is to say, he ordered his scholars to inscribe the Dharma on rocks for the purpose of spreading it and making it widely known throughout his empire. Therefore, it is likely that the Buddhist scriptures had been written in letters and it's unlikely that learning and telling by mouth (mukhapātha) were used, since the style and fashion of presenting the teachings are quite ancient both in terms of the authors' inclinations (adhimutti) and the use of language. However, the presentation style and the use of language, compared with the inscription on rock, appeared to have been made shortly after the Ashoka's Reign. But some scriptures including the commentaries contained the later style, which are believed to be written during the epoch of Sri Lanka. However, some suttas have been added at a much later time, such as the Subha-Sutta of Dīgha-Nikāya, the Sīlakhanda-Vagga, which Venerable Ānanda preached to a young man named Subha Toteyyaputra, and the Madhura-Sutta of Majjhima-Nikāya, Majjhimapannāsa, which Venerable Kaccāyana expounded to the King of Madhurā."[7]

How much confidence in the Devadūta-Sutta shall one have?

Since Krompraya Vachirañanavaroros is popularly considered a great Thai Buddhist scholar, his investigation and view on the Doctrine and Discipline of the Buddha are taken seriously by the learned Thai Buddhists. The detailed description of hell in the Devadūta-Sutta, if one believes it to be the Buddha's authentic utterance, one would see as a comparison that he made to benefit us all in the following two ways:

---

[7] Translated from the Forward to *Dhammavicharn*.

1. For those believing in the above-mentioned sutta, there will be no problem, since [the teaching here] is good, [leading readers to become] healthily ashamed of doing evil things [and] since it is quite essential to apply skillful means to living a life in, and to dealing with, the current of the world, [most helpful here] because some people are unable to understand the Dharma (Truth) by way of logical reasoning.
2. For deep thinkers who possess sharper intellect and wiser intelligence, they will attempt to make out the meanings of those things described in the sutta, and hopefully will find a profound dharmic indication, which will be highly beneficial to living the worldly life.

If the Devadūta-Sutta was not the Buddha's discourse, but written by a certain Buddhist scholar and put in the Buddha's mouth for purpose of making it sacred and respectable, the supposed-to-be author would aim at helping the readers and those who happened to know about it feel healthily ashamed of committing evil things. If that is not the case, the story told in the sutta might have been well known at the time of writing it since the Brahmins did believe in such a kind of hell. So the author of the sutta might have tried to convert some Brahmins into Buddhism by demonstrating a similar story of hell in the Buddhist scripture, which could be another reason for making up a false Dharma in Buddhism. However, the story of hell described in the Devadūta-Sutta could do good only for people in those days, but will not be beneficial for modern people at present time since it is so superstitious that no one would believe in it.

For hell to be taken into account is that hell experienced through our six senses as already explained with the authentic evident made available by the Buddha.

Krompraya Vachirañanavaroros's investigation of hungry ghosts

In addition to the issue of hell, there is another interesting matter concerning hungry ghosts, which many people are doubtful and also curious about. In the Buddhist scriptures, this matter is written and talked about quite often. In fact, if we understand the issue of hell as previously described, it will be reasonably easy to comprehend this matter of hungry ghosts (peta). In order to help the reader understand it with clarify, I would like to quote the detailed investigation by Krompraya Vachirañanavaroros as follows:

"To clarify the plane of hungry ghosts (pettivisaya or petavisaya), it is very essential that the Brahmins' tradition regarding their ancestor be related here. The Brahmins hold the practice of sacrifices and perform meritorious ceremonies for transferring merit to their ancestors, which is technically known as shrāddha, both occasionally on the occasion of cremation and annually at the anniversary of the ancestors' death, sometimes at the beginning of the month and other times at the beginning of the year. They divide the generations of their ancestors into three; namely, parents, grandparents, and great-grand-parents, who deserve to receive their sacrifices of rice lumps, called sapinda, meaning, for the ones sharing lumps of rice (growing up together through consuming rice). As for distant ancestors counting the generation from the great-grandparents upward, and those relatives who do not descend directly through the same blood, they would deserve to receive the transference of water called samānodaka, which means for those sharing water together. However, the Brahmins also transfer water to their first three generations of ancestors, and the way of transferring water is to pour it into the river, taking the water in one's palms and letting it rinse little by little while thinking of the dead and wishing them freedom from thirst. This traditional practice has entered into our Thai practice of the Khao Pinda (originally, Sapinda) by putting cooked rice into large leaves, turning them over and placing them together with the eatable, cooked material on trays, decorated with flowers or other decorating material as deemed fit. This is to be done on the Sart (Sārda or Shrāddha in Sanskrit) day, or on the festival period, or in the Songkran Day (the Ancient Thai New Year or the Water Festival). Originally, this kind of practice aimed at transferring merit to one's ancestors, just as the Brahmins do, but later on we Thai Buddhists do this in worshipping the Buddha.

"This way of transferring the merit to the dead by pouring the water through the palm or the fingertips has been practiced until this present day, with monks chanting appropriate long mantras and chanting blessings. According to the Brahmanic tradition, after the sacrificing ceremony is over, they throw away the rice lumps to animals, birds, pets, and crows, particularly crows, which are believed to be the representation of ghosts, and if they would eat the sacrificial offerings, they would not cause troubles to the ancestors.

"Furthermore, in the Brahmin merit-transference ceremony on Shrāddha, they invite learned Brahmins to have a feast together, and then give away the offerings, including clothes, which they consider very significant since they do not want their ancestors to be thirsty and naked. The offering of clothes in the merit-transference ceremony is also found in our Thai practice, but with the difference that some monks who undertake the austerity practice as regards the collection of the clothes left on the dust or on bushes, do not receive the clothes from the donor's hands. In connection with the Shrāddha ceremony, the other classes of people such as landlords and warriors embrace the same practice as the Brahmins do, although the feast for the Brahmins is not mentioned since they do not eat food prepared by the other castes. Nonetheless, they are understood to be the recipients of the offerings.

"The Brahmins believe that the dead would have gone to be born in various planes of existence, but because of love and respect that they have for their ancestors they consider that those ancestors are still together with them in form of invisible bodies, adissamāna-kāya, and have a place for living called petaloka – the realm of hungry ghosts. This kind of feeling we Thai Buddhists take from the Brahmins with an additional new understanding that those ancestors live in their same house with the new name of Ghost House.

"The practice of the Shrāddha ceremony by Brahmins has been admitted into Buddhism with the new name in Thai of Pubbetaplee, following the Ādiya-Sutta of Pañcaka-Nipāta, Anguttara-Nikāya, which stresses that it is the necessary function that the Householder Noble Disciples of the Buddha should carry out. Also, it is said in Khuddaka-Nikāya, Petavatthu thus:

> *"A good person taking into account either his/her ancestors or the guardian spirits should not be stingy, but should give offerings.*

"Now, let me elaborate the pittivisaya (or petavisaya, realm of hungry ghosts), which is understood to be derived from the pitṛloka (loka or world of the pitṛs, or deceased ancestors) of the Brahmin tradition. In the commentary, the terminology of either petaloka or pittivisayo is used, which is translated as plane or realm of preta (preta, Sanskrit; in Pali, peta) or hungry ghost. Peta placed after the prefix pubba (meaning before) becomes pubbapeta, which derives from pettika or petika, which has two meanings: the dead and the ancestors.

"Therefore, pittivisaya is likely to refer to the ghosts of ancestors, although I failed in my attempt to find a description of pittivisaya in the Pali texts. Nonetheless, such ghosts should not be classified as bad ghosts that live in the painful plane of life, but should be regarded as earthly devas (bhumma-deva). The reason for classifying the ghosts of ancestors as pitiful beings belonging to the painful plane of life is not found in any texts. But in the Dhanañjāni-Sutta they are put in a better position than that of the animal kingdom, which is appropriate. However, the commentators of much later period of time gave the meaning of pittivisaya as hungry ghosts that are very thin and have deformed bodies, and appear both frightening and pitiful. I understand this kind of expression by those Buddhist commentators as the contempt to the ancestors of the Brahmins in exactly the same way as Brahmins insult us Buddhists.

"The Brahmins are very afraid that their ancestors would be poor, hungry, thirsty, and naked, and therefore they make the sacrificial offerings, as described. We may mention some more features of these hungry ghosts, who are said have a very large stomach and a very small mouth (as small as the hole of a needle), and so, as much as they eat, they can never feel full or free of hunger, instead they become more anxious and restless concerning hunger and thirst, as if they were on fire. In this way, the classification of them into the pitiful beings in the hard, painful plane of life is sufficiently reasonable.

"Nonetheless, in some suttas there are sayings that there may be risk to those performing merit-transference by offering necessary things either to Buddhist monks or to Brahmins as the case may be, in delivering those symbolic offerings to their ancestors and relatives. The reason is that those beings would consume the food that is available in the plane of life where they were born into, and would not receive the transference of merit dedicated to them. Only when they were born in the plane of life belonging to the hungry ghosts would they be able to receive the offerings transferred to them through the said ceremony. So, bear in mind that those who were born in hell, in the animal kingdom, or in heavenly world will not receive the offerings from their human family members and relatives since they are obliged to live on food and/or on consequences of their karmas done in the human world.

"Arriving at this point let me summarize the categories of hungry ghosts (preta) as I remember them described in certain texts as follows:

"1. Those hungry ghosts that are starving, with the deformed, thin, and hungry bodies.

"2. Those hungry ghosts whose physical bodies are distorted, for instance, the physical bodies are human while the heads belong to such animals as crows, pigs, or snakes, etc.

"3. Those hungry ghosts whose physical bodies appear extremely peculiar as the results of the evil karmas, suffering their own karmas individually.

"4. Those hungry ghosts that appear pretty much like the normal human beings, some are quite beautiful and handsome and have their own paradise as day-time residence, but at night they must get out of the residence to suffer their karmas until the dawn of the new day. Those ghosts are called vimānika-peta – the ghosts that live in the paradise during the daytime."[8]

Is it possible to be born an animal?

According to the Buddhist scriptures there are four categories of the non-progressive plane of existence (apāya-bhumi), namely, hell, animal kingdom, realm of hungry ghosts, and asurakāya, and we have already discussed at some length two of these four. As for the animal kingdom, it's so obvious that there is no need to discuss it, nevertheless, there might be a question whether those performing bad karmas would be born as animals after death? In fact, this question is not so difficult to answer since we humans have, to some extent, a direct or indirect relationship with the animals, and in the scriptures there is a clear indication that those who would be born animals would be because of possessing an animal character. But, noble, enlightened people will not be born animals since they no longer keep the animal character in their psychophysical systems. However, we human beings, although some of us might be very bad, are still considered the outstanding beings that live on earth. Therefore, it doesn't seem reasonable that the humans would be born as ants, mosquitoes, and other small animals, but it might be probable that some humans would be born animals that are very close to them such as dogs, cats, and cattle; this is in accordance with the story told by the Buddha in Kukkurovāda-Sutta as follows:

At one time the Buddha was staying in the village, *Haliddavasana* by name, in the State of Koliya. At that time, a son of the Koliyans, named Punna, underwent the practice of the character of a cow and a naked mendicant, named Seniya, adopted the behavior and character of a dog as his practice of life. They both went to see the Buddha and asked him this question, "Blessed One, the honorable Seniya has been practicing on a regular basis for a long time the character and behavior of a dog and living on food buried in the soil, which most people find it difficult to do. What will be his plane of life after his death?" "Punna, let the question be. Do not ask me hurriedly," said the Buddha. But Punna persisted and asked him two more times, and at the third time, the Buddha answered it, "If I do not reply to your question, you will try and try again to press me with such a question. All right, I will answer you, so please listen

---

[8] Translated from *Dhammavicharn*, pages 86-93.

attentively. Punna! Someone in this world practices dog character, dog behavior, the dog way of life, dog consciousness, and the dog habitual way of thinking to full scale and with no flaw. After death, such an individual will enter into the friendship with dogs (meaning, will be born as a dog). If he or she would hold the view that by practicing, cultivating the character of a dog, and living the dog's life totally, he or she will become a deva (heavenly being) and will be born in a happy plane of existence, certainly, such view is totally wrong and heretic in all its aspects. So, Punna! I would say to you that the person with such a practice and such a view will be born either in hell or in the animal kingdom." After hearing the Buddha's direct reply Seniya, the naked mendicant, was crying and weeping painfully.

Then, Seniya put another question to the Buddha: "Blessed One! Punna Koliyaputta has been carrying on practice of the character of a cow perfectly and without any flaw for a very long time. What will be his plane of life after his death?" Once again, the Buddha was trying to stop him, but he continued asking that same question three times; and then the Buddha answered him saying, "Seniya! Someone who cultivates the character of a cow, cow behavior, cow consciousness, and practices the cow way of life with holding the totally erroneous view that such practice would lead him/her to heaven, will certainly enter into the friendship with the cows (that is, be born a cow), if not in hell. Seniya! This is my answer to your question." After hearing the Buddha's straightforward reply Punna was crying and weeping painfully just as Seniya was.

Finally, those two men became totally convinced of the Buddha's Dharma and therefore took it to their hearts and minds completely. They requested him to preach to them further the meaningful and significant Dharma, which he did. At the conclusion of his discourse, Punna pronounced himself a devoted disciple of the Buddha, while Seniya gave up his robe of a naked mendicant and asked the Buddha to admit him into the Buddhist Order of Monks, which he honored with compassion.[9]

What is asurakāya?

There is another thing related to the issue of hell, which we need to know about, and that is the asurakāya. Krompraya Vachirañanavaroros explains it this way:

"The matter of asurakāya is rather absurd, which is not mentioned at all in the Pali texts, and the name is found only in the commentaries. In the Sanskrit Dictionary asura means the one who stays, referring to the category of the invisible bad ghosts or the nameless ghosts that frighten human beings deceivingly. A ghost is distinct from a hungry ghost (preta or peta) in the way that the hungry ghost does not frighten people invisibly, but only people themselves happen to encounter it by accident, or when it wants to ask for something it simply appears. It's not clear if the hungry ghost is in the category of the invisible body (adissamāna-kāya). The food for the beings in hell is said to be their karma, while the animals live on a variety of distinct categories of

---

[9] Translated from Majjhima-Nikāya, Majjhimapannāsa 17/55.

food depending on what type of animals they belong to. However, the hungry ghosts' food is both their karma and the meritorious offerings that the relatives in the human world transfer to them. On the other hand, the asurakāya's food is not mentioned specifically, but is compared to the bad kind of food for the giants or the things that grow in the physical bodies of animals whether good or bad, dirty or clean."

Then, Krompraya Vachirañanavaroros has made a comparison regarding those beings of the non-progressive plane of existence as follows:

"The beings in hell are like the prisoners sentenced to various punishments according to the variety of crimes they have committed, but the government feeds them and so they are not the hunger driven beings. The hungry ghosts are compared to those who are very poor, deprived of food, clothes, and sometimes housing as well. They have great difficulty in earning a living, and make a living by begging. The asurakāyas are partly like the hungry ghosts in terms of being poor and lacking food and clothing, and earn their living by robbery and burglary particularly at night and/or cheating, stealing, and robbing the people's possessions and properties by deceit and by force."[10]

Four sources of origination

According to the various sources of the Buddhist Tipiṭaka, we find four categories of life origination in various forms in the entire universe, technically known as four types of yoni (yoni refers to the origination or birth of life). These four sources of life origination the Buddha himself was expounding to Sāriputta, his Right Hand Disciple whose expertise is knowledge and wisdom as follows:

"Sāriputta, there are four categories of life origination; they are andaja, jalābuja, samsedaja, and oppātika. Sāriputta, what does it mean by andaja? Those beings that are born of eggs belong to this category of andaja-yoni (anda, egg; ja, born of). Sāriputta, what is the meaning of jalābuja? Those beings that are born of the mother's womb belong to this category of jalābuja-yoni (conception in the womb). Sāriputta, what is the meaning of samsedaja? Those beings that are born of the rotten dead fishes, of rotten corps, or of the bad, rotten food, or of the filthy water in ponds, in canals et cetera belong to this category of samsedaja-yoni. Sāriputta, what is the meaning of oppātika? Those devas (heavenly beings), the beings in hell, certain types of human beings, and certain categories of hungry ghosts, all belong to this category of oppātika-yoni.

"Sāriputta, there are only these four categories of life origination."

Some explanations on the four categories of yoni (life origination)

In the commentary, Papañcasūdanī by name, the commentator (Buddhaghosa) explained the first three categories of yoni in exactly the same way as the Buddha did in Majjhima-Nikāya, Mūlapannāsa, as translated and given above. However, as regards the oppātika-yoni, the Papañcasūdanī's commen-

---

[10] Translated from the Dhammavibhaga, volume 2, pages 37-38.

tator explained that it refers to the beings born without dependence on the conditions as the previous three categories do, and that when they are born, they just appear as grown up beings suddenly as if emerging from nowhere.

Therefore, the oppātika-yoni is the type of life origination free of parents or of those who provide the source of birth or of coming into existence. So, considering the example given by the Buddha, we understand that all beings in hell and in heaven are born without any sexual contact/intercourse between the male and female entities.

However, in that same just-mentioned commentary there are some more examples provided, especially with respect to heavenly beings or devas. It explained further that the devas here refer to those devas of the four retinues (cātumahārāja) up to the highest class of devas, while the earthly devas (bhummadevatā, those living on land) belong to all four categories of yoni. As for certain human beings that belong to this category of oppātika, there was no example given; however, we may hold the view that the Buddha could mean those original humans that lived on the planet earth for the first time according to the description in the Aggañña-Sutta already shown in the first chapter of this work. On this, Krompraya Vachirañanavaroros said, "Those oppātika beings just emerge and grow into adulthood suddenly without having been children before. When they die, they merely disappear with no trace."

Let us look further into the issue of heaven and its implication in terms of consciousness. Here is my concise description of it:

> It is said that there are six classes of heaven lying on top of another. Beginning with the lowest class they are:
> 1. the heaven of the four kings who take their positions at the four quarters of the firmament (cātummahārājika);
> 2. the heaven of the thirty-three gods headed by Indra (tāvatimsa);
> 3. the heaven of the Yama gods, the governing gods (Yāma), which may be compared with a government body or administration of a country;
> 4. the heaven of delight (tusita), which is the dwelling place of the wonderful and highly developed beings such as Bodhisatvas who live and fill themselves with ecstatic joy, bliss, love, and compassion;
> 5. the heaven of the gods who rejoice in their own creations (nimmānarati), which could refer to the highly creative people, the artists, and the psychically rich people; and
> 6. the heaven of the gods who make others' creations serve their own ends (paranimmita vasavatti), which symbolically refers to those deposed monarchs, retired leaders of nations, rich or poor, who do not have to do anything to earn their living, for they have good pensions and have accumulated much wealth, whether properly or improperly, during their time of being in power.

It is quite clear that all forms of heaven are really found within us human beings who exist in the comprehensive world of consciousness. Some of us can make use of the healing energy through our own psychic channels, while others are prone to act as mediums through whom the heavenly beings or gods or spirits materialize themselves and function as helpers, teachers, healers, etc. Perhaps many of those who are qualified healers, clairvoyants, and prophets actually come from heaven number five. Nonetheless, what I am saying is that devas are both inside and outside of our human form as energy fields and stations of consciousness (viññāna-ṭhiti). Comprehending this, we shall never be surprised when being exposed to the medium, the shaman, or the psychic healer through whom a certain deva or spirit guide is manifesting and offering services out of love, caring, and compassion for humanity. But at the same time, we should investigate the qualities and the teachings as well as the acts of those spirit teachers or spirit healers so that we will understand what class of heaven the belong to. This will help us see more profoundly what kind of consciousness is manifesting and at what level it is operating. To do so is nothing but the study of consciousness by direct observation (Vipassana Practice), at many different levels through its actual manifestations at the moment.

Bear in mind that all the devas or heavenly beings still enjoy sense-pleasures, even more than we humans do. They do not believe in celibacy yet, and there is no monastic institution offered to them as an alternative. So, they spend their lifetimes consuming the pleasures of senses with great rejoicing. Due to the temporary absence of suffering as a challenge, they don't seem to make any further progress in their lives in terms of spiritual development or material production. It seems as if they were stuck with sensual pleasures until the extinction of their ages has come and they disappear from their heavens. I wonder if anybody wants to live the form of a deva life for long?

Archetypes symbolizing four planes and sixteen grades of jhānic bliss (meditative absorptions), or altered states of consciousness that transcend sensual pleasures, symbolically refer to the beings living in such a realm of jhānic consciousness, which are called brahmas. They are divided into sixteen grades according to the four stages of jhāna as follows:

1. The plane of the first jhāna comprises three grades of brahma:
    1. the realm of the Brahma's retinue (Brahma parisajjā)
    2. the realm of Brahma's Ministers (Brahma purohita)
    3. the realm of Great Brahma (Maha Brahma)
2. The plane of the second jhāna also comprises three grades of brahma:
    1. the realm of minor lustre (parittābhā)
    2. the realm of Infinite lustre (appamānābhā)
    3. the realm of the radiant brahmas (ābhassarā). It is said the rays of light, like lightening, are emitted from the bodies of the radiant gods.
3. The plane of the third jhāna consists of:
    1. the realm of brahmas of minor aura (parittasubhā)
    2. the realm of brahmas of infinite aura (appamānasubhā)
    3. the realm of brahmas of steady aura (subhakinha, lit. good light, meaning a mass of steady light emitted from a body.
4. The plane of the fourth jhāna consists of:
    1. the realm of brahmas of great reward (vehapphala — abundant reward, resultant from the jhāna practice)

      2. the realm of brahmas without ideation/perception (asaññāsatta)
      3. the realm of the pure abodes (suddhāvāsa), which are further subdivided into five:
          a. the durable or immobile realm (avihā)
          b. the serene realm (atappā)
          c. the beautiful realm (sudassā)
          d. the clear-sighted realm (sudassī)
          e. the supreme beings of the highest realm (akaniṭṭhā).[11]

A conclusion on the issues of heaven and hell

The world in which we live can be either a heaven or a hell depending on what we do to it, and on how we humans relate to one another in the entire world regardless of East, West, race, color of skin, or the place of birth. When the human rights and the common or indisputable moral principles (including human conscience) are genuinely respected and cared for by each human being, each nation whether powerful or power-less militarily and/or economically, and we are all working for peace and living in peace and in dynamic harmony with one another, then our world is a heaven. On the contrary, when the bigger, the more powerful, and wealthier take advantages of, or seize possession by immoral means or by force either of the properties belonging to other people or even of the country that appears potentially dangerous, and therefore human morality decreases and human rights are not respected, then our world becomes a hell. In such a hellish world, the wealthy neglect the poor or even take advantage of them by various possible ways and means, the more powerful dominate the less powerful, the conservatives are against the socialists and vice versa, the employees fight against the employers, et cetera, so there is no peace, there is no harmony, there no unconditional love or real caring regardless of culture, religion, race, or nation, and there is no respect for one another. Instead hate, violence, and egocentric activity are on the increase. Such is indeed the obvious hell in the human world.

The world of hell on earth may be big or small, more brutal or moderately gentle, more frightening or less fearful, more painful and tormented or bearable, depending on human-made law, its reinforcement, and the government's policy imposed either on the criminals of all kinds or on those holding opinions, viewpoints, philosophy, political ideology, and economic management against those in power or in the government of the country. The ways by which all the countries of the world today treat prisoners, captives, and opposition elements are more or less very similar to the detailed description of the variety of hell in the Devadūta-Sutta. So, if those in power and we humans in general are authentically working together and moving forward toward creating peace, harmony, mutual understanding, and mutual respect, we will be able to build a true heaven on our planet earth. It's up to us all!

---

[11] See details in the author's book, *Turning to the Source* (1990).

=7=

NIRVANA, THE ULTIMATE TRUTH

Without realizing nirvana there is no understanding of life

In dharma studies and practices, if there is no actual realization of nirvana, the knowledge and comprehension of life will not be complete because the Buddha dharma lays a strong emphasis on the total understanding of life as it is. Since nirvana is the final destination of one's life journey and the ultimate goal of the dharma practice, one must reach it so that the journey of life will be completed. In the Brahmajāla-Sutta, the Buddha's Discourse about the Noblest Net (Network), there is a very clear indication that the spiritual masters and distinguished scholars during the Buddha's time still held some wrong views on the Truth because of not *realizing nirvana experientially* for themselves. The Buddha was the first Master who discovered nirvana through his own experiential realization and therefore, he became the Authentic All-Knowing One. Moreover, all the enlightened disciples who realized nirvana as it truly is could comprehend totally and accurately the issue of life and death, including the cycle of kilesa-karma-vipāka (mental, psychological, and spiritual impurity or contaminations, the full law of karma, and karma's consequences) and the substance of heaven and hell. As previously stated, only the noble sekhas (those attaining the earlier stages of enlightenment up to the arahatta-magga) can understand the issue of life in this world and in other worlds (planets) since they realize nirvana experientially. Although they might not have the scientific and/or biological knowledge about life, about the universe, and about the physical, phenomenal worlds, or might not have studied psychology as many of us do at present, even so the Buddha emphasized that sekhas and only the sekhas realize life and all its aspects thoroughly. This implies that knowledgeable others apart from the noble sekhas, although they might be specialized in science, in biology, or in psychology, or might have the indisputable authority of world religions, may not possess the fully accurate knowledge of life and death unless they have realized nirvana in this life on earth.

Some misunderstandings of nirvana

The majority of people tend to misunderstand nirvana by holding the erroneous view that nirvana is a matter only for those renouncing the world, such as monks, nuns, yogis, and people of that category, and that nirvana is not a necessity required for achievement in life. Furthermore, quite a number of people misunderstand nirvana as something to be achieved after death, or as a matter of not being born again and of total annihilation, which gives them an impression that nirvana is not an interesting, meaningful subject, since life without nirvana is quite enjoyable, although one may experience unhappiness and suffering from time to time. With such misunderstandings, those people turn their back on nirvana and leave out the most significant theme of life which needs to be fulfilled before the king of death calls upon us or the messengers of either heaven or hell give a knock at the door.

Nirvana is the issue for all humans

In fact, nirvana is the most desirable thing for everyone since one of its meanings is *peacefulness and luminosity*. We all need peace and light since life in the world is so complicated, complex, and full of dangers, and in addition there are so many dark forces both within and outside that try desperately to influence or run the show on the life that each of us lives individually and collectively as well. Usually, our ordinary, common minds are on fire since they get burned constantly by the fires of kilesa (inner contaminations and disturbing influences), particularly the fire of desire or craving. Nonetheless, from time to time we manage to calm them down, bringing them to drink the elixir of peace, tranquillity, and non-activeness when the mental, inner verbal, and energetic bodily activities technically known as sankhāra slow down and are at rest. At such moments we feel at ease, relaxed, and able to put our feet up, our minds may reach the desirable, psychological state of calmness and dynamic stillness without any preoccupations, restlessness, and concerns. This is entirely contrary to the moment when the mind is filled with, or dominated by, the struggling desire and thirst, which tends to beget pain or suffering or at minimum an uneasy feeling or mental discomfort.

Please observe what actually happens when the mind comes to a rest. Is there peacefulness and a tranquil atmosphere spread out all over our inner world? One will answer "Yes." Therefore, what we mean by *happiness* is the peacefulness and the resting stillness of the internal activities or sankhāras, so all forms of happiness whether mundane or supramundane are the outcome of the peacefulness and restfulness of all sankhāras. For this reason, the Buddha declared in the Dhammapada of Khuttaka-Nikāya thus:

There is no happiness aside from peacefulness.
(Natthi santiparam sukham.)

Considering the time of being happy, we see that our mind (sometimes body too) is at peace and comfortable since it's satisfied with what it has, what it achieves, and it's not driven by the internal forces, especially desire. For those living their lives in the world, if their minds are on fire and without peace most of the time, they are likely to suffer neurological illness, particularly anxiety and fear (for example, fear of not getting what they want and of losing what the have gotten). This is in accordance with the principle of the dependent origination that shows the process of the arising of dukkha (suffering): *"If a feeling or sensation is strong, desire or craving becomes strong; with the driving power of desire, attachment is powerful; and with the domineering power of attachment, the feeling or sensation becomes increasingly strong. On fulfilling and satisfying one's desires, one is happy, on the contrary, when unable to succeed or get that which one wants, suffering or unhappiness reigns on one; and with more suffering or more happiness the desire is burning."*

Therefore, peace of mind is very essential for the capacity to live a happy life, and without it there will be no *real* happiness. Now, nirvana as the most peaceful state of mind/consciousness, refers to the highest, ever-lasting peace, the peace that arises together with the totally enlightened wisdom and the perfect understanding of life with all its conditions and situations. So, the peace of nirvana is absolutely distinct from the ordinary peace in the world since the peace that we achieve from time to time in the world is just temporary and non-enduring, and, in turn, may become a cause of war, for example, when a certain country is at peace and not involving itself with a war, but at the same time such a country is producing weapons and undergoes exercising its military armed forces, which could become a potential cause of a war or of the international tensions on top of its efforts to protect such fragile, worldly peace.

The peace that arises and prevails permanently through the full realization of nirvana is the type of peace that can purify and completely transform all kinds of kilesa; and the completely transformed kilesas will *not* be able to return to their former state of existence. This is like a piece of burning firewood thrown into water, thereby fully extinguishing the fire for all time. The simple reason for all the transformed and purified kilesas being unable to become effective again is that the total realization of nirvana brings about the luminous light that can shine forth eternally together with impeccable awareness and indisputable, ever-lastingly enlightened wisdom that are able to stay present all the time. So, the mind and consciousness of those who realize nirvana experientially will always be prone toward such everlasting peace and therefore all kinds of kilesa totally eliminated through the nirvanic realization will never be able to become alive since their roots have been taken out and put away lastingly. This may be compared to the completely extinct fire without the remainder of fuel, which will be unable to produce any burning effect after all.

According to the law of dependent origination, these four kilesas, namely, ignorance (avijjā), feeling/sensation (vedanā), desire/thirst (taṇhā), and attachment (upādāna), *are interdependent and interrelated by conditions*. So, if the desire, craving, or thirst has no remaining fuel within one's character and the unconscious, avijjā and upādāna will no longer exist, either. With the non-existence of avijjā, taṇhā, and upādāna, a kind of feeling or sensation (vedanā) that is influenced or conditioned by those three principal kilesas cited above, will not come into existence; and without such a feeling or sensation in operation, the three powerful kilesas of avijjā, taṇhā, and upādāna cannot continue operating. In the case of the arahats who have transformed and transmuted all kinds of kilesas totally and enduringly, although they still have feelings and sensations since their sense modalities that provide the source of contact still operate, nonetheless their feelings and sensations are totally free from impurity, blemish, and contamination.

Bear in mind that the peace of nirvana is not the kind that is dull and with no juice, but is the peace that is transparent, joyful, and vibrantly alive. The mind or consciousness of those who have realized and entered nirvana is clear, spacious at all times, full of light emitting everywhere, and endowed with the deepest and complete understanding of life. Since impeccable awareness and insightful wisdom are always present in the nirvana-realized people, they are able to know and see things as they are and at the very moment of their appearing, so that it becomes impossible for them to be deceived or to get lost in anything that enters their senses. Therefore, in those who have realized nirvana experientially, there is no regression, weakening, nor is there any disgust toward anything.

Furthermore, with the experiential realization of nirvana, there will a wonderful thing that happens, and that is the profound understanding of nature. This is because nirvana is the background of nature: How either nature or the law of nature comes into existence will be comprehended without much difficulty; and the profound understanding of all the issues regarding nature will help us achieve perfect freedom, which is the consequence of realizing nirvana with actual experience.

With all the briefly described benefits that would arise from the nirvanic realization, we emphasize nirvana as the essential issue for everyone and as a matter of unlimited value for all the people in the whole world to appreciate and realize. We may begin our study of nirvana with the recognition that eternal living peace, everlasting luminous light, and total purity of heart and mind are attributes of nirvana, and that these are absolutely desirable and constantly sought for by all the mindful humans of all times. Since these mindful people do not misunderstand nirvana as something to be fulfilled after death, or something centered on the matter of not being reborn (as many unaware people comprehend erroneously), they thus become convinced that nirvana is to be realized here and now, in this life on earth. We occasionally experience peace of mind, some light of consciousness, and some pure heart/mind, which are our actual experience, although they are not truly authentic (in the sense of the absolute), as those attributes belonging to nirvana. In order to achieve the absolute attributes of nirvana, in addition to realizing it experientially, one must discern deeply and totally the three dharmas; namely, *the three characteristics of existence, the four noble truths, and the law of dependent origination – the process of the arising of suffering and the process of arriving at nirvana at the complete cessation of suffering.*

However, we should keep in mind that there various steps of realizing nirvana, namely, the initial step is called *stream-enterer, or sotāpanna*, which refers to those who have entered the stream of nirvana. Although the sotāpanna's realization of nirvana is not quite at the same level in its depth and totality as the nirvanic realization of the arahats who have entered it completely, with stream-entry, the sotāpannas have eradicated and transformed totally the *three samyojanas* (the mental and spiritual contaminations that bind us humans to the lower world of sensuality and form), namely, the *wrong view on self and ego, skeptical doubt or indecisiveness, and superstitious practices together with their belief systems.*

The second step is a *once-returner*, referring to the sakadāgāmīs (those who will return to be born human beings once more after their achievements of the nirvanic realization). Also, the sakadāgāmīs have transformed and transcended those three samyojanas, and in addition have reduced tremendously the other two samyojanas, namely, lustful desire and ill-will.

The third step is a *non-returner or anāgāmī*. This term implies that those nirvana-realized people will never return to the human world or to any lower worlds, but will be born in the pure abode realm of consciousness technically known as *suddhāvāsa*. They have utterly transmuted and entirely transformed the five (lower) samyojanas: the three samyojanas that the sotāpannas have eliminated and the other two that the sotāpannas have not eliminated but have significantly reduced. Since those five samyojanas are binding us humans to the lower world, so long as we do nothing to transform them we will remain under their dictates and are bound to live in this kind of world unless we enter the third step of nirvanic realization and become the anāgāmīs naturally. For those arriving at the third enlightenment of the anāgāmīs one very noticeable thing is their wisdom becoming much more profound and much more articulate than those two previous noble enlightened persons in that they understand fully that kilesa is not a natural thing at all but a visiting element since the kilesa, for instance sensual desire, can be eliminated (totally transformed) with no remainder. In addition, the anāgāmīs comprehend further that the sexual organs are the source of the arousing of the passion of sensual, lustful desire since without sensual objects and sexual organs there will be no stimulant to bring up sensual, lustful desire. On the contrary, when sensual, lustful desire has been transformed totally and its energetic passion no longer exists even in form of dormant or latent tendency within the consciousness and in the character, although the external stimulants still exist, they cannot have any influence or power to beget sensual, lustful desire. This is like a completely extinct fire with no more fuel to feed its continuity: even if someone puts in some firewood, there will be no effect in terms of burning. Also, the anāgāmīs realize fully that after death they will no longer return to this world of sensuality, but will born in the other world where it is pure and free of all the sensual energies. Since their psychophysical systems have been transformed with the total eradication of energies of the sensual realm of consciousness, they are unable to provide an appropriate condition for such consciousness to run the show of life as they previously could. This is in accord with the principle of dependent origination that makes it lucidly clear that the form of life with all its conditions must be appropriate and coherent with the rebirth consciousness present at the moment of conception in case of being born in a mother's womb or at the moment of appearing suddenly in case of oppātika beings. In short, we may state here that the anāgāmīs' realization and purity are much more complete than those of the sotāpannas and the sakadāgāmīs.

As for those attaining arahatship, the other five samyojanas binding the human beings to the higher world will be utterly eradicated and totally transformed on top of the lower five samyojanas utterly eliminated by the anāgāmīs. Those higher samyojanas are *attachment to, or longing for the jhānic meditation regarding form (rūpa-rāga), attachment to, or longing for the formless jhānic meditation (arūpa-rāga), pride (māna), restlessness (uddhacca) and ignorance (avijjā — referring to not realizing fully the four noble truths)*. For this reason, all the anāgāmīs must continue working toward full enlightenment and the complete realization of nirvana, while the arahats have completed their work and their journey in all forms and at all levels of consciousness, and therefore they are the most peaceful, the most luminous in terms of light of consciousness, and the purest of all.

A definition of nibbāna according to the Buddhist Canon and teachings

In the Chakka-Vagga of Anguttara-Nikāya the Buddha said:

"Monks, a monk who is endowed with the six dharmas will be able to realize the *supreme cooling off* (in Pali, sītibhāva, an equivalence of nirvana, which signifies the synonymous expression of extinction of all the inner fires and heat)."

These six dharmas are:

1. Training his mind whenever mental training is required.
2. Sustaining his mind whenever mental sustenance is needed.
3. Cheering his mind whenever mental cheering is necessary.
4. Neutralizing his mind whenever mental neutralization and equilibrium becomes significant.
5. Possessing fine character.
6. Taking his delight in nirvana.

In another place the Buddha was talking about the feeling of those having realized nirvana through their experiential touch on it. As soon as their consciousness enters the stream of nirvana, all of them would express to themselves quietly and mindfully the following feelings:

"Oh, peaceful indeed is nibbāna (the Pali word equivalent to Sanskrit nirvana)! Oh, marvelous indeed is nibbāna! Here, in nibbāna there is complete freedom from (mental and spiritual) intoxications, total (quenching) transformation of thirst/craving, thorough abandonment of longing, the utter cutting off of samsara (the cycle of birth and death, and the cycle of kilesa-karma-vipāka), absolute relinquishment of lustful desire, hatred, and delusion, and extinction without remainder of all the kilesas. This indeed is nibbāna."

In the Dhammapada the Buddha confirmed those feelings as follows:

"Those who have tasted the flavor of the utter peacefulness from kilesas and the stilling of sankhāra and have drunk it all, are completely free from anxiety and preoccupations, transcend all the evil once and for all, and abide in the dharma drink forever."

"The dharma drink brings happiness and joy in the dharma, with clarity of consciousness and awakened mind. The wise always take delight in the dharma proclaimed by the noble, enlightened ones."

While in the Navaka-Vagga of Samyutta-Nikāya he declared:

"Here, in this peaceful and marvelous nibbāna all the conditioned things (sankhāra) reach their stillness, the attachment to all aggregates of existence is relinquished, all kinds of craving/thirst become extinguished, and all the mental and spiritual contaminations are totally cleansed off and utterly transformed. Such indeed is nibbāna."

The unborn and uncreated

So far as we are aware, the realization of nirvana is natural to all human beings, which is similar to the common fact that everyone after being born into life will have to decay, to get ill, and to die, with no exception. The consciousness of those who discern life totally and profoundly is getting closer to the vicinity of nirvana since nirvana is a natural state or an existential origination source (āyatana, more on this, below) without any creation or anyone to make it up. This may be compared with wherever and whenever darkness has been cleared away by light, then what prevails is light with all its luminosity. In exactly the same way, when the dark force of ignorance (avijjā) and the fire of craving/thirst (taṇhā) have been absolutely removed from our consciousness, then what prevail are ever-shining light and endurable peace. One metaphor for this is a diamond covered by the mud, and so cannot shine forth, but as soon as the mud is removed, then the diamond can be seen with its brightly shining light. Like this indeed is the realization of nirvana!

Since nirvana *is,* it is not born and not created, and therefore the Buddha declared precisely in the Udāna of Khuttaka-Nikāya as follows:

"Monks, there exists the unborn, unbecoming, uncreated, and unconditioned. Monks, if there were not the unborn, unbecoming, uncreated, and unconditioned, there would not appear the deliverance of the born, the becoming, the created, and the conditioned. But because there exists the unborn, unbecoming, uncreated, and unconditioned, therefore, there appears the deliverance of the born, the becoming, the created, and the conditioned."

Nirvana is an origination (energy) source (āyatana)

Once again, in the Udāna of Khuttaka-Nikāya, the Buddha said this about nirvana as the origination (energy) source or āyatana:

"Monks, there exists the āyatana in which there is earth, no water, no fire, and no wind, which is neither the infinite space (ākāsānañcāyatana) nor the infinite consciousness (viññāṇañcāyatana), neither this world nor the other world, neither the moon nor the sun. Monks, I do not say that such an āyatana has a coming, a going, a standing, a deceasing, a birth; and that the said āyatana has no stationary status and is without an object. That is indeed the ending of suffering (dukkha)."

Although the term 'āyatana' used by the Buddha with reference to nirvana in this Udāna means an origination source, this does not mean that nirvana is the origination source of a form of consciousness, as in the interpretation of some learned Buddhists (that nirvana shines forth in a form of consciousness), or as some other people misunderstand, that nirvana is God, who in the theistic religions can create all things and all beings: *this is absolutely* not *the meaning of the Buddhist nirvana*. The real meaning of nirvana as the āyatana is that it is the object of the dharma (dhammārammana), which is the dharmic object that the consciousness can hold onto firmly in its movement toward the supramundane (transcendental) dharma. According to the section on Knowledge and Wisdom (Paññā-Nidesa) in the Visuddhimagga (Path of Purification), Buddhaghosa, its author, explained it this way: At the moment when the consciousness is about to cross over from the puthujjana (unenlightened) realm to the noble enlightened realm, nirvana appears to that consciousness just like the full moon (emerging and shining forth brightly). In the case in which the kilesas or sankhāras are not decreasing or not lessening or not arriving at peacefulness and tranquility, the appearing of nirvana will not be clear, just as when clouds cover and pass in front of the moon at the full moon night. If this is the case, what the yogi (meditator) should do is to contemplate intently on the nature of impermanence (anicca), dissatisfactoriness (dukkha), and the truth of no permanent self or entity (anattā) existing anywhere, whether inside or outside of the five aggregates of existence. By so doing, the remaining kilesas that cover up and determine the consciousness will gradually fade away, and then the nirvanic appearing will become clearer and clearer within the consciousness. For this reason, nirvana earns the title of *āyatana – origination or energy source,* which is the dhammāyatana (origin/energy source of the dharma) or dhammārammana (object of the dharma) and is counted as the sixth external object in pair with the mind modality (the sixth sense).

For obtaining a deeper and more precise comprehension of nirvana, we should contemplate the following words uttered by the Buddha in the same text of Udāna, in the Khuttaka-Nikāya:

"Monks, in those who depend on craving/thirst, there is a wavering mind, while there is no such mind in those who do not depend on craving/thirst. When there is no wavering mind, tranquillity sets in, with the existence of tranquility, there is no more longing (or wanting to be gratified). Without the longing or wanting a gratifying sensation, there is no coming and no going; and without the coming and the going, there is no death and no rebirth. With no existence of death and rebirth, there is no this world, no other world, and no world between the two. That is indeed the cessation of suffering (dukkha)."

From the above-quoted discourse delivered by the Buddha himself we learn the practical way leading on to the realization of nirvana in addition to the Buddha's demonstration of how it is possible or impossible for death and rebirth to continue or to cease their processes. Furthermore, that discourse shows us obviously the sequence of mind or consciousness on the way to nirvana. If you, my reader, have not studied the teaching of dependent origination, please do so thoroughly and read with full and vital attention the above discourse so that you will have a clearer understanding, not only of the above-cited discourse but of how the process of becoming leads on to, or begets, birth.

Nirvana is not void or emptiness

Up till now, it has become quite clear that nirvana undoubtedly exists, and it is something void or empty. In this connection, the great Buddhist commentator, Buddhaghosa, said about it in his famous treatise of the Visuddhimagga (Vsm.vi.796) as follows: "Nirvana is actually the existential thing, it is not something that anyone has invented through imagination; it is not an imaginative dream or a piece of fantasy that the conscious mind or the unconscious process has made up. The turtle's moustache and the rabbit's horns are non-existential things, which have never existed at any epoch in human history or in pre-history for that matter; and no one has ever seen a turtle's moustache and a rabbit's horns. But nirvana is in no way the same as the turtle's moustache and the rabbit's horns, because nirvana is real and truly exists; but its existence is unmanifested and without any event; the arising, the manifesting, and the passing away are the characteristics of all conditioned things (sankhāras), but as for nirvana there is no arising and there is no passing away. What actually appears as nirvana is the existential reality that *is* such, eternally."

Nirvana is not a consciousness

Another thing that we should realize fully and precisely is about the consciousness that has been deliberated and freed, through the uprooting of all the kilesas and all the contaminations; this consciousness is technically known as the consciousness attaining nirvana. This does not mean that such a purest consciousness is nirvana itself since the said consciousness is that conscious process which will eventually disappear or pass away for good just like all other phenomenal existences. Therefore, the Abhidharma texts have discussed this issue as follows:

"Which dharmas are called consciousness? Eye-consciousness, Ear-consciousness, nose-consciousness, tongue-consciousness, body-consciousness, mind-consciousness, and heart-consciousness, all these dharmas are called consciousness. Which dharmas are not consciousness? The aggregate of feeling/sensation, the aggregate of perception, the aggregate of sankhāras (light and dark forces within the conscious and unconscious processes), all kinds of form, and the uncreated, all these dharmas are NOT consciousness".[1]

The word 'asankhatadhātu' used (in the original Pali text here; meaning the unconstructed, unconditioned, uncaused element) refers to nirvana. The above-mentioned text of the Abhidharma has made it absolutely clear that nirvana is NOT a consciousness.

What is meant by nirvana as the void?

As already stated, nirvana is an existential truth, and it is not emptiness like space or nothingness. If nirvana were simply an element of space or ākāsa-dhātu, it would be something quite shallow and not the most profound dharma; but as the Buddha said about it in the Dhammapada of Khuttaka-Nikāya: "*All the Buddhas declare nirvana as the highest dharma (truth).*" So, when he said that *nirvana is utterly empty — Nibbānam paramam suññam*, he simply meant to say that *nirvana is absolutely **devoid** of nāma-rūpa — the psychophysical phenomena or systems of the body and mind*. He did not mean that nirvana is nothing whatsoever, which itself is merely one of the higher states of the formless, meditative absorptions.

---

[1] Abhidhammattha-Sangahapāli, 34/332.

Nirvana is not another aggregate

When we say that one of the significant meanings of nirvana is the *enormously refined peacefulness*, we merely refer to an important attribute of nirvana, which is easily seen and immediately encountered at the moment the pure and luminous consciousness descends into it. Also, at that particular timeless moment, several other significant fruitions manifest evidently, for example, there arises the complete fading away of mental and spiritual intoxication, cognitive or optical delusion, and psychological narcotization. Since nirvana is the existential reality outside of the consciousness or mind that forms the fifth aggregate of our human existence, some inexperienced and unwise people misunderstand it and mistake it as another (sixth) aggregate. Such a most grave cognitive error and distorted (mistaken and misleading) discernment regarding the ultimate truth of nirvana cost the Buddha Dharma very dearly. In this connection, the highly respected commentator of the Abhidharma Pitaka, the Venerable Anuruddha, who was specialized in the third force of the Buddha's teachings, made it very clear in the Abhidhammattha-Sangaha thus:

"Nirvana is beyond (above) the assembly of the aggregates (or the classification into an aggregate) because of lacking a category (or being undivided) — bhedābhāvena nibbānam khandhasangahanissatam."

Nirvana is the immortal dharma

With respect to the immortality of nirvana, its eternity, and its total freedom from decay and death, the Buddha declared it heroically in the Salāyatana-Vagga of Samyutta-Nikāya as follows:

*"Monks, I shall uncover for you all, the **uncreated** (nirvana), which is the highest truth, the other shore, the most difficult thing to be seen, the decay-free, the eternal, the dharma totally free from all the things that delay the journey toward completion (wholeness), the immortal, the shiva, the authentically secure, the wondrous, the devil-free dharma, the suffering-free thing, the purest, the island (symbolic refuge), the well-protected, and the true sanctuary."*

Since all those words uttered so eloquently and poetically by the Buddha have many significant implications and some of them are related to the concepts used in Brahmanism, I would like to illustrate the original language to you, my reader, especially those of you who have some knowledge of the Pali language as follows:

"Asaṅkhatañca vo, bhikkhave, desessāmi saccañca parañca sududdasañca ajajjaraca dhuvañca nippapañcañca amatañca sivañca khemañca, abbhūtañca anītikañca avyābajjhañca visuddhiñca dīpañca tāṇañca leṇañca vo, bhikkhave, desessāmi."

Of those words, two are of need for clarification here: Nippapañcañca means without the kilesas that delay the journey (progress of practice); these specifically refer to taṇhā (craving/thirst), māna (pride), and ditthi (opinion or points of view). If anyone possesses those three principal kilesas, his or her progressive practice or journey toward the realization of nirvana will be delayed (making only very slow progress). Therefore, it is denominated "papañca-dharma," and the prefix "ni" here indicates "without," so nippapañca is another synonymous word for nirvana — without those three principal kilesas.

As for the word 'Siva,' there are various connotations such as *Shiva, the godhead* (one of the three godheads in Brahmanism/Hinduism), *the highest blessing, and the authentic security*. But the commentator of the Samyutta-Nikāya explained that the reason for calling nirvana "Siva, Pali, or Shiva, Sanskrit) is because nirvana is the highest blessing: sassaririkatthena sivam — it is denominated Siva because of bearing all the blessings.[2]

Is nirvana the same as the godhead Shiva?

Since the Buddha used the word 'Siva' or 'Shiva' ('Śiva') in reference to nirvana, it becomes relevant to study some of the philosophy advocated by the Brahmins and the Hindus, in order to enable us to comprehend the real meaning of Shiva as the godhead. Swami Satyanandaburi, the author of the *Philosophy of Yoga* (in Thai), Sutra 24, 25, said that the godhead Shiva is a special person who is not tied up with kilesa, karma, vipāka (consequences of karma), and taṇhā (craving/thirst). Within Shiva there always exists the seed of all-knowing (sarvajñu).

Actually, the original source of the above-cited statement was the Sutra written by Mahāmuni Patañjali not long after the final passing away of the Buddha.

According to Miss G. Constant Lounsbery in her book *Buddhist Meditation in the Southern School: Theory and Practice for Westerners*, yoga in the Hindu tradition existed before the birth of the Buddha and that his first and foremost Teachers were Ālāra Kālāma and Uddhaka Rāmaputta who specialized in yoga practice. But the Buddha (or rather the monk Gotama as he was originally called before his achievement of Buddhahood) realized through his completion of practice of yoga under those two distinguished masters that the methods of yoga practice did not lead to true deliverance, and therefore he left those two yoga schools.

She further points out that yoga practices were not at first well organized, but became so at the time of Patañjali. Relatedly, she quotes Bhikkhu Mahāpaṇḍita Rāhula Sāṅkṛtyāyana (1893-1963), who stated that yoga during the days of Patañjali "seems to have come under the influence of Buddhism." Furthermore, Miss Lounsbery explained the words 'yoga' and 'atta' as follows. She explains that the word 'yoga' used in the context of Hinduism indicates union with Brahma (the Supreme Being; in Buddhism, brahma is a superior or higher state); in Buddhism yoga is a method of discipline helpful for obtaining nirvana. Further, the term 'attā' (Sanskrit, ātman) used in Hinduism means the immortal soul, while Buddhism employs the word to mean personality or

---

[2] Commentary on the Samyutta-Nikāya, 3/174 Mahachula.

individuality, never something immortal. If anything, attā is understood as a mortal and constantly changing process.[3]

According to Swami Satyanandaburi's Forward to his book mentioned just above, *The Philosophy of Yoga* (in Thai),

> The method for the preparation of yoga was first found in the Upanishads, such as *Maitrāyanī Upanishad and Yogabindu Upanishad*. Later on, the great yogi, Patañjali, was compiling all those existing methods for preparing yoga so that there would be a new order created for the yoga practice. Since then the text that we adopted as authorizing the authentic principles and practice of yoga was Patañjali's *Yoga Sutra*.

> Patañjali was the reformer and re-regulator of yoga. The regulation and methods of practice that appeared in the Upanishads such as the Maitrāyanī Upanishad were quite distinct from those re-organized by Patañjali. That is to say, according to the Upanishads, the yoga body (components of yoga) consisted of *prānāyāma, pratyāhāra, dhyāna, dhāranā, tarka, and samādhi*, while in the *Yoga Sutra* of Patañjali there are *yama, niyama, āsana, prānāyāma, pratyāhāra, dhāranā, dhyāna, and samādhi*. A very noticeable thing is that Patañjali removed *tarka* from the yoga body.

> Furthermore, in the Buddha's Brahmajāla-Sutta there appeared that certain doctrines and belief systems include *takka* (logical reasoning; Sanskrit, tarka) as a factor leading on to samādhi, which makes us think and ponder that during the Buddha's days the factors or components of yoga along the line of the Upanishads were wide spread. But he raised the objection against the principle that *tarka* was the factor for helping develop samādhi as *impossible* by any means. So, in the Patañjali's period we find the similar view on *tarka* since he cut it off from the factor for the yoga practice. Therefore, we may come to the conclusion that Patañjali's days were certainly right after the Buddha's.

> On the other hand, in the book entitled *Carakasamhitā* (medical science), Caraka, the author, referred to the Patañjali's opinion and viewpoints, which indicates that Patañjali was born and carried out his teachings before Caraka. He (Caraka) was the doctor at the court of King Kanishka, and his reign existed around the first century C.E., therefore, Patañjali's period must be from around the fourth century B.C.E. to the first century C.E. Nonetheless, the various statements in the *Yoga Sutra* pointed out clearly that the previously mentioned book, *Carakasamhitā*, must have been compiled and written at the period of time when Buddhism and Brahmanism were still in agreement and walking hand in hand with each other, which referred to the period not after the second century B.C.E. Based on the fore-cited reasons, we (so writes Swami Satyanandaburi) come to the conclusion that the arising and existing time of Patañjali should be between the fourth and first century B.C.E.

---

[3] G. Constant Lounsbury, *Buddhist Meditation in the Southern School: Theory and Practice for Westerners* (1973 edition), p. 77.

According to the history of the *Carakasaṃhitā*, scholars held the view that it must have been published (or made public) at the time when Brahmanism was under the influence of Buddhism. However, the attribute of Shiva as expounded in that book is considered a *fundamental book* in which the Brahmanic Philosophy was lucidly and distinctly explained, that is to say, the book under discussion explained Shiva's attribute extremely similarly to that of the Buddhist nirvana. But the differences lie in the fact that the Brahman Philosophy explained nirvana in the personalization form and maintained the definitive view that to realize and to attain to the ultimate goal of Brahmanism is the *full realization of Shiva*, which implies that those who have realized or attained to Shiva would become exceptionally special persons just as Shiva himself. (Please notice that Shiva is totally free from the kilesas and is said to be the all-knowing one or sarvajñu, in Pali, sabbaññū.)

In this same book, *The Philosophy of Yoga*, Swami Satyanandaburi presents a key attribute of Shiva as follows:

There is nothing in the entire universe that is above and beyond Shiva or Ātman, that is to say, all things exist in Shiva or Ātman — Shiva or Ātman holds up and maintains all things.

The comprehensible distinctions between the Buddha's nirvana and Shiva of Brahmanism

Up until now, we have understood that according to the Brahmanic philosophy, Shiva or Ātman is the upholder and maintainer of the entire universe and at the same time spreads out widely and permeates everything, and that those realizing this state of truth become completely free and liberated from all kilesas, all karma, and cease to die and to be born again (here ends samsara). These principles are extremely similar to those maintained in Buddhism.

However, Buddhism unwaveringly maintains that "the consciousness that has reached nirvana will disappear at the time of death or at the ending of life, and the disappeared or extinguished consciousness becomes extinguished with no remainder, but what we call nirvana still remains." Also, bear in mind that the indisputable position of Buddhism regarding nirvana is that "nirvana is *not* consciousness."

Considering the above statement, it seems that nirvana appears to be something quite mysterious and rather uninteresting since it is not really connected to the benefit of everyday living. In addition, in nirvana, the consciousness becomes extinguished as well, but the attainment of nirvana according to the meaning given by the Brahmanic philosophy seems much more appealing.

However, keep in mind that the true objective of the Buddhist practice is the cessation of suffering once and for all. So, Buddhism has provided the perfect ways and means for achieving the cessation of suffering, which will bring about the desirable fruition to those putting them into practice diligently and intelligently. The most significant thing is that the Buddha taught us to think about the obvious fact and the plain truth that is evident to our human mind and consciousness without involving us in any way with any speculative thinking or any conjecture, or by just logical reasoning. Whatever one can affirm is that which one sees for oneself, which implies the actual exercise of free thinking and self-determination on the matter at hand.

Nonetheless, the Buddha accepted the fact that the consciousness that has arrived completely at nirvana would become the all-knowing (omniscient) one, but *this omniscience or all-knowing consciousness has a limited significance*. That is to say, it simply refers to all-knowing with respect to the birth or arising and the passing away of life, as well as the effective method for accomplishing the cessation of, or the release from, suffering or dukkha, and *apart from this, there is no other especial knowledge, even for the arahats*.

Does an arahat become annihilated after death?

If anyone would ask such a question as the above-posed one, the Buddha replied to it indicating that any speculation is not welcome. In this connection, let us listen to his response to the young man named Upasīva as follows:

Upasīva asked, "For those who have become the arahats and have been absolutely liberated from all kinds of kilesas, does their consciousness become completely extinguished after their parinibbāna (final passing away), or does it still remain somewhere?

The Buddha responded, "To the flame that has been blown out totally, there is no word to describe adequately where it has gone. Just like that indeed for the sage, who, having been released from the burden of the psychophysical aggregates, disappears after death, there is no adequate language to say what would happen next."[4]

As a matter of fact, non-speculation or non-conjecture is the most significant art as the way of putting an utter ending of dukkha since the matter of speculating or conjecturing may begin with clarity of mind but ends up in doubt, uncertainty, and confusion. Since doubt, indecisiveness, and confusion are all kilesas in themselves, they keep the mind restless and far away from being at peace or even at ease most of the time. When the mind is unable to reach utter peacefulness, the taṇhā or craving/thirst will not fade away entirely from the consciousness; and as much as the taṇhā remains intact within the consciousness, that much of avijjā or the lack of realizing the four noble truths will continue living in the bhavanga (similar to the notion of the Unconscious in Jungian Psychology). So long as taṇhā and avijjā (causes of suffering/dukkha) still remain latent in the bhavanga consciousness, it will be impossible to be totally liberated or delivered from dukkha/suffering.

---

[4] Cūlaniddesa of Khuttaka-Nikāya.

Therefore, the very basic Buddhist practice for the cessation of suffering is to contemplate impermanence (anicca), dissatisfactoriness (dukkha), and the lack of a permanent self or entity regarding all conditioned and unconditioned things, as well as the law of dependent origination that illustrates both the process of arising of suffering (the dukkha process) and the process of cessation of suffering (the nirvana process). This way of contemplation is looking at the observable facts, which will lead to overcoming skeptical doubt and the confused mind concerning confusing matters. By so doing, the desirable result is that the mind will be in profound and endurable peace and will reach complete tranquillity and stillness of the internal activities (sankhāras). Certainly, this is the highly effective way to end all kinds of suffering once and for all.

As for the Brahman practice for the ending of suffering, it lays an emphasis on the contemplation of Shiva, which will bring about delight, joy, and rapture when the practitioner has entered the union with him or has realized Shiva experientially. In addition, there is an idea that being in union with Shiva or realizing him through the actual experience will make one become somebody very special or superhuman. This way of thinking and believing will most easily beget self-aggrandizement and ego-inflation strengthening taṇhā (craving/thirst), upādāna (attachment), and avijjā (lacking profound insight and authentic, non-distorted vision), in an extremely subtle, unconscious way. So, it is impossible for this method of practice to lead on to the cessation of suffering. Instead, it will prolong dukkha since ego-inflation and self-aggrandizement are in fact conditioned or psychological dukkhas themselves (sankhāra-dukkha).

From the Buddha's viewpoint, theory is not as important as the practice that will be conducive to the sought-after result and therefore, he prefers to put the practice above (on top of) the theory, which will help his followers move forward directly toward the experiential realization of the set goal. As for the issue of what actually happens to arahats after death, which is totally involved with speculative viewpoints and conjecture, it's rather a waste of time and energy since it will not lead to enlightenment and/or to the definite release from suffering. In this connection, let us listen attentively to the very interesting discussions between the monk, Yamaka by name, and the most venerable Sāriputta, the Right-hand Disciple of the Buddha, as follows:

The story was that the monk Yamaka held an extremely wrong view about the annihilation of the arahats after their death, and many fellow monks were trying their best to help him abandon such a wrong view, but failed to do so. Therefore, they approached Sāriputta asking him to convert Yamaka to the right path, and so Sāriputta went to see him at his residence and inquired about his view on the arahat's death, which he affirmed with clarity and certainty. Then, Sāriputta put to him the following questions:

"Yamaka, what is your understanding concerning form (or materiality, rūpa), feeling/sensation (vedanā), perception (saññā), sankhāra, and consciousness (viññāna)? Are those aggregates the arahat?"

"No, venerable sir," replied Yamaka.

"Do you think and see that the arahat exists in one of those aggregates or in them all?"

"Not so, venerable sir."

"Do you view the arahat as separated from rūpa, vedanā, saññā, sankhāra, and viññāna?"

"Not so, venerable sir."

"Do you comprehend that the arahat has no rūpa, no vedanā, no saññā, no sankhāra, and no viññāna?"

"Not so, venerable sir."

"Yamaka, since you cannot find the arahat in those five aggregates of existence at all, even here at present, is it appropriate to make an unwavering assertion that you know all the dharmas (teachings) proclaimed by the Buddha and dare to put in his mouth that the arahat becomes annihilated after death?"

"Venerable Sāriputta, Sir! Before I did not realize the truth of the matter under discussion, so I held such a gravely wrong view. But now, on hearing your excellently lucid clarification and demonstration of the truth, I am hereby relinquishing pride together with such an evilly erroneous view and hereby am attaining to an extraordinary dharma as well."

"Yamaka, if someone would ask you such a question as this, 'Yamaka, what will happen to the arahat after death?' what would be your response?"

"My response to the supposed question will be like this, 'Rūpa, vedanā, saññā, sankhāra, and viññāna are impermanent; whatever is impermanent is also dissatisfactory (dukkha), and dissatisfactory things finally become extinguished.'"

"Well said and well done, Yamaka, I would like to use a metaphor for helping you deepen your discernment regarding this matter. Yamaka, consider a householder or his son/daughter who is wealthy, filled with treasures, and all is well protected and securely guarded. But suppose that there would be a certain man who would wish him all disasters, disadvantages, insecurity, and the ending of his life, and such a man would approach the wealthy householder and ask for a job as a servant so that he could be closely associated with him and his family. By so doing, the servant would do everything to the best of his ability to serve his master seemingly sincerely and honestly until the master and his family members placed their trust and confidence in him, loved him dearly, and had no suspicion about any evil hidden plot that he might have against them. So, one day when the wealthy householder went to be alone in his private place, the evil servant immediately seized the opportunity and killed him mercilessly with his sharp sword."

"Yamaka, all the time throughout the servant's stay with the wealthy householder, he did not know that the man would kill him, and even when he was enjoying his privacy in his isolated, exclusive place, he did not know at all that the servant would end his life. Is that true, Yamaka?"

"That is correct, sir."

"Just like that, indeed, Yamaka, the person who has not heard the dharma, has not seen the noble ones, has not been wise in the dharma of the noble ones, has not been trained in the noble ones' dharma, has not met with the wise, has not been wise in the dharma of the wise, has not been trained in the wise ones' dharma, will perceive the material form, feeling/sensation, perception, dark and light forces, and consciousness as a self, or will see that the self has the material form, has feeling/sensation, has perception, has the dark and light forces, and has consciousness, or will perceive the material form, the feeling/sensation, the perception, the dark and light forces, and the consciousness as existing in the self, or will see the self as existing in the material form, in feeling/sensation, in perception, in the dark and light forces, and in consciousness. Since the material form, feeling/sensation, perception, the dark and light forces, and consciousness are each and all impermanent, dissatisfactory, and without a permanent soul or an ever-lasting entity as well as are conditioned or made up as the aggregates, they are compared to the servant who kills the wealthy householder because of his non-realization of the impermanency, the dissatisfactoriness or the conflicting nature, the non-self, and the conditioned processes of those five aggregates as previously cited. In addition to such a lack of realization, the killer becomes blindly attached to the five aggregates and considers each one or all of them as his self; and therefore, the five aggregates being so rigidly attached and held on to will lead to the disastrous situations of life with no benefit whatsoever, and to suffering for a long, long time."[5]

There is another interesting sutta, Aggivacchagotta-Sutta by name, in which the mendicant named Vacchagotta went to the Jetavanārāma Monastery where the Buddha was staying and asked him many questions, one about what would happen to arahats after their death, whether they would be reborn or not. These are the questions and answers between the mendicant and the Buddha:

"Monk Gotama, will the monk who has been freed of all the kilesas be reborn somewhere?"

"There is no such word as 'born' or 'reborn' for him," replied the Buddha.

"That means 'no birth,' is that right?" asked again Vacchagotta.

"There are no such words as 'no birth' for him," said the Buddha.

"That means 'both birth and no birth,' is that correct?" asked Vacchagotta.

---

[5] Khandha-Vagga of Samyutta-Nikāya.

"There are no such words as 'both birth and no birth,'" replied the Buddha.

"If so, you mean 'neither birth nor no birth,' am I right?" asked once more Vacchagotta.

To Vacchagotta's final question the Buddha flatly gave the negative answer.

When the mendicant Vacchagotta inquired into the Buddha's reason for all his negative replies, the Buddha simply told him that this dharma was very profound, extremely hard for those holding another viewpoint, having the preference of another teaching, endeavoring differently, or being guided by another master, to understand.

Therefore, to help Vacchagotta view things correctly, the Buddha went on to question Vacchagotta in another way.

Then he put to the mendicant Vacchagotta the followings questions:

"Vacchagotta, if the fire is burning strongly in front of you, will you know it?"

"Monk Gotama, Sir! Certainly, I will know it."

"With what is the fire burning?"

"It is burning with the fuel such as hay or dry wood, Sir!"

"If the fire is blown out in front of you, will you know it?"

"Yes, Sir!"

"Where has the fire gone?"

"There is no answer because the fire was burning with hay and dry wood. When the fuel has been exhausted and no new fuel is added, the fire has no more "food-fuel" to feed it, and so the fire has gone out completely."

"Just like that fire, indeed, Vacchagotta, the monk who has abandoned the five aggregates of existence, is regarded as having been totally liberated from the five aggregates, is absolutely profound, immeasurable, and fathomless. He is like the great ocean and for him there is no such words as 'born or not born' and so on and so forth."

At the conclusion of the dialogue Vacchagotta was so convinced of the Buddha's discourse that he asked to be admitted a disciple and therefore became the "lay devotee" who took the refuge in the Triple Gem (Buddha, dharma, and sangha).

A comprehensive comparison between Shiva and nirvana

First of all, let us listen to what Buddhadasa, a great Thai Buddhist scholar, wrote about Shiva and Nirvana. Published in the magazine called *Buddhism* (in Thai), in 2485/1942; this may help us understand this issue more easily.

Buddhadasa wrote thus:

The viewpoints of the Upanishads that appeared just before the Buddha's time claimed to have discovered ātman or the *unmanifested*, which is difficult to understand since it is opposite to the world, is uncreated and unconditioned, but remains in existence at all time and exists everywhere seemingly similar to the *universal consciousness*. It is taught that if anyone would purify and transform his mind from avijjā (ignorance as regards the four noble truths), he would be able to see ātman with the *eye of wisdom* and at the same time the mind of such an individual would be ultimately happy as well. Then, the Buddha arose in the world and became the *fully enlightened one*, and he further discovered that the unmanifested nature which the Upanishads denominate as *ātman* really exists, but it is not something that has an *attā or atman (permanent self)* since it is *anattā (no-self)* and is neither the one that does (active voice or doer) this and that, nor the thing that is done (passive voice) by someone such as a creator. It is the *dharma or the purely natural*. So, it is not at all appropriate to take it for granted that it is *attā or ātman*. The contemplation on, or searching for, the ātman was done in such a way that *attachment* becomes a powerfully dominating factor (not with a freedom of thought and/or of contemplation), while the right thing to do is to see for certain whether one's mind has relinquished and let go of all things including attachment to the concept of ātman that is believed to be existing in all things and in all places. If one's mind or consciousness has been totally free and liberated from the attachment to both the eternal, supreme self or paramātman and the permanent soul (jīvātman) that is believed to be wandering from one physical body to the next, and from all kinds of craving, whether the craving for getting, the craving for having, the craving for becoming, and the craving for neither having nor becoming, then one is on the right path. If one's mind or consciousness has not reached such a goal, one must continue treading the eightfold path or the Middle Way with more perseverance, more diligence, and more intelligence until the ultimate goal of the total, immeasurable freedom and the complete transformation have been accomplished. For those undertaking practicing Buddhism there is the stable point (the fixed goal) that is known as *nirvana*: the cessation and extinction of all clinging to the idea of attā or ātman (in the sense of a permanent entity existing somewhere inside or outside of the human form) and the total extinction of all kilesas as well as the complete cessation of all suffering. When all suffering has come to a complete extinction, one knows it for oneself and also knows the state in which all the suffering becomes extinguished (nirvana); even so, one does not become attached to it believing it to be a self or ātman/attā since it is purely natural and ought not be clung to.

Whatever one has released and let go should not be brought back by clinging and becoming attached to once again. One should abandon them all once and for all, without looking back in longing for any of them. All the existential realities once met with or discovered should not be the objects of attachment, but one should just let them be. This is accordance with what the Buddha said, *'Once the burden has been laid down, one should never pick up another for clinging to again, or once craving/thirst has been uprooted, one should just be it remain extinguished for good.'* However, the denial of everything as not a self or as what ought not to be clung to, is in complete agreement with the Buddha's teaching that says, 'All things or dharmas are without a self – sabbē dhammā anattā,' or 'All things ought not be attached to.' The word 'dhammā' ('Sanskrit dharma') refers to all things and everything, whether conditioned/created, or unconditioned/uncreated such as nirvana, which is the state where all kinds of suffering cease forever.

Specifically speaking, the Upanishads' points of view maintain the existence of *ātman* and explain its attribute as uncreated, which is similar to the Buddhist nirvana. This is because the philosophy of this kind derives from the principle that there is a self (attā or ātman), but later on when they discovered that the body and mind are not a self, they became astonished and therefore eager to know where is the self, then? The discovery of the reason why the body and mind are not a self is because they are created, put together, assembled with various parts, and basically illusory perceptually. Now, the next search lays a strong emphasis on what the self or ātman really is; and then there is a discovery of the uncreated (asamkhata), which further brings about the inference and the logic (reasoning) that point out that the uncreated is absolutely in opposition to the body and mind (the created), which is an illusion (māyā). But the new discovery gives rise to a conviction that the uncreated exists universally and can be encountered anywhere and everywhere, and therefore the final conclusion is reached in that they affirm it by stating, 'This is the ātman or the self. Whoever I am, that you are. Who the Brahma is, that I am,' which means that I have a self that is the same as the Brahma, and the Brahma is the ātman in every place. This point of view is very similar to that of Buddhism: the only difference lies in the fact that the Ātman of Brahmanism is covered by, and wrapped up with the mundane things and then becomes liberated from them, which is actually known and realized fully by the consciousness. But in Buddhism there is no such thing as ātman, nonetheless it is the consciousness that is covered with the kilesas (contaminations), and when the consciousness is liberated and freed from the kilesas, it knows for itself and by itself that it has been released and delivered (*without any self or ātman as the liberator or freer*). The freedom or deliverance here refers to *being in contact* with, or encountering *nirvana*, and then the consciousness itself puts the complete cessation and absolute extinction to the feeling, 'I am or have a self, this is my self,' and therefore there is no more suffering or dukkha to arise again. *There is no everlasting ātman as maintained by the Upanishads*.

Also, in another (Thai-language) book by Buddhadhasa, *Magguddessika of viññāna*, page 23, he wrote, describing this Upanishadic sense of ātman:

> The ātman, after having been released and liberated from the mundane things, when it belongs to anyone, is identical and all the same with no distinction whatsoever. That is to say, there is no master, no servant, no good, no bad, within the ātman, which is compared to the air contained in the different trays, is impeded by those trays, but is essentially part of the air that prevails in the vast sky and on the extensive earth. When those trays get destroyed, the air, which is now without any container, becomes exactly the same as the air at large.

According to Swami Satyanandaburi, in *The Philosophy of Yoga*, already cited, the existence of ātman was explained in this way:

When the yogi has done the preparation and meditated on aum (om), there will be two results, namely,

1. The yogi can realize the ātman that permeates everywhere.
2. All kinds of dangers that hinder or obstruct the attainment of samādhi will become extinguished.

Further, regarding the preparation (parikamma) or initialization and meditation on aum, the yogi always perseveres in withdrawing or separating consciousness from its mundane or worldly manifestations, and after having succeeded in doing so, that state which cannot be obstructed by place and time (kāla desa), is considered as undivided or inseparable into categories or parts. For this reason, it is called *pacceka*, meaning, One with no two.

Such a state of truth is regarded as the absolutely pure and clean state, totally free from all blemishes and flaws of the mundane world or from the *not knowing inwardly* (aññāna), which is actually the *authentic insight* technically known in the Upanishads as *cetana*, including very high forms of consciousness. Combining the *absolute oneness* and the *true insight* together there arises the real state of *paccekacetana*, which is ātman itself.

Therefore, the initialization and meditation on aum will uncover pacceka-cetana, the truly authentic state of truth, thus shown clearly to the yogi.[6]

The word aum (continuing here the presentation by Swami Satyananda-buri) sometimes represents Shiva, other times represents ātman as the Brahman Philosophy prefers to say. This indicates, Swami Satyananda-buri continues, that those worshipping Shiva use aum to replace Shiva in their chanting or meditation, and that those remaining in ātman also use aum in place of ātman. However, the fundamental attributes of both Shiva and ātman are quite common, which is the attribute of aum as well. To put

---

[6] Swami Satyanandaburi, from *The Philosophy of Yoga*, vol. 1, pages 107-111.

it in another way, the standardized attribute of Shiva or ātman refers to the fact that both Shiva and ātman are not obstructed and hindered by anything at all, for example, time cannot hinder Shiva or ātman and therefore, in creating a terminology that symbolizes Shiva or ātman, it is essential to respect the described attribute as the basic principle. As we know, every sound can be defined by its origin, for instance, the sound ka originates in the throat, while cha (or ja) originates in the palate, and therefore the word combined with those sounds must be confined in the throat and in the palate according to these origins. If any word can pass through all possible origins (locations in the mouth, etc. making speech sounds), it signifies that such a word is not obstructed by any means. That is to say, the word must be endowed with the Shiva's or ātman's common attribute, and various sounds that originate from the navel up to the head, which are aum consisting in A, U, and M. The way of pronouncing aum is to be done with a long pronunciation which takes three instances (moments) and begins at the navel right up to the head; for example, A covers the areas from the navel to the chest and takes two moments, U covers the areas from the chest to the throat and takes one moment, and M covers the areas from the throat to the head and takes one half moment. Combined together, aum covers the areas from the navel to the head and takes three and a half moments, on the other hand, the word aum is not obstructed by any situation and any circumstance unlike the other words that are often hindered by some things. Since the attribute of aum is in agreement and in harmony with the Shiva's or ātman's attribute, the wise utilize it (aum) to represent the name of Shiva or ātman.

Apart from the above described common attribute (Swami Satyanandaburi, continuing here), both aum and Shiva or aum and ātman still possess another common attribute, that is to say, as we have previously mentioned, the principle that there is nothing in the entire universe that stands above or beyond Shiva or ātman. Meanwhile, all the names that symbolize all things exist in the aum because the aum spreads out and prevails in every alphabet and therefore, it permeates in every origin of the name that is composed of such and such alphabet. For this reason, Shiva or ātman upholds all things just as aum does, that is, maintains and upholds all the names or the symbols of all things in the universe. Therefore, aum is the representation that indicates the Shiva's name.[7]

Shiva is the energy source of the consciousness in all living things

As we have learned that the Buddha calls nirvana an āyatana, which means an origination source, for example, the eye faculty is called āyatana because it is the source or base wherefrom the eye-consciousness arises. But the āyatana as the name for nirvana does not mean that nirvana is the source or base from which the consciousness arises or that nirvana shines forth in some form of consciousness. It simply signifies that nirvana is the energy source where consciousness cleanses itself and becomes totally purified and

---

[7] The preceding passages render Swami Satyanandaburi, *The Philosophy of Yoga*, pages 103-107.

luminous, and such a consciousness finally turns into extinction at the moment that life reaches its ending.

However, the Brahmanic philosophy maintains the viewpoint that consciousness stems from the ātman, or, to put it in another way, proceeds from Brahma or Shiva, who appears to be the universal consciousness or consciousness of the cosmos, the core of all things. It is this thing that, according to the Brahman philosophy, is considered the āyatana, the origination source or the base wherefrom consciousness of all things comes into existence. Since consciousness is covered by ignorance (avijjā), it deceives itself by mistaking itself for the self or ātman, attā. But when this ignorance has been removed, the misunderstanding consciousness will disappear or become extinguished, and then the ātman as asamkhata – the uncreated and as omniscience – sabbaññu, will appear, which is in accord with the Yoga philosophy: *"Yoga is the cessation of the manifestation of consciousness, and after that the seer will remain straight fast in its own form."*

As for the statement that says, *"Consciousness arises from ātman,"* we will see the explanations given in the *Philosophy of Yoga* as follows:

> The receiver or the seer (witness) of the manifestations is purusha or ātman that lives in the physical body, but the instrument for receiving or the active one in charge of receiving is *consciousness*, and the consciousness is merely an executive function of purusha or atman; that is, consciousness is able to carry out its function because there is the purusha or ātman remaining in the position of the witness. This is like the magnet that is conducive to iron objects and makes them move, although the magnet stays still or immobile. The mere immobility of the magnet can produce the movement of the iron because of the magnitude of the (magnetic) current that flows out of the magnet into the iron; in exactly the same way, the current or stream of ātman or purusha flows constantly into the consciousness and therefore, the consciousness can function as the executor, director, or manager (the one in charge). In fact, ātman and consciousness are two separate things just as the magnet and the iron, but because the avijjā overpowers consciousness, it then mistakes the ātman for the consciousness itself. That is to say, because avijjā impedes the stream of our insightful inner eye, we hold on to the manifestations of consciousness as the manifestation of ātman, just as those who do not see the magnet may consider the movement of the metal objects as their own free movement (and not as originated from the magnet), or may perceive all metal objects as being themselves the magnet, without the right understanding that all the metal objects are merely conductors relaying the power of the magnet. Like that indeed is the misunderstanding of the manifestations of consciousness as the manifestation of ātman, or the erroneous discernment that the manifestations of consciousness and the manifestation of ātman are the same things, which is termed *asmitā*.[8]

---

[8] From *Philosophy of Yoga*, pages 206-208.

The word 'asmitā' is a Sanskrit term that means holding on to consciousness as ātman — literally, I am-ness: asmi (I am) + tā (-ness) — which is in agreement with the word 'asmimāna' in Pali, signifying the taking of the five aggregates of existence as attā or self, or assuming that the five aggregates have a self or attā. Holding a point of view that one (a person, an individual) is this or that, while in reality there is no self at all, is asmimāna. Nonetheless, the Brahmins teach their followers to search for the ātman, while Buddhism does not urge Buddhists to seek after something that doesn't exist; instead, it instructs them to contemplate the three characteristics of existence, namely, impermanence, dissatisfactoriness (including conflict, crisis, and suffering), and anattā or anātman (the lack of a permanent self, soul, or entity anywhere, whether in human aggregates or in the relative world) or to contemplate the law of dependent origination (the interdependence and interrelatedness of things). The search for a self, from the Buddhist viewpoint, is like looking for an authentic picture in the mirage!

According to Buddhism the most important thing is to be *fully aware* and *widely vigilant* in every moment when the conscious process is in operation, in order to see ongoingly that all types of consciousness, intellect, and even wisdom, that all operate through the six sense modalities or that remain dormant in the bhavanga (the unconscious), are all dependent on certain conditions for appearing, existing, and disappearing momentarily. When the conditions for keeping it going and manifesting have become extinguished, the consciousness will also reach its extinction.

This way of contemplating and meditating will help the consciousness liberate itself from the dark force of ignorance and delusion (*avijjā and moha*), and then the consciousness will realize by itself the attributes of nirvana. As for those who haven't entered the stream of nirvana and have not removed utterly avijjā and moha from their consciousness, they will be unable to comprehend this state of affairs (nirvana) exquisitely. This is like a blind person unable to see all kinds of pictures as does the person who is fully equipped with the healthy eye-sight faculty.

What happens to the consciousness after the final passing away?

As we are aware, consciousness by its real nature is neither materiality (rūpadharma) nor the result or product of the material conditions, since it can exist without depending on materiality such as the consciousness of the brahmas with form and the consciousness of the formless brahmas,[9] and the state of consciousness existing in the formless plane of life is said to last epochs and epochs of time, even much longer than the age of our planet earth. This makes us think that consciousness can live for incalculable time![10]

Thinking along this line it seems that the consciousness that has realized nirvana, and then has become extinguished, simply refers to the fact that all

---

[9] Those who have attained various stages of both jhāna with form and the formless jhāna earn the title of brahma, meaning excellent beings. See the section on such consciousness in the previous chapter.

[10] See Chapter 1, above. For details, see Aggañña-Sutta, Sutta or Discourse 27 in the Dīgha-Nikāya (D.iii.80).

forms of consciousness covered up with avijjā and all other kilesas have reached their utter extinction, while the unmanifested consciousness with all its intrinsic nature of purity and luminosity still exists.

However, this way of explaining consciousness may be easy to understand, but, alternatively, might be confused with the Brahman Philosophy as already discussed. In this respect, some Buddhist scholars subscribe to such a view on the consciousness, particularly some learned Mahāyāna Buddhists. But as for the Theravāda Buddhists, they have found various sources that indicate the fact of the arahats' consciousness disappears for good after death or final passing away, and there is no word from the Buddha to support the view that the pure consciousness exists after the final passing away (parinibbāna or parinirvana) of the arahats. In case of any questions about what really happens to the arahats' consciousness after their parinibbāna, please review the Buddha's responses to Vacchagotta in the previous section of this chapter.

Bear in mind that the consciousnesses that arise or is manifest in the variety of forms through our six sense-modalities, are all dependent on the appropriate conditions giving rise to or manifesting any of them. For example, any sense modality (āyatana) can provide the base wherefrom a consciousness may arise or manifest, only when the psychophysical systems are still alive and functioning.

When the consciousness has disappeared for good as in the case of the final passing away of the arahats, we do not have any criterion to determine what really happens then. In fact, we cannot find any adequate word or language to describe the utterly extinguished consciousness of the arahats and therefore, the Theravāda Buddhists do not say that *the pure consciousness continues to exist after the final passing away of life* since all words and all languages are merely symbols or symbolic signs, while such pure consciousness has no sign or symbol attached to it.

However, in the Kevaṭṭa-Sutta (or Kevaddha-Sutta), the Buddha used the word 'viññāna' for nirvana as follows (a full translation appears below, p. 191):

> Viññānam anidassanam anantam sabbatopabham
> Ettha āpo ca pathavī ca tejo vāyo na tāyati
> Ettha dīghañca rassañca anum thūlam subhāsubham
> Ettha nāmañca rūpañca asesam uparujjhati
> Viññānassa nirodhena etthetam uparujjhati.

There exists that consciousness which is invisible through the eyes (visual contact), incomparable to anything, infinite, shining forth brilliantly, and is attainable through all the methods of meditation. In such consciousness there is no water, no earth, no fire, and no wind.

Within such consciousness there is nothing that is long, short, small, big, beautiful, not beautiful (ugly), and here in this consciousness the nāma-rūpa processes (psychophysical phenomena) become extinguished without remainder since, in this, the consciousness (the one that is influenced by avijjā, the consciousness that arises through the six sense bases) reaches its utter extinction, and here is the place where all nāma-rūpa disappears utterly.[11]

According to the commentary to the Dīgha-Nikāya the word 'viññānam' was translated as the state to be realized. Since the commentator explained that word as *that which is to be realized*, which refers to nirvana, so, the nirvana is anidassana in the sense of invisibility through the eyes and also in the sense of not having an example for comparison. Here in particular nirvana covers those two meanings since it cannot be seen by the naked eyes or eye-perception, and there is no adequate metaphor to illustrate the total significance of nirvana.

The word 'anantam" according to the commentary signifies the ending of birth, which implies that there is neither origin (beginning) for nirvana nor is there the ending of its cessation. Hence, the commentator meant to say that nirvana has no beginning and has no ending since it *is*, with no conditions for creating it (the uncreated), with no changes according to time (the eternal), and *is* so (thus) as it actually *is*, infinitely.

The word 'sabbatopabham' is derived from 'sabbato' and 'pabham.' The commentator explained the word 'pabham' as derived from 'papam' by changing *p* to *bh* grammatically. Papam or pabham means entrance to water (such as the entrance or entry to a river, or to a beach by the sea) and therefore, sabbatopabham signifies that nirvana has an entrance where anyone may enter or descend, and in actuality the entrance here refers to the meditation practice which leads the practitioner to descend into nirvana.

However, a great Sri Lankan Buddhist scholar and sage or saint, Dhammapāla by name, who was the founder president of the Mahabodhi Association in India, translated this word 'pabham' as rays of light or radiance, and the entire word 'sabbatopabham' as Infinity of Bright Radiance. Another great scholar of Thai Buddhism, Ajahn Sujeev (Sujīva) Puññānubhāva who was once a Buddhist monk with the name of Sucīvo Bhikkhu, wrote an article on this topic of sabbatopabham that was published in the Buddhist magazine called *Dharmachakshu*, where he wrote as follows: "This terminology is popularly used in Mahayana Buddhism, which appears in Sanskrit language as *sravatoprabha*." As a matter of fact, in all places the word 'pabham' is always translated as (rays of light – radiance), so if we would translate it this way, saying that nirvana has *radiance shining forth everywhere* (or has the *bright radiance all around*), it would not be a mistake since the Buddha said:

"*In nirvana there is no moon, no sun, no shining stars, even so there is no darkness in nirvana.*"[12]

The above messages were the partial exclamations that the Buddha uttered in connection to the final passing away or parinibbāna of the monk,

---

[11] For details, in the Dīgha-Nikāya, in the section entitled the Sīlakhanda-Vagga, see the Kevaddha-Sutta (or Kevaṭṭa-Sutta), Sutta or Discourse 11 (D.i.211).
[12] Khuttaka-Nikāya, Udāna-Vagga.

Bāhiya, whom he praised as the *extremely fast enlightened one*. The full text is as follows:

"In the place where no water, no earth, no fire, and no wind stand fast (are found to exist), where the stars do not glow with dazzling light, the sun does not appear with its brilliant rays, and the moon does not shine, (even so) in such a place the darkness does not exist.

"Whenever the brahman who becomes a sage out of insight, knows such a place by himself, he will be freed from the world of form and the formless world and therefore, will be totally liberated (released or transcended) from both happiness and suffering."

In this context, let me quote here Buddhadasa's translation of the verses beginning with "Viññānam anidassanam" and ending in "etthetam uparujjhati" (as given above, p. 189):

"One thing to be realized, which is unmanifested, infinite, and is having the practices that can lead on to it by all means and all ways, does exist. Within such a thing earth, water, fire, and wind cannot descend (since it's fathomless), and in that very thing the length, the shortness, the smallness, the bigness, the beauty, and the ugliness cannot stand fast or be measured, and in such a thing indeed the nāma-rupa reach their utter extinction. The nāma-rupa disappear utterly in that very thing because of the extinction of consciousness."[13]

What is the technical meaning of nibbāna (nirvana)?

The word 'nibbāna' literally means extinction or easefulness, which is a noun, while in form of a verb it appears like this word 'nibbāyeyya' or 'abhinibbuta.' As the Buddha said in Uparipannāsaka of Majjhima-Nikāya:

"Those who see the danger of attachment which is the cause of birth and death, become liberated out of non-attachment as the result of nirvana, which is the cessation of birth and death. Such liberated persons attain to the highest security and become genuinely happy, and so, reach the extinction (of all the kilesas) in this very life." In Pali the text goes as follows:

> Upādānena bhayam disvā jātimaranasambhave
> Anupādā vimuccanti jātimaranasamkhaye
> Te khemappattā sukhino ditthadhammābhinibbutā.

The word 'abhinibbuta' (which signifies extinguishing), the commentator of the above-cited scripture explained as the extinction of all kinds of kilesa (mental, psychological, and spiritual contaminations).

In Nidāna-Vagga of Samyutta-Nikāya the Buddha used 'nibbāna' in the form of verb ('nibbāyeyya') as follows:

---

[13] Translated from the magazine, *Buddhism*, page 164, published (in Thai) in 1954.

"Evamhi kho bhikkhave mahāaggikhandho purimassa upādānassa pariyānā aññassa ca anupahārā anāhāro nibbāyeyya evamevam kho bhikkhave upādāniyesu dhammesu ādinavānupassino viharato taṇhā nirujjhati."

"Monks, the big pile of fire becomes extinguished because of the exhaustion of the former fuel and lacking the new fuel to put in (or to add up to), just like that indeed, monks, the taṇhā (craving/thirst) of those who contemplate constantly on the danger of attachment reaches its utter extinction."

The extinction as the literal meaning of nibbāna refers to the utter extinction of all the fires of kilesas (the mental, psychological, and spiritual fuel that burns our lives), which is accord with the Buddha's utterance:

"Taṇhāya vippahānena nibbānam iti vuccati." This is its translation: "It is called 'nibbāna' because of the total transformation of taṇhā."

In this connection, once the mendicant named Jambukhādaka asked the Venerable Sāriputta, "Venerable Sāriputta, Sir, what do you mean when you often say, 'nibbāna, nibbāna'?"

"The utter extinction of lustful desire (rāga), the utter extinction of hatred (dosa), and the utter extinction of delusion (moha), all these are called nibbāna (nirvana)," responded Sāriputta.

In addition, nibbāna also means the extinction of bhava – the becoming process, which is nāma-rūpa (the psychophysical systems) as said once more Sāriputta, "Bhavanirodho nibbānam," meaning, the utter extinction of bhava is nibbāna.

Sa-upādisesa nibbāna and anupādisesa nibbāna

Usually nibbāna is divided into two categories, namely, sa-upādisesa nibbāna and anupādisesa nibbāna. The former is translated as utter extinction of all the kilesas with the five aggregates still remaining, while the latter's translation is: utter extinction of all the kilesas and the five aggregates also become extinguished with no remainder. These two categories of nibbāna the Buddha was talking about in Itivuttaka of Khuddaka-Nikāya as follows:

"Monks, there are two elements of nibbāna (nibbāna-dhātu), namely, sa-upādisesa nibbāna-dhātu and anupādisesa-nibbāna-dhātu.

"Monks, what is the sa-upādisesa nibbāna-dhātu? Monks, the monks in this dharma (doctrine) and vinaya (discipline) become arahats (fully enlightened) whose contaminations and fetters have been totally transformed and utterly extinguished, who have done what ought to be done, have laid down all the burden, have fulfilled their own benefits, have utterly eradicated all the kilesas that bind them to various planes of existence and to the process of becoming, have been completely free and liberated because of their all-knowing (omniscience). Nonetheless, their faculties still remaining in operation since they have not been damaged or perished, those arahats experience some agreeable things, some disagreeable things, some happiness and some pain. Now, their sensual desire, their hatred, and their delusion have been uprooted totally, which I call, monks, sa-upādisesa nibbāna-dhātu.

"Monks, what is the anupādisesa nibbāna-dhātu? Monks, the monks in this dharma and vinaya become arahats, whose contaminations and fetters have been totally transformed and utterly extinguished, who have done what ought to be done, have laid down all the burden, have fulfilled their own benefits, have utterly eradicated all the kilesas that bind them to various planes of existence and to the process of becoming, have been completely free and liberated because of their all-knowing (omniscience). Monks, all their feelings and sensations, which no longer make them become attracted to, will reach their utter extinction here in this world (life). Monks, such is called anupādisesa nibbāna-dhātu."

The stream-enterer is considered the nirvana-realized one

The term 'sa-upādisesa nibbāna-dhātu' (the nibbāna-dhātu with the remaining upādi) is composed of 'sa' (to have), + 'upādi' (five aggregates) + 'sesa' (remaining) + 'nibbāna-dhātu' (the nirvana element), while 'anupādisesa nibbāna-dhātu' (the nirvana with no remaining upādi), consists of 'ana' (no) + 'upādisesa' (remaining upādi) + 'nibbāna-dhātu' (nirvana element).

According to this sutta, those considered to have realized nirvana are only the arahats, but those noble, enlightened ones of the earlier stages of the enlightenment, who are of the lower grades in comparison with the arahats, are considered to be *not-yet* nirvana-realized ones. Bear in mind once again, the word 'nibbana' or 'nirvana' here refers to the utter extinction of rāga (sensual desire), of dosa (hate or hatred), and of moha (delusion).

However, the word 'upādi' also means upādāna (attachment/clinging). As for the initial noble, enlightened persons such as the stream-enterer or sotā-panna, although their rāga, dosa, and moha have not been entirely uprooted, it is still said that their consciousness has reached the stream of nirvana. For this reason, all the sotāpannas are certainly the nirvana-realized ones since the minimum requirement of the three lower fetters for extinguishing has been accomplished. In this connection, the Buddha spoke about it in the Navaka-Vagga of Anguttara-Nikāya; the story goes thus:

"At one time, the Blessed One was staying at the Jetavanārāma near the City of Sāvatthī. One morning Sāriputta after dressing himself with his robes took his bowl and entered the city for collecting food. Since it was too early to go for food, he was then thinking about entering the monastery of the mendicants who followed the other doctrine different from his, which was situated nearby. Thus thinking, he went into their monastery, seated himself at a proper place, and took up some conversations with them with friendliness and loving words. At that time those mendicants were holding a meeting at which they were discussing about those who have attained the sa-upādisesa nibbāna after death will not go to hell since they have been freed from it through their insightful wisdom (all-knowing wisdom). Nonetheless, they maintained the view that those nirvana-realized ones would be still subjected to the animal kingdom, the realm of hungry ghosts, and the non-progressive planes of existence."

Sāriputta, after listening attentively to such conversations of those mendicants, did not express his disagreement and at the same time did not raise his opposition either, but got up from his seat and went his way quietly. He actually thought that he would hear the truth of the matter at his Master's (Buddha's) place at the appropriate time. Therefore, after his going round for food has ended, he approached the Buddha and reported to him all the conversations he had heard from the mendicants, and then the Blessed Master said to him the followings:

"Sāriputta, the mendicants of the other doctrine, some are quite ignorant and unwise, while some others know the sa-upādisesa nibbāna as it is, and know the anupādisesa nibbāna as it is. Sāriputta, these nine categories of the noble people who have realized the sa-upādisesa nibbāna, after death will be free and liberated from all the obligations to go to hell, and also from going to the animal kingdom, from the realm of hungry ghosts, and from all kinds of non-progressive planes of existence.

"Who are those nine kinds of noble people? Sāriputta, some people in this world have perfected themselves in sīla (precepts, ethical conduct, and discipline of consciousness), in samādhi (meditation), but have only done some work on the cultivation of wisdom. Inside them the first five fetters that bind us humans to the lower world have been transformed and uprooted utterly; some of them will enter the parinibbāna at the time when their age has not reached its half, while some others will enter into it at the time when their age has passed its half, and still some others will enter the parinibbāna without making great efforts. Sāriputta, some noble people will enter the parinibbāna with great efforts, some will not enter it in this life, but will be guided by the supreme current (in the cosmos) and will be born in the realm of akanittha (one of the brahma worlds) and enter the parinibbāna there. Sāriputta, these five categories of noble people (the non-returners – anāgāmī) have realized the sa-upādisesa nibbāna with the upādi still remaining, after death will be free from hell, from the animal kingdom, from the realm of hungry ghosts, and from all kinds of the non-progressive planes of existence.

"Sāriputta, still there are some others in this world who have perfected themselves in sīla, have done some considerable work on the cultivation of samādhi, and have done some considerable work on the development of paññā (all-knowing wisdom). They have transformed and uprooted utterly the three fetters or samyojanas and have reduced to a great extent rāga, dosa, and moha, and have become sakadāgāmīs (once-returners) who will return to this world only one more time, and then will accomplish (put an end to suffering) the cessation of suffering. Sāriputta, the sixth type of noble ones has also realized the sa-upādisesa nibbāna, and after death will be free from hell and from all the rest as already mentioned above.

"Sāriputta, further still, there some noble people in this world that have perfected themselves in sīla, have done some work on samādhi and some work on paññā. Such noble ones have transformed and uprooted utterly the three samyojanas (fetters) and have become ekabījī (having the seed of one more birth), which indicates that they will be born in the human form once more and then will terminate all kinds of suffering. Some of this type of the noble ones may wonder from family to family (kolamkola), two to three times and then will put a complete end to suffering; and the third category of this type may go on with birth and death up to seven lifetimes (sattakhattuparama), which means that they may be born in the heavens and in the human world not more than seven lives before accomplishing the total termination of suffering. Sāriputta, the seventh, eighth, and ninth noble ones have also realized the sa-upādisesa nibbāna, so after death will free from hell and all the rest.

"Sāriputta, among the mendicants of the other doctrine, some are quite ignorant and unwise, while some others know the sa-upādisesa nibbāna as such, and know the anupādisesa nibbāna as such. Sāriputta, those nine kinds of noble people have realized and become sa-upādisesa nibbāna, so after death will be free from hell and all the rest."

According the above-cited sutta we have gotten the nine types of noble enlightened people, namely, three categories of the sotāpannas, one sakadāgāmi, and five anāgāmīs, who have achieved the sa-upādisesa nibbāna, the nirvana with the remaining upādi. As we know, upādi means fuel, which refers to upādāna, or attachment/clinging, which is the fuel for becoming. Depending on becoming birth comes into existence according to the law of paticcasamuppāda or dependent origination. Those who have extinguished the fuel of birth utterly are only the arahats.

It is quite noticeable that upādi here signifies upādāna, but in the terminology of sa-upādisesa nibbāna or that of anupādisesa nibbāna, upādi refers to the five aggregates, and both meanings came from the Buddha. Therefore, we may come to a conclusion that upādi in one place means upādāna while in another place it signifies the five aggregates, depending on the context to which it refers at the time.

Therefore, there are two general categories of nirvana-realized persons: one is the arahat; the other consists of the initial enlightened ones beginning with the sotāpannas, although their realization of nirvana is not quite complete, since their upādāna has not been totally uprooted. However, those who have reached the sotāpannaship will never fall back, but will only move forward toward full enlightenment.

As a matter of fact, the above-mentioned sutra or suttanta is very significant in the sense that it helps many of us understand and appreciate the realization of nirvana more easily since it recognizes the sotāpanna or stream-enterer as a nirvana-realized noble person, which a number of Buddhists or students of Buddhism do not know about.

The significant key for actually realizing nirvana

Up till now, we have learned about nirvana from various sources of the Buddhist scriptures, especially from the Buddha's own words. However, there is still one more significant key for actually realizing this ultimate and exceedingly desirable truth. This kind of key regarding the proper practice that leads on to the realization of nirvana is not very well known to the seekers after truth and therefore, I would like to present the Venerable Sāriputta's discourse recorded in the Navaka-Vagga of Anguttara-Nikāya for helping all of us deepen our wisdom and enlarge our awareness with regard to the nirvanic realization. Sāriputta spoke as follows:

"Monks, what is the reason for my saying that the extinction of all contaminations depends on the attainment of the first jhāna (meditative absorption)? Monks, the monk in this dispensation (or teaching, sāsana), aloof from sensual things, detached from all unskilful things, attains to the first jhāna in which exist the act of lifting the mind up to the meditation object (vitakka), the mindful act of cuddling and drinking in the meditation object, just like a bee on a flower (vicāra), and this monk is experiencing an ecstatic joy and happiness resultant from the inner solitude. Whatever dharmas exist in the first jhānic meditation, namely, the material form (rūpa), the feelings/sensations (vedanā), the perceptions (saññā), the conditioned things or activities (sankhāra), and consciousness (viññāna), such a monk contemplates their impermanence, their dissatisfactoriness or conflicting nature, their void of substantiality or essence, and their lack of a permanent and everlasting self. He maintains his consciousness to stand fast in those dharmas (keeping the conscious and aware mind on the insight into the nature of impermanence (anicca), into dissatisfactoriness, and/or conflicting nature (dukkha), and into the no-self (anattā), which are the indispensable characteristics of each one of the five aggregates. After having maintained his consciousness and mindfulness on those five dharmas (aggregates), after having seen precisely the three characteristics of existence, he will settle his consciousness in the deathless (nirvana) exclaiming silently thus:

" 'Here is so peaceful! Here is so wonderful! Here indeed is the stilling of all the activities (sankhāras), is the relinquishment of all the upadhi[14], is the extinction of craving/thirst (taṇhā), is the complete release from all contaminations, is the utter extinction, is nibbāna itself.'

"The monk who stands fast in those dharmas achieves the extinction of the mental, psychological, and spiritual fermentations (āsava); and if such attainment is not accomplished because of still being attached to those dharmas (five aggregates and what he has achieved) and because of being excessively delighted in those dharmas, since his three lower fetters (samyojanas) have been extinguished, he will be born in the realm of oppātika (in the pure abodes of the highest brahmas, technically known as suddhāvāsa) and will

---

[14] Upadhi refers to two things: One is *attachment*, another is the emotional, psychological, and/or spiritual *blocks* (blockages) buried in certain parts of the physical body and in the psyche.

enter parinibbāna there without coming back to the lower worlds including the human world."

From the above-cited discourse delivered by Sāriputta we have learned another practice or the other precisely pointed-out way leading on to the realization of nirvana. Here we may summarize it for our practical purposes:

1. We need to meditate by cultivating a firm samādhi (stabilized mind and firmly focused consciousness) until the first jhāna (first stage of meditative absorption) is achieved. This first jhāna consists of five very noticeable factors, namely, vitakka, vicāra, pīti, sukha, and ekaggatā, the meanings of which will be explained below.
2. We must train the mind properly so that it could reach the stilling of the sankhāras or internal activities and therefore can be comfortably at ease and perfectly at peace, and in such completely peaceful state the mind is entirely free from all the unwholesome (unskilful) things (which normally disturb and distract the mind when they are in operation). So, with their operation coming to a complete stop, the mind is naturally at peace.
3. From now on, the yogi (meditator) will have to contemplate the impermanence, dissatisfactoriness or conflicting nature regarding the material form, the feelings/sensations, the perceptions, the dark and light forces (sankhāras), consciousness, and the absence or lack of an existential everlasting soul or self either within or outside of those five aggregates of existence.
4. After that the yogi will be able to focus his or her consciousness on the *unique object* exclusively, and that is *nirvana* itself. By so doing, such unwaveringly focused consciousness will become inwardly unified wholly (one with the wholeness of *being* or *essence*).
5. Once nirvana has been taken as the *sole* object of meditation, the yogi will enter its stream or energetic current that flows incessantly and eternally. Right here the all-knowing wisdom and profound insight will arise to do the job of transforming all the kilesas patiently awaiting this thorough transformation and total purification.

Let me now elaborate the meanings of those technical terms forming the five factors of the first jhāna:

Vitakka here does not mean a kind of preoccupation or obsession with regard to sensuality (kāma-vitakka), the will to destroy or cause harm to others vyāpāda-vitakka), and the violent thought (vihimsa-vitakka), but being a factor of the jhānic meditation, it refers to the act of *lifting the mind up* to the meditation object, whatever it may be at the moment, since the nature of the mind is habitually prone to distractions and is often carried away from the creative present by some distracting objects near and far. With such act of lifting the mind up, when it becomes slackened, or bringing it back, whenever it drifts off, to the focusing object, the mind will stay focused firmly so as to enable the jhānic meditation to become fully established and securely stabilized.

Vicāra means that the mind in this stage of jhāna is cuddling and drinking in mindfully the meditation object all around, just like a bee on a flower. It does *not* imply the act of *reasoning* or *attempting to make out* some things either by way of conceptualizing or through intellectualizing.

Pīti signifies the *inner fullness* in which nothing is lacking. Sometimes, we prefer to use such an expression as *ecstatic joy*, which refers to those moments when the mind feels completely *full* and is totally *filled* with the joy of ecstasy.

Sukha simply means the *feeling at ease* and the state of consciousness where *spaciousness* permeates beyond any boundary, both within and without, in which the mind becomes exceedingly satisfied and exceptionally happy.

Ekaggatā refers to the uniqueness and oneness of consciousness wholly unified with the meditation object on which the mind is exclusively focused with resolved, definitive, and unwavering attention and inner stability.

What we call nirvana will appear at the moment when we understand profoundly and thoroughly that *that which is denominated as I, you, or we is nothing but the combination of five aggregates of existence. Apart from those aggregates there is no other thing else worthy for naming a self (I, you, or we).*

However, the combination of five aggregates commonly considered a self (such as oneself, myself, yourself, himself, herself, ourselves, themselves, and so forth) is merely the denominated (supposed-to-be), conventional self coming into a conventionally acknowledged existence through a grave optical delusion of consciousness (a severe cognitive error), sheer ignorance, craving/ thirst, and attachment. Without those three principal kilesas in existence and in operation, there will be no naming (meaningful label), and without naming and labeling, the feeling of "I am" will no longer exist. Right here consciousness disappears. When consciousness has disappeared, nāma (feeling/sensation, perception, and sankhāras) and rūpa (form or materiality) become extinguished. In this very extinction without remainder appears nirvana.

At the instance of such disappearing of nāma and rūpa, there will appear at once the *luminously brilliant light* together with the genuine contact with the *outstandingly pleasant and exquisitely clear extinction*. Such is the **realization** of nirvana. In this connection, the Buddha declared in the Dhammapada of Khuttaka-Nikāya thus:

Phusanti dhīrā nibbānam   yogakkhemam anuttaram.

The wise touch nirvana, which is the excellent dharma, totally freed of the passions of yoga.[15]

---

[15] The word 'yoga' is used here to represent kinds of kilesa. The three yogas (also called āsavas, variously rendered as fermentations, influences, cankers, corruptions) or categories of yoga-kilesa, are (1) the kilesa or contamination/defilement binding or tying us humans to sensuality (kāma-yoga), (2) the contamination binding or tying us to becoming (bhava-yoga), and (3) the contamination binding or tying us to ignorance. Note that ignorance has two significant meanings: one is the grave cognitive error regarding the real and the unreal; another is the lack of realizing the four noble truths.

However, the realization of nirvana, or in another word, the attainment of the distinctly peaceful and exquisitely luminous state, will appear more clearly or less lucidly, depending on the greater or lesser degrees of understanding life with all its aspects laid out in the teaching of dependent origination. Also, this depends on the common principle that the more avijjā (ignorance) is removed, the brighter and more profound is the all-knowing wisdom (paññā); and the more taṇhā (craving/thirst) is uprooted, the more pleasant is the state of being.

Please bear in mind that the efficiency of contemplating life according to the law of dependent origination, sometimes called the wheel of life, is to be done during the meditation where the mind is firmly stabilized. The reason is that during such a period of the securely stabilized mind, the internal disturbing influences (another meaning of kilesa) become calm and at peace, and the mind or consciousness is luminous and pure. In this way, the mind will find itself in complete accord with the dharma and therefore, will not become arrogant or stubborn like during the period of being greatly influenced by the kilesas.

Why is the dharma-knower unable to eradicate the kilesas?

There is a query based on the recognition that some people whose minds have reached a peaceful and neatly refined state, still have not been able to eradicate the kilesas! The reason may be because, on one hand, their minds are not really prepared to give up the kilesas, since at the deeper level of the psyche, such as at the bhavanga (unconscious) level, there is some attachment to certain kilesas and the bhavanga-citta still grabs onto certain values of the subtle and more refined kilesas. Further, certain knowers of the dharma are still satisfied with the way of life that they have been living and therefore do not want to let go of it yet; and when satisfaction (the milder form of attachment) still remains in the consciousness, avijjā cannot be removed and uprooted entirely from the unconscious (bhavanga).

At this point, let us look once again into some partial order of dependent origination: "Satisfaction is a feeling or an evaluation of experience (vedanā), which is a condition for the arising of taṇhā (craving/thirst); and then taṇhā becomes a condition for the birth of upādāna (attachment/clinging), and the upādāna causes avijjā to come into play. In the reverse order we have gotten avijjā > taṇhā > upādāna > vedanā." For this reason, Sāriputta made it clear to his fellow monks thus: "The monk who has established himself in such dharma (in the profound insight into the three characteristics of existence, namely, anicca, dukkha, and anattā, which is insight fully integrated with samādhi), but has not been able to accomplish the total extinction of all the āsavas (fermentations/contaminations) because of being still attached to that dharma (the previously mentioned insight) and still deriving the satisfaction or delight from it."

Another significant key for realizing nirvana

The most important thing to acknowledge is that nirvana must not be *considered* a permanent, everlasting self, although it is the *special dharma, the ultimate truth, and the eternal dharma*, since the Buddha Dharma lays a strong emphasis on non-attachment regarding all things and everything including nirvana and the *very special insight* leading to the full realization of it. One of the four categories of attachment is clinging to the notion or idea of self – attavāda-upādāna, so, the attachment to nirvana as a self is dead wrong and is absolutely against the Buddha Dharma. With respect to this truth, the Buddha uproariously declared: "All dharmas (things) are anattā – without a self," or "All dharmas ought not to be clung to, or are not worth clinging to." In addition, he said about this in the Mūlapannāsa of Majjhima-Nikāya as follows:

"Monks, a certain monk who is a sekha,[16] has not attained the arahatship yet, but aspires to the dharma that is utterly secure and totally free from all the yogas (āsavas), although he has a glimpse of nirvana and therefore knows it as the nirvana, must not consider nirvana as a self (or take it for granted that it is a self, mine, or belonging to me), and must not take enjoyment in it (meaning, he must not regard nirvana as his, or himself as the possessor of it). Why? Because, I say that nirvana is the thing to be fully realized only (here and now).

"Monks, a certain monk is an arahat, having reached the total extinction of all the āsavas, having lived completely the entire holy life (brahmacariya), having done what ought to be done, having laid down all the burden, having fulfilled his own benefit (goal), and having relinquished all the fetters (or samyojanas, those kilesas that bind the human beings to the process of becoming), is irreversibly liberated and immeasurably free because of his all-knowing wisdom. Such a monk, since he knows precisely nirvana as it truly is, does not regard it as his, and does not take pleasure in it. Why? Because, I do say that nirvana is the thing to be fully realized only (here and now)."

The theory of consciousness and the realization of nirvana

Consciousness is the process indispensably connected with energy, and both energy and consciousness are constantly together: Whenever one is found, the other is also discovered. Sometimes we say this: Consciousness is underneath energy, and energy is underneath vibration, while vibration is on the surface since it is the vibration of the energy. For example, fear is a certain type of energy and has a certain vibration quite distinct from the vibration of anger, which is another type of energy. When one recognizes the particular vibration, one will discover certain energy underneath it, and with the continuity of looking and searching one will find a consciousness underlying both the vibration and the energy. To put it in another way, we may formulate the theory that *consciousness* is the *carrier* of energy and vibration, or that both vibration and energy are the manifestations of the consciousness.

Theorizing consciousness in a scientific way, we may simply state that consciousness is a form of mental and spiritual energy permeating and prevailing in all things, is the energy source of the nature's law and the natural law or order such as the order of plants (bīja-niyāma), the order of seasons (utu-niyāma), the order of karma or karmic energy (karma-niyāma), and the order of consciousness itself (citta-niyāma). Therefore, if one can absolutely overpower the consciousness, one may ride above the nature and its natural

---

[16] Self-educator (the one who is still learning and self-educating).

law, for example, those yogis who have developed various supernatural powers successfully are able to stay above the law of nature.

Naturally, consciousness is the process that exists and continues its existential process in the same way as matter and material energy. How and when do matter and energy originate or come into existence? Where do they come from? How or where will they reach their cessation or extinction? No one, whether a scientist or a highly developed spiritual person, actually knows the perfect, indisputable answer to those questions. We merely know that the entire universe is so vast and so infinite that it becomes a puzzle and a koan (riddle) for everyone to penetrate and to discover its whole truth. We know that the substantial core of the universe is matter and energy, and that both matter and energy cannot be destroyed or become extinguished, they can only change the form and the quality from one to the other and vice versa (since the matter is another form of energy or is the energy in a structure or in a physical unit, so everything is concluded in the term 'energy').

Likewise, the energy of consciousness can never be destroyed either, but can change the form, the structure, and the attributes. From its existence in non-living things, consciousness evolves and becomes a conscious process in living things and living creatures, including humans. Therefore, the manifestations of the consciousness process can be recognized through the events and forces of nature demonstrated in various forms and in different ways, depending on the appropriate conditions at the time and in the place.

The appearing and disappearing of consciousness is the process of change and transformation in the variety of forms within the realm of consciousness, which is tremendously vast and absolutely infinite just like the element of space (ākāsa-dhātu) with its vastness and infinitude. In the case of a human individual's death and rebirth, here a certain group of conscious energy provides an appropriate condition for the arising of a new form of life. At the cessation of such a life form, the group of conscious energy will cause a certain movement to take place within the world of consciousness through the power of the karmic energy and the influence of the kilesas, and such a pulsating movement will effectuate a certain form of life awaiting its origination. Then, the new life form will emerge into its existence with the reinforcing power that prevails in the form prior to death, which possesses the approximate quality transferred to the rebirth consciousness (meaning, the rebirth consciousness will receive the fairly accurate quality of life from the death consciousness when a certain person dies so that it may form the new life accordingly and with the additional new environment and new circumstances.) For this reason, the dead person and the re-born individual, although they are neither the same nor different persons,[17] will possess a similar character and a seemingly identical personality, which will help those familiar with such an individual to recognize him or her. So, each one of us has our own uniqueness and differentiation at the same time.

---

[17]   In the Pali language: Na ca so na ca añño.

From the theory of consciousness eloquently explained up to this point, some readers might take into account and conclude that consciousness is permanent and everlasting, which will be fitted with the erroneous, heretic theory called sassata-ditthi, or eternalism, which refers to the view that *everything is permanent and unchangeable*. But, in fact, the observable fact shows us that it is not so since the intrinsic nature of consciousness is subject to appearing and disappearing, arising and passing away momentarily, and is in constant change. In addition, one should keep in mind that consciousness is not a thing in itself, and cannot exist independently by itself, but its existence, operation, and manifestation depend on certain appropriate conditions at the given moment. The basic conditions for the appearing or coming into existence, and disappearing or passing away from moment to moment of consciousness are avijjā, taṇhā, and upādāna.

However, this way of presenting consciousness might also instigate some of you, my readers, to imagine it this way: *Certainly, nirvana is the purest consciousness that is utterly free from all the kilesas and is unmanifested.*

Nonetheless, the author does not intend to create such a poor imagined understanding in his readers before they attain to arahatship. Once full enlightenment or arahatship has been achieved, all questions about consciousness will be naturally answered indisputably and undoubtedly.

Concerning the subscription to a certain theory and speculative view prohibited and proscribed by Buddhism, let us listen to the Buddha's conversations with the young man named Upasīva, which will help us understand the position of Theravada Buddhism more clearly. In addition, the following conversations will clarify the differences between the philosophy of Brahmanism, the philosophy of Mahāyāna Buddhism and the philosophy of Theravāda Buddhism.

The story goes like this: Upasīva was one of the sixteen young men[18] who were the close disciples of the great Brahmin Master, Pāvalī by name. He formulated certain questions for them to defeat the Buddha through debate and counter-debate. Being habitually doubtful, Upasīva put several questions to the Buddha, and in turn he responded to him as follows:

Upasīva: Please tell me something really concrete for helping me cross over the sea of mental contaminations (kilesa/āsava).

The Buddha: You should practice meditation by focusing firmly on, and penetrating deeply this conception of "nothing whatsoever" and maintain clear awareness at all times. Overcome thus the sensual desires, cross over all doubts, investigate and penetrate at all times the dharma that can bring about the extinction of taṇhā. By so doing, you will overcome all kinds of doubt and indecisiveness, and will realize the noble truth experientially day and night.

---

[18] See the detailed discussions between those young men and the Buddha in the author's book entitled *The Unity of Crises and Solutions*.

Upasīva: Once such a meditation has been achieved, is it possible to fall off from it?

The Buddha: No, with such achievement one can never fall off, but will remain firmly in that formless meditative absorption and therefore, will attain full enlightenment there.

Upasīva: If that is so, when such a person dies, what will happen to his or her consciousness?

The Buddha: Just as the flame being blown by the wind disappears with no trace, the person who has been liberated from the attachment to the aggregates of nāma-rupa (psychophysical phenomena or mind-body systems) ceases without remainder. It cannot be said where he or she has gone!

Upasīva: When the said person vanishes after death, does he or she disappear forever? Or, has only the physical body disappeared? Does he or she remain pure and permanent somewhere?

The Buddha: When the five aggregates of attachment that belong to the said person have been totally transformed in which no mental contaminations whatsoever remain to be effective. Then, there is nothing to be born after the death of such aggregates. In fact, there is nothing to be talked about since it is a complete cessation with no remainder.

In connection with the investigation and penetration of the specific dharma that leads on to the complete transformation (the traditional use of language is "utter extinction") of taṇhā (craving/thirst) I would like to present to you, my reader, the method that the Buddha taught Moggallāna, his Left hand Chief Disciple, Sāriputta's counterpart. The method is quite simple and therefore, is suitable for those who are not familiar with the Buddhist practice.

The story began with Moggallāna citing his duration of only seven days of practicing meditation under the Buddha's guidance and attaining to the arahatship on the seventh night of the practice. He then asked his Master the following questions:

"Most Venerable Sir! Briefly, please tell me that kind of practice that can help a monk move his mind toward Nirvana, the dharma by which the extinction of taṇhā can be accomplished. With such attainment the monk will have reached his ultimate goal, being ultimately free from all kilesas and therefore, having his mind totally purified and made brilliantly luminous, fulfilling his practice of the holy life, completing his journey, and thus considered the best among men and devas." The Buddha then responded:

"Moggallāna, a monk in this dharma and vinaya, after having heard that all the dharmas ought not to be clung to, learns to understand all those dharmas. After having learned and comprehended them all, he should realize the impermanence, dissatisfactoriness and conflicting nature, and the absence of a permanent self in all things. After achieving such realization experientially, if he would encounter any sensations or feelings, be they pleasant, unpleasant, neither pleasant nor unpleasant, he would contemplate on the impermanence of those feelings/sensations, seeing it in his profound wisdom so that he could become unattached (or healthily non-attached) and mobilizing such wisdom to transform thoroughly all the kilesas as well as to uproot once and for all the attachment to any feelings or sensations.

"Having been contemplating all the time in this manner, he no longer gets attached to anything in the world, and without attachment there is no fear, and being free from fear he attains the highest degree of tranquillity and everlasting peace by himself. Then, he will realize fully this truth: *Birth has ceased, the holy life has been totally lived, what ought to be done has been done, and other things to get done in this way are no more.*

"Moggallāna, briefly speaking, such described practice will help the monk move his mind upward toward nirvana, the dharma that transforms completely all kinds of taṇhā. In so doing, the monk will accomplish his final goal, being absolutely free from all the kilesas with his consciousness shining forth luminously — he is the highest brahmacārī (practitioner of the holy life) and has reached the completion of journey and therefore, becomes the best among men and devas."[19]

Summarizing the practical side of the sutta

For the practical purposes I would like to summarize the practical side of this sutta for the practitioner to grasp the essence of the practical teaching as follows:

1. *Studying certain dharmas that are basic[20] for the practice and the movement toward attaining enlightenment and realizing nirvana.*
2. *Contemplating all the dharmas in light of impermanence, dissatisfactoriness/conflicting nature, and the void of a permanent self/soul or an everlasting entity existing anywhere, whether inside of life or somewhere else in the entire universe. This is for the goal of achieving the highest virtue of non-attachment.*
3. *Meditating on feelings/sensations first, to see what kind of categories each one belongs to; second, to see its momentary arising (origination) or appearing, and its momentary passing away or disappearing (extinction); third, to see in profound wisdom its impermanence, its dissatisfactoriness/conflicting nature, and its utter emptiness of substantiality and/or voidness of a permanent soul or self.*
4. *Transforming all kilesas (mental, emotional, psychological, and spiritual contaminations or impurities) and uprooting the attachment of all forms to all things.*

---

[19] Translated from Anguttara-Nikāya, Sattaka-Vagga.
[20] Those dharmas are: the three characteristics of existence, the five aggregates, conditioned genesis or dependent origination (paticcasamuppāda), the four noble truths, and the noble eightfold path.

Understanding Buddha Nature

This concept of Buddha Nature (also called the Buddha Nature) is quite well known to the Buddhists of the Northern School of Buddhism such as Mahāyāna and Vajrayāna, while the Theravāda Buddhists lack such terminology, even though there is the reality of the so-called Buddha Nature recorded in the Pali text of Theravāda Buddhism. It is widely believed among the Northern School Buddhists that within each person there is the nature of *awakening* or the *enlightened essence,* which is unmanifested during the period when the mind and the body are covered with the clouds of unknowing (ignorance) and the mud of contaminations, fermentations, and impurities technically known as *kilesas*. As soon as the veil of ignorance is removed by all-knowing wisdom and the kilesas have been transmuted and transformed utterly, the Buddha nature will stand out luminously to the inner eye of such wisdom or the eye of dharma (in Pali, the dhamma-cakkhu).

Metaphorically speaking, during the time of unmanifestation, the Buddha Nature is pretty much like the gem that is totally covered with the mud so that its intrinsic appearance is murky and its luminosity is completely unlit and therefore, one can only see the lump of non-shining mud with its brownish shadowy color. Nonetheless, the gem is naturally pure within and untainted by the temporary mud stains. Or, the Buddha Nature may be compared to space, veiled by clouds, mist, or smog, which obstructs the vision of those on the ground from perceiving and seeing its clearness and its infinitude since it appears thus blurred. But at the moment the clouds, the mist, and the smog have been cleared away thoroughly, infinite, boundless, and clear space appears clearly and flawlessly since it has never been contaminated; instead it remains forever pure and untouched, for however long a period may last of its being covered and veiled by those things. To put it in the third metaphor, it is like water mixed up with soil, which becomes dense and murky for a certain time, although it can be reversible. Since the water and dirt have not fused into an inseparable mixture, the water can always be purified again. The water itself remains basically immaculate. Although the Buddha Nature is at the moment obscured and tainted by gross and subtle blemishes, these can be purged off so that one's natural, unspoiled state of being may emerge unimpedingly.

In chapter five of this work, we discussed at some length the symbolic nāga in the Vammika-Sutta, as the representation of the *enlightened being* within each of us. Please return to refresh your knowledge of such a being and the whole story of how the intelligent Sumedha has discovered it. Honestly speaking, it is the process of the symbolic digging into our psychophysical systems deeply and thoroughly that will help us encounter our enlightened state of being or our Buddha Nature awaiting us at the completion of our digging process. So, Theravāda Buddhism has pointed out quite exquisitely the existence of the Buddha Nature represented by the nāga, or the khīṇāsava — the one whose contaminations or āsava-kilesas have been utterly transmuted and totally transformed, the terminology used by the Buddha himself as he was expounding the meanings of those symbols or mental pictures that appeared during the all-night meditation practice of the monk, Kumāra-Kassapa (the Youth Kassapa). At the moment the young, intelligent man in the story arrived at the nāga at the end of his journey of the digging process, the mature, wise Brahmin who was guiding him all along during such most significant process, told him to approach the nāga and to pay respect to him. As we know, the wise Brahmin in the story symbolizes the Tathāgata (another title for the Buddha), the Buddha Nature manifesting in action, we might say, and the Tathāgata is the completely enlightened one who is always available for helping anyone accomplish his or her process of reaching the full enlightenment.

Therefore, gathering all the precise, untainted, and undistorted information given to us in the Pali Vammika-Sutta we become undoubtedly convinced that Theravāda Buddhism has not only a Buddha Nature, but a double one represented by both the nāga or the khīnāsava and the wise Brahmin or the Tathāgata. So, speaking in terms of the common language, the Theravada Buddhists should be proud of this utmost significant information handed down to them flawlessly through the original Pali text, the sacred language that inscribes all the teachings of the Sakyamuni, Gotama Buddha.

Buddha Nature and nirvana

As we have discussed at some length both the Buddha Nature and nirvana, before leaving this very significant chapter let me shed some more light on these two important subjects so that we could be clearer about them. Concerning Buddha Nature, Dōgen, the Sōtō Zen Founder and the eminent Roshi (Master) of that Zen school, has made it absolutely clear that the Buddha Nature is the *unnameable*, and the *unlimited*, while in the Pali text of Theravāda School of Buddhism describes nirvana as *the unborn, the non-become, the unmade (uninvented), and the uncreated*. From these two viewpoints we draw together that nirvana and the Buddha Nature are identical.

Here I would like to clarify four important points, namely, (1) Buddha Nature and the enlightened essence or khīnāsava, (2) the realization of impermanence is the realization of nirvana, (3) the issue of non-duality, and (4) samsara versus nirvana.

Although the Theravāda Scriptures do not have the concept of Buddha Nature, there is an equivalent concept of khīnāsava – the one who has transformed all the contaminations, the fully enlightened one, or the totally nirvana-realized person, used by the Buddha himself in the Vammika-Sutta (the Discourse about an Anthill) as previously discussed, to signify the Buddha Nature. Therefore, there is no doubt whatsoever in my mind and in my heart that the khīnāsava and the Buddha Nature are utterly identical.

According to the Vammika-Sutta, the khīnāsava was found through the process of digging into the anthill of the human psychophysical systems commonly known as the body and mind. So, the khīnāsava is just there, without the creation or invention by anyone or anything, but is only waiting to be discovered by the wise such as Sumedha who was understood to be the intelligent and diligent digger described eloquently in the cited sutta. In this connection, we become completely convinced of the khīnāsava – the fully enlightened being as the *unnameable, the unlimited*, to use Dōgen's terms, and as the *unborn, the non-become, the unmade (uninvented), and the uncreated*, to use the terminology of Theravāda Buddhism, since the khīnāsava simply *is*, and the khīnāsava is nirvana in action or in mobilization.

When describing the khīnāsava in our common human language we have got a person, a being who has attained the khīnāsavaship, while in the dharma language or in the absolute sense, the khīnāsava is the unnameable (the unnameable always has a name in our human language), the unlimited, the unborn, and the uncreated. Ultimately speaking, there is no person or being to achieve such a state of khīnāsava, just like the Buddha Nature is all the beings and all the beings are the Buddha Nature, which simply points out that there is no achiever, or attainer, or even experiencer of the Buddha Nature apart from the *realization* of that which is unnameable and illimitable.

Let us move on to the second point I would like to clarify here: *the realization of impermanence is the realization of nirvana*. For traditional Theravāda Buddhists, this might sound a bit peculiar since in the Pali text (which recorded the Theravāda teachings), nirvana (in Sanskrit) or nibbāna (in Pali) is described as the permanent, the eternal, the ever-lasting, and the positive, elevated state of the ultimate truth. In addition, the Buddha said in the Dhammapada that *all the conditioned, created things (sankhāra) are impermanent (anicca); while all the created and uncreated things (dhammā) inclusively are without a self or non-substantial (anattā)*. Here the Buddha made a distinction between the impermanence and the non-substantiality, indicating that all the beings (living and non-living, sensible and non-sensible) are subject to impermanence, while nirvana, the uncreated, is not impermanent, but non-substantial. Such an interpretation has been maintained steadfastly by the traditionally-minded Theravāda Buddhists. As for me, although nirvana is not a sankhāra since it is uncreated (asamkhata), we cannot really put it in either category of permanence or impermanence, since by so doing we limit the unlimited, define the indefinable, and name the unnameable. Nonetheless, the impermanence is common to all things and all beings that live in this ever-changing, relative world, the realization of it is most essential for helping us release (or reduce little by little) the passion of attachment, a deeply rooted cause of incessant suffering in our lives. As we know, in Vipassanā Practice, the insight into impermanence is the very basic requirement for reaching enlightenment and for the realization of *nirvana*. So, Dōgen's affirmation of the *realization of impermanence as equal to the realization of nirvana,* is extremely interesting. This is because from the Theravādic viewpoint, it is widely maintained that *whatever is impermanent and subject to change is dukkha (suffering), and whatever is dukkha is anattā* (without a self or substance). Therefore, the realization of impermanence undoubtedly includes the realization of dukkha and anattā at the same moment, which implies that all the three basic characteristics of existence (anicca, dukkha, and anattā) are simultaneously realized, and not one after the other. Since the realization of nirvana is instantaneous and in it is included the realization of all the three characteristics of existence together and therefore, the realization of impermanence is the realization of nirvana.

Also, when the Buddha used positive terms to describe nirvana, he just meant to make it imaginable for the common, unenlightened people so that they may endeavor to realize it, which is merely a teaching technique, I suppose. Since nirvana is disconnected from time and space, meaning, there is no time and no space, or nothing whatsoever in the nirvana apart from nirvana itself, and so the realization of it is, relatedly, timeless. Therefore, to conceive of nirvana as eternal (dhuva), immortal (amata), totally secure (khema), and so forth, is an active imagination method for helping those who are still thick (with kilesas) to perceive a possibility of achieving it, although nirvana is not for achieving or attaining, but only for realization. I understand that the Buddha uses those concepts for the said purpose.

If we say nirvana is permanent, it implies time and in addition, it creates an opposite concept of "impermanent". Dōgen did not say that nirvana is impermanent, he simply says: *Nirvana is impermanence and impermanence is nirvana*, which is entirely different from the nirvana being impermanent. To me, the word 'impermanence' here signifies the negation of time and that of duality, particularly when it is identical with non-substantiality. The impermanence in relation to nirvana is neither bound by time, nor is it limited by space, since it is unlimited and illimitable beyond space and time, and yet exists within time and space with a total freedom from both. Once again, keep in mind that nirvana is the akālika (timeless) dharma, so to take for granted those positive words about nirvana without the true comprehension of the user's specific indications will just keep nurturing erroneous cognition and the delused or radical misunderstanding of consciousness. For this reason, the author would like to suggest that his reader pays more vital attention to the negative terms used by the Buddha so that nirvana will be realized for what it *is*, and not for what it should or would be.

Now, let us penetrate the concept of *non-duality*. As we are aware, the irresolvable problem for the mind is *dichotomy*, the subject-object, the good-bad, the true-false, and so forth. A pair of opposites arises through the thinking mind, and as a result becomes an inevitable cause of conflict both inner and outer. For example, if the words "'agreeable' and 'disagreeable' do not exist in our vocabulary to evaluate or describe our sensation or feeling, then the sensation or feeling would just be a sense experience through the sense contact, and nothing more. Or when we create a self, then the other (otherness) comes into existence, or in terms of psychology, to create is to destroy, since the concept of creating invented by us humans will unavoidably look for its opposite, or its counterpart, and that is destroying. These dualistic things go on and on and on so long as we are under the influence of the thinking mind, and since such a mind can never solve its problem of dichotomy, it will have to live with it and learn to do so wisely so that the problems of inner and/or outer conflicts could be managed more effectively. Maybe, the poetic language that says: *This is not this and not that, but is at the same time this and that*, would be pretty much identical with *non-duality*, since this term is used to mean *the union of opposites or the unity of diving lines such as the unity of the borders between the two countries*. In this connection, physically speaking, the land, the sky, and the water are in themselves not divided, it is the human beings that draw the lines on the map to divide various countries; otherwise there would just be a one country in the whole world.

Since we cannot do much about the language, the politics, the organized religions, and the culture, we can do something intelligent and wise inwardly, and that is abolish the dualistic concepts and mobilize the non-dualistic thinking and the oneness-dimension of understanding and feeling. For example, in the spiritual sense we may take it this way: *The practice is the realization and the realization is the practice, or the realization of impermanence is the realization of nirvana and the realization of nirvana is the realization of impermanence.* In other words, the paradoxical expression must be embraced unconditionally so that any inner conflict may be resolved since the truth is paradoxical.

Let me now elaborate the contrast of samsara versus nirvana. According to the figure below, I understand that the base of samsara is the cosmos while the ego stays on the vertex; and the base of nirvana is the Buddha Nature with impermanence on the vertex. But with the upside-down cone, the ego becomes the base of nirvana with the cosmos at the vertex.

Therefore, I call samsara as **nirvana upside down** since it is in accord with the truth and also fitted with the Zen saying: *Samsara is nirvana and nirvana is samsara (as they are identical)* — another example of non-duality.

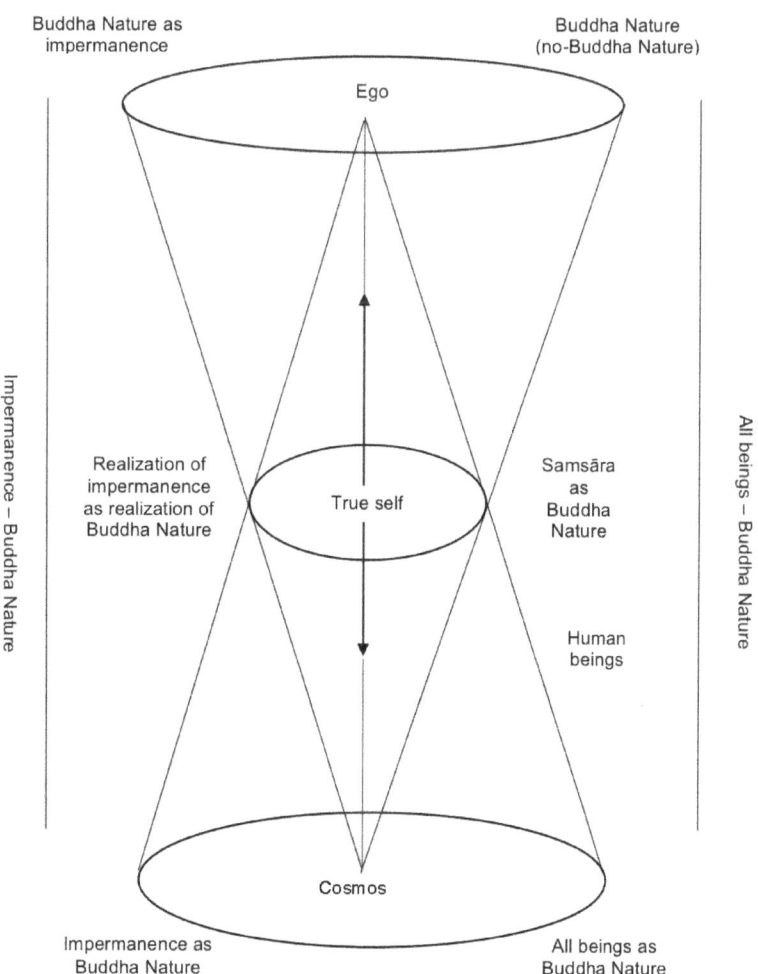

Talking about various dimensions, in the above figure or diagram we have four interesting dimensions, namely, (1) the human dimension represented by birth and death, (2) the life or living dimension represented by origination and extinction, (3) the self dimension represented by appearing and disappearing, and self and no-self, and (4) the cosmic dimension represented by impermanence/Buddha nature. As we can see, out of four the three dimensions point to the same thing, and that is *birth and death*: origination is synonymous with birth, while extinction is equivalent to death, appearing is the same as birth, and disappearing is identical with death, and self versus no-self is still bound by birth and death. Only the fourth dimension is beyond birth and death since the Buddha Nature (as equivalent to nirvana) is the *unborn* and the deathless. Certainly, when we (included here are all the beings) are involved in birth and death, we are in samsara. But as soon as we become dissolved into the realm of nirvana, we are nirvana-realized and therefore, birth and death, origination and extinction, appearing and disappearing, self and no-self (all these pairs of opposites exist only in the world of duality) cannot find our trace (when we arrive at nirvana, figuratively speaking).

One more interesting thing provided in the above-drawn figure is the true self, prevailing in the middle circle of the two cones. This so-called true self or true being is associated with samsara versus nirvana and the realization of impermanence versus the realization of the Buddha Nature. Hence, it has become utterly clear beyond the reasonable doubt that the samsara and the nirvana are identical just as the realization of nirvana is the same as the realization of impermanence. Nonetheless, there is a puzzle about the true being or self in the middle place of the two cones! What does this mean? For me, the middle place means the point of dynamic equilibrium just as the middle point of the see-saw is the place of balance. Regarding this matter of middle place we also say: *it is a sacred* place since it represents the omnipresence, the omniscience, *the complete and steadfast attention.* So, the true being or self is merely a figurative expression, while in truth it refers to the khīnāsava or the Buddha Nature awaiting our discovery or realization.

In conclusion, one may make such a statement as this: *the nirvana-Buddha Nature* is to be realized fully here and now, in this present moment, which is eternal, timeless time. Being the cycle of birth-death, origination-extinction, and appearing-disappearing, as well as the cycle of kilesa-karma-vipāka, samsara is also here and now, with no beginning and no ending; in other words, the beginning of samsara is inconceivable, and so is the ending. Therefore, there is no difference between samsara and nirvana, except the words or concepts covering them both. Nonetheless, in the paradoxical or non-dualistic expression there are both **differentiation** and **integration** of samsara and nirvana. Looking at either of them from the narrow point of view they become different and differentiated, but penetrating them wholly with the luminous light of the profound wisdom and the bottomless insight they are integrated (identical).

=8=

THE BUDDHA'S MIDDLE PATH

Introductory note

The Middle Path is a large subject to consider, because it is not easy to define it or to assert a principle or formula for it. Usually, we look for something very definite, or for something that is clearly stated, defined, or named, so that we can easily follow. You may be disappointed to find that the middle path has no clear definition, and in a way, it cannot have a definition at all.

You may remember that the Buddha, soon after enlightenment, was thinking of giving his first sermon to those who could understand his teaching. First, he thought of the two teachers under whom he had studied and practiced, fulfilling all the necessary spiritual attainments, but whom he had left, realizing that he had still not reached enlightenment. He thought they would understand what he was going to say, but then in his visionary insight he saw that they had already passed away. Then, he saw in his vision the five ascetics with whom he had practiced self-mortification, and whom he had left simply because he realized that their extreme asceticism was not the way. He felt they would understand, so he went and gave the sermon to them at Benares.

In his first sermon, the Buddha mentioned the two extreme practices. The first is self-mortification, believing that by tormenting the body, fasting, lying on thorns or nails, depriving and wearing out the physical form, one will realize nirvana. The other extreme is self-indulgence and hedonism, believing that happiness or joy is the primary goal of life (this can often be seen in the modern spiritual movements which aim for states of bliss).

The Buddha taught the middle path that lies beyond these two extremes. This is the Buddhist way of life, which is called the *eightfold path*: right understanding, right thought, right action, right speech, right livelihood, right effort/perseverance, right mindfulness/awareness, and right concentration/contemplation. These practices are the foundation of the Buddha's teaching or dharma.

We can see that the two extremes are prevalent in our present world. Many people advocate the material way of life, thinking that through material support all happiness must come — but it is not so. We get more and more comfort and pleasure, but we are still not happy because we are not free. Our problems may increase, because when sense desires are continually gratified and the body is richly fed, the mind becomes poorer and more disturbed — it has more thirst, more craving and clinging. With an unstable mind, we go to extremes. When there is no balance in the mind, then there is no balance in life, and this we can see clearly.

The other extreme concerns a "Spiritual" life, in which people may drop away from the material world, refusing to face what is arising in their lives. They may give up their work and responsibilities, renouncing the world without insight into what it is that really needs to be renounced. In fact, the world cannot be renounced, because the world means human relationships and life situations, which reappear in different forms. If we turn our face away from these, it is the ego rejecting the natural path provided. Even those who go into the forest or become sanyasis need to accept material things to support their life, and monks and nuns living in a monastery or a convent exist within a community. Those who insist on rarefied conditions and resist what is being given to them by life are usually being driven by spiritual ambition. They may become famous teachers, but will still be bound by their own self-importance and desire for power. Their work may appear more profound and valuable than the materialist, but in fact they are developing an equally superficial side of life, limited by what might be called spiritual materialism.

It is not very easy to practice the middle path, but this does not mean that it is difficult for us to begin. We have to see the extremes we are practicing in life, and to watch ourselves, attending to all our activities. The middle path is the way of balance, neither to the left nor to the right, neither to the wrong nor to the correct, but we shall not have this balance through trying to grasp it. It will come when the extremes are properly looked at and dissolved. The mind is always wanting to grasp something in order to stay with it and not let it go, but in doing that it is not open, and for the middle path, it needs to be open. As soon as we are closed to any event, any situation, we fall asleep psychologically. In sleep we feel comfortable and secure, but there is no freedom. You might say that of course there is freedom, because you can do what you think is right, but that is like the freedom of prisoners to decorate their prisons — they are still living in the prison. It is essential to look at the mind and how it creates things to reassure itself.

The middle path is not just the path between two poles, but is beyond them. In the ultimate sense, we can say that the middle path has no concept of what is right or what is wrong, what is good or what is bad. When we have concepts we try to justify our behavior by them. Our concepts impose upon us so that we don't really look into the action in order to see it as it is.

Usually things are judged according to a standard or an authority, whether religious, political, social, legal, parental or personal. This sort of standard is secondhand. But if we look for ourselves, without denying any authorities but understanding things first-hand, we shall have the basis for a balanced way of life.

Guidance is important, but is something we can find within us, which fully relates us to the teachings of life without being imposed upon us. What is that something? The guide within is insight, which arises naturally through the operation of awareness and observation. What does it mean to have insight? It does not mean that you have seen something very mysterious, beyond the reach of human intelligence. It is something well within the capacity of human beings, although not necessarily expressed in words or concepts. It is the guiding principle (the guiding light of wisdom) in the middle way, but is not a fixed principle and cannot be obtained from studying or any other external source. It's already within every one of us, but its flow is totally blocked by the ideas that prevent the seeing within, the *in-sight*. To have insight means the *clear seeing* not only of what lies inside us, but also outside us, without involving knowledge (pre-accepted ideas), but leading to the *illumination* of knowledge. That kind of seeing has no position it is trying to establish, and is therefore free and open to everything.

Let us take the example of insight into pain, which may arise in the body while sitting in meditation. Your first reaction to physical pain may be to try to alter your position in order to be more comfortable. When the pain continues or increases, another kind of pain arises — in the mind, which cannot accept the pain and tries to escape or fight it. If we can *bear* to watch, and keep on watching, we can exercise insight into the situation of pain and of our reaction, which leads to greater insight. Bearing with patience is the key, because when we are watching, this does not mean that pain must disappear. We have to allow pain, or even agony, yet without forcing toward a goal of mastery. Let everything happen. If you want to cry, cry, and continue to look. Sometimes, the mind and the body are suddenly released from pain, and you experience a very pleasant sensation — then look at that too, without interference.

This kind of situation during sitting meditation can give us a practice in looking, which we can use in life situations. Suppose you are attached to something or somebody, and you lose them. You may feel great loss, and have nothing to cling to. You may feel very lonely, without help from anything external. This is the time to meditate, not in the sense of turning inward for serenity and security, but in the sense of facing the emptiness and the feelings of loneliness and grief. Look at the situation of loss, and you will have insight into attachment, if you keep on looking penetratingly long enough. Go into it fully, with courage. It is the painful way of working, but it is the middle path, which eventually dissolves the problem because it turns toward the source — not an imagined source of peace and beauty, but the source of our troubles. When we can look facing the cause of our pain, it ceases to have such power over our lives.

Who can help us to be free unless we are prepared to look? People may give comfort in words and assertions, but this will only be temporary if we do not tread the path ourselves. The problem remains, rooted in the mind, and we have to be willing to experience and investigate it properly, seeing all its aspects. We may sometimes feel despair at the long road ahead, but being prepared to look fully, just once, our situation changes immediately because we have set our feet in the right direction. Time does not matter; it is the direction that counts. We need not believe what somebody tells us — we need only experiment, and we shall see for ourselves what our path is.

You may ask whether insight give us any conclusions about what should be done in life. No, "Should be" and "Should not be" are merely ideas. What is so is what we deal with, as it arises, and insight will guide our actions. We remain free to act, to lose, to look, to receive, without any rigid decision about what is right or wrong. You may reply that you don't trust your insight at present. But all our actions are based upon something — either our insight or our reactions or desires — so we have to trust the situation that arises. One of our greatest fears is to *be* ourselves, to accept ourselves as we are. You have to be honest, and not set up high standards, as this can be a form of arrogance. To be yourself is to be alone with what you are, looking at it and at your own reactions to yourself, free from beliefs and objectives. If you say "It is terrible to be like me. I cannot be like that" you are attempting to escape what *is*. Reality is not something mysterious and inaccessible — it is what *is*.

Loneliness can make us feel terrible, because we cannot face ourselves as we are. If we look into the conditioned mind, we shall see why we cannot be alone with it. Can we be alone during our lives among people? To be truly alone within life does not mean withdrawal, indifference, and pride. It means the allowing of emptiness through which there is the freedom to open and to listen. If you have the capacity to listen you have the weapon that renders powerless the enemy of authority and compulsion. We cannot listen freely because we still have authority in us, the authority of knowledge, belief, and experience. Sometimes, we don't hear other people talking because we are listening to ourselves, interpreting, commenting, rejecting, building up attitudes or evolving questions. With all these, we cannot be alone.

The best relationships are based on aloneness, when you do not need to use others for your own happiness or support. Such needs destroy relationships because exploitation is based upon ego-centered wanting, which prevents the giving and accepting of love. If you can lose and be alone, you can share everything with everybody.

With such a relationship you will not look back — you can finish with every moment as it passes. Then you do not cling to pleasure. People may think this sounds like being a vegetable, without feeling. But at the moment of experience you have pleasure without thought, and that is true pleasure. If desire gives attachment to the experience, and you wish to regain or repeat it, you become out of balance. Leave it alone, so that when you don't regain it, you understand, or when you do, you appreciate it freshly. This is the stage of freedom from experience and non-experience. We don't look back or forward, we don't carry anything with us, so we can travel lightly and freely.

Thinking ahead is often necessary, but when there is attachment to our own wish for success and fear of failure, fear concerning the future creates psychological tension and even paralysis. One cannot act, and it is very difficult to live. But if we live our life in every moment, appreciating it fully, we can leave it when it is finished.

Life has everything to give, it has all the treasures, but it also has pain because conflict is there. We have to accept life as it is, and in fact we can learn more from conflict than from pleasure. Without conflict we may just continue to sleep in life, without learning anything. So any unpleasant experience in life can be used as a teaching, an awakening, to bring wisdom. All spiritual masters, like the Buddha or the Christ, had painful experiences in their lives through which they discovered what was important. It is not a matter of avoiding suffering nor of seeking it out, but of going through it, working through it.

We need insight, and this cannot be given by anyone. It is within. What can we do in order to develop insight? With this question, we come here to the basic thing, which we call meditation. To meditate is to be simply aware of what is going on here and now; it is to find the capacity to live fully and creatively in the present, without being swayed by the past or the future. Insight does not always arise during a period of sitting meditation, but often comes afterward. To meditate is in a way like a hen hatching eggs. During her period of sitting, the chickens do not emerge, but her sitting is necessary for them to come out later. If we sit and meditate without any expectation of insight, it will arise more easily. But if we sit with expectancy and impatience, disappointment and suffering arise.

The motive for meditation is to see, to look, to go through one's own conditioning, or to take a journey through oneself. You see what kind of person you are, what your particular weaknesses, qualities, and characteristics are, dominant or secondary, without having to be told by anyone, without being tested, interpreted or diagnosed. You can be your own analyst by looking into yourself, seeing each particular for what it is and how it manifests every moment. You are sitting, reading, talking with friends, going somewhere, being emotional — in any situation you can observe what is happening. When you see unpleasant things in yourself, a further reaction often arises — feelings of self-dislike, self-blame or guilt — but do not let this prevent you from continuing to *look and accept*. Without acceptance, seeing can become a form of self-torture and self-hatred, which can never lead to freedom.

It is a matter of seeing, without even categorizing. If you say "I am such-and-such a person," this creates a fixed idea. Then when you look at yourself you see the image held in your mind, instead of seeing yourself as you are at that next moment. When you look at what is there, without ideas, you can see objectively. In that seeing, there is balance. You are not emotionally involved or distracted or overwhelmed, yet you allow feeling to arise without attempting to ignore or repress it. Feeling arises naturally with intelligence and seeing – it is flowing at all times, and does not become negative unless it has been blocked or denied. So, even if the feeling is unpleasant, there is no distortion unless it is not seen and accepted. If the intellect is overdeveloped, the energy of feeling is channelled into attitudes and judgments.

You can learn to meditate at any time, but it is essential that we have a certain period of training to begin with, because most people are not strong enough to look into themselves properly. This is a problem of fear, and of not understanding psychological and mental processes. When you come across something that appears harmful and destructive, and you have no guidance, there may be a withdrawal and a reinforcement of fear so that further meditation is avoided. Or, on the other hand, there may be a blissful experience that the meditator would like to repeat, so that desire is strengthened and meditation is used as a substitute for drugs. Another pitfall (especially frequent in Hindu forms of meditation) is the wish for detachment, in which the mind finds relief in a suspended state dissociated from the flux and conflict of what is actually arising at every moment. Or refuge is sought in a higher being, God, or guru, which are trusted blindly to the exclusion of all else. Such a fixed state of belief brings a form of security which people long for, but lacks the flexibility upon which true freedom and contentment are based.

We have to allow continuous inquiry. This is not the compulsive questioning of the skeptic, but an open flow that can investigate everything without getting brainwashed. And a very important factor in this is *honesty*. Be honest with yourself, be frank, without trying to hide yourself, or prove you are right, or saying that you are always wrong. To be honest is to be objective, to allow criticism without rejection. When we understand our habits and tendencies, and accept them, we shall be able to understand and accept others. *This is the way in which harmony is established between individuals, where we are neither naïve nor judgmental about one another.*

What does it mean to be honest? First of all, you may see that you are not honest, and if you look into this, you will see the reasons why, not in theory but in practice. In working toward honesty we do not use ideas or principles, or philosophies, but we look at dishonesty in action. When the causes of dishonesty and our need for deviation are seen through, then honesty becomes easier and the direct path is taken. That is why, in the explanation of nirvana the Buddha expressed it in non-assertive terms: It is not the moon, not the sun, not the earth, not the planets, not the stars, not the color, and so on and so forth. Therefore, the mind cannot hold on to a definite, fixated idea. Another way of doing this is through paradox, in which something is described as *both* this and that, apparently opposite and therefore impossible, but perfectly possible to a non-dualistic understanding.

This deep understanding creates inward flexibility. One moves freely from point to point, and this is pleasant because movement is natural to living. Flow also clears away obstacles and prevents stagnation, so that it is self-cleansing. If the mind becomes fixed, like the water in a pond, it becomes polluted and can be dangerous; it cannot see beyond its own boundaries. But if it can move on with awareness, it does not get stuck and remains young in the sense of having vitality, openness, and flexibility. The body may grow old, but the free mind, the mind with clear insight, is always young, and moves along the middle path.

There are two basic types of thinking: One is concentrative, which may be powerful, but can also be dangerous because of an inability to bend. It is linear and exclusive, rather than lateral and inclusive. This way of thinking has strong attachment to support it, and certainly lacks flexibility. At times we may need to use it for certain things, but it is unwise to do so for long, and in particular it should not be used with psychological problems, nor on the spiritual path. The other type of thinking we may call thinking from the heart. Of course this does not mean the physical heart, which cannot think. What we call the heart here is the center of being — or just *being* (totally integrated self), with no idea of center. Thinking from the heart is an open-ended, total perception of what is actually happening, without logic. It does not operate from any point, any angle, or any principle, but passes through us from whatever arises, from the situation here and now. Being is not somewhere, but anywhere, everywhere, and nowhere in particular, because it has no special place. Like the free man or woman, the mind that thinks from the heart has no fixed abode or plane of existence. Its path is that of intuitive insight, the way of awareness and wisdom, and as the Buddha said, wisdom and insight spring from mediation. Such a meditative, aware mind does not draw its power from the explosive energy of suppressed conflict, from the attempt to make itself still, but from the *nourishing flow of insight*, when it (the mind) becomes still naturally and the middle path can be truly lived.

The significance and factors of the path

The path that we have been discussing is simply called the *middle path,* which consists of three principal groups, namely, the *wisdom group,* the *meditation group,* and the *ethics group.* There are two factors that make up the wisdom group. They are *complete understanding and rightful viewing*, and *heartfelt thinking and authentic intention.* As for the meditation group, there are three factors that compose it, to wit, *total awareness, wholehearted perseverance, and firmly stabilized mind.* Similarly, there are three factors that constitute the ethics group, and these are *right action, right speech, and right livelihood.*

First of all, let us consider the wisdom group since it plays a very significant role in bringing about transformation and enlightenment. The first factor of wisdom refers to the direct or experiential knowing and complete understanding of the truth of life, which involves suffering and the cessation of it, as well as definitive characteristics of existence. Generally speaking, this refers to the understanding of four fundamental things concerning life, namely, *what is* — meaning *whatever it is that happens in life and in the world, how it arises, where it ends (its solution), and the path leading to the ending or real solution of it.* As a matter of fact, one cannot understand what is with all its total structure if the causes or conditions that gives rise to it is not completely comprehended. Furthermore, to comprehend fully what is, requires a thorough viewing of where and how the real solution is to be found.

The second factor of wisdom involves the qualities of heart, which embrace the thoughts based on emphatic feeling in regard to *self-sacrifice, compassion, and non-violence.* Self-sacrifice is, in fact, the relinquishment of the ego's compulsive patterns of conditioning that obstruct the way of freedom and naturalness. This kind of sacrifice originates in the heart, the strong feeling and willingness to leave one level of consciousness, and ascend to another level, for example, giving up bad habits, addictions, and attachments to some things or to certain people. For this reason, self-sacrifice plays a very important role in self-development work since without it, there will be no forward movement toward growth in all directions and full development. Therefore ego *must* be prepared and willing to let go of all its uncreative and compulsive patterns of conditioning, in other words, to *de*condition itself, which is an enormous sacrifice. If this is done, undoubtedly there will be a big leaping forward, a conspicuous shift in consciousness; otherwise, the stagnant and sluggish state of affairs will dominate and damage the development process.

As for compassion, we see it as an outstanding quality of the heart because it points to the empathic feeling for those who suffer or are in troubles, and at the same time, there is the willingness to help in all possible ways. Compassion goes together well with wisdom as the union of the pair of opposites, and without one, the other cannot operate effectively. The reason for this is that compassion alone or wisdom alone is conducive to extremity, for example, wisdom sees ultimately that all things are empty and that the world is an illusion, since it doesn't exist in reality and therefore, that there is no world to be saved. Hence compassion is essentially needed in order to render services to humanity and to the world; otherwise wisdom will make us merely sit there, idealizing and contemplating the fertile void of all phenomena in life and in the world. In the similar way, compassion without the supportive guidance of wisdom will inevitably put us in a position of exercising the feeling function in an extreme manner up to the point of lacking balance in rendering services. Such an extreme implementation of compassion will lead to making use of sacrifice in the wrong way, as it lays a strong emphasis on offering external services exclusively, without attending to personal growth and self-transformation. It is erroneous thinking and wrong believing to try to make a sacrifice with no reference to self-growth and to the transformational process in the way of putting compassion into practice. Therefore, those two qualities of the heart must be closely linked in practice so that both the self and the other (or others) can gain similar, mutual benefit — meaning that no one is left out from getting needs met and from moving forward toward fuller and fuller being.

Let us now turn to the third quality of the heart, non-violence. Again, this matter of non-violence is indispensably linked to those two previously discussed qualities of the heart since it lays a very firm foundation for actualizing compassion and sacrifice wisely and correctly. Non-violence is the most powerful action to be taken in regard to all human world affairs, including politics, psychotherapy, and spirituality. In a sense, it is a high self-respect and respect for the others, because in actual fact, no one wants to be hurt either physically or emotionally, and for that matter everyone wants to be treated with a genuine respect, without causing any damage to any human realities. With non-violence in the heart, compassion in the mind, and sacrifice in consciousness, one will be able to grow into full humanness, bringing along with one all the fellow beings that live in the world and walk on the planet Earth without any discrimination. In this way, peace, safety, and prosperity will prevail, and consequently we all will be happy, healthy, and in harmonious coexistence.

Another essential group that forms the middle path is meditation. By meditation we mean the total self-development through bodily and mental training, throwing light into the dark places within, and bringing the unconscious up to the conscious plane of existence so that the two streams of consciousness can merge and form the one powerful stream in life. Take a close look at the three factors of the meditation group: total awareness, genuine perseverance, and firmly stabilized mind (samādhi). They are all very strong and potent forces that can bring about complete transformation and full enlightenment. Let me give you a brief description of these factors: Awareness operates by way of feeding the correct information into the ego to enable it to become an *aware ego*, a fully conscious and totally awake functioning. Meanwhile, perseverance constantly puts energy into making use of the awareness until it becomes part and parcel of life, a constant companion that never leaves and is available at all times. The firmly stabilized mind lays a strong and secure foundation for the other two factors to operate effectively, for without it, awareness and perseverance will become dormant and inactive due to the dominance of the habit tendencies and conformative ego patterns that run the show of life.

The last group of the middle path is the ethical guidance that helps shape moral conduct regarding action, speech, and the right way of earning a living. Unlike the other five factors of the path, these three factors are not absolutely required for attaining enlightenment and total transformation, although they provide some convenience with respect to adopting acceptable behavior and righteous means of conducting life, businesses, and personal relations with another human beings. They are the ethical guidelines concerning the right and wrong, the good and bad, and the harmonious and disharmonious in regard to the type of action to be taken, the manner of speech, and the livelihood to be engaged in. For example, killing, stealing, and committing adultery are considered wrong actions; instead, loving-kindness, respect for the others' possessions and properties, and faithfulness and devotion to one's husband or wife should be practiced.

With regard to right speech, one should not speak a lie, one should not use accusing and manipulating words in speaking, one should not make use of improper, rude language in speech, and one should not engage in vain talk. As for right livelihood, the occupation of selling and buying meat, the trade of destructive weaponry, intoxicating drinks, tobaccos, drug trading, and slavery trading or unlawful use of labor, are all wrong ways of earning a living.

Balancing power and love, wisdom and compassion

These two pairs of opposites play a very significant role in the path of transformation because each element in each pair is extremely strong by its nature and is in complete opposition to the other in their functioning. For transformation to take place we need to bring them into balance; otherwise, there will be no real solution to inner conflict. The first pair of power and love may be considered the most difficult pair to balance. As we know, power indicates strength, authority, manipulation, and control, while love signifies the sense of caring, the feeling of connectedness, and the energy of wholeness. The former is dominant and, without love, has the possibility of being cruel, devilish, and totally heartless. On the contrary, the latter is nurturing, inviting, unifying, integrative, and is always concerned with keeping all beings in oneness consciousness.

Now, the question arises: how can one bring about the balance of the pair of opposites? First of all, one must make sure that one has the properly developed awareness, the highly effective tool for bringing out the penetrating insight into each component of the pair, that is, into power and love. This means that the exercise of power should be carried out with clear awareness, and not with the egocentric manipulation. Such a way of using power will ease the one-sided ambition of the mind and at the same time soften the heart so that the element of love, in the sense of caring and feeling sympathetic, will be brought into operation. Furthermore, in the mind and heart of those who execute power through the guiding light of awareness and insight, there will be a gesture of balance and a sense of equipoise, which in turn will make them feel more humane and more satisfactory in life and at work. As they grow into carrying out power in this manner, love in their hearts will flow more strongly both inwardly and outwardly so that the power, while maintaining its strength, will be integrated with love. In this way, the balance between power and love can be achieved.

As for those who are the upholders of love, it is very essential for them to understand clearly that love without power becomes very weak and impotent. They need to bring the element of power into love in order to sustain it and help it flow more powerfully so that the upholders of love will be both amiable and resolute. It is like balancing *yin* and *yang* in the world of manifestation. Love is yin and power is yang. They must be utilized proportionately for the purpose of keeping balance in being and becoming; otherwise we will be thrown into the extreme ways of living and mobilizing in the world, swinging back and forth, with no sight of the center or middle place.

When power and love are in harmonious operation, the negative aspects of each element will be transformed. For instance, power will remain as *creative energy* with inexhaustible strength and abundant ability to carry out functions and activities; while love will stay as the *nurturing agent* for living and functioning. In this fashion, one can live a balanced life and be able to function harmoniously and fully, making use of all possible human resources without getting hindered by the destructive forces. Once again, bear in mind that *awareness and insight* are the golden key or the most potent means of access to such accomplishment.

As for the pair of wisdom and compassion, we find another extreme polarity that keeps sustaining our inner conflict and prevents full functioning and wholeness of development. Certainly, one-sided development is extremely dangerous not only to fellow beings that walk on earth but to self-growth and self-transformation. This is because in the eccentric, one-sided way of life, one is under the strong dominance and great influence of the egocentric personality with its burning pride, arrogance, and total alienation from essence.

Wisdom in its extreme sense sees nothing concrete and practical in life in the world, but concludes that all is absolutely void and illusory. According to this extreme wisdom, there is no world to serve and the beings to be saved do not exist; all that appears to exist is just illusion. If one carries this form of wisdom through life, all things become meaningless, irrelevant, and insignificant, including life and living; there is nothing-worthwhile doing. It sounds completely negative and definitely undesirable, to say the least. Nevertheless, although it appears to the unenlightened mind or lop-sidedly trained individual as a form of mental sickness, this level of wisdom is not a schizophrenic, lunatic illness. In fact, it is a completely healthy state in which the perception and comprehension of reality takes place in the ultimate, absolute level of consciousness. At that level, everything is viewed from the eye of the absolute truth, with no reference whatsoever to relative truth. For this reason, it becomes an utterly extreme view that is absolutely unpractical in the practical world; nonetheless, it is a philosophical entertainment. In order for wisdom to be balanced and practicable it becomes ultimately essential to add the element of compassion to it because compassion plays the active role of emphatic understanding with the willingness to help. Compassion operates in the relative world, while wisdom renders its service in the absolute world; and this is just like heaven and earth. When the two worlds are brought together in harmony and compatibility, this is the balancing of heaven and earth. Compassion alone is not adequate for dealing with complex human beings and the complex world; we need wisdom to shed light on what is happening so as to enable us to discover the related conditions and causes of the happenings. Wisdom has two main aspects: one being the intellectual understanding; another is *insight and profound, inner vision*. With those two aspects combined, there comes into operation the ability to be and live in accordance with that which one knows either intellectually or directly (through sharp insight and profound vision).

Finally, let us put it this way: wisdom renders its service in bringing about the precise and total understanding of things and life situations as they occur, together with the right solution; while compassion focuses on taking the appropriate actions to help those in pain and suffering. In addition, compassion also mobilizes our energies to rescue the risky and dangerous situations in this rapidly changing world so that it can make a safe, secure, and better place to live in. Without compassion, the world will be divided and therefore there will be a big gap between the rich and the poor, between the black and the white, and between the peoples of different religions, cultures, races, or backgrounds of upbringing. The more divided we are, the more dangerous we become as hatred toward, and illusion about, one another are due to be on the increase. As a result, violence and terrorism will spread over all places to the point of total chaos and disorder, so that no one can be safe anywhere in the world. There can be no peace for the world in this situation.

Compassion is greatly needed not only for community, society, nation, and the whole world, but for each individual as well. Each one of us needs to feel compassion for ourselves; particularly when we have done something wrong or bad, because in such wrongdoing, we suffer a great deal. In place of blaming, condemning, or putting ourselves down, we can exercise a compassionate feeling for ourselves, or at least for a certain part of us that has been led into doing so. With compassion, we can emerge from pain and suffering, and then will be able to review our situations correctly, so that we may begin anew or find a new way of doing things without repeating the old pattern. If you see in yourself something bad or unacceptable, the first thing to do is to render the service of compassion to it, recognizing it and letting it be as it is. Then, compassion will help you understand the unacceptable or the so-called bad thing, because compassion is closely associated with intellect, and with precise intellectual understanding, there is the possibility of acceptance. With acceptance comes loving-kindness that will strengthen compassion and will lead you on to transformation, to a definite shift in your consciousness.

Integrating head, heart, and soul

Let us consider the following passage written by Alexander Lowen, MD:

"In the course of evolution, the energy level of some organisms increased greatly, with the result that in the higher animals the charge at both ends of the body became strong enough to form two centers. The upper center became the brain; the lower center became the sexual and reproductive system. The middle center of activity became the heart, from which blood pumped to both ends of the body connects them energetically to the center... In a tree, that connection is made by the upward and downward flow of sap... The movement of fluid is related and dependent on a corresponding energy flow in the form of waves of excitation that traverse the organism. In the human body these waves of excitation are the force that maintains its erect posture. In general, these waves are stronger during daytime periods of activity than during nighttime periods of rest.

"It is a basic rule of bioenergetics that energy charge cannot exceed energy discharge. Although it is possible to eat more food than one needs for the production of energy at a given time, the excess will be stored as fat, ready to be converted into energy when needed. Similarly, if one is in dire straits – for example, in the midst of famine – one may spend more energy than one takes in, but the body's energy reserves will be so severely depleted that the end result may be death. The body's equilibrium may be altered momentarily – by holding the breath, for example – but it must be restored if life is to continue.

"The balance of opposing forces is inherent in the phenomenon of pulsation, which underlies life itself. Pulsation, which describes a process of expansion and contraction, is apparent in respiration, peristalsis, the beating of the heart, and other bodily functions. It is basic to all living organisms, regardless of size. In the case of the human body, it occurs not only in the total organism but also in every cell, tissue, and organ.

Energy centers of the body

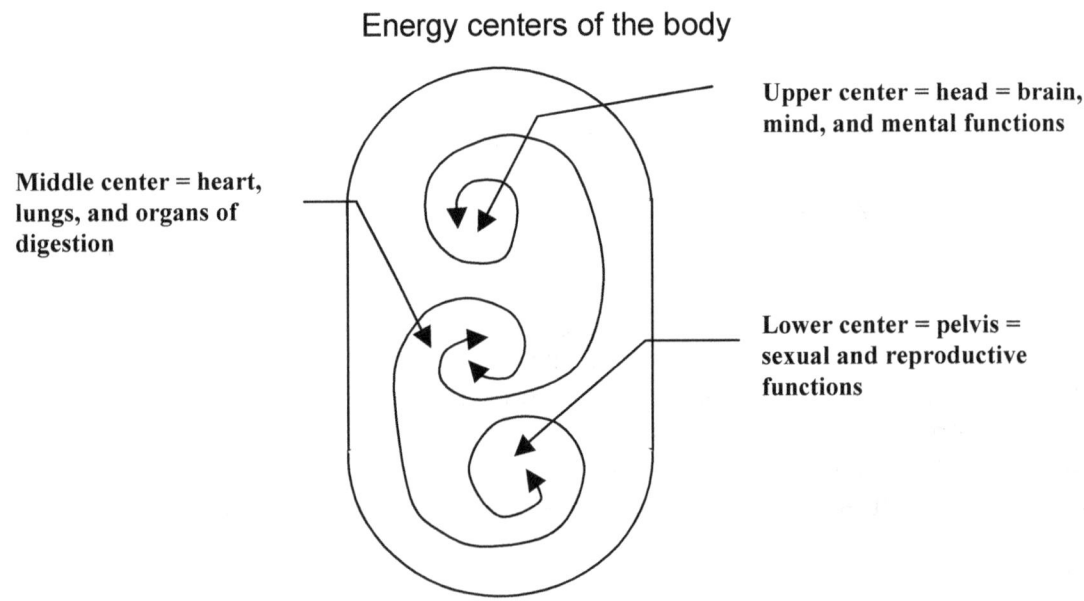

"This model applies to behavior as well – the alternation between reaching out and withdrawal is a form of pulsation. Reaching out leads to contact with the world outside one's self, while withdrawal leads to contact with the self. This alternance is influenced by the diurnal rhythm. We are more outgoing during the day and more withdrawn into ourselves at night when we sleep. Neither state is superior to the other, and are both necessary to good health. To be stuck in either is pathological, for life depends on the pulsation, on the ability to move out or withdraw as the situation requires."[1]

As for the knowledge of basic pulsation both in a single-cell organism and in humans, please take a closer look at the following two diagrams.

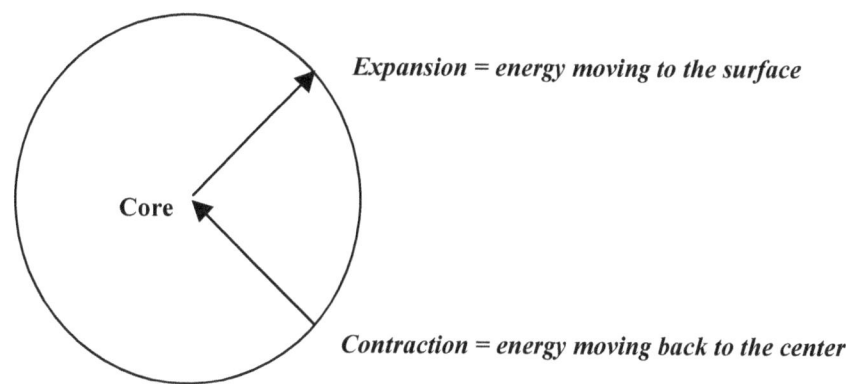

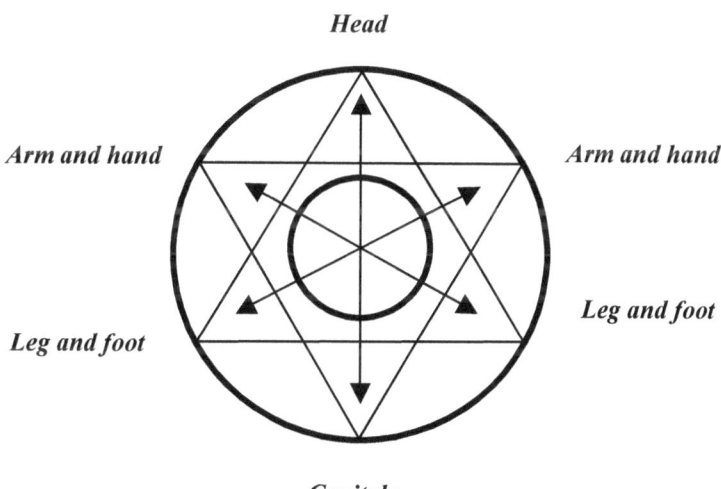

Expansion and Contraction in the body
(Upper diagram) Basic pulsation in a single cell organism
(Lower diagram) Basic pulsation in humans

This is a scientific and bioenergetic approach to the body and mind, which helps us understand the interconnection of the three principal centers of our psychosomatic systems. They are *upper center* (head, brain, mind and mental functions), *middle center* (heart, lungs, and organs of digestion), and the

---

[1] Alexander Lowen, *The Spirituality of the Body*, from text and diagrams on pages 126-129.

lower center (pelvis, sexual and reproductive functions). According to this thesis, the three centers are correlated both in functioning and in getting affected when something wrong happens. For example, a major disturbance in the body can be in correlation with an equally significant disturbance in the personality, which is the phenomenon of splitting. Psychologically speaking, there are people who have split or schizoid personalities and some individuals have even been described as having multiple personalities. The split comes into running the show as the result of losing the feeling of connection between those three centers. We often encounter the people whose heads are not connected to their hearts and whose hearts are not connected to their genitals. As a result, the head dominates the genitals, while the heart becomes quiescent and inactive because of lacking the opportunity to display its energy. This is often found in some people's sexual activities in which the lovemaking is not done with love but with the idea of fulfilling pleasure or the necessity of removing tensions either physical or emotional. In this fashion there is a big gap and discontinuity of cooperation between the head and the heart, which can lead to further division, a more dangerous split between the two centers. Eventually, if no essential action is taken to narrow the gap and to heal the split, or to create a bridge for the head and the heart to reconnect, those undergoing such splitting may suffer a severely pathological illness.

As we know, the head is the boss in conducting life and all the world affairs, and we obey it submissively. In this connection, the Buddha states it very clearly in the Dhammapada (words of wisdom):

> *The mind (head) is first and foremost; the mind is the chief. When one speaks or acts with the disturbed mind, suffering follows one just as the wheels of the cart follow the footprints of the oxen.*
>
> *But when one speaks or acts with the clear, healthy mind, happiness follows one just as one's shadow never leaves.*

From these statements we can see precisely the interrelatedness between the state of mind and the action or the speech. That is, the state of mind from which we act or speak determines how an action is to be taken, or how speech should be formulated. Not only that, all our behavior patterns and the ways we think are influenced and directed by the mind, or, to be precise, by the mental state that is in charge at the moment. Happiness or suffering in life comes about not because of external conditions but depends on what kind of mind and mental attitude one has toward life and also toward the world.

As for the heart, it is feeling that knows the free flow of life and evaluates life experiences through sense contact. At the point of contact, whether through the eyes and visual objects, the ears and sounds, the nose and smell, the mouth and taste, the body-touch and tangible objects, or the mind and all of mental world, a feeling arises. The feeling evaluates the sense experience as pleasant, unpleasant, or neither pleasant nor unpleasant, depending on the quality of contact. Bear in mind that when talking about contact we refer to the presence of three factors, namely, the sense organ, the corresponding object, and consciousness. So, the quality of feeling as the evaluating agent springs from the attribute of the sense contact. That attribute stems from the combination of the state of sense organ, the quality of the corresponding object, and the condition of consciousness. In this way, the heart knows the world of senses and evaluates them accordingly. But there is the sixth sense through which the heart is in constant contact with the inner world and therefore knows exactly what is going on. For this reason, we *must* listen to the heart to hear what it's trying to tell us, or what it is that it's speaking about, sometimes in a very still voice. By listening to the heart one dwells in the higher level of knowing, that is, knowing *directly*, without using the thinking mind, but only with full, vigorous attention. In the case of needing a solution to any difficulty one has, just put a precise question to the heart and do so three times; after that, merely listen attentively with the gesture of stillness and with both hands touching the heart center (middle of chest). After all, the heart is the seat of consciousness, while the brain (head) is the operating center of the mind. So, it's not a new conception when we talk about the heart knowing and speaking, because cultivated, refined consciousness operates from there. In other words, it may be equally correct to say that it is the heart consciousness that knows and speaks to us because consciousness arises through five physical sense doors and through the sixth sense door of mind and heart.

Now let us consider soul. Generally speaking, there is an understanding in many traditions that an entity exists in man that is permanent, eternal, absolute, an immutable substantiality behind the changing phenomenal world. According to some religions, each human being has such an individual soul as created by God, which lives eternally after death, now in hell, now in heaven, and whose destiny depends on the judgment of the Creator. Some others maintain that this entity passes through numerous lives until it reaches complete purification, and finally becomes united with God or Brahma, the universal soul where it originally comes from. This soul in man is the thinker of thoughts, the feeler of feelings and sensations, the receiver of rewards and punishments from all the actions, whether good or bad.

In Buddhism, there is no such a thing as briefly described above. The soul is not something that wanders about at night, or leaves a physical body and enters another body in case of death and reincarnation as traditionally maintained. The soul is not a figure of speech or a superstition. It is, in its true sense, the *inner directedness and mediator between the ego and the unconscious*. According to Robert A. Johnson, there are three things that Jung said of soul that can guide us as we make this inner journey of discovery. First, the soul is a psychological reality, an organ of the psyche; it lives on the unconscious side, but it affects our lives profoundly. Our soul is that part of the unconscious that is outside the ego (conscious mind), out of sight, yet mediates between the unconscious and the ego. Dr. Jung said that the soul is "both receiver and transmitter," the organ that receives the images of the unconscious and transmits them to the conscious ego-mind.

Second, the soul manifests itself, and the unconscious, by means of symbols: these are the images that flow from the unconscious in the form of dream, vision, fantasy, and all forms of imagination. The vital thing that Jung has discovered for us is that we have lost our sense of soul because we have lost our respect for symbols; our modern mind is trained that symbols are illusion. We say, "It is only your imagination," not realizing that all the missing parts of ourselves that we long for, the "lost lane into heaven," are constantly mediated to us through the forgotten language of the soul: the symbols and images that emanate through dream and imagination.

Third, for men, the symbol of the soul is the image of woman. If a man is aware of this and knows when he is using the image of woman as the symbol of his own soul, then he can learn to relate to that image as a symbol and to experience his soul inwardly. Jung says, "It belongs to him, this perilous image of woman." When a man understands that this image is his, and that it "belongs to *him*," then he has taken the first step toward consciousness in romantic love. He begins to see that "every beloved is forced to become the carrier and embodiment of this omnipresent and ageless image."

Now we have arrived at the frequently asked question: how can one integrate those three significant parts that make up each of us humans? The best way to achieve this integration is to bring each one of the three to harmonious, full development. The head must learn to listen to the heart and the soul through the realization that it cannot continue its solitary journey, because such a journey is terribly lonely and dangerous to harmonious self-development. To be able to listen properly to those two parts, the head must develop the right hemisphere of the brain so that the *receptive* mode can be opened for use, and at the same time the proportionate activity of the left hemisphere of the brain can be reduced. In this way, both hemispheres of the brain are utilized in a dynamic balance so as to enable one to have all possible means available for leading life and conducting businesses.

The receptive mode can be developed in the practice of mindfulness meditation that covers the whole magnitude of human activity and consciousness. Whatever one does, if it is done in the spirit of awareness and vigilance, is mindfulness or insight meditation. So, this form of meditation is very practical in all aspects of the earthly life, let alone in the significant spiritual part of life. One can do it literally anywhere, any time, regardless of formality or informality by just being aware and keeping awake at all times.

Having the receptive mode open and right at hand, one will be able to hear the voices of the inner world and to receive all essential, unthinkable information that is most beneficial to one. Operating with this receptiveness is what Robert A. Johnson calls "slender threads," which is a kind of *open hand* or the gentle, still voice that we have previously mentioned. The heart is quite accessible to this invisible, powerful force, and so is the soul, particularly because the soul lives in the deepest level of consciousness, that is, the unconscious where both dark and light forces reside. Attentive and freely flowing listening is the best means for the meaningful and profitable contact with the unconscious (the unknown or hidden) elements within us. The reason for this is that this listening is a form of solitude, solitude not in the sense of the physical or emotional isolation but in its true sense of inward silence and stillness where all the senses (including the sixth sense) are totally alert and mindfully receptive.

To illustrate the integration of head, heart, and soul, I would like to cite the Greek myth of Cadmus who undergoes the search for his lost sister, Europa, for a long, long time. The story begins with one beautiful, sunny afternoon in Boeotia (a part of Ancient Greece that included the city of Thebes) where King Agenor lives with his Queen, Telephassa, and his three sons, Cadmus, Phoenix, and Cilix, and their youngest, a beautiful daughter, Europa. It happens that that lovely afternoon those princes and their sister go out to play in the beautiful meadow by the shore. While the three brothers are enjoying their leisure time with sports, Europa, who is the favorite of everyone, is lying on the soft, green grass looking up to the clear, beautiful sky and fantasizing all the possible gorgeous things that she could imagine. As a matter of fact, she is having a great time. But soon after returning to her immediate environment and opening her eyes she sees a gigantic, snow-white bull standing right there in front of her, which is quite an amazing and at the same time a frightening sight for her. Nevertheless, she is not too afraid, and can remain more or less calm, and is able to watch the bull with astonishment. It becomes quite obvious that the bull doesn't want to harm her; instead, he is very friendly and even charming with her. She then picks the grass and feeds him, which he eats with pleasure out of her hand. While walking around eating the grass beside her, the bull at an unexpected moment kneels down, indicating that she could get on his back and he would give her a pleasant ride, and this she does. Now Europa is very happy and excited being on the back of the bull since it is really a very special event for her. She thinks it would be good to show this to her brothers, and probably let them have the ride with her. To her great surprise, the bull runs out in full speed to the middle of the field, and she with one hand holds on to the beautiful horn of the bull and the other hand waves to her brothers who are obviously having great fun. At a glance of their sister riding on the exquisite, gigantic, snow-white bull, they are so delighted for her that they just leave her alone with the bull and continue playing. By the time they take another look at her, they realize that the bull is carrying her out to the middle of the sea, which troubles them tremendously. Although she is yelling for help, they cannot hear her, for she is too far away, and it is too late to rescue her. So, the last sight remaining in their memory is the picture of Europa riding on the gigantic snow-white bull with one hand on the bull's lovely horn and another hand waving to them, racing at full speed. They just don't know what to do since there is nothing they can undertake.

Now they have no choice but to return to the palace, which they do with grief, guilt, and distress in their hearts and minds. They inform their father, the king, about the loss of their sister. King Agenor is so furious and overwhelmingly upset that he tells them to leave home and the kingdom in search for her immediately, and never return until or unless they have found Europa and bring her back with them. In this story, Europa is an extremely special child to King Agenor, and he loves her with all his heart and mind. So, the loss of such a darling and beautiful daughter is a great blow for him, and he can neither sleep nor eat without her.

The three sons are totally shocked and become stressful because they have no idea of where to go and how to search for their sister. They don't know what to do, as it all happened so suddenly; furthermore, they haven't eaten anything yet, either, and have got no time even to change their clothes. At that moment, the mother, Queen Telephassa, appears and tells them that she will go with them. They tell her that the journey will be very long, and will be extremely dangerous, so she should not accompany them, but should remain in the kingdom waiting for the news. She then says, "What's my life for, when all my children are gone? I would rather go and die with them wherever they would be." Hence, she takes leave from home with her three sons, in search for Europa.

On their uncertain journey, whomever they meet they constantly ask one and the same question, "Have you seen a beautiful, beautiful princess riding on top of the snow-white bull racing like the wind?" The answer they get is always negative, "No, no, no such a thing has been seen. There is neither the princess nor the bull to be seen." Everyone begins to think that these people must be crazy looking for such a nonsensical thing. Still, they carry on journeying, searching, and putting that same question to everyone over and over again, because they cannot think of anything else to ask. Probably their mind might have been out of touch with reality as it only focused on the picture of Europa riding on the gigantic, snow-white bull racing through the vast, infinite sea.

After a long, long journey, they arrive at a magnificently beautiful valley surrounded by lovely green hills and mighty mountains with abundant water in the land. The middle son, Phoenix, says to his search party that he doesn't want to go on in this journey any longer; for one thing, he says, it is already too long; the sister is dead, and if she were still alive we wouldn't recognize each other. He further tells them that he has decided to stop searching for Europa and plans to build a house to live here, because he doesn't see any more meaning to the indefinite search for her. They are all very sad to hear that from him, but respect his decision and integrity, and therefore help him build a beautiful house. They are quite envious of the peace that he is going to have, living in such a beautiful place. Nevertheless, they leave him there and continue their journey to find Europa.

Soon after that, many newcomers arrive and Phoenix tells them his story and his travels. After listening to all the interesting things, they appreciate him and love his place so much so that they all settle there with him. Then the first kingdom is established around that spot, and Phoenix becomes the leader of that kingdom. (This is the land to become known as Phoenicia.)

The family, now consisting of the queen (the mother) and the remaining two brothers, goes on undertaking the enduring journey and continues asking everyone they come across the same question, "Have you seen a very beautiful maiden riding on the gigantic, snow-white bull racing like the wind?" Of course, the answer is always "No, no, there is no such a thing." That question has been asked hundreds of times, thousands of times, but the answer is the same "No, no, nothing like that."

Once again they arrive at another beautiful, beautiful place. Now, the youngest brother, Cilix, says, "I don't want to go on searching for our sister, Europa, any more. I want to stop the journey and build a house to live here."

They help him build a lovely house using the natural things of the land; and then they continue their journey in search for Europa. Again, another kingdom is set up and Cilix becomes the leader of this kingdom. (This region will become known as Cilicia, in Asia Minor, south of Cappadocia and the Anatolian plains of modern central Turkey.)

Now we have only two people left: Cadmus and Queen Telephassa. They go on searching and traveling across many lands and many seas, through unknown countries and unknown places, until one day the queen sits down and tells her son, Cadmus that she has to rest. Cadmus responds to her by saying, "You can rest as long as you want, mother!" She then says to him, "Cadmus, the rest that I am talking about is not the ordinary rest that we need when we get tired, I mean the eternal rest. My time to die has come." Cadmus bursts into tears because all these years he has been close to his mother; and her death would mean that he would be alone, totally alone. His mother continues to say, "But before I die, I want you to promise me something," to which Cadmus replies, "I can promise you anything, mother. Whatever you want me to do, I will carry it out." She then tells him to stop searching for his sister, Europa, and to go to the oracle at Delphi to seek direction. Having said all those things, Queen Telephassa lays back and a few moments later she is dead.

Now Cadmus is truly alone: he has no father, no mother, no brother, and nobody in his life. He does not know what to do apart from wandering around, asking the same question that he always asks since it has become the way of life for him and he has no other question to ask. In fact, all the things that his mother told him do not really mean anything to him, although he listens to her sincerely. Nevertheless, his journey eventually takes him to Delphi and he goes to the oracle, following his mother's advice as he had promised her. He puts his ears to the oracle and asks, "What shall I do? Why am I here?" He then waits and listens carefully until the wind comes through, which indicates that the oracle is about to talk to him. Then he hears the message "You must stop searching for your sister, Europa. You must stop searching for your sister, Europa. You must stop searching for your sister, Europa." He continues waiting and listening and then there comes another message "You must follow the cow. You must follow the cow. You must follow the cow." Then there is a period of silence. After that he hears the final message from the oracle that says repeatedly three times "Where the cow stops, you must build your kingdom. Where the cow stops, you must build your kingdom. Where the cow stops, you must build your kingdom." Of course, Cadmus merely listens without understanding anything that the oracle has said to him. He then leaves the oracle and continues his journey.

While roaming about alone, not knowing exactly where to go and what to do next, he encounters many interesting young people to whom he tells the story of his life. They love it so much and become attracted to his presence. So, he has friends, new friends, and they walk with him, sharing their experiences with him, hanging out with him wherever he goes. One day, he happens to see a cow and thinks to himself, "That must be the cow that the oracle was talking about." He looks at the cow and the cow looks at him. He then walks to the cow, and the cow walks away. In this way, he ends up following the cow. After a long while, they come to a very beautiful place with fertile lands and greens around, a lot of water, and a lovely forest and mountains surrounding it. There, the cow stops! Cadmus then knows for sure that now he must build the kingdom. So, he sends his young friends out to fetch some water and to cut down some trees in the forest for use as the building material so that the construction work can begin the next day.

Then, Cadmus lies down on the green grass looking up at the sky and absorbing the peace of that beautiful, beautiful land. Suddenly, he hears cries and screams coming out of the forest where his friends have entered. He leaps up right away and rushes toward the direction from which the noises come. Cadmus is now quite berserk, and is no longer afraid of anything. Arriving there, he sees a huge dragon standing and eating up all his friends, actually finishing up his last young friend. He throws himself inside the dragon through its open mouth, and then begins to cut up all the internal organs until the dragon falls over dead. Then he comes out and stands there bloody from having fought with the dragon. After recovering from the heavy fight, he contemplates what to do next. In the silent state of mind and inner stillness, he hears the voice saying, "Cadmus, now cut out all the dragon's teeth." As there are hundreds and hundreds of the teeth in the dragon's mouth, it takes him quite some time to finish the job. After getting it done, he stands still and waits. Then another voice comes up and tells him to plough the land, dig holes, and bury all the dragon's teeth; and this he does. While standing still and waiting, he hears the third voice commanding him, "Now, Cadmus, step back and watch them grow."

To his horrid amazement Cadmus watches something emerging from each buried tooth. First, he sees faces, then necks, shoulders, torsos, and finally entire gigantic human bodies. They are the warriors of the dragon's teeth. Now hundreds and hundreds of them stand with swords drawn in the large field ready to fight. During his silently watching, Cadmus hears the inner voice speaking to him, "Cadmus, throw a stone in their midst." He then picks the stone and throws it in their midst and it hits one of them, who immediately turns to the one next to him assuming that his neighbor hits him. In this fashion, they start to quarrel and eventually all of them go into conflict and fight fiercely among themselves all day long. Many, many warriors of the dragon's teeth die in that battlefield until only the fiercest and most powerful five warriors are left. They are all facing one another, getting ready to finish the final fighting. At that moment, Cadmus hears the voice from inside him saying, "Cadmus, step in their midst and make them yours so that they can help you build the kingdom." With no hesitation, Cadmus steps into their midst, draws his sword, swirls it, and gives them his command: "Now, sheath your sword and there will no more fighting." Then, all five worriers sheath their swords and wait for the next command from their new boss, Cadmus, who now speaks with great authority since he has had so many experiences in dealing with people and things.

As night falls, they all go to bed and get a sound sleep and a peaceful rest. Waking up in the morning, it is a great, happy surprise for them to see a beautiful, enormous castle built specifically for Cadmus by Zeus. Although the five powerful worriers are puzzled by this extraordinary event that happens to

Cadmus, they undoubtedly have complete confidence in, and total respect for, him.

Cadmus, then, leads them to the entrance gate in front of the castle where he sees a beautiful, young woman at a distance. She at first appears to him to be his sister, Europa, but when she approaches him, he realizes that she is a combination of his sister, Europa, his mother, Queen Telephassa, and some other woman. Her name is Harmonia. She is Zeus's gift for Cadmus, to be his wife. They do marry and live happily together. Cadmus and Harmonia have five daughters, and one of them is Simile, who gives birth to several sons, including one whose name is Dionysus, the god of wine, experience, and ecstasy.

From this myth, we understand that the journey taken by Cadmus is a head or father journey since he is under the command of his father in search for Europa, his sister. All forms of searching fall in the category of head activity because it is the head that plans its trips of seeking and looking for something that is missing or lost. As in the above-cited myth, pure femininity, represented by Europa, is carried away by Zeus, the symbolic bull. The central focus of personality (the king) lacks an essential element for competent operation, so that a search for it must be done. The search always begins with the dominance of the head, thinking out and planning the journey so that the missing part of consciousness may be found. Since the head doesn't really know where exactly to search for, it sets out the uncertain trip with a great idea, and then ends up in confusion. For that matter, so many questions are asked a hundred times, a thousand times, and the answers received are always negative, that the search must go on until the realization of its fruitlessness is reached. In our story, Cadmus's head journey is stopped by his mother (the feminine principle) as she makes him promise to go to the oracle (inner knowing) to seek direction. This means that the useless, time- and energy-consuming search must come to a stop, and the hero or the central focus of consciousness must shift to the inwardly directed energy source. That is the only way to enable the hero to find the right path that will lead on to discover the uncovered, *Harmonia,* or the complete sense of equilibrium of a fully developed self.

The stopping of the head journey in this story indicates that to continue with such an extreme path is very much out of balance, and that there is a need to establish a genuine sense of balance in life. For this reason, the heart and the soul must be brought into full operation so that they can play an efficient, active role in completing the journey. This Cadmus has done well, and we should follow his good example.

The role of morality in the journey to complete transformation

When talking about morality, we usually refer to certain rules of conduct laid down by the organized religions or certain spiritual masters. Those who are religious and obedient to the tradition's rules, such as monks, nuns, and devoted lay followers, know exactly how to behave accordingly, without even questioning their authoritative standards of conduct and disciplinary regulations. But when the rules are broken through transgressions, the transgressors either suffer guilt or make a confession, disclosing their wrong doing to the other members of the monastic community, if they are the monks such as Buddhist monks, or to the priests if they are lay devotees. By so doing, the guilty feeling or sense of remorse could be relieved, which will help them become more mindful of their future actions and behavior so that they might think twice before taking similar actions and conducting their daily lives.

There is another type of morality that is not well known to the majority of people, and that is *the postulate of conduct revealed through meditation or mental culture*. This, according to the Buddhist practice, is technically known as *bhāvanā sīla*, which is equal to flashes of insight that show the right way of behaving and conducting oneself at the moment. This is not a set of rules, which one can conform to easily, but it is an immediate insight arising as a response to a situation or a circumstance at the given moment. Being a guiding light, it is available to those who practice *Insight Meditation* wholeheartedly or live the meditative way of life genuinely. By providing hospitality for insight to arise through waiting upon full attention and wakefulness, one does not have to be concerned about the moral rules or social precepts embraced by society and abided in by most people, because one is inwardly directed.[2]

As the aims of morality are to protect us from suffering, guilt and remorse, and to lay a strong foundation for achieving *purity of conduct*, a solid foundation for bodily and psychic transformations, we should fulfill the moral standards of living. Being born and having grown up in a certain culture, it becomes inevitable for anyone of us not to experience guilt and/or remorse painfully when a moral rule is transgressed or the righteous thing is not carried out (when what should be done is not done). *Once guilt has been felt, and then buried in the psychophysical systems, it is absolutely essential to process it through either meditation or therapy if the transformation is to be achieved.* When the physical body and the psychic center become clean and clear of all contaminations (these and others), we then reach the freedom from the buried energy patterns, including guilt and remorse, and therefore purity of conduct is naturally attained. A complete transformation cannot be accomplished so long as guilt and remorse as well as the other locked-in energy patterns still predominantly contaminate our psychophysical systems. Still, so long as our action and speech that form the moral aspects of our conduct are not clean and pure, we will have much inner work to do in order to enable us to process all those contaminated actions and speeches deposited in our body-mind systems. This is because whatever action (including reaction) we take, and whatever speech we express, whether good or bad, negative or positive, will be accumulated as buried energy patterns in our body and in our psyche. There is no way that we can escape this reality. For this reason, the issue of morality in the context of purity of conduct plays an important role in the transformation process.

---

[2] Compare Mitchell Ginsberg, *The Far Shore: Vipassanā, The Practice of Insight* (1980), speaking of vipassanā practice or vipassanā bhāvanā (the cultivation of insight): "With vipassanā there is also a morality or way of right acting. Now, the way of right acting that comes from vipassanā does not come through following rules. The way of right acting through vipassanā is seeing what is to be done." Quotation is from the chapter entitled "The Far Shore's Under Your Feet" (at p. 28).

Bear in mind that the complete transformation under discussion is not confined only to psychological and spiritual transformations, but includes the other aspects of transformation, such as the transformation of the physical body, the transformation of the emotional body, and the transformation of the mental body. If all of our realities are still not transformed, the work for achieving total freedom, for accomplishing complete transformation and for full enlightenment, is *not* done, life is *not* totally lived, and the cycle of birth and death is *not* yet cut off. On the contrary, the inner work has been completed, life is fully lived, and this is the final birth since the samsaric cycle of birth-life-death has been utterly cut off, when total freedom, complete transformation, and full enlightenment have been accomplished.

ABOUT THE AUTHOR

*****

Born in a remote village in North-eastern Thailand, **Dhiravamsa** grew up in a rather primitive world, helping his parents grow rice and rear animals. He joined the Buddhist Monastic Order at the age of thirteen. During the next twenty-three years he became one of the well-educated and well-trained monks both at the Traditional Monastic Schools for Dharma and Pali Studies and at the Buddhist University, Mahachulalongkorn Rajavidyalaya. His accomplishments in the Thai Buddhist monastery include the position of *Preceptor (Upajjhāya), Abbot (Chao Āwās)* of the Wat Buddhapadīpa (Thai Temple) in London, Britain, *Chief of the Thai Buddhist Mission* in the West, and being recognized as an *International Insight Meditation Master.* In addition, in 1966, when he was only *thirty-two* years old, he achieved the appointment to the rank of *Chao Khun* (Honorable Title of a Higher Rank for a virtuous and well educated monk in Thai Sangha hierarchy), with the Royal Name of *Phra Sobhana Dhammasudhī* (the wise and beautiful in the Dharma).

He began his psycho-spiritual work in the capacity of a Teacher/Helper in Britain in 1965. He gradually became internationally known, particularly in Europe and North America, where he rendered most of his services to those seeking psycho-spiritual advice and assistance. In England, Chapter House, the spiritual/therapeutic community and retreat center, was established under his personal advice and guidance. Also, he did a similar thing in the United States and established another *Vipassana (Insight) Meditation Center* on San Juan Island, Washington State, to use for his psycho-spiritual work as well as his home base. Here he began to use extensively (1983) the Enneagram System of Personality to help him work more successfully with those coming to study and practice with him the Holistic Vipassana Meditation in which he incorporates the compatible Western Psychology (e.g., Jungian, Gestalt, and Humanistic Psychologies) and certain therapeutic techniques.

With regard to literary works he wrote and published several articles and books on the subject of Vipassana and self-growth, some of which have been translated into **French, German, Spanish, Italian, Dutch, Greek,** and **Russian**. At present he has completed three more books: **Union of Opposites** (A Memoir), **Selected Stories of Dhammapada with the Buddha's verses and the author's psycho-spiritual analysis,** and the **Testimony of Conscious Love** (a classical Thai tale of Srīthon & Manorah on their genuine search for love). These three books are available in Spanish.

Immediately after obtaining the First Degree in Buddhist Studies, Comparative Religion, and Modern Subjects, he was appointed an Instructor in Educational Psychology and in the English language at the Mahachulalongkorn University. Also here at his beloved educational institution he rendered special services for two years, establishing, administering, and teaching the First Buddhist Sunday School for Thai children and young people. Before accompanying his Principal Vipassana Master (the late Most Venerable Phra Dhammadhiraraj Mahamuni of Wat Mahadhatu, Bangkok) to Britain, 1964, he held the position of Headmaster of a private school in Prachinburi Province and raised the standard of education to the point where the Provincial Authority of Education at the Ministry of Education recognized it.

In addition to teaching courses in meditation and related activities, he spends his time writing and living a meditative life. He travels a great deal to carry out his work in all the Continents of the Western world, including the Continent of Australia; and loves it with all his heart and mind. Methodically speaking, he has honored both Apollo (the god of light, order, and structure) and Dionysus (the god of ecstasy, experience, and play). It has proven wonderful for him to be able to leap up to the transpersonal realm of spiritual experience and yet, be grounded and firmly connected to the earthly realm. In other words, he balances heaven and earth within himself. On the physical plane he becomes king ...symbolically speaking ...and inwardly he is a sage. All these symbolic notions indicate the union of opposites on the energy level within human consciousness.

Dhiravamsa has lectured and taught Vipassana Meditation extensively in United Kingdom, on the Continent of Europe, in North America, and in Australia. He first visited the United States in January 1969, when he conducted a meditation workshop at Oberlin College and lectured at several colleges and universities. Since then he has regularly returned to Canada and to the States for periods of two to five months, invited by many universities and colleges including Swarthmore, Haverford, the University of Pennsylvania, Princeton, Colgate, Amherst, Earlham, Carlton, Middlebury, Florida State, and Chicago Presbyterian Seminary.

In September 1971, Dhiravamsa gave up the robe after twenty-three years as a Buddhist monk. Now he leads a simple, meditative life in the world and in the Dharma, continuing his work of teaching Vipassana Meditation and other related activities such as **Vipassana Dream work, Active Imagination,** and **Holistic Healing**.

www.ingramcontent.com/pod-product-compliance
Lightning Source LLC
Chambersburg PA
CBHW081358160426
43193CB00013B/2060